ReMaking America

Edited by Richard McCormack

14.95

ALLIANCE FOR
american
manufacturing

The Alliance for American Manufacturing is a non-profit, non-partisan partnership formed in 2007 by some of America's leading manufacturers and the United Steelworkers to explore common solutions to challenging public policy topics such as job creation, infrastructure investment, international trade, and global competitiveness. We believe that an innovative and growing manufacturing base is vital to America's economic and national security, as well as to providing good jobs for future generations. AAM achieves its mission through research, public education, advocacy, strategic communications, and coalition building around the issues that matter most to America's manufacturing sector.

The Alliance for American Manufacturing
711 D Street, 3rd Floor Washington, DC 20004
www.americanmanufacturing.org

TABLE OF CONTENTS

Authors

ERIC GARFINKEL

Eric Garfinkel is a member of the adjunct faculty of the University of Colorado Law School. From 2010 to 2011, he served as Chief Counsel for China Trade in the Office of the U.S. Trade Representative. He had previously served as Lead U.S. Negotiator for Antidumping and Industrial Subsidies during the Uruguay Round Multilateral Trade Negotiations and as Assistant Secretary of Commerce with responsibility for antidumping and countervailing duty enforcement for the Foreign Trade Zone program.

Mr. Garfinkel was General Counsel of the Overseas Private Investment Corporation from 1987 to 1988, Deputy Assistant Director for Commerce and Trade in the White House Office of Policy Development from 1982 to 1983 and Attorney-Advisor at the Office of the U.S. Trade Representative from 1981 to 1982. Between government positions, he practiced international trade law at several law firms.

He has been a senior fellow at the Wharton School of Business, the Huntsman Center for Global Competition and Innovation and the Council on Competitiveness in Washington, D.C.

From 1992 until 2002, he was President of Back to Basics Toys, a catalog and Internet toy retailer.

Mr. Garfinkel is a graduate of the University of Maryland (B.A., 1976) and of the Emory University School of Law (J.D., 1979).

LEO HINDERY, JR.

Leo Hindery, Jr. is Chairman of the Smart Globalization Initiative at the New America Foundation and is Managing Partner of InterMedia Partners LP, a New York-based media industry private equity fund. Until 2004, he was Chairman and Chief Executive Officer of The YES Network, the nation's largest regional sports network and the television home of the New York Yankees, which he founded in 2001. Previously, he had been President and Chief Executive Officer of AT&T Broadband, which was formed out of the 1999 merger of Tele-Communications, Inc. (TCI) into AT&T. At the time of the merger, Mr. Hindery was President of TCI and its affiliated companies, which then made up the world's largest cable television system operator and programming entity.

A former Chairman of C-SPAN and of the National Cable Television Association, he is currently Chair of the Horizon Project, a group of CEOs and senior public policy professionals developing economic and trade policy recommendations for Congress. In addition, he is an Executive-in-Residence at Columbia Business School, a member of the Board of Visitors of the Columbia School of Journalism, a member of the Council on Foreign Relations, a Trustee of The New School and a Director of both the Library of Congress Trust Fund and Teach for America.

Mr. Hindery is the author of *The Biggest Game of All and It Takes a CEO: It's Time to Lead with Integrity.* He received an MBA from Stanford University's Graduate School of Business after doing his undergraduate work at Seattle University.

KEN JACOBSON

Ken Jacobson, co-editor of this book, is a Philadelphia-based journalist specializing in business, technology and economics. Currently senior editor of *Manufacturing & Technology News* and an associate of the nonprofit Academic-Industry Research Network (AIRnet), he has headed two specialized newsletters, New York-based *Metals Week* and Washington, D.C.-based *New Technology Week*, and reported from Paris for *Business Week* and from Amsterdam for the Associated Press. An investigator on the Democratic staff of U.S. House of Representatives' Science and Technology Committee between 2007 and 2011, Jacobson has also contributed to numerous published reports of the National Academies' Board on Science, Technology, and Economic Policy (STEP Board) and is the author of the 1994 book *Embattled Selves: An Investigation into the Nature of Identity Through Oral Histories of Holocaust Survivors*. He is a graduate of the University of California at Berkeley.

SRIDHAR KOTA

Sridhar Kota is the Herrick Professor of Engineering at the University of Michigan. He has authored over 200 technical papers on product design and bio-inspired engineering systems. He holds more than 25 patents and has served as an engineering consultant to numerous organizations.

Prof. Kota is the recipient of the American Society of Mechanical Engineers' Machine Design Award, the Leonardo da Vinci Award and the Outstanding Educator Award. He is the founding President and CEO of FlexSys Inc., a company that specializes in bio-inspired design of aircraft wings and wind-turbine blades.

Between 2009 and 2012, Prof. Kota served as the Assistant Director for Advanced Manufacturing at the White House Office of Science and Technology Policy. In this role, he developed policy recommendations and implementation strategies for enhancing U.S. manufacturing competitiveness and fostering innovation-based manufacturing and the commercialization of emerging technologies. He played an instrumental role in launching several initiatives, including the National Manufacturing Innovation Institutes, the National Robotics Initiative, Connecting American Manufacturing and the National Digital Engineering and Manufacturing Consortium.

RICHARD McCORMACK

Richard McCormack is Editor and Publisher of *Manufacturing & Technology News,* a 20-year-old news journal based in Washington, D.C., that focuses on issues related to manufacturing policy and global trends impacting American industry and jobs.

He has worked as a journalist in Washington for 30 years, starting as a reporter at *The Energy Daily* and becoming Founding Editor of *New Technology Week* in 1987, *High Performance Computing and Communications Week* in 1991 and *Manufacturing & Technology News* in 1994. He has won awards for investigative and interpretive journalism.

Mr. McCormack is author of the 2002 book *Lean Machines, Learning from the Leaders of the Next Industrial Revolution* and was editor of the 2009 Alliance for American Manufacturing book *Manufacturing a Better Future for America.* He received a B.A. in English and Political Science from University of the Pacific. He has been the golf coach at Annandale High School in Virginia for 16 years.

HAROLD MEYERSON

Harold Meyerson is Editor of *The American Prospect*, the Washington-based current affairs magazine, and since 2003 has written a weekly op-ed column in the *Washington Post.*

From 1989 through 2001, he was Executive Editor of the *L.A. Weekly*, the nation's largest metropolitan weekly. His articles on politics, labor, the economy, foreign policy and American culture have also appeared in *The New Yorker, The Atlantic, The New Republic, The Nation, The New Statesman,* the *New York Times* and the *Los Angeles Times*, as well as in numerous other publications. He is a member of the editorial board of Dissent. His writing has won numerous awards.

From 1987 to 1988, Mr. Meyerson was a regular commentator for the *Los Angeles Herald-Examiner*, and from the late 1970s through the mid-1980s he was a political consultant to a range of progressive organizations and candidates. From 1991 through 1995, he hosted the weekly show "Real Politics" on radio station KCRW, the Los Angeles area's leading NPR affiliate.

Mr. Meyerson was educated in Los Angeles public schools and at Columbia University.

HARRY MOSER

Harry Moser is Founder of the Reshoring Initiative, which he created in 2010 with the intent of bringing industry and jobs back to the United States. Before that, he served as Chairman Emeritus of Charmilles Technologies Corp., now GF AgieCharmilles.

Mr. Moser is a member of the board of the National Institute of Metalworking Skills, an institute providing credentials for skilled manufacturing, and President of the Swiss Machine Tool Society.

He has spent his life in the manufacturing sector, having worked summer vacations during high school and college at the Singer Sewing Machine factory in Elizabeth, N.J., where his father, a manager, and his grandfather, a foreman, had both worked. The Singer factory is one on a long list of American manufacturing plants and companies that are now gone due to decades of offshoring.

Not wanting to see even more U.S. manufacturing jobs disappear, Mr. Moser decided to start the Reshoring Initiative to help companies recognize that manufacturing in America is often the most profitable choice. The initiative works with U.S. manufacturers to help them recognize their potential for profit should they produce in the United States, as well as the critical role they could play in strengthening the economy by utilizing local sourcing and production.

Mr. Moser received a B.S. Degree in Mechanical Engineering and a M.S. Degree in Engineering at MIT. He received an MBA from the University of Chicago.

SCOTT PAUL

Scott Paul is President of the Alliance for American Manufacturing (AAM), a partnership established in 2007 by some of America's leading manufacturers and the United Steelworkers union. Mr. Paul and AAM have worked to make American manufacturing a top-of-mind issue for voters and national leaders through advocacy, research and public relations.

Prior to forming AAM, Mr. Paul worked on the legislative staff of the AFL-CIO and served on Capitol Hill at various times between 1987 and 2001. He concluded his work in Congress as the Chief Foreign Policy and Trade Advisor to House Democratic Whip David Bonior (D-Mich.).

He has testified before seven committees of the House and Senate, frequently appears on television news shows and regularly blogs at the *Huffington Post*, CNBC and *Industry Week*.

Mr. Paul earned a B.A. in Foreign Service and International Politics from Penn State and an M.A. with honors in Security Studies from Georgetown University's School of Foreign Service.

IRENE PETRICK

Irene Petrick is a Penn State University professor and is Managing Director of Trend-Scape Innovation Group. An internationally recognized expert in strategic roadmapping, she has research interests that include technology forecasting, collaborative innovation and business ecosystem development.

Prof. Petrick is actively engaged in the innovation and technology strategy activities of numerous organizations, including 12 *Fortune* 100 companies, the U.S. military and a wide variety of small and medium-sized enterprises. She has over 25 years of experience in technology planning, management and product development in both academic and industrial settings.

She has been named a CSC Faculty Intern in India and a Boeing Welliver Fellow and, since 2010, she has spent considerable time with Intel Corp., focusing on innovation strategies. Dr. Petrick is author or co-author of more than 135 publications and presentations. She received a Ph.D in Engineering Science and Technology Management from the Colleges of Engineering and Business Administration at Penn State. She holds an M.A. in Economics and a B.S. in Business, also from Penn State.

CARL POPE

Carl Pope is a veteran environmental leader, having served with the Sierra Club for more than 30 years as Political Director, Conservation Director, Executive Director and Chairman. He stepped down as Chairman in 2012 to become an independent consultant working at the intersection of sustainability and economic development.

During Mr. Pope's tenure as Executive Director, the Sierra Club added 400,000 new members and supporters, growing to approximately 1.2 million. It led the campaign "Moving the United States Beyond Coal" and campaigns to establish new regulations to drive the auto industry into an era of fuel efficiency.

STACEY JARRET WAGNER

Stacey Jarrett Wagner is Manager of Workforce Systems Development at the National Institute of Standards and Technology's Manufacturing Extension Partnership (MEP) program. She has more than 20 years of experience in workforce development, having conducted research and provided technical assistance for the American Society for Training and Development, the National Association of Manufacturers, the American Association of Community Colleges, the National Center for Education and the Economy, the Center for Energy Workforce Development, ARAMARK and the National Fund for Workforce Solutions, among others.

Her work for MEP includes integrating workforce development as a critical business strategy in the program's Next Generation Strategies initiative.

From 2002 to 2007, Ms. Wagner was the Managing Director of the National Association of Manufacturers' Center for Workforce Success, where she was responsible for strategic planning and research programs. From 2008 to 2010, at FutureWorks LLC,

she worked with rural and urban regions on job creation and skills development. During that time, she was a member of the technical assistance and program support team for the National Fund for Workforce Solutions.

She has served as a member of the National Science Foundation's Advanced Technology Education Center's initiative in the pulp and paper industry, as a board member of the Precision Metalforming Association, and as a member of the Heritage Foundation's 21st Century Workforce and National Security Working Group.

Ms. Wagner has a B.A. in International Relations from American University and a certificate in Corporate Social Responsibility from Harvard Business School. She has done graduate work in Organizational Development at George Washington University.

Introduction

When we released *Manufacturing a Better Future for America* in 2009, industry in America was experiencing perhaps its worst year on record: Manufacturing in America was left for dead. That book, deftly edited by Richard McCormack, described in 332 pages exactly how we got there. The authors collectively noted an urgent need for policy changes to address trade imbalances, globalization of supply chains, automation, the workforce and other important issues.

The book was cited in numerous publications, including *Make It In America* by Dow Chemical Chairman and CEO Andrew Liveris, as well as in Commerce Department research. In an important way, it set the stage for the renaissance we now see in manufacturing policy.

Today, we stand on different ground. Better ground. Our national leaders, smartest academics and most prominent think tanks are engaged in a vibrant competition of ideas on how to restore America's manufacturing leadership, which they all agree is essential. There is no longer a shortage of books on manufacturing, and many that I've read are excellent contributions to the growing body of thoughtful policy work.

ReMaking America adds a new level of detail and sophistication to the policy debate, and I could not be prouder of the result. Our authors are experts and leaders in their respective fields, and they view the challenges and opportunities for manufacturing in America through unblinking eyes. We offer bold policy prescriptions: It will take more than just a dash of innovation, a splash of job training and a sprinkle of trade enforcement to return manufacturing to its proper place in the U.S. economy. This book makes the argument for much more. We must realign our economic policies to support American manufacturing or resign ourselves to a shrinking share of the global employment and growth pie.

I want to extend a personal thank-you to all of the amazing authors who contributed to this book. These ideas will make a difference. Richard McCormack, the editor of this volume (as well as of our 2009 book) and author of its first chapter, deserves special thanks. He has managed to shape extraordinarily different perspectives into a cohesive set of ideas. His writing inspires me. For years, Richard was one of the lonely voices in the wilderness speaking on the outlook for American manufacturing. Now, he has the ear of our leaders. I hope they will listen.

Thanks also to the stakeholders of the Alliance for American Manufacturing, who make our work possible. The United Steelworkers and its industry partners prove that business and labor can work together to make a difference. This introduction would not be complete without a hearty thank-you to several other individuals who have made important contributions and suggestions along the way: Ken Jacobson, Michael Wessel, Steven Capozzola, Matt McMullan, Tracy Sefl and Shatterbox. It's an honor to work with them.

Scott Paul
Washington, DC
May 2013

Here's a synopsis of this new volume.

MANUFACTURING: WHERE AMERICA STANDS

by Richard McCormack, Editor of *Manufacturing & Technology News*

Recently there has been widespread recognition of the importance of manufacturing, which can play a central role in restoring growth to the U.S. economy. McCormack looks at dozens of market and economic indicators and manufacturing sectors and finds that if there is an industrial turnaround, it is not yet nearly strong enough to restore American prosperity. It will take a concerted effort to rebuild the U.S. economy.

CAPITAL FORMATION FOR A STRONGER U.S. MANUFACTURING SECTOR

by Leo Hindery, Jr., Chair of the U.S. Economy / Smart Globalization Initiative at the New America Foundation and former CEO of AT&T Broadband

Hindery proposes a "sturdy tripod" of manufacturing policy reform: access to financing for small- and medium-sized enterprises; tax credits for research and investment; and broad tax reform undertaken with the goal of encouraging the reshoring of production. He also urges the creation of a National Infrastructure Bank that would support the revival of American manufacturing.

TRADE: WHY STRENGTHENING THE ENFORCEMENT PROVISIONS OF THE WTO IS IMPORTANT FOR AMERICAN MANUFACTURING

by Eric Garfinkel, Member of the Adjunct Faculty at the University of Colorado Law School and former Chief Council for China Trade in the Office of the U.S. Trade Representative

The World Trade Organization's rules are not being enforced due to structural flaws in its system. Cases that are filed on behalf of U.S. manufacturers are not being adjudicated quickly, and when a final decision is made, there are no consequences for countries that break the rules. "The time for reforming the WTO's dispute-settlement system is ripe," writes Garfinkel.

ENERGY MANUFACTURING: THE LINCHPIN FOR AMERICA'S FUTURE

by Carl Pope, former Executive Director and Chairman of the Sierra Club

The United States is in the midst of an enormous political struggle between fossil-fuel energy monopolies left over from the 1930s and an innovative, disruptive set of high-tech renewable-energy technologies. America's destiny "depends on getting on the right side of history — the side of energy innovation," writes Pope, who describes how this can be done.

RESHORING: TURNING A TREND INTO A TORRENT, A STRATEGY FOR REBUILDING A STRONG ECONOMY

by Harry Moser, Founder of the Reshoring Initiative and Chairman Emeritus of Charmilles Technologies Corp.

Companies have started to reassess where they should locate manufacturing capacity, and, for the first time in a generation, the economics are beginning to favor U.S. production. New tools allow companies to determine the true costs of offshore production. Those costs turn out to be much higher than many companies may have realized. Moser describes what will be required for the United States to become more cost competitive.

A MANUFACTURING RENAISSANCE FOR WHOM?

by Harold Meyerson, Executive Editor of *The American Prospect*
and columnist for the *Washington Post*

The semi-renaissance of American manufacturing is an encouraging trend, but its benefits — like the benefits in other sectors of the economy — are not being shared with American workers. With the number of unionized manufacturing workers in steady decline, wages are down in the sector even as production, productivity and profits rise. Unions can combat these trends by working with companies to provide skilled workers and innovative processes, as they have done at ArcelorMittal, Boeing and Spirit Aero. But to take full advantage of workers' skills and potential, to enable workers to reap the rewards of their work and to create a political force that can foster more domestic manufacturing, workers and their unions need to become more powerful.

THE FUTURE OF MANUFACTURING

by Dr. Irene Petrick, Director of the Enterprise Informatics and Integration Center
at Pennsylvania State University

The combination of cloud computing, which enables every company
to access sophisticated modeling and simulation software for designing
new products and production processes, with additive manufacturing
and other advanced automation technologies is creating new business
models that are transforming global manufacturing supply chains. Petrick
describes how these trends will favor local manufacturing over centralized,
economies-of-scale production models based on offshore outsourcing.

THE ROLE OF INNOVATION AND MANUFACTURING R&D

by Dr. Sridhar Kota, Professor of Mechanical Engineering at the University of Michigan
and former Assistant Director for Advanced Manufacturing at the White House Office
of Science and Technology Policy

The United States spends more than any other country on basic research,
but it has fallen behind in commercializing R&D. Creating and designing
new technologies in the United States for production in foreign countries
"is neither economically sustainable nor governmentally justifiable," writes
Kota, who describes a new innovation policy that will reverse that trend.

CREATING A SKILLED MANUFACTURING WORKFORCE

by Stacey Jarrett Wagner, Manager of Workforce Systems Development at the
National Institute of Standards and Technology's Manufacturing Extension Partnership

Manufacturing employees will need to be adept at maneuvering within
high-tech, information-loaded, fast-paced, multidimensional, multinational
work environments. Wagner discusses the need to create a workforce
training system to help the United States regain its competitive edge.

THE BLUEPRINT FOR REMAKING AMERICA

by Scott Paul, President of the Alliance for American Manufacturing

We need a new manufacturing policy in America, one that garners
broad public support and shifts economic policy back to favoring domestic
production by adopting tax, trade, monetary, education, innovation,
energy, infrastructure and other policies that create an America that
is truly "built to last."

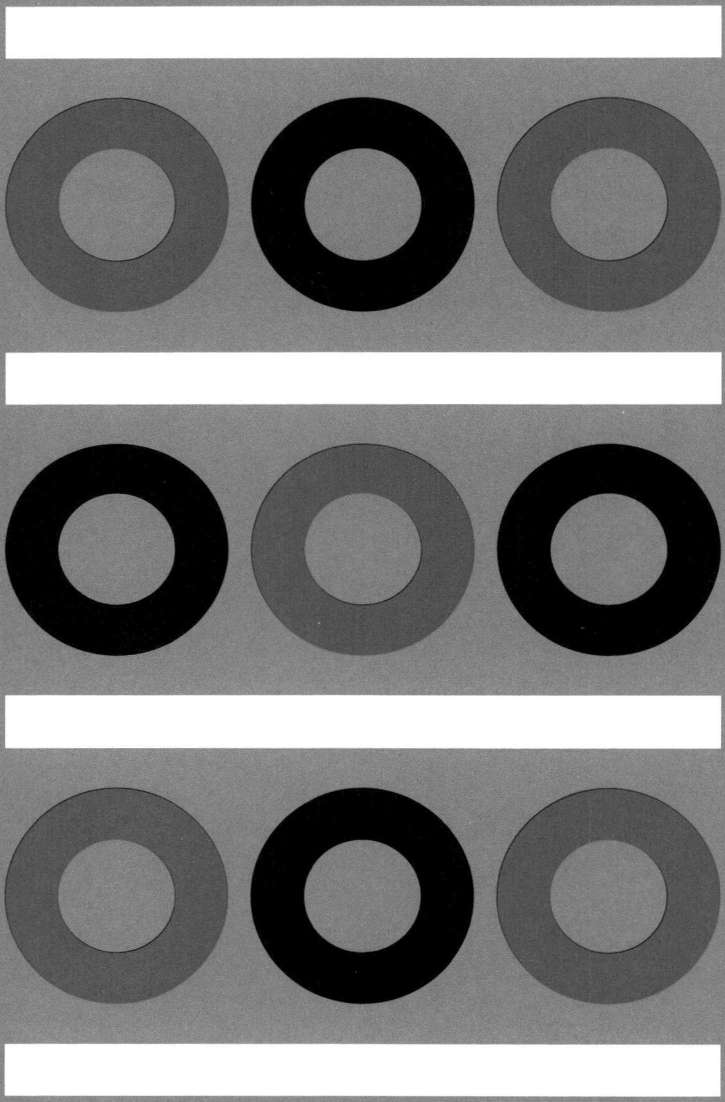

CHAPTER I

The State of American Manufacturing

Richard McCormack

Five years after the U.S. financial system collapsed in October 2008, the U.S. economy continues to struggle. The traditional measures used to shake off a typical cyclical recession through fiscal stimulus are not working: Efforts to renew economic growth and generate jobs by reducing taxes, boosting government spending, keeping interest rates low, printing money and then cutting government spending have come up short. There is growing recognition that the one way to restore growth and, with it, hope to millions of Americans is to revive the U.S. manufacturing sector and to reinvigorate innovation, commercialization of American technologies and their high-volume production in the United States.

Putting borrowed money into the pockets of American consumers has merely allowed them to buy a greater number of products made overseas, enriching America's competitors and leading to the continued loss of its most important industries. Since 2001, 63,300 factories have been shuttered in the United States.[1] A few are beginning to reopen due to declining costs of labor and energy in the United States, but entire industries have disappeared, taking along with them their supply chains and millions of American jobs. Reconstituting America's industrial base will be a tough task.

Nevertheless, for the first time in more than a generation, there is talk about an industrial revival. Executives and workers, management consultants, economists, academics, policymakers — in fact, Americans in general — are beginning to realize that the United States may not survive if it holds to its present economic course. A discussion has started about what it will take to bring manufacturing back to the country and why it is important to do so. There is a recognition that manufacturing is not a relic of the past but a force for progress for the future.

The United States does not have much time to lose. Changing the incentive structure to make the United States a place where companies want to invest in plants, equipment and workers must become a policy priority. By 2013, however, those things had yet to happen. Simply counting on a rapid rise of exceedingly low wages paid in China while American wages remain stagnant or decline will not turn the tide; that is a strategy of winning by losing. The country must adopt a range of policies that foster investment in manufacturing. If it doesn't, the future will not be bright for the United States as it heaps mountains of debt onto its mountains of debt to keep the U.S. economy on life support.

The intent of this chapter is to describe the state of U.S. manufacturing at a time when many in the media have proclaimed that manufacturing is staging a miraculous comeback. These pronouncements have left policymakers in Washington feeling that there's not much of anything to do to shore up America's global economic competitive standing.

Such thinking is dangerous. Other than anecdotes about Wham-o Frisbees or General Electric water heaters now being made in the United States, there is only little evidence that U.S. manufacturing is undergoing a renaissance. Even growth in the U.S. auto sector must be viewed through the lens of international trade: Imports of automobiles, parts and engines are reaching unprecedented levels, jumping to a record $300 billion in 2012 from $256 billion in 2011. The U.S. trade deficit in automobiles and parts increased by $30 billion in one year alone, from $117 billion in 2011 to $147 billion in 2012.

The principal message is this: With a depleted industrial sector and the corresponding reduction in wealth creation, millions of Americans cannot afford the products made in China, even at prices lower than if they had been made in the United States. The world's largest retailer has figured this out; without manufacturing, there are not enough American jobs paying high enough wages for Wal-Mart — or any other large retailer — to grow, according to Wal-Mart President and CEO Bill Simon. Encouraging the rebirth of manufacturing will "revitalize the communities we serve," said Simon in early 2013.[2] New factories would "have ripple effects in their communities," he said. "Factories need raw materials to supply them, trucks to deliver to them and, yes, retail to serve them."

Having failed to invest sufficiently in innovation, equipment, commercialization and production technologies, the U.S. economy has reached a critical juncture. It is not creating enough jobs for the millions of Americans who need them.

A GROWING CHALLENGE

From 2000 to 2012, the U.S. population increased by 33 million, from 281 million to 314 million. Yet, at the end of 2012 there were 134.7 million payroll jobs in the United States, 3.4 million fewer than in 2007. Only 2 million more people were in payroll jobs in 2012 than in 2001, despite the more than 10 percent growth in the population over the period.[3] The economy is not generating the millions of good-paying jobs in the globally competitive tradable sectors necessary for the United States to regain prosperity.

And still, legions of economists and columnists continue to proclaim that the United States does not need manufacturing — and, further, that the millions of Americans reduced to poverty when their jobs were shipped abroad are now better off because they have access to cheap consumer goods made by people in the developing world who are happy to work for desperately low wages.[4]

These same experts dismiss the manufacture of commodity products as too low-tech to merit a place in the United States' advanced economy. But a high-volume manufacturing facility, one that turns out tens of thousands of items every week, is one of the highest-tech enterprises ever to exist, arrayed with robotics, automated machinery, sensors, information technologies, advanced supply chain software networks and skilled workers, many of whom are not on the factory floor. Its products may be "low tech," but the processes involved in making them for billions of people are not.

It is also imperative for these same pontificators to realize that, although technology may displace some manufacturing jobs, those service-sector jobs that require skilled workers and pay a livable wage largely owe their existence to manufacturing. Service-sector jobs supported by industry — jobs in research, design, accounting, legal services, marketing, logistics, maintenance, information technology and software — pay more than a livable wage. On the other hand, many service-sector jobs that cater to private individuals — those in health care, food service, tourism and retail — require few if any skills and pay wages that may well consign a worker to a life of poverty.

Also calling into question the conviction of many economists that the United States does not need to be making "low-tech" goods is this fact: The country has lost the capability to make the highest-tech products, like cell phones, laptops, computers, tablets and HDTVs — products that are made by the same "advanced manufacturing" systems used for "low-tech" products. The United States became a superpower because of its embrace of all manufacturing. China has become a world power by following a similar path.

AMERICAN INDUSTRIES ARE NOT COMPETITIVE

There were 1.75 billion cell phones made in the world in 2012.[5] In one hour, 199,635 mobile phones were being produced globally, or 3,327 per minute. Not one of those phones was made in the United States. Only two of the 10 largest cell phone producers were U.S. companies — Apple and Motorola — with a combined global market share of under 10 percent (and Motorola is sinking fast). It is projected that by 2017 the total number of cell phones made each year will be 2.6 billion, or almost 300,000 phones *per hour*. That is a lot of jobs making what is, in effect, a supercomputer.

In 2011, Americans purchased a total of 2.297 billion pairs of shoes (two billion pairs of which, worth $16.4 billion, were from China), or an average of seven pairs of shoes each.[6] Ninety-nine percent of the shoes Americans purchased in 2011 were imported.[7] That means every day in 2011 foreign workers produced 5.48 million pairs of shoes for American consumers. That breaks down to 228,310 pairs of shoes being made every hour by foreign workers for American shoppers. That is a lot of shoes, a lot of jobs and a lot of money — $22.2 billion — disappearing from the U.S. economy.

But who wants to make shoes? It's a terrible job, isn't it? "Come to one of our factories in Maine and tell someone who has worked there for six months, or 20 years, that their job doesn't matter," says Matt Lebretton of New Balance, the last remaining large shoe manufacturer in the United States. "It is a job that they are able to feed their family on and make a good wage. A lot of people would take a job in a factory whether it's a low-tech product or a high-tech product. Really, it matters."

In 2001, the U.S. printed-circuit-board industry was generating $11 billion in revenue, selling its output to American electronics companies that were then the world's biggest. The printed-circuit-board industry is an essential foundation for the electronics and defense industries. Without it, a country cannot consider itself to be among the world's top competitors in high technology. But by 2011, the industry's revenue had collapsed to $3.3 billion, or 5.5 percent of the $59.5 billion global industry.[8] Sales continued to decline in 2012, going down by another 5.5 percent. Of total global revenues in 2011, $53 billion was generated in Asia.

The United States produced 86.6 million tons of steel in 2012, 5.7 percent of global output.[9] Compare that to China's output, which was 827 percent greater at 716.5 million tons, 46.3 percent of the total global production of 1.548 billion tons.

Also in 2012, the U.S. machine-tool industry accounted for only 5 percent of global output. In the important category of machine-tool consumption, which provides a clear indication of the vibrancy of an industrial economy, the United States installed $8.7 billion worth of machine tools, a fraction of the $38.5 billion worth of machine tools China installed that year.

It was the same story with industrial robots, which are essential to increasing automation and productivity. Of 160,000 industrial robots purchased by the world's manufacturers in 2011, the United States accounted for only 12.5 percent, or 20,000 units. The World Robotics Institute says that U.S. production of industrial robots was so small it was not even measurable.

To create most any product requires the expertise and skill of tool-and-die shops. When Apple CEO Tim Cook was asked in 2012 whether his company could bring manufacturing back to the United States from China, where Apple's contractors employ 1.5 million production workers, he said it would be all but impossible. "How many tool-and-die makers do you know in the U.S. now?" he asked. "I could call a meeting around the United States and say, 'Would every tool-and-die maker come to this room tonight?' and we wouldn't fill the room. In China, you would need several cities to fill with tool-and-die makers." Cook did go on to say that the microprocessor Apple uses in the iPhone and iPad is made in Austin, Texas. But what he didn't mention is that the chip is produced there by South Korean tech giant Samsung.[10]

In 2011 and 2012, there were 36 major semiconductor fabrication plants under construction throughout the world. Twenty-one were being built in China, only one in the United States.

The United States invented the personal computer. Now the two largest American brands — HP and Dell — are quickly losing market share. In 2012, HP shipped 7 percent fewer PCs worldwide than in 2011, while Dell's shipments were down by 13 percent. In contrast, Beijing-based Lenovo Group Ltd., which purchased IBM's PC division in 2005, experienced sales growth of 19 percent in 2012, coming up just short of HP in total sales.[11]

The United States accounted in 2011 for only 1.5 percent of global production of crystalline solar photovoltaic (PV) cells, a technology it invented, and even that portion is in jeopardy. China's share of the global market in that same year was 64 percent. Subsidized Chinese production has led to the closure of almost all U.S. PV capacity.[12]

In wind energy, of the top 10 global producers of wind turbines in 2011, only one (General Electric) was an American company, which accounted for 8.8 percent of the global market. Four of the top 10 firms were Chinese.[13]

In 2011, the United States imported 1.976 billion pieces of luggage, travel bags, leather bags and backpacks, 1.797 billion of which were made in China. The United States imported 245 million women's handbags, 224 million of which came from China.[14]

Ceramic tile can be found in virtually every building in the United States. U.S. ceramic tile producers were responsible for producing 60 million square meters of ceramic tile in 2010.[15] It sounds impressive, but the output accounted for well less than 1 percent of total global production of 9.52 billion square meters. U.S. production of ceramic tile has stayed steady since 2006. During that same period, China's production increased from 3 billon square meters to 4.2 billion. Its global market share: 44 percent. Portugal, Thailand, Indonesia and Egypt are among 17 countries that produce more ceramic tile than does the United States.

What has happened in semiconductors, tool-and-die making, industrial robotics, machine tools, steel, shoes, ceramic tile, printed-circuit boards and mobile phones has occurred in other major industries as well, including consumer electronics, household goods, furniture, textiles and apparel.

As companies offshored production and eliminated millions of U.S. jobs over the past decade, U.S. consumers didn't stop spending. Imports skyrocketed, leading to a most inauspicious development: The federal government lost its tax base. For the period 2002 through 2012, federal budget deficits totaled $8.567 trillion, rising from an annual deficit of $158 billion in 2002 to an astounding $1.33 trillion in 2011.[16] All during those years, as manufacturing was fleeing the country, budget deficits climbed, the financial system collapsed and millions of Americans were left in economic despondency. Why don't the economists make the connection? No industry means no economy. It is pretty simple, and yet there are only a handful of economists who insist on the need for a robust and innovative manufacturing sector. The rest are guided by outdated theories and a refusal to confront the reality of today's world economy.

At exactly the same time that the federal debt was ballooning, America's trade deficit in goods and services was soaring. Between 2000 and 2012, the United States imported $7.08 trillion more than it exported. The direct loss of wealth to foreign competitors over that period averaged $22,556 for every American.[17] For a family of four, the trade deficit represents a loss of $90,224 since 2000. How many American families saved $90,224 over that time?

The trade deficit ballooned even though the U.S. dollar depreciated by 27 percent against the world's major currencies.[18] The dollar's depreciation should have made American exports competitive in world markets and should have sharply reduced America's trade deficit. It did not.

As imports soared, employment in the U.S. manufacturing sector experienced its largest decline in the history of the country, dropping precipitously from 17 million jobs in 2001 to fewer than 12 million less than a decade later. That means that for every 100 Americans, in 2012 only three were in payroll jobs making products. By contrast, from 2001 until 2008, the number of manufacturing jobs in China grew by 14.1 million (to 115.7 million), its increase in seven years alone exceeding the total number of manufacturing jobs in the United States.[19] And the Chinese are not making only low-value, high-volume junk. The percentage of exported products made by unskilled labor in China is declining rapidly, falling to 25 percent in 2006, while high-technology-intensive exports jumped to 32 percent.[20]

The loss of American manufacturing jobs did not occur because of increased automation and productivity. That's a myth, as recent research from the Upjohn Institute and the National Institute of Standards and Technology has proven. Production growth and productivity gains appeared in the manufacturing sector only because the natural evolution of the performance of computer chips skewed the numbers to make it look like U.S. industrial output was growing robustly, while it wasn't.[21] This statistical error led numerous economists to wrongly conclude that the United States is still the largest manufacturing nation in the world. America's flawed measuring systems for industrial output, outsourcing and productivity produce results that "are not representative of what is happening in most manufacturing," notes Upjohn's Susan Houseman.

Why do American politicians fail to see the correlation between skyrocketing debt and a growing inability to finance government services on the one hand and, on the other, the outsourcing of production that has led to the surge of trade imbalances and the loss of both industry and manufacturing jobs? Why have they ignored the crisis at hand? Why have they not spent every moment of their time in Washington debating, adopting, implementing and fine-tuning policies that address America's global trade imbalances, its lack of industrial competitiveness and its loss of so many well-paid jobs?

For those who consider themselves "innovation" economists, the answer is simple: The country continues to be run by neoclassical and Keynesian economists who promote and pursue the application of outdated theories of fiscal and monetary stimulus. These economists control policy throughout the government. They occupy all of the top positions at the White House, Federal Reserve, Treasury Department and all levels of the U.S. academic and industrial enterprise. There are legions of them employed by Washington think tanks and policy institutes. They remain perplexed as to why the economy has stopped generating jobs. "Ultimately, it's a bit of puzzle," says Robert Moffitt, an economics professor at Johns Hopkins University.[22]

No it isn't. It is not a puzzle at all. Without a strong manufacturing base, the economy has no capacity to create good jobs. Manufacturing, with all of its supply chains, is the great economic multiplier.

Still, their repeated prescription for America's ailments is either to spend more federal money or to cut taxes so that Americans can shop. When President Obama demanded in the summer of 2011 that Congress pass his "jobs bill" providing a $1,000 payroll-tax deduction for every employee and extending unemployment benefits to 99 weeks, he rationalized it this way: "It will put money in people's pockets and more customers in the stores."

He never seemed to realize that this policy prescription — either through tax cuts or increased spending programs — has been implemented a dozen times over the past decade. After all, President George W. Bush at a press conference in December 2006 said the solution to America's economic problems was for Americans to "to go shopping more."

The result is a first-ever U.S. bond-market-rating downgrade, massive accumulation of debt, a dispirited workforce with less income and few job opportunities, blighted cities and little sign that America's politicians have a pulse, save for when they are attacking each other.

THE U.S. POLITICAL SYSTEM IS "NOT RESPONDING"

Through the first half of 2013, there was still little talk in Washington of the need to restore industrial capacity or to address skyrocketing imports of both advanced-technology and everyday goods. America's economic policy seems to be a mix of avoiding fiscal cliffs, sequestration, continuing resolutions and debt ceilings.

At the time President Obama was pressing for his payroll-tax cut, he blamed America's problems on "a string of bad luck — things that we could not control," such as the Arab Spring, which drove up the price of oil, the debt crisis in Europe and the earthquake and tsunami in Japan. George Bush did the same thing in 2003, blaming anemic economic growth and the loss of more than 100,000 manufacturing jobs per month on the terrorist attacks of 9/11, the dot-com bust and the war in Iraq. Again, there was no mention of staggering trade deficits and outsourcing, which were viewed by Bush's top economic advisors as being beneficial to the economy. In fact, former top members of Obama's economic team also argued in favor of outsourcing as being beneficial to the U.S. economy and were replaced in Obama's second term by supporters of domestic production.

But when Obama was insisting that his tax cut be adopted to promote shopping, his top economic advisor was Christina Romer, an economist who ultimately returned to her post as a professor at the University of California at Berkeley. Romer revealed the administration's bias against manufacturing in a February 2012 *New York Times*[23] editorial: A policy that promotes the production of "real things," she wrote, is misguided because "American consumers value health care and haircuts as much as washing machines and dryers."

Obama's other top economist, Lawrence Summers, head of the National Economic Council, sneered at policies that would lead to the re-industrialization of the United States, stating shortly after he left the post that there was "no going back to the past," when manufacturing was a dominant part of the economy.[24] He said the new economy was built on "health care, retail, services, recreation, education, haircuts and insurance policies, hotels and houses."

Gregory Tassey, senior economist at the National Institute of Standards and Technology (NIST), says most economic oracles like Romer and Summers suffer from an "installed wisdom" effect. The justifications for their policy prescriptions "have become entrenched and therefore persist, even in the face of accumulating evidence that change is imperative," he writes in a courageous paper published by NIST.[25] "Neoclassical economists dominate the economics profession. They are the ones with a history of publications. They have stature. It's natural that they get picked for the policy positions. To the best of my knowledge, there has never been an innovation economist who has been a member of the White House Council of Economic Advisers." The result, says Tassey: "We are in a competitive environment and we are not responding."

With Summers, Romer and so many like them in control, it isn't too hard to figure out why President Obama has been only marginally successful in rationalizing his economic policies to the American electorate.

During the presidential debate on October 3, 2012, Mitt Romney and Barack Obama focused on the economy and job creation. In 90 minutes of discussion, noted Economic Strategy Institute President Clyde Prestowitz, there was no mention of "the loss of U.S. international competitiveness, the continuing chronic U.S. trade deficit, the offshoring of U.S. jobs and technology, the low rate of U.S. investment compared to countries like China and Germany, and the abysmal state of U.S. infrastructure compared to other leading countries. Insanity has sometimes been defined as continuing to act in a particular way while expecting a different result. Neither of these candidates showed any awareness of the deep underlying currents that continue to erode the country's productive capabilities."[26]

Still, in 2012, Obama's team started talking about the need for a new economic policy focused on rebuilding the manufacturing sector. In March, Gene Sperling, director of the National Economic Council (NEC), spoke about the sector's importance to the larger economy at a conference sponsored by domestic manufacturers. Manufacturing requires "preferential treatment" from the policy community, he said, because of its role in funding innovation, producing spillover economic impacts and creating wealth. "If an auto plant opens, a Wal-Mart can be expected to follow," he told the Manufacturing Renaissance Conference. "But the converse does not necessarily hold — that a Wal-Mart opening brings an auto plant with it."

But Sperling, the main architect of China's 2001 accession to the World Trade Organization (WTO) while serving as NEC director under President Clinton, made no more public mention of a manufacturing policy initiative for the remainder of 2012. His March 27 speech was greeted with skepticism, being viewed as a means to counter challenger Mitt Romney's focus on the issue in the industrial swing states.

Obama made the same promises during the 2008 presidential campaign about rebuilding the U.S. manufacturing sector and reforming trade policies, but then did nothing, most notably failing to address the renminbi-dollar exchange rate. Shortly after the November 2012 election, the Department of the Treasury released its biannual report on international currency practices and, adhering to a decade-old precedent, failed to recognize China as a currency manipulator. The Treasury's decision drew the customary wrath of U.S. domestic manufacturers, who for years have been pleading with the U.S. government to represent their interests rather than the interests of the Chinese government or of those in the United States whom it has hired to do its bidding.

The majority of elected officials have refused to recognize that manufacturing is the engine of a modern economy and that, without it, the country has gone broke. Without a manufacturing base, the service economy has little to serve, save for French fries and margaritas. Without manufacturing, the United States has proven unable to pay off its debts, support the aging baby boomers, restore its educational system, maintain a healthy military, rebuild its infrastructure and continue as a prosperous nation. Yet a majority of Americans know that manufacturing is essential to economic revival. They want the country's elected officials to implement an economic strategy that leads to the rebirth of American industry. In a survey conducted in 2012 by Republican and Democratic pollsters,[27] 89 percent of voters said they favor a strategy for supporting U.S. manufacturing.

In early 2013, President Obama re-started his push for a manufacturing agenda, promoting the creation of a $1 billion National Network of Manufacturing Innovation, but the American political system has been incapable of adopting a pro-manufacturing strategy.

Nevertheless, manufacturing jobs started growing modestly in 2011 through early 2013 for the first time in decades. Exports of goods and services picked up modestly. There is fresh talk about "insourcing" or "reshoring" production back to the United States from China. A growing abundance of cheap natural gas is fueling new investments in energy-intensive process industries. Companies are growing increasingly concerned about global supply chain interruptions caused by floods, earthquakes and labor issues at the ports. Americans say they prefer to buy products made in the United States. And, most important of all, there is recognition — coupled with an immense amount of fear — that the country cannot remain on its present course of going deeper into debt and needs a strong manufacturing base. That's the good news, and it is good. It is essential for the United States to build upon the fledgling growth of its manufacturing sector.

But, by other measures, America's global competitive standing is not yet improving. Through 2012, the U.S. trade deficit continued at record highs, sapping production and jobs out of the economy. China continued to subsidize its industries and exports, engage in illegal manipulation of its currency and restrict exports and imports of products, technologies and materials. Other nations that had massive trade surpluses with the United States followed China's lead into illegal and mercantilist trade practices.

In addition, many countries continued to allow the wanton exploitation of their environment and their workers. Why are foreign-made products that could not be manufactured legally in the United States allowed to be sold in the United States?

In 2012, the U.S. trade deficit with China reached $315 billion, almost $1 billion per day, a disparity between two countries greater than any in history. A calculation based on a conservative estimate of $1 billion equaling 5,000 jobs, a ratio of one job for every $200,000 of GDP, puts the cost to the United States of its $863 million daily trade deficit with China at 4,315 jobs per day in 2013.

In January 2008, U.S. manufacturing jobs fell to their lowest level since 1941, with 11,458,000 Americans employed in the sector. Things turned around from January 2010 to June 2012, as U.S. manufacturing employment increased by 527,000 jobs, to 11,985,000, an average of

17,112 new manufacturing jobs per month. But the increase represented a mere 10 percent of the manufacturing jobs lost since 2000, and at that pace of growth all of the six million manufacturing jobs lost from 2001 to 2009 would not be recovered until 2042, one-third of a century from now. In that time, it is projected, the U.S. population will grow by 66 million people, to 380 million.

To understand the shift in the American economy from production to consumption, it's worth comparing the recent histories of Wal-Mart and General Motors. At the end of 2011, Wal-Mart had 1.4 million employees in the United States and was the country's largest employer. It employed 2.2 million workers worldwide. Its sales in 2012 were $466 billion, almost equaling the budget of the U.S. Department of Defense. On the other hand, General Motors, one of the nation's largest manu-facturing companies and its leading employer as recently as 1990, had a U.S. workforce of 77,000 in 2011, only 5.5 percent the size of Wal-Mart's U.S. workforce. GM had 130,000 employees located outside the United States, almost twice as many as its domestic workforce. More than one-third of GM's American employees, 29,000, were salaried workers while the remaining 48,000 were hourly workers. Amazingly, GM had 520,000 former employees receiving retirement benefits, 120,000 of whom had been salaried workers and 400,000 hourly workers. GM employment has been in steady decline, from a peak of 618,365 in 1979 to 207,000 worldwide at the end of 2011. The automaker's total 2012 revenues of $152 billion were less than one-third those of Wal-Mart. GM claims to be on the road back to health and prosperity, and there are some positive indicators, but the company will remain a shadow of its former self.

At the beginning of 2013, the 12 million Americans who were officially unemployed outnumbered the 11.9 million working in the manufacturing sector. Almost twice as many Americans worked for the government (21.8 million) as worked in the manufacturing sector.

While the total number of Americans employed has hardly budged since 2002, the number of Americans receiving Social Security benefits has increased by 9 million, to 55.4 million by the end of 2011. The number of Americans on Medicare increased from 41 million in 2002 to 49 million in 2011 and Medicare's cost increased over those years from $266 billion to $549 billion, or 3.7 percent of U.S. GDP.[28]

The growth in the number of people receiving food stamps has also far exceeded the number of new jobs created in the United States. In 2000, there were 17 million Americans enrolled in the Supplemental Nutrition Assistance Program (SNAP). In 2012, that number had almost tripled, increasing by 30 million, to 47 million.[29] SNAP cost American taxpayers $95 billion in 2012, not including another $19 billion for the School Lunch Program.

The amount spent on Social Security, Medicare and food stamps in 2012 — more than $2.06 trillion, or 13 percent of the U.S. GDP of $15.68 trillion — is more than the manufacturing sector's total contribution to GDP of $1.837 trillion, or 12.2 percent.[30] Incredibly, imports of goods and services, at $2.74 trillion in 2012, represented 17.5 percent of GDP.[31] Is it possible for the United States to continue paying for these social programs without a robust industrial sector and with only 11 million people producing products?

Re-energizing U.S. manufacturing and putting people back to work making products would go a long way toward resolving the U.S. employment crisis and reducing the cost of the safety net. Evidence comes from three major U.S. global competitors: Germany, Japan and South Korea. In the United States, 10.2 percent of all workers were in the manufacturing sector at the end of 2011. In Germany, employment in the manufacturing sector stood at 20 percent,[32] while Japan and Korea both had 17 percent of their workforces in manufacturing. All three countries had unemployment rates that were substantially below that of the United States at the end of 2011: Germany's was 6 percent, Japan's was 4.2 percent and South Korea's was 3.4 percent. The United States' official unemployment rate at the time was 8.9 percent.[33]

CALL TO ACTION: AMERICA'S CEOS, ACADEMICS AND THINK TANKS ADVOCATE FOR A MANUFACTURING REVIVAL

Since 2009, some of America's most prominent business executives have grown so concerned about the country's loss of industrial capability that they have written books, hosted major conferences and gotten personally involved in policymaking. They want the United States to get back on track by embracing manufacturing as the central pillar of economic policy.

Ford Motor Co. CEO Bill Ford wants the government to "develop a national manufacturing strategy that re-establishes an environment for U.S. business to thrive and compete on a global basis." Along with Andrew Liveris, chairman of Dow Chemical Co., Ford hosted a meeting of the Detroit Economic Club for the purpose of calling on the federal government to "define an industrial policy that creates a framework that allows [U.S.] companies to compete fairly and freely" on the world market.[34] Some 4,000 people from 550 organizations attended the event.

The "only chance" for the United States to turn things around "is to remember, revive and revolutionize what made us great for so long — the manufacturing sector," writes Liveris in his book *Make It In America: The Case for Re-Inventing the Economy*. Without a strong manufacturing base "the United States no longer has an economic model that's sustainable," he states. Yet, "it seems no one's talking about a fundamental fix." Liveris got so fed up that he got involved, becoming co-chairman of the Advanced Manufacturing Partnership, a federal council that is advising the government on manufacturing policy.[35]

Hank Nothhaft, former CEO of Tessera Technologies, a producer of high-tech manufacturing production equipment, attributes the decline of California's economy to a process similar to what occurred a generation earlier in the industrial Midwest. "I did not work my whole life creating jobs and wealth just to spend my golden years in some Banana Republic of Silicon Valley," he writes in his book *Great Again: Revitalizing America's Entrepreneurial Leadership*. Without a manufacturing base, "the clock is ticking on America's future," Nothhaft warns.

The biggest cheerleader in the private sector for U.S. manufacturing —
or at least the one with the most visibility — has been General Electric
CEO Jeffrey Immelt, who said: "We have to make things here. We
have to know how to make things. It's like night follows day. There was
a macroeconomic misstep that has taken place over 25 or 30 years that
we could go gently from being a technology- and manufacturing-based
economy to a service-based economy and that we could run $1 trillion
trade deficits, and nobody fundamentally cared. That has been quite
a big misstep."[36]

Others who have jumped onto the "manufacturing-is-essential" book-
writing bandwagon include Richard Dauch, co-founder and chairman
of American Axle & Manufacturing Inc., with *American Drive: How
Manufacturing Will Save Our Economy*; former Deputy Assistant
Secretary of Commerce and Silicon Valley congressional hopeful Ro
Khanna with *Entrepreneurial Nation: Why Manufacturing Is Still Key
to America's Future*; and Pulitzer Prize-winning journalist Hedrick
Smith with *Who Stole the American Dream?*

Old bastions of academia are also galvanized. The Massachusetts Institute
of Technology (MIT) initiated a major cross-disciplinary study in 2011
on the importance of reviving American manufacturing. The "Production
in the Innovation Economy"[37] project concluded in early 2013 that the
United States has lost the ability to scale new innovations into commercial
products. The problem afflicts every sector of the American economy.
High-tech startups, heartland manufacturing firms and multinational
corporations alike can no longer scale up production in the United States.
"It's not just that factories stand empty and crumbling," according to
the MIT study, which included 20 faculty members. "It's that critical
strengths and capabilities have disappeared that once served to bring
new enterprises to life." The situation has caused "alarm bells to sound
loud in our halls," says MIT.

In late 2012, Harvard University professors Gary Pisano and Willy Shih,
in their book *Producing Prosperity: Why America Needs a Manufacturing
Renaissance*, wrote that the United States has been engaged in the "grand
economic experiment" of allowing its manufacturing sector to atrophy

under the false assumption that embracing services and the IT sector would lead to growing prosperity. "If, in the end, the 'manufacturing does not matter' hypothesis proves wrong — and we think that's exactly what's going to happen — the United States … will have a big problem on its hands."[38]

Management consultants are on board as well: Having made millions advising American companies on how to outsource production and jobs to foreign nations, they have now switched to marketing the notion of "insourcing" or "reshoring." The most famous of these about-faces comes from the Boston Consulting Group (BCG), whose 2012 paper on insourcing[39] touched the hearts of American journalists seeking to write a contrarian story about manufacturing. The BCG study found that manufacturing was going to return to the United States — to places like Mississippi, where employers have traditionally paid low wages and provided few benefits, and where the cost of employing American workers could become competitive with Chinese labor rates. According to BCG's calculations, as many as five million jobs could return to the manufacturing sector by 2015 and generate an additional $100 billion in annual output.

Booz & Company's contribution to the discussion, *Manufacturing's Wake Up Call*, says that U.S. manufacturing "is at a moment of truth." If the manufacturing sector continues to be neglected, U.S. industrial output "could fall by half … and U.S. manufacturing capabilities could then erode past the point of no return."[40] And PricewaterhouseCoopers joined the discourse, stating in its September 2012 report *A Homecoming for U.S. Manufacturing?*[41] that transportation and energy costs, along with currency fluctuations, are "the most salient reason United States manufacturers will choose to produce closer to their major customer base."

Some of the country's most influential think tanks are also fully engaged in the manufacturing-is-necessary campaign. The United States could generate up to four million direct and indirect manufacturing jobs if the country were to eliminate its trade deficit, says the Progressive Policy Institute (PPI).[42] A target of 15.5 to 16 million manufacturing jobs —

representing a one-third increase over today's 12 million — "gives policy-makers something explicit to aim for." With the elimination of the trade deficit, the U.S. budget deficit would fall by as much as $250 billion, the unemployment rate would fall by as much as 2.3 percentage points and GDP would increase by up to 2 percent, says PPI.

The Brookings Institution has produced its own major study, in which it states that manufacturing is "indispensable to the U.S. economy."[43] And through its "Charter for Revitalizing American Manufacturing," the Information Technology and Innovation Foundation (ITIF) brought together a diverse group of organizations that ordinarily would not agree on most anything to endorse policies promoting U.S. manufacturing. ITIF has become a prominent Washington economic think tank due to its unapologetic embrace of "innovation economics" and its ability to make and promulgate the intellectual argument in favor of American manufacturing.

The White House Office of Science and Technology Policy put its own stake in the ground in 2012 with a long-delayed report, *National Strategic Plan for Advanced Manufacturing*, in which it stated: "Manufacturing capability gaps in the United States have led to the loss of substantial economic benefits."

What is the common conclusion of these myriad books and studies? That the American political system has proved incapable of addressing the policy issues that are crucial to revitalizing domestic industry. The political process has failed to deal with restructuring the tax system; to address some trading partners' illegal currency practices, subsidies, incentives and barriers to American exports; to eliminate red tape and regulations; to restructure work-training programs; or to adopt a range of policies that encourage investment in innovation, production over consumption and exports over imports. Such a Herculean effort will require every office of government, from bureaus within the Defense Department to civilian agencies, to reorient its operations and policies toward the goal of enhancing job creation and economic growth, just as is done in every local, regional and national government agency in China, Germany, Korea and Japan.

A MORE FAVORABLE LANDSCAPE FOR MANUFACTURING

Global conditions have changed slightly in America's favor through 2012 and early 2013, but not because its political system has been activated or even alarmed.

Rising wages in China are making the United States' workforce more competitive. But an American worker with three dependents and an hourly wage of $13.97 or less is eligible for food stamps. In all, 40 percent of the 46 million people receiving food stamps in 2012 lived in households meeting those criteria.[44] That means American companies that don't pay their employees enough to buy groceries — much less health care — are effectively being provided with tens of billions of dollars in a form of corporate welfare by the federal government. Corporate profits and management pay may be on the rise, but adequate worker pay is not.

And anyone who thinks Chinese wages are quickly catching up with America's minimum wage of $7.25 an hour would do well to look at the federal government's research on Chinese manufacturing compensation, conducted by the Bureau of Labor Statistics (BLS). According to the BLS International Labor Comparisons program (killed in 2013 due to budget cuts),[45] the average total hourly compensation for a Chinese manufacturing worker at the end of 2008 was $1.36 an hour, including all wages, bonuses and allowances paid in cash or in kind; sick leave, medical insurance and vacation time; and employer payments for social benefits, unemployment insurance and pension funds.

But that is the average compensation package for all manufacturing workers in China. The compensation of a manufacturing worker outside an urban area was the equivalent of $0.82 per hour in 2008 — which multiplies out to $156 per month or $1,870 per year. Manufacturing in China is migrating to these lower-cost areas.

So, although total average compensation costs for manufacturing workers in China are rising, they began at an exceedingly low level. In 2002, they stood at $0.57 per hour, doubling by 2007 to $1.06 per hour and stretching to $1.36 per hour in 2008. If the total compensation cost for a manufacturing worker in China goes up by a factor of 10, it will still be only one-third of the total compensation cost for an

American manufacturing worker, which stood at $35.53 an hour in
2011. This includes a wage of $23.70 and all benefits and payments
made by employers, including sick pay, pension and 401(k) contributions,
vacation pay, unemployment and health insurance, social insurance
and payroll taxes.[46]

FIGURE 1: *Index of Hourly Compensation Costs in Manufacturing,
Selected Countries and Areas, 2008*

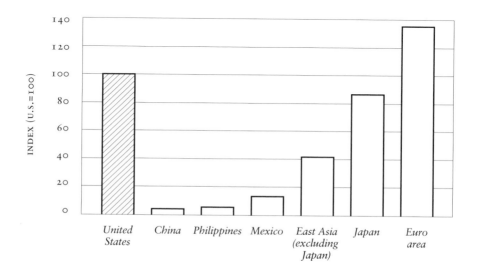

*(Source: "China's employment and compensation costs in manufacturing through 2008,"
Judith Banister and George Cook, for the Bureau of Labor Statistics International Labor
Comparisons Program, March 2011.)*

"As measured in U.S. dollars, Chinese hourly labor compensation costs
in manufacturing were roughly 4 percent of those in the United States,"
said the International Labor Comparison program.[47] India's manufacturing
workers are just as poorly paid. At the end of 2007, the latest year
for which data was available, India's average hourly compensation rate
in U.S. dollars was $1.17, about 3 percent of the level of workers in
the United States.[48] Other countries in the same category include the

Philippines at 3.6 percent and Sri Lanka at 2.3 percent. The total hourly compensation cost for a Mexican worker in 2011 stood at $6.48 per hour. Conversely, Norway had the highest-paid manufacturing workers, with an average hourly compensation of $64.15. Germany's manufacturing workers averaged $47.38 per hour in total compensation.

If manufacturing returns to America based on depressed wages, its return will be of little benefit to the U.S. economy. In fact, reshoring is already "accelerating the decline of the middle class," as southern states are luring foreign automobile and aerospace manufacturers with the country's lowest wages, notes Northwestern University economist Robert Gordon.[49]

"This in turn puts pressure on legacy firms in the North to introduce two-tier wage systems that pay new entrants half the traditional union wage, as has occurred in the Midwest auto industry in the past few years," Gordon writes. "The 'revival of American manufacturing' is heralded in the media without recognition that this is part of an ongoing process that erodes the number of high-paying middle-class jobs available to those without a college education."

U.S. TRADE FIGURES TELL THE AMERICAN ECONOMIC STORY

There are not many measures of a country's global industrial competitive position, but there is one that can be used: the trade balance. Evidence provided by trade figures suggests that reshoring on a measurable scale is not yet taking place, at least not through the first half of 2013. The United States continues to rack up the largest trade deficits in history. If the country is wondering why it is broke — and why it can't afford to do anything about it — it has only to look at where its money is going: overseas, to foreigner competitors.

America's trade deficit in goods was $736 billion in 2012, which divides out to $2.02 billion per day, or $6.41 per American per day. Over the course of a year, that equals a loss of $2,340 for each American or $9,362 for a family of four.

Total imports of goods and services in 2012 were $2.736 trillion, which works out to 17.3 percent of U.S. GDP of $15.83 trillion or a daily import stream of $7.5 billion. Dividing total imports by the U.S. population in 2012 of 315 million equals $23.81 per day of imported foreign goods and services for each American. In 2012, therefore, each American spent $8,690.65 on imported goods and services and a family of four spent $34,763. This amount is equal to the yearly take-home pay, before taxes, for an American earning $18 an hour. Virtually all of that money goes abroad.

How many manufacturing jobs were lost due to the $736 billion trade deficit in goods in 2012? The Commerce Department calculates that one U.S. job was created for every $185,000 in exports,[50] so by this measure the $736 billion goods deficit cost the United States 3,978,378 manufacturing jobs in 2012. If one job is created for every $92,000 in government spending, which it is according to another measure provided by the White House,[51] then the 2011 trade deficit in manufactured goods cost the United States 8 million direct manufacturing jobs.

Here's yet another measure: George Mason University calculated that one American job would be lost for every $78,571 in budget cuts due to sequestration.[52] By that measure, the $736 billion trade deficit in goods in 2011 equals the loss of 9,367,323 jobs. By any measure, manufacturing job loss due to burgeoning trade deficits is enormous.

Perhaps even worse is the fact that so much of what the United States imports comes from countries that do not abide by the environmental and safety rules that are imposed on U.S. manufacturing companies — which is one of the reasons their prices are so low. Many imported products being sold in the United States would not be allowed to be manufactured under the same conditions in the United States. A recent case: the September 12, 2012, fire at the Karachi, Pakistan, textile factory that killed at least 250 people who were locked in the factory by its owners. The last time something like that happened in the United States was on March 25, 1911, when the Triangle Shirtwaist factory caught fire in New York City and hundreds of people on the streets watched as 146 women perished, many jumping to their deaths. At the time it was called "one of the most tragic events in the history of the world." But 70 percent more workers died in the Karachi fire.

Who were the buyers of the Karachi factory's output? Francesco d'Ovidio, the head of the International Labor Organization's office in Pakistan, said "production was primarily for the export markets of Western Europe and North America." Press reports in Pakistan said the denim produced in the factory was purchased by Levi's and Wal-Mart.[53] Wal-Mart, Sears and Disney were implicated in a November 24, 2012, Bangladesh garment factory fire that killed 112 workers according to the Associated Press, whose reporter, in searching the charred ruins of the factory, "found these and other clothes, including sweaters from the French company Teddy Smith, among the equipment."

Five months later, the worst industrial accident in the history of the world garment industry occurred — again, in Bangladesh. The horrific collapse of the Rana Plaza building in Dhaka on April 24, 2013 killed 1,127 people who were making the lowest wages of garment workers in the world. Newly ordained Pope Francis shortly thereafter called those in the business, financial and political communities who have constructed this global economic system a "virtual tyranny, which unilaterally and irremediably imposes its own laws and rules, [and whose] attitude is a rejection of ethics."[54]

Another example of a company that could not operate in the United States in the manner it does in China is Hon Hai Precision Industry, or Foxconn. Apple Inc. has hired Foxconn to produce most of its gadgetry. Here is what Foxconn CEO Terry Gou said in early 2012 about his employees: "Hon Hai has a workforce of over one million worldwide and, as human beings are also animals, to manage one million animals gives me a headache." He added that he would like to learn how to manage animals from the director of the Taipei Zoo — who was in the audience at the presentation. In 2010, 18 Foxconn employees tried to commit suicide at work, jumping out of factory windows. In response, Foxconn installed nets below their upper factory floors to catch jumpers.

It wasn't long thereafter that Terry Gou's "animals" rioted. On September 23, 2012, a Sunday, 2,000 of the 73,000 workers at Foxconn's Taiyuan, China, plant grew violent over grievances they had against the security forces guarding the dorms where they live. The factory was temporarily shut down. The *Washington Post* account of the event quoted

Liu Kaiming, executive director of the Beijing-based labor-rights group Institute of Contemporary Observation, as stating: "Such riots have become in some ways inevitable."

There are stories almost every week in American newspapers about workers in developing nations, many of whom are children, who live and work in desperate conditions, exploited by their employers — all making products for consumers in the United States. The Department of Labor's annual "List of Goods Produced by Child Labor and Forced Labor"[55] says that adult forced laborers in China — a communist country with only 4 percent of the population identifying as Christian — are producing Christmas ornaments. The U.S. Department of Labor says that other goods produced in China by forced labor include artificial flowers, cotton, electronics, fireworks, footwear, garments, nails and toys. Child labor is being used in the production of cotton, bricks, electronics, fireworks, textiles and toys.

Dozens of countries are exploiting millions of workers, including children, according to the Department of Labor. There were "at least 21 million individuals, including 6 million children, in forced labor, including commercial sexual exploitation and debt bondage, at any point in time during the 10-year period of 2002 to 2011," says the department. The most recent global estimate found that between 2004 and 2008 there were 215 million child laborers, 115 million of them doing hazardous work.

Most every year, the National Association of Manufacturers (NAM) produces a report on how much more it cost to make products in the United States than in other countries. American manufacturers complain that overzealous regulation contributes to America's lack of competitiveness. NAM's 2012 study said U.S. companies had costs that were an average of 20 percent higher than their foreign competitors', due in large part to burdensome rules from the Environmental Protection Agency (EPA) and the Occupational Safety and Health Administration (OSHA).[56]

Is there a chance that the United States government could impose an import fee at the rate recommended by NAM — 20 percent — on imports from countries whose regulatory standards do not measure up to America's? If this payment were imposed as a fee, it would be called a "tariff" and those promoting it would be labeled "protectionists," a pejorative used in Washington to immediately bring discussion about trade policy to a halt.

Yet an import tax could be the most effective way to level the playing field. By directing such a tax at nations that are exploiting their workers and the environment and are cheating in the global market, the United States could raise hundreds of billions in revenue — revenue that it could use to pay off its debts to these very trading partners. All this could be done while avoiding tax hikes on Americans and offsetting the cost disadvantages that domestic manufacturers face when competing with foreigners who do not have an EPA or an OSHA to worry about.

Donald Trump's 2012 presidential campaign gained traction among Americans based entirely on his strident advocacy of slapping a 25 percent import fee on all Chinese imports. Former Republican congressman and Louisiana governor Buddy Roemer tried to compete in the 2012 Republican presidential primaries by promoting a "fair-trade adjustment" tax on the Chinese. "The *Wall Street Journal* already labels me a protectionist," said Roemer at the start of the Republican primary season. "And I am proud of it. I am going to protect American jobs from child labor, prison labor, forced labor and standards where it would be illegal to have such plants in America. A level playing field is not protectionism. That is solid American security. What kind of nation would we have if 15 percent of the people are out of work permanently? We would be Greece. We would be Portugal. We would be in trouble. Well, I've got news for you, we're in trouble." Republican presidential nominee Mitt Romney was a trade hawk, stating repeatedly in his stump speech through the Midwest that, "On day one, I will label China a currency manipulator, which will allow me as president to be able to put in place, if necessary, tariffs where I believe that they are taking unfair advantage of our manufacturers."

But powerful financial forces and multinational corporations that benefit from overseas production through its cheap labor, lack of worker rights and environmental protection, subsidies and tax breaks would oppose such a "fair-trade adjustment" fee. They could be counted on to argue that it would be the American consumer, who at this point can ill afford it, paying the duty — making it, in effect, a regressive tax. Still, such an import fee could help improve the United States' cost competitiveness, making it a more attractive place to build a factory that could hire some of the welfare and food stamp "takers," who could then both contribute to U.S. consumer demand — as Wal-Mart CEO Simon would hope — and pay taxes.

Exploited workers overseas and America's unemployed millions have something in common, and that is a growing sense of unfairness. There were 60 million fewer jobs in the world in 2012 than in 2007, with 225 million people unemployed worldwide. The global economy needs to create 400 million new jobs over the next decade.[57] The planet has 900 million working poor, 456 million of whom live on less than $1.25 per day, the internationally accepted standard for extreme poverty. At least 870 million of the world's people are undernourished.[58]

While U.S. exporters face high tariffs on the goods they sell to foreign nations, the United States allows the vast majority of imports into the country without any duty whatsoever. In 2012, average U.S. import duties were a mere 1.3 percent applied to only 31 percent of all imports. The remaining 69 percent of imports entered the country duty free. Those import duties — tariffs — contributed $37.2 billion in revenue to the U.S. Treasury in 2011, up from $32 billion in 2010. The increase in government revenues from tariffs was due to the growth of imports. Of course, U.S. Customs and Border Protection, which collects duties, hailed the surge of imports as being great for the American economy. "A 10.5 percent increase in imports over fiscal year 2010 import values reflects a positive outlook for a recovering economy and increased consumer purchases," says the first line of the agency's 2011 annual report.[59] Acting Customs Bureau Commissioner Allen Gina gushed: "As many of you know, domestic economic health can be measured by the value of our imports." From his perspective, the fact that the United States imported so much more in 2011 "is an encouraging sign not just for the trade community, but for the American economy in general."

Historically, U.S. import duties of 1.3 percent on 31 percent of imports are very low. The 1828 Tariff Act raised the average import duty to 62 percent, and tariffs funded all of the activities of the federal government for the better part of 100 years. Between 1871 and 1913, when the federal income tax became permanent under the 16th Amendment to the Constitution, U.S. "tariffs never fell below 38 percent," according to Clyde Prestowitz of the Economic Strategy Institute. In 1922, tariffs were set at 38.5 percent. During the Kennedy Round of the GATT negotiations ending in 1967, U.S. tariffs on imports declined from 12.2 percent to 8.6 percent. If that rate had been applied in 2011, the U.S. Treasury would have collected $229 billion in revenue from imports.

According to U.S. Customs, in 2011 China paid more U.S. duties than any other country, its $13 billion "exceeding the total of Japan, Germany, Vietnam and Indonesia combined." With Chinese imports close to $400 billion in 2011, the $13 billion collected by the federal government represents an average duty rate of 3.25 percent for all Chinese goods. And, according to a 2013 study by the Government Accountability Office, countries easily skirted paying duties due to inadequate enforcement efforts by the U.S. Government.[60]

China's government collected a lot more than did the United States in import duties. In 2011, China's customs duties on imports increased by 29 percent over 2010, to $256 billion, according to Yu Guangzhou, chief of China's General Administration of Customs.[61] China's average import-duty rate is 10 percent on goods, a decrease from 15 percent when China joined the WTO in 2001, according to the Chinese government.

A CLOSER LOOK AT AMERICAN IMPORTS AND EXPORTS

To an alarming extent, the United States imports high-value-added manufactured goods and exports waste paper, scrap metal, raw materials, bulk food, forest products, animal feed and chemicals — products that are more typical of a developing country's exports than those of a high-tech industrial power.

In 2011, Wal-Mart was the country's leading importer of goods entering via container ships, according to the Port Import Export Reporting Service (PIERS). Wal-Mart imported 710,000 containers in 2011, an increase of 418,100 containers over 2002.

In 2011, the second-largest importer of containers was another big American retailer, Target, with 472,000 containers, followed by

Home Depot (296,800 containers); Lowe's (228,000); Dole Food (223,000); Sears (207,700); Heineken (129,000); Philips (127,200); LG (120,000); and Chiquita Brands (117,500 containers). The 10 largest importers of containers into the United States accounted for 3,450,900 containers in 2011.

Not far below 2011's top 10 importers were a who's who of retailers: IKEA, Samsung, Costco, Nike, Ashley Furniture, General Electric, Family Dollar Stores, Whirlpool, Dollar Tree, Williams-Sonoma, Gap, Kohl's and Staples, as well as many other name brands, major global manufacturers and retailers (Bridgestone, BMW, Adidas, Panasonic, Best Buy, Toyota, Hewlett-Packard, Nissan, etc.). In 100th place on the PIERS annual compilation of importers was Mando America, a South Korean company that imported 11,600 containers of automobile brakes and steering and suspension systems.

The export side of America's international trade-in-containers ledger is not nearly as pretty. For the eleventh year in a row, America's largest exporter in terms of containers was the Chinese-owned company American Chung Nam. This exporting powerhouse shipped 354,000 containers, mostly to China, every one of which was filled with waste paper. As has been the case for a decade or more, America's number-one export via ocean container remains junk.

In second place among American exporters by containers in 2011 was Koch Industries' subsidiary GD Harman Recycling. Its exports: 144,000 containers of paper. Third place among America's largest container exporters was International Paper (135,000 containers of paper and waste paper), followed by Sims Metal Management (116,000 containers of scrap metal); Weyerhaeuser (109,100 containers of paper); Dow Chemical (105,800 containers of bulk chemicals); Newport CH Intl. (98,200 containers of waste paper); DuPont (93,800 containers of bulk chemicals); Shintech, a Japanese company that produces polyvinyl chloride (91,200 containers); and ExxonMobil Chemical (82,100 containers of bulk chemicals).

Of the top 100 American exporters via containers in 2011, 22 were exporting waste paper. In 100th place among exporters of containers from the United States in 2011 was SP Newsprint at 13,600 containers full of, you guessed it, recycled paper.

Americans were once proud of their ability to sell value-added products to global consumers — the 1935 slogan "Trenton Makes, The World Takes" still illuminates a major bridge crossing the Delaware River into New Jersey's capital. But the tables have turned. While the top 10 importers of containers into the United States brought in 3.45 million, the top 10 exporters shipped out only 1.32 million That is a lot of empty containers headed back to foreign competitors.

What happens to the wastepaper, newsprint and cardboard that is shipped from the United States to China? It is turned into boxes used to pack manufactured goods headed back to the United States, many of which are imported by Wal-Mart, Target, Home Depot, Lowe's and other retail giants and global manufacturing firms.

Joseph Bonney, senior editor at the *Journal of Commerce*, which produces the PIERS report, says there is little indication of "reshoring" in the import/export data. "As far as packing up an entire plant in China and moving it back here, I don't see it," he says. "You see a lot written about manufacturing coming back here, but I just don't see it. I'm a skeptic of all of this reshoring."

DRILLING DOWN INTO TRADE WITH CHINA

The Census Bureau's monthly trade data provides further insight into America's trade status.[62] It breaks out the precise dollar amount of imports from and exports to every country that trades with the United States. Its findings are surprising: When it comes to trade between the United States and China, it is the United States that looks like the developing nation and China that looks like the industrial and technological powerhouse.

In 2012, the largest U.S. export to China was "oil seeds" — mostly soybeans — at $15 billion. By comparison, China's largest export to the United States was telecommunications equipment at $58 billion (up from $45 billion in 2011). U.S. exports of the same equipment to China were a fraction of that amount, only $1.9 billion. The second-largest import category from China in 2012 was computers at $55 billion (up from $47.2 billion in 2011). The United States, considered by some to be a computer superpower, exported to China computers worth only $1.1 billion.

The same imbalance exists in dozens of other advanced product categories: industrial machinery, semiconductors, scientific machinery, automotive parts and accessories, electrical parts, generators and transformers, industrial engines and scientific and medical equipment. The trend lines of surging Chinese exports to the United States and diminishing U.S. exports to China have not changed over the past 10 years. Indeed, the U.S. went from having a surplus in advanced-technology products trade of $32 billion in 1997 to a deficit of $92 billion in 2012, a staggering shift of $124 billion.

As the U.S. trade deficit worsens, China's global trade surplus continues to expand. In 2012, China's trade surplus jumped by 15 percent to $755 billion, $315 billion of which was with the United States. From 2009 to 2012, total Chinese exports increased by $809 billion, up 71 percent, while total U.S. exports increased by $337 billion or 39 percent. At the current rate of growth, President Obama's stated goal of doubling exports by 2014 will not be reached, with the latest projections calling for an increase of 43 percent. China will almost achieve the doubling that Obama set for the United States, however, with its exports expected to increase by 83 percent over the five years ending in 2014.

"This continues the dramatic rise of China from 2000, when U.S. manufactured exports were almost three times larger than Chinese exports, to 2012, when Chinese exports are projected to be 58 percent larger than U.S. exports and on track to double U.S. exports by mid-decade," according to analyst Ernest Preeg of the Manufacturers Alliance for Productivity and Innovation (MAPI).[63] As its annual trade surplus reaches $1 trillion, China will have vast financial resources that it can use to continue to increase its global economic power and influence.

Preeg estimates that the increase of $169 billion in the U.S. trade deficit between 2009 and 2012 resulted in the loss of between 700,000 and 1.4 million U.S. manufacturing jobs — or more than 10 percent of total U.S. manufacturing employment. Typically, one manufacturing job generates four jobs in the service sector, so the increase in the U.S. trade deficit with China cost the United States upward of one million jobs in 2012. The total number of jobs the United States created in 2012 was 1.88 million. "The most disturbing development of all for U.S. manufacturing jobs and production is the surging trade imbalances with China," says Preeg.

Other economists have put a specific number on U.S. job loss due to the trade deficit with China. Rob Scott of the Economic Policy Institute says the United States has lost 2.7 million jobs due to trade with China since that nation joined the WTO in 2001.[64] Of that total, 2.1 million were in manufacturing. "These lost manufacturing jobs account for more than half of all U.S. manufacturing jobs lost or displaced between 2001 and 2011," says Scott. The manufacturing sector that experienced the largest loss of jobs was computers and electronics, where 1.065 million jobs were displaced by Chinese production, or 39 percent of the total number of manufacturing jobs lost in that sector between 2001 and 2011.

It did not stop after the collapse of Wall Street, either. From 2008 to 2011, the United States lost 662,100 jobs to Chinese trade, "even though imports from China and the rest of the world plunged in 2009," says Scott. "The growing trade deficit with China has cost jobs in all 50 states and the District of Columbia and Puerto Rico, as well as in each congressional district."

California's economy has been hammered, with the loss of 474,700 manufacturing jobs, or 2.9 percent of total state employment, due to the trade deficit with China since 2001 — and that is not including the multiplier effect created by each manufacturing job. Texas lost 239,600 manufacturing jobs due to unbalanced trade with China, or 2.3 percent of total state employment. Even in a small state like New Hampshire, the loss of 20,400 manufacturing jobs due to the trade deficit with China represented 3 percent of total state employment. Scott says that his numbers are conservative.

Another study, done by economists at Yale University and the Federal Reserve, found that the U.S. manufacturing sector would have gained more than 4 million jobs for the seven years ending in 2007 "without the effect of PNTR" — Permanent Normal Trade Relations, which was signed with China in 2000.[65]

Research conducted by David Autor of MIT found that imports from China accounted for 25 percent of the decline in U.S. manufacturing employment between 1991 and 2000 and explain "41 percent of the decline between 2000 and 2007." These, he said "are economically sizable effects."[66]

MAPI's Ernest Preeg believes that such lopsided trade with China can't continue for much longer. He is convinced that the United States must confront China over its practice of currency manipulation and must do so quickly and forcefully. He is stunned that the U.S. Treasury Department, in its biannual report on foreign currency practices, has not labeled China as a manipulator of its currency. The issue flared up in the 2012 presidential campaign when Mitt Romney made the point in hundreds of commercials aimed at the industrial swing states. Obama postponed release of the scheduled October 2012 currency manipulation report until after the election. Issued late in the day on November 27, a Friday — the deadest part of the weekly news cycle — it said that "no major trading partner of the United States met the standards" used to determine whether a country conspicuously manipulates its currency. But tucked on page 14 of the report was this: "China's exceedingly high foreign exchange reserves relative to those of other economies, the persistence of its current account and trade surpluses, and the insufficient degree of appreciation of the RMB (renminbi), especially given rapid productivity growth in the traded goods sector, suggest that the real exchange rate of the RMB remains significantly undervalued and further appreciation of the RMB against the dollar and other major currencies is warranted."

Preeg notes that the International Monetary Fund (IMF) defines currency manipulation as protracted, large-scale central bank purchases of foreign exchange that hold down the exchange rate. Since 2002, he says, China has made $3 trillion in such purchases, "by far the most protracted and largest-scale purchase[s] in the history of the IMF, while its trade surplus in [manufactured goods] has increased tenfold."

Yet both the Bush and Obama administrations have refused to act. "This American policy of head-in-the-sand denial needs to end," declares Preeg. If the country continues to hemorrhage so many of its industrial resources, it will no longer be able to achieve "technology-driven growth and defense modernization."

THE SUCCESS OF INDUSTRIAL POLICY:
IN RARE EARTHS, CHINA HAS THE WORLD IN ITS GRIP

China brags that its long-term strategy of capturing an entire industrial supply chain has worked. In a June 2012 report the Chinese government issued to defend its rare-earths industrial policies, it said that China can now produce more than 400 varieties of rare-earth products to more than 1,000 specifications.[67] China's rare-earth materials industry generated $15 billion in revenue in 2011 and accounted for more than 90 percent of global production.

China's success in rare earths goes well beyond the mining and refining industries. "[I]ndustrialization has been achieved in using rare earths to produce permanent magnet, luminescent, hydrogen storage catalytic materials and other new materials, providing support for the restructuring and upgrade of traditional industries and the development of emerging industries of strategic importance," states the Chinese government. The Chinese in essence told the United States and the rest of the world that they had won the economic battle for future technologies without the United States' even realizing that it had lost.

It wasn't long ago that the United States was the dominant global supplier of these materials. For 50 years beginning in the 1940s, the Mountain Pass mine in California produced most of the world's rare-earth materials. But everything changed in the 1990s, when China started flooding the market with rare-earth minerals, more than tripling global supply. "During this time, Chinese rare-earth-producing firms were largely unprofitable but were allowed to survive through direct and indirect support by the Chinese government," says Jeffery Green, president of J.A. Green & Co. and former staff director to the House Armed Services subcommittee on Readiness. "This backing enabled China's rare-earth industry to continue to mine and export these materials at prices far below the actual costs of production."

Once China controlled almost 100 percent of the world's rare-earths mining and processing industries, it put its industrial policy initiatives into overdrive. In 2011, it strengthened its export restrictions on rare-earth materials, which it had done every year since 2006, driving prices up dramatically over that period. The intended effect was to force companies that use rare earths in their products to set up manufacturing operations in China in order to have access to supplies. "China strictly controls the total volumes of rare earth mining and production and takes restrictive measures on the mining, production, consumption and export of rare-earth products simultaneously," says the Chinese government.

Rare earths are not some esoteric commodity with limited importance. On the contrary, rare earth elements and the products made from them are increasingly used as vital components in high-technology products and defense components. From hard disk drives to the guidance systems used in "smart bombs," rare earths play a critical role.

In its 2012 annual report to Congress, the U.S.-China Economic and Security Review Commission stated that China is using its dominance in rare earths "as leverage for political purposes" in its dispute with Japan over fishing rights. A Chinese embargo on rare-earth exports to Japan "suggests that China is willing to use its position as the world's primary source of these materials as a political weapon," says the U.S.-China Commission. "As China continues to tighten control over its rare earth industry, this threat becomes more acute. . . . The United States is vulnerable to such developments due to its reliance on minerals imported from China."

Twenty years after Chinese premier Deng Xiaoping stated that "there is oil in the Middle East and there are rare earths in China," the United States, Europe and Japan finally took notice. On June 27, 2012, the three filed a case with the WTO asking for the creation of a dispute-settlement panel aimed at eliminating unfair Chinese practices related to rare-earth materials. The United States Trade Representative (USTR) said it was necessary to take action because Chinese export duties and quotas on rare earths "appear to be part of a troubling industrial policy aimed at providing substantial competitive advantage for Chinese manufacturers at the expense of foreign manufacturers." The USTR added that it was "vital that U.S. workers and manufacturers obtain the fair and equal access to raw materials like rare earths that China specifically agreed to when it joined the WTO."

DEFENSE "SEQUESTRATION" REVEALS
U.S. MANUFACTURING WEAKNESS

The weakness of the U.S. manufacturing sector was further exposed when the threat of "sequestration" consumed the defense industry in 2012. As part of the congressional controversy over raising the nation's debt ceiling in August 2011, which led to the first-ever downgrade of U.S. debt, members of Congress and the President agreed to a mandatory 10-year spending reduction of $1.1 trillion starting on January 1, 2013. As part of the compromise, the Defense Department would have to take half of that cut, amounting to $55 billion in 2013. The prospect sent shock waves through the defense industry, galvanizing its most active lobbying campaign in 50 years.

Such a cut would lead to the loss of at least 473,250 defense-industry manufacturing jobs, according to an analysis conducted for the Aerospace Industries Association by Stephen Fuller, director of the Center for Regional Analysis at George Mason University. That means the United States would lose 5 percent of its manufacturing jobs, all because of a reduction in military spending of $55 billion — which represents a mere 0.37 percent of the nation's $15 trillion economy. That is quite an impact from a one-year, government-wide cut of $110 billion, which represents one month's worth of the borrowing needed to cover the federal government's deficit spending.

Traditionally, when defense budgets have entered periods of decline, the biggest cuts have been made in the procurement account. Between 1985 and 1998, the military budget fell by 36 percent, and the procurement account dropped by 66 percent. "When the defense budget declines significantly, the procurement account is the easiest to cut and becomes the bill payer," says Gerald Abbott, former professor of acquisition at the National Defense University's Industrial College of the Armed Forces. "We are about to enter another period of significant defense budget decline and history will repeat itself particularly in the procurement account.

This does not bode well for either the manufacturing base or the defense manufacturing base." The proposed cuts in defense will likely represent the most significant percentage decline since the Korean War.

U.S. TAX POLICY PROMOTES THE WRONG INDUSTRIES

The incentive structure in the United States is not aligned for the era of globalization of technology and investment, and the proof is found in the U.S. tax code. Tax breaks provided to Americans for housing totaled $104 billion in 2011. For companies that provide health insurance, 2011 tax breaks were $177 billion. For pensions and 401Ks, the tax break totaled $142 billion.

By comparison, the R&D tax credit, which helps increase productivity, innovation and strategic investment in physical capital, came at a cost of $8.5 billion, a trifle compared to the $423 billion total for the three other sets of tax breaks. "In fact, Congress has consistently done virtually everything conceivable to direct household savings into real estate — the most unproductive of all asset classes with respect to economic growth," according to NIST economist Gregory Tassey.[68]

And even the R&D tax credit is weak. In 2012, the United States ranked in 27th place out of 42 countries in terms of R&D tax incentive generosity, down from the 23rd position in 2007, according to ITIF.[69] "This statistic is unmistakable and troubling," notes the think tank. "When firms look for countries in which to invest in R&D, many other nations have a distinct, and in many cases, large tax advantage over the United States. This means that the United States loses out on the capital investment, economic growth and the high-wage R&D jobs that these investments would bring. Even more worrying, our low R&D tax credit gives other countries an innovation advantage over the United States, as their companies, both large and small, invest more heavily in R&D and gain the competitive advantage that stems from it."

FORTUNE 500 LIST OF GLOBAL CORPORATIONS

Over the 10 years ending in 2011, the number of American-based companies on the Fortune 500 list of the largest global companies by revenue fell by 33 percent, from 172 to 132.[70] During the same decade-long span, the number of Chinese companies on the list jumped by 663 percent, from 11 in 2002 to 73 in 2012.

"One of the more remarkable shifts has been in the number of Chinese companies on the list," said *Fortune* magazine in presenting the annual ranking. On the other hand, "no country has lost more companies during the last decade" than the United States.

By the end of 2011, only four U.S. companies remained among the world's 10 largest companies, down from six in 2005. None of the four U.S. companies on the 2012 list — ExxonMobil in second place, Wal-Mart in third, Chevron in eighth and Conoco Philips in ninth — was a manufacturing firm. General Motors, Ford and General Electric were all in the top 10 in 2005. By the time the 2012 list came out, GM had fallen to 19th place, General Electric to 22nd and Ford to 27th.

Wal-Mart is the only U.S. company ranked in the top 10 globally in number of employees, with IBM and McDonald's being the only American companies joining Wal-Mart in the global top 20. IBM, in 13th place with 433,362 employees, has fewer than 100,000 workers in the United States.[71] McDonald's, in 15th place, has 420,000 workers. Of the global top 50 employers, only 11 are American, and only three of those are industrial companies: IBM, followed by Hewlett-Packard in 24th place globally with 349,600 employees and by General Electric in 37th place with 301,000. Here are the top 10 global companies by number of employees and their headquarters:

1. Wal-Mart, U.S., 2,200,000

2. China National Petroleum, China, 1,668,172

3. State Grid, China, 1,583,000

4. Sinopec Group, China, 1,012,979

5. Hon Hai Precision Industry, Taiwan, 961,000

6. China Post Group, China, 889,307

7.   U.S. Postal Service, U.S., 601,601

8.   Volkswagen, Germany, 501,956

9.   China Telecommunications, China, 491,447

10. Aviation Industry Corp. of China, China, 480,147

IN GLOBAL INNOVATION, THE U.S. TUMBLES

The United States no longer ranks at the top of the annual "Global Innovation Index."[72] In the 2012 rankings, America was in 10th place, behind Ireland — which is hard to believe, since ninth-place Ireland does not have a single major research university, high-tech company or global brand, save for Guinness. The United States, after having held down the top spot for the last time in 2009, came in 11th in 2010 and improved to seventh in 2011 before backsliding again in 2012. Why did America fall out of first place, and why has it been floundering? According to the World Intellectual Property Organization, it is because the United States lacks exports of computers and communications equipment; sends few students to study abroad, particularly to China; has a growing level of xenophobia and disregard for immigrants; and has a failing educational system, including a university system that has become overpriced and unaffordable. Despite its huge university network, the country ranked 74th on the Innovation Index in graduates in science and engineering.

The United States' fall from the summit had been abrupt. In 2007, the Innovation Index said the United States was "in a league of its own as far as global innovation is concerned." At the time, the United States was best in the world at "translating ideas into value-added products and services." But when the United States dropped from first to 11th place three years later, the Innovation Index sponsors wrote: "As Andy Grove of Intel says, paranoia is what makes one competitive and retain the edge in any niche." America had, however, lost its "paranoia when it comes to technological superiority," and had yet to recognize that "the nature of global competitiveness in business had fundamentally changed." In short, the United States had lost its "capacity for sustaining a culture of innovation."

U.S. CONSTRUCTION COMPANIES
IN THE GLOBAL ECONOMY

The construction industry helps drive the manufacturing sector, since it consumes so many industrial materials and goods. But large American construction companies are few and far between. Five of the world's top seven construction companies in 2011 were Chinese, including the three largest: China State Construction Engineering Corp. in first place, China Communications Construction Group in second place and China Metallurgical Group in third. Just two American companies were ranked in the top 20: Bechtel, the only U.S. construction company in the top 10 globally, was in ninth place, and Fluor Corp. was in 11th.[73]

Between 2006 and 2011, China's share of the global construction industry doubled, reaching $344 billion in revenue, or 23.2 percent of the $1.48 trillion in revenue amassed by the world's 200 largest construction companies. Meanwhile, the U.S. share has been halved, to 12 percent of global revenue in 2011, or $179 billion. Japanese construction companies generated $211 billion in revenue that year, more than their U.S. competitors and 14.2 percent of the global total.

The companies that fell the farthest on the 2011 list of the 200 largest construction firms were both American: Pulte, which fell from the 70th position in 2010 to 88th in 2011, and DR Horton, which fell from 74th place to 98th.

U.S. STANDING IN KEY INDUSTRIAL SECTORS

Many Americans believe the United States remains an industrial powerhouse, but when the output from individual industries is analyzed against global competitors, the results present a startling reality: The country has only a minor presence in many important industries.

No one organization in the country, and certainly no office of the U.S. federal government, keeps abreast of the health and global economic position of the country's leading industries. In 2000, the Commerce Department decided to cease publication of its annual "U.S. Industry and Trade Outlook," an 800-page publication that the agency itself described at the time as being "essential for market researchers, executives, analysts, strategic planners and economists," since it offered a "comprehensive understanding of the economy and its effects on world trade."

When it stopped publishing the "Outlook," the National Technical Information Service said the Commerce Department's International Trade Administration would "redevelop the Outlook as a web-based product only."[74] But no such product appeared. Ever since, the U.S. government and those making economic policy have been without data on the real health of the 200 industrial sectors that were once tracked by government specialists.

What follows is an analysis of some of these sectors. None of the data is easy to find, since virtually all market information is now gathered and sold by trade associations and market research firms, and in many cases is considered proprietary.

MINERALS AND MATERIALS

One good measure of a nation's industrial activity that is not generally considered by economists is minerals and materials production and consumption. Both play an essential role in an industrial economy. Virtually all manufactured products start from minerals. For the most important materials used in manufacturing, China's consumption is three or four times greater than that of the United States.[75] But for some construction materials, China's consumption is astronomically higher. For instance, the United States consumed 69.5 million metric tons of cement in 2010, a scant 3.7 percent of China's consumption of 1,867 million metric tons.

For copper, an essential mineral used throughout industry, China's consumption in 2010 was 7.6 million metric tons, up fivefold from 2000, when the country consumed 1.94 million metric tons. By comparison, U.S. consumption in 2010 was less than China's in 2000, at 1.73 million metric tons, and down dramatically from 2.73 million metric tons ten years earlier.

A similar story can be told for virtually every other refined metal and material: As China's consumption soars, U.S. mineral consumption recedes. Compared to China's, America's consumption of major mineral commodities is downright puny.

China's consumption of aluminum increased by a factor of five from 2000 to 2010, from 3.7 million metric tons to 19.8 million. By comparison, U.S. consumption of aluminum plummeted from 9.37 million metric tons in 2000 to 6.8 million in 2010. In a decade, U.S. consumption of aluminum has gone from almost triple China's consumption to only 34 percent of it.

The same is true of zinc (U.S. consumption in 2010 of 901,000 metric tons compared to 6 million metric tons for China); tin (U.S. consumption of 17,000 metric tons in 2010, or 10 percent of China's consumption of 167,000 metric tons); and lead (U.S. consumption of 1.5 million metric tons in 2010, or 35 percent of China's consumption of 4.24 million metric tons).

Things are even more lopsided on the production side of the minerals industry. China is the world's largest producer of 80 of the most important industrial mineral commodities. China accounts for more than 80 percent of the world's output of antimony, magnesium, rare earths and tungsten, and for between 50 and 80 percent of the global production of more than a dozen major other minerals and materials, including pig iron, bismuth, silicon, cement, fluorspar, natural graphite, lime and natural zeolites.

By comparison, the United States is a major importer of most mineral commodities. "U.S. import dependence has increased significantly since 1978, the year that information was first reported," according to the U.S. Geological Survey. In 1978, the United States was 100 percent import dependent for seven mineral commodities. By 2011, that number had increased to 18 major minerals. In 1978, the United States was more than 50 percent dependent on imports for 25 major minerals. By 2011, that number had increased to 47.

China's mineral statistics become even more interesting when one looks at per-capita consumption rates. For industrial minerals, China's per-capita consumption is still below that of the United States, "suggesting that China's consumption of these minerals is likely to continue increasing for some time to come," says David Menzie, chief of the Global Minerals Information Center of the U.S. Geological Survey. "For the United States, a particularly worrying trend is the declining domestic consumption of a number of processed metals — aluminum, copper, lead, finished steel, tin and zinc — both in terms of absolute consumption and in terms of per-capita consumption. The declines in per-capita consumption follow decades in which the per-capita consumption of many metals was stable."

MACHINE TOOLS

One of the most important strategic industries is machine tools. Domestic machine-tool production provides a competitive advantage to industries that can use the latest manufacturing technologies. The United States has given up that advantage over the past few decades. The U.S. industry accounts for only a small share of global machine-tool output, its 2012 production of $4.98 billion amounting to only one-fifth of China's.[76] In fact, America's machine-tool output ranked seventh in 2012, behind those of Taiwan ($5.4 billion), Italy ($5.68 billion), South Korea ($5.7 billion), Germany ($13.6 billion) and Japan ($18.2 billion) as well as China, whose $27.5 billion figure put it in first place by a wide margin. The U.S. machine-tool industry accounted for only 5.3 percent of the combined output of the world's 28 largest producers.

Machine-tool consumption is another important indicator of the health of an industrial economy. China's consumption in 2012 stood at $38.5 billion, double its 2009 consumption of $19.8 billion. By comparison, U.S. consumption of machine tools, at $8.7 billion, came to only 23 percent of China's. Still, of the world's leading consumers of machine tools in 2012, the United States had the highest growth rate at 19 percent and was the world's second-largest consumer behind China. With imports accounting for 43 percent of its market, the United States ranked 27th among the 28 countries tallied in balance of trade in machine tools. The U.S. machine-tool trade deficit increased from $2.6 billion in 2011 to $3.74 billion in 2012. The only country with a larger deficit was China, at $10.9 billion, while Japan led the world with a 2012 machine-tool trade surplus of $10.8 billion.

INDUSTRIAL ROBOTS

Industrial robots are another important advanced technology required by manufacturers to increase output and productivity. Again, the United States is hardly a player in the production of industrial robots, nor is it one of the world's largest purchasers of robotics. The United States accounted for 20,555, or 13.4 percent, of the 160,028 industrial robots purchased by manufacturers globally in 2011.[77] Japan was the biggest market for robots in 2011 with purchases of 28,000 units, followed by Korea at 25,500, China at 22,600, the United States and, in fifth place, Germany at 19,500.

China's figure represents a 51 percent surge in its purchases of industrial robots. "In the 50 years of history of industrial robots there is no other country with such a dynamic growth of robot installations in such a short period of time," according to the International Federation of Robotics in Germany, which projects that China will soon become the world's largest market for industrial robots. "In order to have the same robot density in China as in Germany or Japan, about one million new robots will have to be installed in the coming years in China," says the Robotics Federation. "The global suppliers are aware of this potential and are increasing their capacities. Furthermore, the Chinese robot suppliers are in the process of entering the market or have already entered the market."

With regard to the production of industrial robots, the United States is not even a blip on the global landscape. Japan accounted for 65 percent of the world's production, and "virtually all of the rest of the world's industrial robots were produced in China, Korea and Europe," says Nina Kutzbach of the Federation's Statistical Department. "The number of robots produced in America is small."

How small? Neither Kutzbach nor others who track the industry could say because doing so would disclose the output of the lone American producer, Adept Technology. But even Adept admits that it is not a true manufacturer of robots. "We outsource most of our manufacturing functions and obtain many key components, materials and mechanical sub-systems from sole or single-source suppliers," the company states in SEC Form 10-K for its fiscal year ending June 2012. Adept sold only 28 percent of its output in 2012, worth $18 million, in the United States.

SEMICONDUCTORS

Semiconductor chips represent the top of the global electronics-industry pyramid, as they determine the performance of every high-tech device available to consumers, businesses and scientists. The industry has long been considered the most important strategic economic asset a nation can possess. The United States, however, is no longer among the countries where companies are building their new semiconductor fabrication plants, or "fabs."

In 2011, of the 27 high-volume semiconductor fabs under construction in the world, only one was located in the United States, while 18 were in China, four were in Taiwan, two were elsewhere in Southeast Asia and one was in Japan.[78]

In 2012, construction started on nine new high-volume fabs around the world. None was in the United States. In 2013, construction was expected to start on another six fabs. Again, not one of them was planned for the United States. In all, between 2011 and 2013 construction was expected to start on 42 new fabs, only one of which was to be in the United States.

By a similar measure, the number of high-volume fabs that started operations in 2011 was 49. Three of these were in the United States, six in Europe, three in Korea, two in Southeast Asia, seven in Taiwan — and 26 in China. In 2012, another 23 high-volume fabs were scheduled to begin operations. Again, only two of those were in the United States, while 15 were in China. To sum up, between 2011 and 2013, there were 81 new fabs expected to begin operations throughout the world: six in the United States, and 50 in China.

The United States' downward slide in semiconductor fabrication is a long-term trend. In 2003, North America ranked in second place globally in semiconductor capacity, but it is projected to fall to fourth place by 2013 behind Japan, Korea and Taiwan. In 2007, the United States was home to 123 fabs. That number is projected to decline to 95 by 2017.

As the industry has shifted offshore, the supply chain has gone with it. When the electronics-packaging industry moved to Asia, "a lot of people thought that once it became more automated, it would move back to the United States because it would not be so dependent on labor costs," says Bill McClean, president of IC Insights and a leading semiconductor industry analyst. But as production moved, so did the manufacturing and management expertise. "It's not a case of comparing labor costs anymore," says McClean. "It is comparing where the expertise in manufacturing is: It doesn't make sense to move it back here."

Semiconductor manufacturers need to be close to the systems houses that purchase their chips. With so much electronics production taking place in Taiwan, China and the rest of the Asia Pacific region, "the goal is to be near the customer," says McClean. With so little electronics system assembly in the United States, "it has become less important to manufacture here."

SEMICONDUCTOR MATERIALS AND EQUIPMENT

As for the materials that are used for the production of semiconductors and semiconductor packaging, North America in 2011 accounted for only 10 percent — or $4.9 billion — of global consumption of $48.6 billion.[79] The U.S. market for packaging materials in 2011 was $720 million, or 3 percent of the total global market of $24 billion. Virtually the entire packaging industry is located in Asia.[80] And in the category of semiconductor equipment, the United States accounted for $9.3 billion of the total global output of $43.5 billion in 2011, with Asia Pacific accounting for $30 billion. U.S. equipment makers saw their percentage share of the global market slip below 40 percent in 2011 for the first time in history.[81]

AUTOMOBILES AND AUTOMOBILE PARTS

The revival of the U.S. automobile industry has played an essential role in preventing the 2008 financial collapse from turning into something far worse. U.S. production of cars and light trucks in 2012 increased by 19.3 percent, to 10.33 million units.[82] That is a big jump from the trough of 2009, when U.S. production collapsed by 34 percent, to only 5.7 million vehicles.

U.S. auto factories are getting closer to the 13 million vehicles they produced in the peak year of 1999, but imports, at 4.15 million vehicles in 2012, continued to displace a large portion of U.S. production. Imported automobiles accounted for 29 percent of the vehicles sold in the United States in 2012.

U.S. production pales in comparison to that of China, which in 2012 produced almost double the number of vehicles that the United States did: 19.3 million. In 2001, when the United States was producing 11.4 million cars and trucks, China's production was only 2.3 million. Since then, Chinese production of cars and trucks has grown by 839 percent, while U.S. production is down by 21 percent.

The United States auto industry accounted for 12 percent of the world's production of 84 million vehicles in 2012. Japan, with about one-third the U.S. population, produced 9.9 million vehicles in 2012, almost as many as the United States. Germany, with one-quarter of the U.S. population at 82 million, produced 5.6 million vehicles, and South Korea, with one-sixth of the U.S. population at 50 million, produced 4.6 million vehicles.

The automobile trade figures indicate that the United States continues to get whipped in global competition. Combining automobiles and auto parts, the country ran a $147 billion auto-sector trade deficit in 2012, a surge of $30 billion from the 2011 deficit of $117 billion. The figure for 2009, $75 billion, was only 51 percent of that posted in 2012.

Exports of passenger cars from the United States increased to $53.5 billion in 2012, from $47.5 billion in 2011. But imports totaled $147 billion in 2012, up from $128 billion the previous year, for a total trade deficit in automobiles alone of $93.5 billion.

The auto-parts trade deficit is gargantuan, and it is growing. It has almost tripled in four years, going from $20 billion in 2009 to $56 billion in 2012.[83] China's exports of auto parts to the United States are surging at an incredible pace and pose a significant threat to the U.S. auto-parts sector. They increased from $10 billion in 2004 to $60 billion in 2012, an average annual rate of almost 30 percent.

Imports into the United States of Chinese aluminum wheels increased from eight million units in 2009 to 18 million units in 2011. Imports of radiators from China increased from three million in 2009 to more than four million in 2011. Imports of laminated safety glass windshields from China increased from six million units in 2009 to more than 10 million in 2011. Brake-lining imports from China surged from 15 million in 2008 to more than 40 million in 2011. Imports of Chinese engine-ignition coils increased from less than four million in 2009 to more than 14 million in 2011.

In 2012, the U.S. trade deficit in auto parts with China stood at $13.2 billion, a 32 percent increase from $10 billion in 2011 and more than 10 times higher than in 2001. Over that same period, the United States lost more than 400,000 automobile-industry jobs.[84]

If China successfully implements its latest five-year economic plan, which targets a 35 percent annual growth rate in auto-parts production, the United States' trade deficit with China in auto parts could top $100 billion by 2020 — and that is a conservative estimate, according to Terence Stewart, managing partner in the Washington trade-law firm of Stewart and Stewart.

China's government has committed an "overwhelming force" of $1.5 trillion to developing seven strategic industrial sectors,[85] including automotive. It has put in place a system of export restraints on raw materials important to the production of automobile parts, making them cheaper to manufacture in China and forcing production to move there. It has export duties on cobalt used in rechargeable batteries; on copper used in wiring and cables; on germanium used in transistors; on manganese used in making aluminum alloys; on rare earths used throughout the electronics supply chain; on titanium; on tungsten; and on tin and vanadium used in alloys and plating. "That may be good for China, but it is bad for the United States and it is contrary to China's WTO obligations," says Stewart.

China has also implemented a sales-tax waiver on electric and alternative-fueled vehicles manufactured there, and it imposes the sales tax — along with a value-added tax — on imports. China has "basically told foreign auto companies that, 'if you want to play in our market, you have to move your technology and production here,'" says Stewart.

"That changes the outcome of the game, not based on competition but based on the iron fist of government saying 'you can't play if you don't shift where you produce.' That is not how the system is supposed to work. That is not how comparative advantage is supposed to be determined. And it is the reason that we lose hundreds of thousands of jobs to China in various sectors."

In addition, the Chinese government is ramping up all of its subsidy programs for the country's auto sector,[86] making loans directly to Beijing Automotive Industry Holding, Brilliance China Automotive Holdings Ltd., FAW Group, BYD Automotive and others. It is boosting incentives for companies to invest in hundreds of different auto parts and systems, among them LED headlamps, high-strength steels, composite plastics, transmission-control units, electric air conditioning, electric braking, idle stop-start systems, electronic parking systems, battery packs, engine air-intake superchargers, hydrogen storage systems and many more.

STEEL

The U.S. steel industry in 2012 produced 88.6 million tons of steel, an increase of 2.5 percent from 2011.[87] But that production level equates to only 12.4 percent of the 716.5 million tons produced by China in 2012, up from 683 million tons produced in 2011. China's steel output that year increased 9 percent from 2010 and was up by 474 percent over that of 2001, when the country produced 151 million tons. Its share of 2012's world steel output of 1.548 billion tons rose to 46.3 percent, while the U.S. share was 5.7 percent. U.S. production is still below where it was in 2006, when U.S. output reached 99 million tons before falling off a cliff in 2009 to only 58 million tons.

In 2012, the United States steel industry was also outproduced by Japan (107 million tons), Russia and the CIS (113 million tons) and the EU (169.4 million tons). U.S. output in 2011 was below that of every year in the 1990s except 1992. As long ago as 1981, the U.S. produced 110 million tons of steel, and its annual output had been at least 120 million tons throughout the 1970s, reaching a peak of 151 million tons in 1978. The only foreign producer that was even in a league with the United States at the time was the Soviet Union, which during the 1970s was producing between 152 million tons and 187 million tons per year. Over the same years, China's output ranged from 16 million tons to 34 million tons.

Imports continue to make up a large portion of the U.S. market, reaching 30.4 million metric tons in 2012, up from 26 million metric tons in 2011. The value of steel imports in 2012 reached $34 billion, up from $30.5 billion in 2011 and $17 billion in 2009.[88] "The reason we are seeing this import surge is that, while America is a free market, many major steel producing countries are not," says John Ferriola, President and CEO of Nucor. China's market is closed to foreign competitors. "The government owns 100 percent of 16 of China's 20 largest producers," says Ferriola. "China's steel industry has 35 percent more capacity than it needs," with capacity rising in 2012 to "an astounding 970 million tons, compared with about 120 million tons for the entire U.S. steel industry."[89]

In the area of specialty steels, imports into the United States rose by 12.4 percent in 2012 to 879,879 tons and accounted for 35 percent of the U.S. market of 2.5 million tons.

FURNITURE

The U.S. furniture industry is being inundated by imports, and there are few signs of the "reshoring" of factories from overseas locations. "The problem with wood furniture is that it is a dirty industry with emissions, finishing sprays and dust-collection problems," says leading furniture industry analyst Jerry Epperson, managing director of Mann, Armistead & Epperson of Richmond, Va., a privately owned investment banking firm. "Once those factories close, they pretty much stay closed due to the difficulty of getting permits."

In 2011, household furniture imports accounted for 52 percent, or $18 billion, of the total U.S. market of $34.5 billion.[90] The import-penetration rate decreased slightly from 2010 to 2011, but that turnaround was a "blip" says Epperson. "While the domestic industry gained a tiny bit of share back in 2011, it has reversed itself in 2012." Imports continue to gain strength in the U.S. market.

In the wood household-furniture category, imports accounted for almost 70 percent of the U.S. market in 2011, or $10.2 billion of a market of

$14.7 billion. The U.S. market for wood household furniture remained depressed in the wake of the housing bust. In 2006, the total U.S. market was worth $20.7 billion, $6 billion more than in 2011. China has been the source for most of the imports. In 2002, Chinese furniture exports to the United States reached $5 billion; a decade later, in 2011, they had more than doubled, to $11 billion.

A few factories have been opening in the United States. IKEA opened a plant in Danville, Va., and is considering opening another. "But it's not significant in any way," says Epperson. "The most likely thing is, we will fill up the existing factories first before we even think about building anything new." The only sign of "reshoring" — if it can be called that — is plants returning from Asia to Mexico. Ethan Allen, Furniture Brands and La-Z Boy have opened plants south of the border, but not in the United States.

Some companies are adding 30 or 40 jobs, but no big factories have reopened, none like the ones with 500 or more employees that closed over the past decade, notes Andy Johnson, editor of *Hardwood Review*. "Jobs are trickling back here, but most of the furniture production is moving from China to other parts of the Far East, and some is coming back to Mexico," says Johnson.

CHEMICALS

The U.S. chemical industry is in its most propitious moment in 75 years, thanks to the discovery of plentiful and cheap natural gas from tight shale formations. "It is an exciting time to be in this industry," says Thomas Kevin Swift, chief economist and managing director of the American Chemistry Council. But the industry is still recovering from years of stagnation, and its output now pales in comparison to that of China.

U.S. shipments improved in 2011 to $569 billion, up from $515 billion in 2010 and $434 billion in 2009. But on an index scale with 2007 representing 100, U.S. production in 2011 stood at 88.2, the same level as in 2003. On the same index, production in Asia has increased from the 2007 baseline of 100 to 137.3 in 2011, with China having an index score of 149.[91]

Any growth of the U.S. industry is small compared to that of China's. From 2000 to 2010, the Chinese industry increased in size by almost ninefold, its output growing over the decade by almost an order of magnitude: from $105 billion to $903 billion.[92]

China's share of the $3.01 trillion global market for chemicals surged from 6.4 percent in 2000 to 30 percent in 2010. The U.S. share of the global chemical market headed in the opposite direction: from 28 percent in 2000 to 19 percent in 2010. China's production is projected to grow by another 66 percent between 2012 and 2020. Meanwhile, China's investment in capital equipment, which surged to over $300 billion in 2010, accounted for more than 70 percent of the entire global investment of $464 billion in 2010.

U.S. chemical-industry employment remains much lower than a decade ago. In 2000 there were 985,000 workers employed in the industry. By late 2012 that number had dropped to 797,000.

U.S. chemical exports have increased significantly, rising from $172 billion in 2008 to $198 billion in 2012, but imports were up by a slightly larger amount, from $180 billion in 2008 to $214 billion in 2012. The industry is the largest exporting sector in the United States, "larger than both agriculture and aircraft and aerospace," says the American Chemistry Council.

Capital expenditures increased in the United States chemical industry from $27 billion in 2010 to $33 billion in 2011, but the majority of that, 39 percent, was for information technologies, while process equipment represented only 26 percent. The majority of the industry's capital expenditures went to replace existing plant and equipment (24 percent) and to expand capacity for existing products (27 percent), while only 5 percent was for new capacity for new products. U.S-based companies invested far more in their overseas operations, however: $141 billion in 2010, up from $96 billion in 2007.

MANY INDUSTRIES IN THE UNITED STATES
WILL BENEFIT FROM CHEAP NATURAL GAS

For the first time in decades, low-priced natural gas is leading to the growth of new, energy-intensive industrial capacity. The average price for natural gas paid by industrial customers dropped from $5.90 per million cubic feet in 2010 to $3.70 per million cubic feet in 2012.[93] Proven reserves reached more than 300 trillion cubic feet in 2010, the largest recorded in the history of the United States.[94]

The boom in shale natural gas production created 334,000 jobs in natural gas-dependent industries between 2010 and 2011, according to the American Gas Association.[95] Between 2007 and 2009, almost 85,000 natural gas wells were drilled and completed in the United States, which pumped business into industries like steel and heavy machinery. Gas production has increased by 33 percent over the past two decades, growing from 17.2 trillion cubic feet in 1990 to 23 trillion cubic feet in 2011. The United States has now surpassed Russia as the world's largest producer of natural gas.

PricewaterhouseCoopers estimates that the lower prices will help U.S. manufacturers reduce their natural gas expenses by $11.6 billion annually through 2025 and will lead to the creation of one million new manufacturing jobs by that year.[96] "Historically, there has been an indirect relationship between the level of energy prices and the level of domestic manufacturing employment, as manufacturers consume approximately one-third of all energy produced in the United States," according to the consulting firm. "Consequently this relatively abundant domestic energy source has the potential to drive an uptick in U.S. manufacturing over the long term and create new jobs in the sector."

The American Chemistry Council estimates that natural gas abundance will result in the creation of 17,000 jobs in the U.S. chemical industry and an additional 395,000 jobs outside the industry through 2015. Investments made in the chemical industry will lead to a $32.8 billion increase in U.S. chemical production and will generate $132.4 billion in additional U.S. economic output.[97] "Some of these investments are being made in areas of the country that have been hardest hit by declines in manufacturing, improving the outlook in economically depressed areas," says the Council.

Citigroup estimates that the surge in natural gas and oil reserves and production could increase U.S. GDP by a cumulative 2 to 3 percentage points, or by between $370 billion and $624 billion.[98] Of this amount about $274 billion would come directly from the production of oil and gas. The rest would be from potential re-industrialization, which Citigroup says would be "both profound and timely," creating between 2.7 million and 3.6 million net jobs by 2020.

In 2011 and 2012, there were five major new ethylene facilities announced in the United States (Chevron, Dow, Shell, Formosa and Sasol) and a restart (Dow), along with 10 major feedstock plant conversions. "Fertilizer manufacturers, particularly ammonia producers, are also mobilizing to take advantage of cheaper natural gas," Citigroup notes. "Potash Corp. is restarting an idled ammonia plant on the U.S. Gulf Coast and is also expanding two other existing ammonia plants."

The American Chemistry Council tracks the announcements of new manufacturing facilities that use natural gas as their primary feedstock or fuel. It found that in 2012 there were 13 major new iron and steel factories on the drawing boards; three major tire plants; 35 chemical facilities; and 50 new plastic-products plants.[99] "These types of announcements are likely to become more common, with more companies outside the chemicals and metals industries planning new capital expenditures in the United States to take advantage of lower costs resulting from shale gas," according to PricewaterhouseCoopers.

TEXTILES AND APPAREL

Foreign textile and apparel workers keep America clothed. In 2011, the average American purchased 68 new garments, 98 percent of which were imported.[100] The combined value of imports for textiles and apparel in 2012 was $113.4 billion, of which $47 billion came from China, up from $9.7 billion in 2000.

Apparel imports were at $79 billion in 2012, up from $74 billion in 2010.[101] China was the largest exporter of apparel to the United States in 2012 at $30 billion (up from $7.5 billion in 2002), followed by Vietnam, which exported $7 billion worth of apparel to Americans in 2012. The United States ran a trade deficit in textiles and apparel of $91 billion in 2012, or $290 for every American.

SPACE LAUNCH AND SATELLITES

There were 18 commercial satellite launches in 2011, not one of which was marked by U.S. participation. The worldwide commercial launch industry generated $1.9 billion in revenue in 2011. Europe's revenues were $808 million. Russia's revenues were $707 million. China's revenues were $140 million. "U.S. commercial launch revenues were $0 in 2011," according to the Congressional Research Service (CRS).[102]

In the area of satellite construction, the U.S. share of global revenue fell from 75 percent prior to the 1998 congressional adoption of export controls to 52 percent in 2010. Of the 1,012 satellites manufactured worldwide between 2001 and 2010, the United States accounted for 386, or 38 percent. U.S. satellite manufacturers have seen their revenues decline from an average of $6.6 billion per year between 1996 and 1999 to an average of $4.7 billion per year between 2000 and 2010.

What happened? The 1999 version of the annual Defense Authorization Bill classified all satellites and their parts and components as munitions that may not be exported without a government license. The action "was highly controversial within the U.S. aerospace industry, due in part to the decision by the United States to impose unilateral export controls on commercial satellites without corresponding actions by European and Japanese governments," according to the CRS. "Foreign competitors immediately grasped the competitive disadvantage facing U.S. satellite exporters."

U.S. BUSINESS JETS

The U.S. business-jet industry is under assault. U.S. production as a percentage of global production fell from 83 percent in 2008 to 57 percent in 2011, the same period during which global sales were plummeting: Only 485 business aircraft were delivered worldwide in 2011, a decline of 56 percent from 1,121 in 2008. Cessna's business-jet deliveries fell from 466 in 2008 to 183 in 2011; Gulfstream's deliveries dropped from 156 to 107; and Hawker Beechcraft's sales plunged from 160 to 30. In 2012, the number of business jets made in the United States sank to 347, down from 364 in 2011 and 955 in 2008.[103]

"The trend toward increased outsourcing of parts and systems is seen as diminishing the long-term prospects for increasing employment at U.S. business-jet manufacturers, but also the remaining workforce's capacity to innovate," according to the U.S. International Trade Commission (ITC).[104]

Inconsistent funding for the Federal Aviation Administration (FAA) is hurting the U.S. business-jet manufacturing industry. The FAA has become extremely slow in certifying new products and technologies. Upgraded avionics, software, computing systems and composite structures developed by U.S. manufacturers are not making it to market because the agency is currently taking three-and-a-half years to certify them. The FAA is also being inundated by foreign certification agencies' requests for test and production data on U.S.-certified aircraft, "with no commensurate increase in staff or funding" to provide the information. "As a result of these issues, certain U.S. business jet firms have reportedly considered shifting production of complete aircraft outside of the United States to countries where certification agencies are more responsive to commercial needs," according to the ITC.

CONCLUSION

In most of the important and strategic global industries, the United States has lost its leading position. But the United States is not out of the competition. The country has strengths: Strong competitive companies remain in most sectors. It has advantages: Its research enterprise is still the envy of the world. And it has momentum: Companies are re-assessing their plans for locating new factories. There is great potential for a true industrial revival.

America's politicians have a choice: focus on adopting a range of policies aimed at reinvigorating the U.S. industrial sector or continue to sit and watch as the country's foreign competitors target what is left of American manufacturing. Doing nothing will result in mountains of additional debt, with serious financial consequences for tens of millions of Americans. Doing nothing will result in the continued poisoning of the American political system, since the country is not generating enough tax revenue for all of the programs politicians have decided are essential. Doing nothing means the country has to fight about how to carve up a shrinking economic pie. Doing nothing is not a viable option.

It would not be difficult for the United States to engage in the global competitive battle for new manufacturing plants and the attractive jobs they create. It does not take long for a company to open a new factory.

Making the economic conditions favorable for companies to invest in the United States will take resolve and the courage to adopt some new economic policies. Americans are ready. It's the country's politicians who need to be jolted into action. The next nine chapters describe what is required to assure a prosperous future for the United States of America.

1. The manufacturing factory data series is located at the Bureau of Labor Statistics' Census for Employment and Wages database: http://www.bls.gov/cew/. The number of factories in the United States can be tallied by the number of employees at each plant. In the box titled "On This Page," click "QCEW Databases." Click on the green icon "One Screen Data Search." No. 1 box, scroll down and click on "U.S. Total." No. 2 box, click "U.S. Total." No. 3 box, scroll to "Manufacturing" and click on it. No. 4 box, click "Private." No. 5 box, click "All Establishment Sizes." No. 6 box, click the number of establishments. No. 7 box, "Get Data." The number of factories in the United States declined from 398,837 in 2001 to 335,553 at the end of the third quarter of 2012.

2. Bill Simon, president and CEO of Wal-Mart, before the National Retail Federation's 102nd Annual Convention and Expo, January 15, 2013, "A Job To Do: Retail's Role in an American Renewal," http://news.walmart.com/executive-viewpoints/a-job-to-do-retails-role-in-an-american-renewal.

3. Bureau of Labor Statistics. To view the employment data for the entire United States and by every sector of the economy, including manufacturing, go to http://www.bls.gov/. In the top tab box, click on "Databases & Tools"; in the second box, "On This Page," click on "Employment"; in the first category, "Employment, Hours, and Earnings – National," click on the green "One Screen Data Search"; for total U.S. employment, in the first box click on "All Employees, Thousands"; in the second box click on "Total Nonfarm"; in the third box click "Total Nonfarm"; and then hit "Get Data." You can add previous years to the search, produce charts and view historical employment numbers for every sector of the economy.

4. An example of the anti-manufacturing bias that continues to exist among the intellectual class is a February 13, 2013, column by New York University professor Richard Florida, "Sorry Mr. President, Manufacturing Will Not Save Us," *The Atlantic — Cities*, in which he states: "Manufacturing does not translate into local growth and development," http://www.theatlanticcities.com/jobs-and-economy/2013/02/sorry-mr-president-manufacturing-will-not-save-us/4656/. Another appeared in the *Washington Post* on April 7, 2013, written by columnist Robert Samuelson under the title "The Post-Industry Myths," in which he states that an economic revival led by manufacturing "is make believe."

5. Gartner Inc., "Worldwide Mobile Phone Sales in 2012," February 13, 2013, http://www.gartner.com/newsroom/id/2335616.

6. U.S. Department of Commerce, Office of Textiles and Apparel (OTEXA), "U.S. Imports for Consumption for Selected Products — All Footwear," November 2012, http://otexa.ita.doc.gov/FLT/imports/cat10.htm.

7. American Apparel & Footwear Association, "We Wear" brand snapshot, https://www.wewear.org/assets/1/16/WeWear.pdf.

8. IPC - Association Connecting Electronics Industries, "World PCB Production Report" for 2011, published August 2012.

9. World Steel Association, "World crude steel output increases by 1.2 percent in 2012," January 22, 2013, http://www.worldsteel.org/media-centre/press-releases/2012/12-2012-crude-steel.html.

10. "Apple Supplier Responsibility, 2013 Progress Report," January 2013, http://images.apple.com/supplierresponsibility/pdf/Apple_SR_2013_Progress_Report.pdf.

11. International Data Corp., "Soft PC Shipments in Fourth Quarter Lead to Annual Decline, as HP Holds Onto Top Spot, According to IDC," January 10, 2013, http://www.idc.com/getdoc.jsp?containerId=prUS23903013#.UTpL5o6gqbA.

12. U.S. International Trade Commission, "Crystalline Photovoltaic Cells and Modules from China," November 2012, Investigation Nos. 701-TA-481 and 731-TA-1190 (Final), Publication 4360, November 2012, http://www.usitc.gov/publications/701_731/pub4360.pdf.

13. "Renewables 2012, Global Status Report," Renewable Energy Policy Network for the 21st Century, http://www.map.ren21.net/GSR/GSR2012.pdf.

14. U.S. Department of Commerce, Office of Textiles and Apparel, "Footwear, Leather and Fur Products and Travel Goods, Index Page, Imports by Product Group," http://otexa.ita.doc.gov/FLTCAT_imp.HTM.

15. *Ceramic World Review*, "2011 World Production and Consumption of Ceramic Tiles."

16. Office of Management and Budget, "Summary of Receipts, Outlays, and Surpluses or Deficits: 1789 to 2017," Historical Tables, http://www.whitehouse.gov/omb/budget/Historicals.

17.   U.S. Census Bureau, "U.S. Trade in Goods and Services — Balance of Payments Basis," http://www.census.gov/foreign-trade/statistics/historical/gands.pdf.

18.   Gregory Tassey, senior economist, National Institute of Standards and Technology, in "Beyond the Business Cycle: The Need for a Technology-Based Growth Strategy," February 2012, http://www.nist.gov/director/planning/upload/beyond-business-cycle.pdf.

19.   Judith Banister, "China's employment and compensation costs in manufacturing through 2008," *Monthly Labor Review*, March 2011. The total number of manufacturing workers — 115.67 million — includes the 16 million self-employed manufacturing workers that China stopped including in its annual count in 2007. Banister notes that these manufacturing jobs still exist but were not counted. "Breaks in series are not unfamiliar in Chinese manufacturing employment data," says Banister.

20.   Geethanjali Nataraj and Anjali Tandon, "China's Changing Export Structure: A Factor-Based Analysis," *Economic & Political Weekly*, March 26, 2011, http://www.ncaer.org/downloads/MediaClips/Press/GNatraj&AnjaliTandonChina%20ChangingStructure.pdf. Also see "The Growth of Chinese Exports: An Examination of Detailed Trade Data" by Brett Berger and Robert Martin, both of the Board of Governors of the Federal Reserve System, International Finance Discussion Papers, No. 1033, November 2011, which states: "We show that Chinese exports can help account for a significant portion of U.S. job losses at the industry level." It is located at http://www.federalreserve.gov/pubs/ifdp/2011/1033/ifdp1033.pdf.

21.   Susan Houseman, "The Debate Over the State of U.S. Manufacturing: How the Computer Industry Affects the Numbers and Perceptions," Upjohn Institute for Employment Research, July 2012, http://research.upjohn.org/cgi/viewcontent.cgi?article=1197&context=empl_research.

22.   *Washington Post*, "Origins of Job Market Troubles Difficult to Pinpoint," November 16, 2012, http://www.washingtonpost.com/business/economy/origins-of-job-market-troubles-hard-to-pinpoint/2012/11/16/243ca40c-2fea-11e2-9f50-0308e1e75445_story.html.

23.   Christina Romer, "Do Manufacturers Need Special Treatment?" *New York Times*, February 14, 2012, http://www.nytimes.com/2012/02/05/business/do-manufacturers-need-special-treatment-economic-view.html.

24.   Larry Summers, "Summers Delivers Final Public Address at EPI," from the Economic Policy Institute in Washington, D.C., December 13, 2010, http://www.epi.org/publication/summers_delivers_final_public_address_at_epi/.

25.   Gregory Tassey, senior economist, National Institute of Standards and Technology, "Rationales and Mechanisms for Revitalizing U.S. Manufacturing R&D Strategies," August, 29, 2012, http://www.nist.gov/director/planning/upload/manufacturing_strategy_paper.pdf.

26.   Clyde Prestowitz, "Can We Have a Third Candidate?" October 4, 2012, *Foreign Policy*, http://prestowitz.foreignpolicy.com/?page=2.

27.   Alliance for American Manufacturing, "2012 National Poll: Voters See Manufacturing as the 'Irreplaceable Core of a Strong Economy,'" http://www.americanmanufacturing.org/content/new-national-poll-voters-see-manufacturing-irreplaceable-core-strong-economy-0.

28.   "Annual Report of the Trustees of the Federal Hospital Insurance and Federal Supplementary Medical Insurance Trust Funds," April 23, 2012, http://www.cms.gov/Research-Statistics-Data-and-Systems/Statistics-Trends-and-Reports/ReportsTrustFunds/index.html?redirect=/ReportsTrustFunds/.

29.   United States Department of Agriculture, "FY 2013 Budget Summary and Annual Performance Plan," page 56. The total for the Supplemental Nutrition Assistance Program (SNAP, or food stamps) for 2012 includes the "Special Supplemental Nutrition Program" at $6.6 billion, the SNAP program itself at $80.4 billion and an additional $8.2 billion for SNAP provided by the Recovery Act for 2012. The total does not include $48 million for Soup Kitchens and Food Banks, $17 million for the Farmers' Market Nutrition Program, $139 million for Nutrition Programs Administration, $21 million for the Senior Farmers' Nutrition Program and $155 million for "permanent appropriations for Child Nutrition Programs," http://www.obpa.usda.gov/budsum/FY13budsum.pdf.

30. Bureau of Economic Analysis, GDP, "Value Added By Industry." To find the GDP figures by sector, go to www.bea.gov. In the top row of buttons, click on "Interactive Data." In the row of boxes toward the top of the screen, click on the "GDP-by-Industry & Input-Output" button. Click on the big button "Begin Using the Data." The button "GDP-by-industry accounts" should be high-lighted, so click on "Next Step." Click "Value Added By Industry," and then, again, "Value Added By Industry."

31. Bureau of Economic Analysis, "Percentage Shares of Gross Domestic Product," Table 1.1.10 of "Domestic Product and Income" series in the National Income and Product Accounts, www.bea.gov, Interactive Data, "GDP and Personal Income."

32. International Labor Comparisons Program at the Department of Labor's Bureau of Labor Statistics, "Annual Labor Force Statistics, 1970 - 2011, Full Series and Underlying Levels — By Country," http://www.bls.gov/fls/#data.

33. Ibid.

34. "The National Summit: A Gathering To Define America's Future," http://www.nationalsummit.org/.

35. http://manufacturing.gov/amp/amp.html.

36. Export-Import Bank Annual Conference, 2010, http://www.exim.gov/news/annualconf/2010/conversation/Vid1HochbergImmeltTranscript.pdf.

37. Massachusetts Institute of Technology, "Production in the Innovation Economy," http://web.mit.edu/pie/. Its interim report, released in February 2013, is located at http://web.mit.edu/press/images/documents/pie-report.pdf.

38. Gary Pisano and Willy Shih, *Producing Prosperity, Why America Needs a Manufacturing Renaissance,* Harvard Business Review Press, 2012.

39. Boston Consulting Group, "Made in America, Again — Why Manufacturing Will Return to the U.S.," August 2011, followed by a March, 22, 2012, update, "U.S. Manufacturing Nears the Tipping Point: Which Industries, Why and How Much?"

40. Booz&Co, "Manufacturing's Wake-Up Call," in *Strategy and Business,* Issue 64, Autumn 2011, by Arvind Kaushal, Thomas Mayor and Patricia Riedl, http://booz.com/media/file/sb64-11306-Manufacturing's-Wake-Up-Call.pdf.

41. PricewaterhouseCoopers, "A Homecoming for U.S. Manufacturing? Why a Resurgence in U.S. Manufacturing May Be the Next Big Bet," September 13, 2012, http://www.pwc.com/en_US/us/industrial-products/publications/assets/pwc-us-manufacturing-resurgence.pdf.

42. Progressive Policy Institute, "Manufacturing in the App Economy: How Many Jobs Should We Aim For?" May 2012, http://progressivepolicy.org/wp-content/uploads/2012/05/05.2012-Mandel_Carew_Manufacturing-in-the-App-Economy1.pdf.

43. Brookings Institution, "Why Does Manufacturing Matter? Which Manufacturing Matters? A Policy Framework," by Susan Helper, Timothy Krueger and Howard Wial, February 2012, http://www.brookings.edu/~/media/research/files/papers/2012/2/22%20manufacturing%20helper%20krueger%20wial/0222_manufacturing_helper_krueger_wial.

44. The Department of Agriculture does not keep track of which companies' employees are receiving food stamps. "Federal regulations do not require applicants to provide the name of their employer on their Supplemental Nutrition Assistance Program application," according to a Department of Agriculture spokesman.

45. Judith Banister and George Cook, "China's Employment and Compensation Costs in Manufacturing Through 2008," for the International Labor Comparisons Program at the Bureau of Labor Statistics, March 2011, http://www.bls.gov/opub/mlr/2011/03/art4full.pdf.

46. Bureau of Labor Statistics, International Labor Comparison Program, "International Comparison of Hourly Compensation Costs in Manufacturing, 2011," published December 19, 2012, http://www.bls.gov/news.release/pdf/ichcc.pdf.

47. The Obama administration zeroed out funding for the International Labor Comparison program in both the fiscal year 2012 and 2013 congressional budget requests, claiming its data was not useful. With sequestration approved in 2013, the Department of Labor killed the program outright. Some of those who have fought to save the program say the government does not want Americans to know the wages they are competing against globally or the reason why their jobs are being outsourced. Save the BLS International Labor Comparisons Program website: http://www.ipetitions.com/petition/saveilc/.

48. Department of Labor's International Labor Comparisons program, "Labor Costs in India's Organized Manufacturing Sector," May 2010, http://www.bls.gov/opub/mlr/2010/05/art1full.pdf.

49. Robert Gordon, "Is U.S. Economic Growth Over? Faltering Innovation Confronts the Six Headwinds," Working Paper 18315 from the National Bureau of Economic Research, Cambridge Mass., available for purchase ($5) at http://www.nber.org/papers/w18315.

50. U.S. Department of Commerce, International Trade Administration, "Exports Support American Jobs: Updated Measure Will Quantify Progress As Global Economy Recovers," http://trade.gov/publications/pdfs/exports-support-american-jobs.pdf.

51. Executive Office of the President, Council of Economic Advisers, "Estimates of Job Creation from the American Recovery and Reinvestment Act of 2009," May 2009, states on page five that "estimates for the job-years created by direct government spending indicate that it takes approximately $92,000 of spending to create one job-year. Thus, for example, if increased spending in one portion of the program through the end of 2012 is $11 billion, that spending will create about 120,000 job-years during the President's first term," http://www.recovery.gov/About/Documents/Jobs_Report_Final.pdf.

52. Stephen Fuller, Director for Regional Analysis, George Mason University, "The Economic Impact of the Budget Control Act of 2011 on DOD and Non-DOD Agencies," July 2012, http://www.aia-aerospace.org/assets/Fuller_II_Final_Report.pdf. The Congressional Research Service also conducted a study on the jobs impact of sequestration in "Sequestration: A Review of Estimates of Potential Job Losses," Linda Levine, Specialist in Economics, October 1, 2012, which notes various reports estimating the job loss peaking at 1.2 million in 2014, http://www.fas.org/sgp/crs/misc/R42763.pdf.

53. "Karachi Fire Sparks Safety Concerns," *The Friday Times*, September 21-27, 2012, Vol. XXIV, No. 32. Levi's and Wal-Mart were named as companies that purchased the factory's output. The companies were asked by the author to respond to the press report about their buying the factory's output, with the request stating that if they did not reply, then it would be assumed they were buying the output. The companies did not reply.

54. Address of Pope Francis, Clementine Hall, May 16, 2013, http://www.vatican.va/holy_father/francesco/speeches/2013/may/documents/papa-francesco_20130516_nuovi-ambasciatori_en.html.

55. Department of Labor, "List of Goods Produced by Child Labor or Forced Labor 2012," http://www.dol.gov/ilab/programs/ocft/2012TVPRA.pdf.

56. National Association of Manufacturers' Manufacturing Institute and the Manufacturing Alliance / MAPI, "2011 Report on the Structural Cost of U.S. Manufacturing," October 2011, available at the Manufacturing Institute, http://www.themanufacturinginstitute.org/.

57. International Labor Organization, "Global Employment Trends, 2012," http://www.ilo.org/wcmsp5/groups/public/ — -dgreports/ — -dcomm/ — -publ/documents/publication/wcms_171571.pdf.

58. Food and Agricultural Organization of the United Nations, "Hunger," http://www.fao.org/hunger/en/.

59. U.S. Customs and Border Protection, "Import Trade Trends, Fiscal Year 2011, Year-End Report," http://www.cbp.gov/linkhandler/cgov/trade/trade_programs/trade_trends/fy11_yearend.ctt/fy11_yearend.pdf.

60. General Accounting Office, "Antidumping and Counterveiling Duties: Management Enhancements Neeeded to Improve Efforts to Detect and Deter Duty Evasion," (GAO-12-551), May 2013, http://www.gao.gov/assets/600/590917.pdf.

61. *People's Daily Online — English Version,* "Revenues of Chinese Customs Duties Top 1.6 Trillion Yuan," January 13, 2012, http://english.peopledaily.com.cn/90778/7704476.html.

62. To review U.S. import and export data by country and product category, go to www.census.gov. On the top of the home page, click "Business." In the pop-up box, scroll over to the far right column, "Popular Resources," and click on "Foreign Trade." In the top line of buttons under the banner "Foreign Trade," click "Data." In the left gutter under "More Data," click on the "Country/Product Trade" link. In the second main box, "Product Detail and Partner Country," click on "Imports." Scroll to China (or any other country) and click on the link to view imports by NAICS product category from 2002 to the most current year's data. Exports to China from the United States can be viewed in the same data series. As of early 2013, data was available only through 2011.

63. Ernest Preeg, "The U.S. Trade Deficit in Manufactures and the Chinese Surplus Continue to Surge in 2012," February 2013. From the Manufacturers Alliance for Productivity and Innovation.

64. Robert Scott, "The China Toll," Economic Policy Institute, August 23, 2012, http://www.epi.org/publication/bp345-china-growing-trade-deficit-cost/.

65. Justin Pierce, Board of Governors of the Federal Reserve System, and Peter Schott, Yale School of Management, "The Surprisingly Swift Decline of U.S. Manufacturing Employment," December 2012, published by the National Bureau of Economic Research, http://www.nber.org/papers/w18655.

66. David Autor of the Massachusetts Institute of Technology, David Dorn of the Center for Monetary and Financial Studies in Madrid and Gordon Hanson of UC San Diego in "The China Syndrome: Local Labor Market Effects of Import Competition in the United States," http://economics.mit.edu/files/6613.

67. The People's Republic of China's Information Office of the State Council, "Situation and Policies of China Rare Earth Industry," June 20, 2012, http://www.chinadaily.com.cn/china/2012-06/20/content_15514823.htm.

68. Tassey, "Beyond the Business Cycle," fn. 18 supra.

69. Information Technology and Innovation Foundation, "We're No. 27!: The United States Lags Far Behind in R&D Tax Incentive Generosity," July 2012, http://www2.itif.org/2012-were-27-b-index-tax.pdf.

70. *Fortune Magazine*, hosted online by *CNNMoney*, http://money.cnn.com/magazines/fortune/global500/2012/full_list/index.html.

71. *Computerworld*, "In a Symbolic Shift, IBM's India Workforce Likely Exceeds U.S.," November 29, 2012, http://www.infoworld.com/d/the-industry-standard/in-symbolic-shift-ibms-india-workforce-likely-exceeds-us-208028. See also the Communications Workers of America's Alliance@IBM website, http://www.endicottalliance.org/index.php.

72. INSEAD and the World Intellectual Property Organization, an agency of the United Nations, "Global Innovation Index," http://www.globalinnovationindex.org/gii/.

73. KHL Group, "Chinese Contractors Top Global Rankings Once Again," July/August 2012 edition of *International Construction* magazine. A list of top 20 is located at http://www.khl.com/magazines/international-construction/detail/item76550/Chinese-contractors-top-global-rankings-once-again/.

74. National Technical Information Service, "U.S. Trade and Industry Outlook," 2000, http://www.ntis.gov/products/industry-trade.aspx.

75. U.S. Geological Survey, David Menzie, Chief, Global Minerals Analysis Section, National Minerals Information Center, before the U.S.-China Economic and Security Review Commission hearing on "China's Global Quest for Resources and Implications for the United States," January 26, 2012.

76. Gardner Publications' *Metalworking Insider's Report*, "World Machine Tool Output and Consumption Survey," 2012, http://www.gardnerweb.com/cdn/cms/uploadedFiles/2013wmtocs_SURVEY.pdf.

77. International Federation of Robotics, "World Robotics 2012 — Industrial Robots," published August 30, 2012, http://www.worldrobotics.org/.

78. Semiconductor Equipment Materials International (SEMI), "World Fab Forecast for 2013 and 2014, Past and Future Trends for Fab Spending and Capacity," Gartner Market Symposium, July 9, 2012.

79. SEMI, "Total Regional Materials Markets," May 2012.

80. SEMI, "Regional Semiconductor Packaging Materials Market," May 2012.

81. SEMI, "Equipment Producer Share by Region — Percent of Worldwide Sales by Company HQ Region," May 2012.

82. International Organization of Motor Vehicle Manufacturers, "2012 Production Statistics," http://oica.net/category/production-statistics/.

83. The trade numbers for autos and auto parts can be found at http://www.census.gov. On that page, click on the top tab "Business." Scroll over to the right column under "Popular Resources" and click "Foreign Trade." Under "News," click the first link to go to the "Latest U.S. International Trade in Goods and Services Report." Directly above the chart, click on "Previous Releases." Under the first box, "FT900 U.S. International Trade in Goods and Services," select a month (for all of 2012 data click on December 2012) and hit "Go." In the fifth box down "Not Seasonally Adjusted," click the last link, "Exhibit 18, Motor Vehicles and Parts by Selected Countries."

84. Stewart and Stewart, "China's Support Programs for Automobiles and Auto Parts Under the 12th Five-Year Plan," January 2012, http://www.stewartlaw.com/stewartandstewart/ LinkClick.aspx?link=Douments%2fS+%26+S+China+Auto+Parts+Subsidies+ Report.pdf&tabid=119&mid=579&language=en-US.

85. China's 12th Five-Year Plan, issued on March 14, 2011, targets seven strategic industries: new energy (nuclear, wind and solar power); energy conservation and environmental protection; biotechnology (drugs and medical devices); new materials (rare earths and high-end semiconductors); new IT (broadband networks, Internet security and network convergence); high-end equipment manufacturing (aerospace and telecom equipment); and clean-energy vehicles.

86. On September 17, 2012, the United States Trade Representative requested that the World Trade Organization create a dispute settlement consultation concerning China's auto and auto parts export subsidy programs. "The subsidies provide an unfair advantage to auto and auto parts manufacturers located in China, which are in competition with producers located in the United States and other countries," says USTR: http://www.ustr.gov/about-us/press-office/press-releases/2012/september/ obama-administration-challenges-china-auto-subsidies.

87. World Steel Association, "World Crude Steel Output Increases by 1.2 Percent in 2012," January 22, 2013, http://www.worldsteel.org/media-centre/press-releases/2012/12-2012-crude-steel.html.

88. U.S. International Trade Administration's Steel Importing and Analysis System, http://ia.ita.doc.gov/ steel/license/index.html, "U.S. Imports of Steel Mill Products From World," http://ia.ita.doc.gov/steel/ license/SMP/Census/Annual/gdesc52/MMTSum_ALL_wo_9Y.htm.

89. Testimony before the House Energy and Commerce subcommittee on Commerce, Manufacturing and Trade, March 21, 2013, http://energycommerce.house.gov/hearing/our-nation-builders-strength-steel.

90. Mann, Armistead & Epperson, Ltd., Richmond, Va., "2012 Import/Export Study, Furnishings Research Collection."

91. American Chemistry Council, "2012 Guide to the Business of Chemistry," http://www.americanchemistrycouncil.com/store, 301-617-7824.

92. European Chemical and Industry Council, "Facts and Figures 2011, The European Chemical Industry in a Worldwide Perspective," http://www.cefic.org/Global/Facts-and-figures-images/Graphs%202011/FF2011-chapters-PDF/Cefic_FF%20Rapport%202011.pdf.

93. Energy Information Administration, "Average Price of Natural Gas Sold to Industrial Customers, by State, 2010-2012," August 2012, http://www.eia.gov/naturalgas/monthly/pdf/table_22.pdf.

94. Energy Information Administration, *Natural Gas Annual, 2010*, http://www.eia.gov/naturalgas/annual/.

95. American Gas Association, "Energy Analysis, Identifying Key Economic Impacts of Recent Increases in U.S. Natural Gas Production," May 22, 2012, http://www.aga.org/Kc/analyses-and-statistics/studies/demand/Documents/EA%202012-03%20Economic%20Impact%20of%20Increased%20Gas%20Supplies%20May%202012.pdf.

96. PricewaterhouseCoopers, with contribution from the National Association of Manufacturers, "Shale Gas, A Renaissance in U.S. Manufacturing?" December 2011, http://www.pwc.com/en_US/us/industrial-products/assets/pwc-shale-gas-us-manufacturing-renaissance.pdf.

97. American Chemistry Council, "Shale Gas and New Petrochemicals Investment: Benefits for the Economy, Jobs and U.S. Manufacturing," Economics & Statistics division, March 2011, http://www.americanchemistry.com/ACC-Shale-Report.

98. Citigroup, "Energy 2020, North America, the New Middle East?" March 2012, http://fa.smithbarney.com/public/projectfiles/ce1d2d99-c133-4343-8ad0-43aa1da63cc2.pdf.

99. The American Chemistry Council, had this to say on the subject of shale gas: "Access to vast, new supplies of natural gas from previously untapped shale deposits is one of the most exciting domestic energy developments of the past 50 years. After years of high, volatile natural gas prices, the new economics of shale gas are a 'game changer,' creating a competitive advantage for U.S. petrochemical manufacturers, leading to greater U.S. investment and industry growth," fn. 97 supra.

100. American Apparel & Footwear Association, "We Wear," https://www.wewear.org/assets/1/16/WeWear.pdf.

101. International Trade Administration, Office of Textiles and Apparel, "Trade Data, U.S. Imports and Exports of Textiles and Apparel," http://otexa.ita.doc.gov/msrpoint.htm; "The Textile and Apparel Interactive Trade Balance Report," located at http://otexa.ita.doc.gov/scripts/tbr.exe.

102. Congressional Research Service, "The Commercial Space Industry and Launch Market," Glennon Harrison, Specialist in Industry Policy, April 20, 2012, CRS report to Congress, 7-5700, R42492.

103. General Aviation Manufacturers Association, "Quarterly Shipments and Billings, Year End Shipments of Aircraft Manufactured Worldwide," http://www.gama.aero/media-center/industry-facts-and-statistics/shipments-billings.

104. U.S. International Trade Commission, "Business Jet Aircraft Industry: Structure and Factors Affecting Competitiveness," April 2012, http://www.usitc.gov/publications/332/pub4314.pdf.

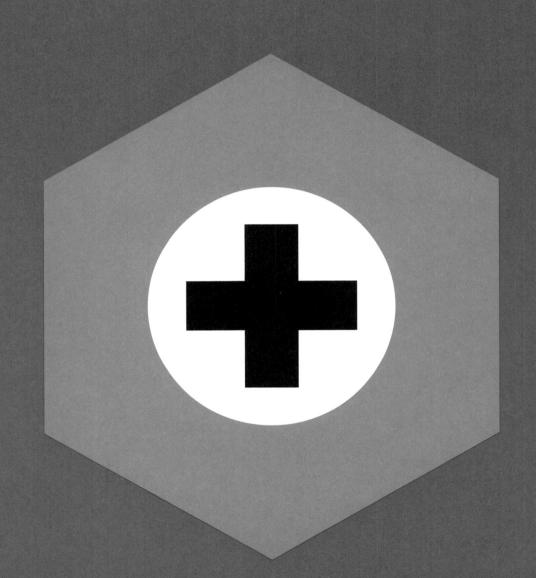

CHAPTER 2

Capital Formation For a Stronger U.S. Manufacturing Sector

Leo Hindery, Jr.[1]
Capital Formation

Manufacturing is critical to the American economy, yet over the past 12 years, U.S. manufacturers have cut 31 percent of their workforce, or nearly 6 million workers. The manufacturing sector's contribution to the U.S. gross domestic product fell to 11.9 percent in 2012 from 22.7 percent in 1970.[2]

While most other major nations have long embraced aggressive economic strategies to help their manufacturing sectors capture global market share in high-value-added industries, the United States has adopted no such "industrial policy." Whether under that name or another, America needs a manufacturing strategy of its own. If it does not adopt such a policy, then the shape of the U.S. economy will be determined by the industrial policies of its commercial and military rivals. Moreover, in the absence of an American manufacturing policy, manufacturing output as a percentage of U.S. GDP will continue to decline and the U.S. trade deficit will continue to balloon, with disastrous economic, employment and, ultimately, national security consequences.

In this chapter,[3] I will outline proposals for the three legs of what should be a sturdy tripod of manufacturing policy reform: access to finance; tax credits for R&D and investment; and broad tax reform undertaken with the goal of encouraging the reshoring of production rather than its continued offshoring. In addition, I will discuss the role that a National Infrastructure Bank might play in supporting a revival of American manufacturing.

THE MANUFACTURING IMPERATIVE

In a compelling statement in defense of the importance of manufacturing both to domestic job creation and to maintaining America's competitiveness and national security, Rich Harshman, President and CEO of Allegheny Technologies Inc., writes: "You can't just have a service sector as the underpinning of a successful, diverse and globally competitive economy. From economic strength to national security, America has great global responsibilities. The type of economic diversification that can support a middle class and meet our international obligations mandates that the U.S. be a successful manufacturer."[4]

John Hofmeister, a former president of Shell Oil Company and the founder and CEO of Citizens for Affordable Energy, has noted that as manufacturing has shrunk, "we've honored the gods of 'rationalization,' 'restructuring' and, the almightiest of all, 'globalization.' Core industry after industry has orchestrated its own decline, facilitated by short-term managerial reward systems. The next decade could see negative growth thanks to our foolhardy fondness for 'free market' philosophies that tell us it's okay to export all our jobs."[5]

The data support the judgments of these American business leaders. The indisputable importance of the manufacturing sector to America and the American economy is many-sided:

1. *Largest multiplier.* Manufacturing has by far the largest employment multiplier of all sectors of the economy, at least three times that of any service sector, including the hallowed financial services sector. In 2010, every dollar in final sales of a manufactured good generated $1.34 in output from other economic sectors, compared to 58 cents of output generated by wholesale trade and 55 cents of output generated by retail trade.[6] The Milken Institute suggests that if, today, the nation's largest industrial states each had a manufacturing sector proportional to what they had a decade ago, their current budget crises would be much less severe.[7]

2. *Productivity powerhouse.* Manufacturing productivity growth consistently outpaces productivity growth in other sectors of the economy. It is on the order of 60 percent greater than in the private, non-farm economy as a whole.

3. *Better wages and benefits.* Manufacturing employees earn higher wages and receive more generous benefits than other working Americans. On average, manufacturing employees earn 23 percent more than workers in other parts of the economy.

4. *Source of innovation.* The manufacturing sector is of vital importance in maintaining America's innovative capacity. Manufacturers are responsible for more than 70 percent of all business R&D, which ultimately benefits both other manufacturing and non-manufacturing activity.

5. *Key to an improved trade balance.* An increase in the production of manufactured exports and import-replacing goods in the United States is the only thing that will bring down America's trade deficit in manufactured goods to sustainable levels and reduce its international debt burden. Eliminating the current massive trade gap in manufactured goods, which is mostly with China, could be achieved without materially reducing Americans' standard of living. In an important piece of research and analysis, Michael Mandel and Diana Carew concluded that achieving this critical aspirational goal would result in a one-time-only rise of just 1.8 percent to 2 percent in overall economy-wide prices spread out over the time it takes to close the trade gap. This is equivalent to less than one-year's worth of inflation.[8] All the while, the United States would be borrowing much less from the rest of the world.

6. *Critical to other high-value-added sectors of the economy.* The maintenance of a strong and vibrant manufacturing sector is essential to other high-value-added sectors of the economy, including design, telecommunications and finance. Perhaps not surprisingly, Mandel and Carew's work concluded that if America is to achieve balanced and sustainable growth, every sector of its economy must contribute. But in light of new calculations showing that the manufacturing sector has much larger job spillovers than commonly thought, revitalizing manufacturing would do more

than any other action in any other sector of the economy to ease the job drought. It would offer millions of Americans a better path to the middle class.[9]

7. *Diversified employment.* Manufacturing employs workers at all skills and educational levels and helps reduce income inequality. For workers without a college education, manufacturing is a crucial source of good, often highly skilled jobs that pay above-average wages. On average, non-college-educated manufacturing workers make around 10 percent more than similar workers in the rest of the economy.

The first six characteristics on this list are integral to a truly balanced and vibrant economy that is globally competitive; the last characteristic — diversified employment — is an ethical imperative in a large society built on immigration.

SIZE OF THE MANUFACTURING SECTOR

What is not yet settled, however, is the size that the manufacturing sector ultimately needs to be, measured by both number of employees relative to the overall workforce and percentage of GDP. Right now, the sector employs only 12 million workers — just around 8 percent of the U.S. civilian labor force of 154.6 million workers — and produces only around 12 percent of GDP.[10]

Work done by the U.S. Economy and Smart Globalization Initiative at the New America Foundation suggests that the American manufacturing sector should have an employment base that is on the order of 20 percent of total U.S. employment and should contribute a fairly similar percentage of the nation's GDP. Put simply, no country as economically mature, large and diverse as America can prosper with only about 8 percent of its workers in its manufacturing sector. It seems from the New America Foundation's findings that if manufacturing employment in the United States is not at 20 percent at the least, a level more closely mirroring those of Germany and China, then only a series of consumer-credit-driven bubbles can sustain the economy — until, of course, each such bubble bursts, as bubbles always do.

Strongly affirming that the decline in manufacturing leads to unsustainable bubbles, research by Kerwin Kofi Charles, Erik Hurst and Matthew Notowidigdo of the University of Chicago documented that the "housing bubble" temporarily papered over the impact of the hollowing out of America's industrial base.[11]

Charles and his colleagues studied the extent to which the U.S. housing boom and subsequent bust during the 2000s masked — and then unmasked — the sharp, ongoing decline in the manufacturing sector. By correlating manufacturing declines and housing booms and then estimating the effects of both shocks on local employment and wages, they assessed how aggregate employment would have evolved absent the housing boom/bust cycle. They found that roughly 35 percent of the increase in non-employment between 2007 and 2011 can be attributed to the decline in manufacturing employment during the 2000s, and that much of the recent increase in non-employment would have occurred earlier had it not been for the large temporary boom in local housing prices.[12]

A NATIONAL MANUFACTURING POLICY

While there are many reasons for the decline in American manufacturing, a primary one is the simple fact that, unlike every one of its large trade competitors, the U.S. does not have a national manufacturing strategy or policy, nor has it established a framework for creating either. Government policies related to R&D, investment tax credits, taxes, access to financing, trade, currency valuation and other foreign subsidies, export initiatives and controls, and domestic procurement have yet to be integrated into a cohesive and effective strategy to restore the U.S. manufacturing sector.

And to counter those who argue that because the U.S. still leads the world in innovation and entrepreneurship it therefore does not need its own manufacturing policy, we have only to ask: "Then where are the jobs and where is the recent large-scale value creation?"

ACCESS TO FINANCING

Inextricably related and, in combination, integral to any meaningful resuscitation of the American manufacturing sector are access to financing, tax credits for R&D and investment and tax reform. This chapter will discuss this "three-legged stool," as well as the biggest single opportunity confronting the entire sector, namely, a National Infrastructure Bank.

Access to financing comes first in the discussion because it is absolutely critical to the prospects of the American small and medium-sized enterprises (SMEs) involved in manufacturing. Robust R&D efforts are important to SMEs and large companies alike, and every part of the manufacturing sector would benefit greatly from thoughtful investment tax credits and fundamental tax reform.

"Access to capital," as access to financing is technically called, covers four categories: daily working capital, term loans, mezzanine or subordinated debt and equity. This chapter will discuss the prospects for each of the three debt categories, since access to equity by the large public companies essentially takes care of itself and there is very little investor enthusiasm for small-company public equities, inherently a risky class of shares. It will also put forward three complementary initiatives that should be undertaken to improve the manufacturing sector's access to capital as Congress independently seeks to fundamentally improve the commercial prospects and dynamics of the sector.

Currently, as the big banks endeavor to rebuild their balance sheets by taking advantage of record-low Fed discount rates and engaging in non-lending-related activities, what lending they will do is mostly to large borrowers. This is because large U.S. companies, especially those that are publicly held and multinational, almost invariably have stronger balance sheets and a greater diversity of products or goods, which appeal to both big lenders and equity investors. These large companies are also greatly advantaged by borrowing because, for businesses, debt interest payments are tax deductible, whereas equity payments, such as corporate dividends, are not. At the margin, this encourages entities to take on more debt than they otherwise would.[13]

Vis-à-vis the smaller manufacturers, the Great Recession of 2007 and the subsequent further consolidation of the banking and financial services industries have, perversely, led to an unfortunate new focus for the nation's banks that can only be characterized as "short-term financialism" and "disdain for patient capital and long-termism."

In late 2012, commercial bank lending to SMEs — encompassing working-capital loans and term loans — was still, despite a recent pickup, down about 25 percent from its level at the beginning of the Great Recession.[14] Yet both types of financing are vital: working-capital loans, which are typically secured by the combination of accounts receivable and inventories, are what turn a company's lights on in the morning, pay its employees their wages, and purchase the raw materials needed for production machines. Senior-term loans, in turn, are needed to give businesses the baseline stability they need to make significant equipment purchases and long-term commitments to customers.

The best solution for turning these two "faucets" back on would seem to be to adhering, as much as possible, to the principles reflected in the Credit Union Small Business Jobs Bill (S−2231), introduced by Senator Mark Udall (D-Colo.) in March 2012. This legislation sought to raise the credit union lending cap to 27.5 percent of total assets from the current figure of 12.25 percent. When Sen. Udall and two of his primary co-sponsors, Michigan Democratic Senators Carl Levin and Debbie Stabenow, saw the dramatic falloff in bank lending to SMEs, they observed that at the same time a large number of the so-called "alternative lenders" — credit unions, accounts receivable financers, merchant cash advance lenders, Community Development Financial Institutions and microlenders — were trying to pick up the slack. They realized that the largest by far of these alternative lenders, the nation's credit unions — which have more than $300 billion that can be lent — could dramatically increase their lending if only their lending caps were increased. With just the increase in the cap proposed in the Credit Union Small Business Jobs Bill, an estimated $13 billion in additional capital would be freed up, which could create more than 140,000 new jobs in the United States.

Unfortunately, but almost predictably, in one of the most arrogant and selfish actions imaginable, the American Bankers Association decided to formally oppose the bill, even though it is the very reluctance of the ABA's member banks to lend to SMEs that prompted the bill's sponsors to put forward the legislation in the first place.

Two responses to the ABA's obstruction are called for, although the first of these is like rewarding the goose who wants to kill off the gander.

First, since the principle behind the proposed Credit Union Small Business Jobs Bill is indisputable — namely, that an increase in the lending cap to certain borrowers leads to an increase in lending — Congress should endeavor to change the commercial banks' reserves rule in such a way that it provides them an incentive to resume lending to SMEs, with additional leeway granted for loans to SMEs in the manufacturing sector.

Second, acknowledging that regardless of any change in their lending caps, many commercial banks simply won't want to lend to SMEs because they think it is unprofitable or too risky, Congress should (as laid out below) create a system of public or nonprofit banks to lend to SMEs.

Another layer of commercial debt financing to be considered is the mezzanine — or subordinated — debt layer. In an ideal capital structure, this layer sits between senior-term loans and owners' equity. It is usually fairly priced at an interest rate roughly halfway between the senior-term-loan interest rate and the desired return on equity (or "cost of equity capital"). Unfortunately, there is now little or no access for the SMEs to this layer of financing. There will likely continue to be none at least until sustained real growth and long-term optimism come back to the national economy, and until the nation has a manufacturing policy in place. As it is now, the interest rates on subordinated loans to manufacturing SMEs are barely lower than the high implicit rates of return that equity investors now demand from SMEs.

In sum, virtually all three of the traditional commercial debt sources — working capital, senior-term loans and subordinated debt — that once provided the capital structure of the manufacturing sector have largely been suppressed by political insensitivity to the sector along with U.S. global trade policies that have run amok, the ongoing effects of the Great Recession and the changed "missions" and loan portfolios of the country's major banks.

ACCESS TO NON-BANK CREDIT

The central strategy for industrial revitalization in America must be expanding access to non-bank credit for all American manufacturing companies and especially those that are small and medium-sized. One of the most important factors in growing any economic sector is reducing the cost of credit for businesses in that sector. In the 20th century, the federal government put a very heavy thumb on the scale in order to provide financial aid to railroads, financial institutions and businesses, and to help farms and homeowners with their credit needs. Now the federal government needs to do more of the same specifically for American manufacturing.

Currently, public-development banks play a major role in economic development and strategy in other countries. Eighty-four percent of development banks around the world target industry and manufacturing along with other related sectors that include infrastructure and agriculture, and 92 percent help SMEs.[15]

In 2012, state-owned financial institutions, of which public development banks are the most important, accounted for 25 percent of the assets of the world's banking system and 30 percent of financial assets in the banking system of the European Union.[16] Public development banks around the world include "megabanks" with more than $100 billion in assets, such as the China Development Bank, Germany's Kreditanstalt fuer Wiederaufbau (KfW) banking system and North Rhine-Westphalia Bank and Brazil Development Bank. In 2012, 74 percent of development banks had 100 percent government ownership, while 21 percent had 50 to 99 percent government ownership. In only 5 percent of these banks does government own less than 50 percent.

Fifty-two percent of development banks engage in both retail lending (direct to customers) and wholesale lending (to other financial institutions); 36 percent engage only in retail lending; and 12 percent engage only in wholesale lending. Ninety percent of these banks provide long-term loans, 85 percent provide loans for working capital and 74 percent provide bridge or short-term loans. Half of all development banks provide credit at subsidized interest rates; of these, 66 percent fund the subsidies by means of government transfers.[17]

Public-development banks are not at all limited to developing countries with undeveloped local banking systems or countries that lack access to global capital markets. The world's leading industrial nations have important public-development banks, except for the United States. Japan relies on the Japan Development Bank, Germany on the KfW, South Korea on the Korea Development Bank and Canada on its Business Development Bank of Canada.

In other nations, public-development banks have engaged in counter-cyclical spending in order to help cushion the impact of the worldwide Great Recession on SMEs and large businesses alike. Mexico's NAFIN, for example, helped Chrysler's operations in Mexico by extending loans.[18]

Other countries use their export-import banks as a tool of national industrial policy far more aggressively than the United States uses its Export-Import Bank. A report by the European Parliament in 2011 concluded that "Chinese export credits have become a competitive threat to exporters from the OECD. China is not a member of the OECD and is therefore not obliged to comply with the OECD guidelines that limit tied aid; regulate credit practices; impose maximum repayment terms, country risk classification and minimum interest rates; require the exchange of information; and impose social, environmental and governance standards on financing activities. This creates an unfair advantage for Chinese exporters."[19]

Michael Lind and Daniel Mandel of the New America Foundation explored these themes and proposed a large-scale program of "Made in America Bonds."[20] It is modeled on the $181 billion Build America Bonds program that was created by the American Recovery and Reinvestment Act of 2009 (ARRA). The Task Force on Job Creation has made a similar recommendation.

Made in America Bonds would be a new class of tax-credit bonds issued by states, local governments and other authorized entities, especially municipalities, to encourage the establishment and expansion of manufacturing in the United States. A tax-credit bond is simply a taxable bond in which part or all of the interest on the bond can be deducted from federal taxes by the bondholder, who may be an individual or a company. This tax credit is really just another "tax expenditure" among the many other tax breaks for individuals and institutions provided for in the federal tax code.

As points of reference, in descending order of size, the most significant tax expenditures accessible today to American taxpayers are the mortgage interest deduction (around $82 billion per year), the earned income tax credit ($61 billion), the child tax credit ($56 billion), the deduction for state and local income, sales and property taxes ($40 billion), the charitable contributions deduction ($35 billion) and untaxed Social Security and railroad retirement benefits ($29 billion).[21]

Even though the credits implicit in a tax-credit bond are undeniably subsidies to the issuers on the part of the federal government, tax-credit bonds have particularly strong political appeal — even in a period of pervasive public concern about high federal deficits — precisely because these federal tax subsidies take the form of a tax expenditure. For example, a number of tax-credit bonds were either introduced or revised in ARRA, such as Recovery Zone Economic Development and Facility Bonds, New Clean Renewable Energy Bonds and Qualified Energy Conservation Bonds. All have been widely embraced politically.

As Lind and Mandel observed, at this challenging juncture the concept of Made in America Bonds as a non-bank credit way to revitalize the manufacturing sector is more important than the actual details, which would inevitably reflect compromises in Congress. This said, the basic features of any Made in America Bonds program should include: a reasonable "volume cap" in order to limit revenue losses to the federal government to a level acceptable politically; fairly loose restrictions on how state, local and municipal governments should be allowed to use the bonds, provided they show verifiable results in promoting new manufacturing investment in their jurisdictions; and, a particularly important point, restrictions on states using Made in America Bonds as a part of a "beggar-thy-neighbor" strategy to rob other states and regions of manufacturing companies.

An important aspect of the Made in America Bonds program should be "employment impact statements" to determine which proposed new or existing manufacturing initiatives are most likely to create and support U.S. jobs. Each of these employment impact statements would contain information pertaining to the jobs that would be maintained or created if the investment was approved.

Finally, as is obvious from its name, the whole intention of a Made in America Bonds program would be to create jobs in the United States, and thus every effort should be made to ensure that "Made in America" meant just that.

No single measure would do more to help resuscitate U.S. employment, particularly in manufacturing, than an all-of-government buy-domestic procurement requirement. Unfortunately, right now the federal government grants too many waivers and considers a product to be domestically manufactured even if it is substantially made up of components produced outside the United States. Before any state or municipality enters into a Made in America Bonds program, it should make sure that the borrower's domestic content calculations are effective and transparent and that not less than 75 percent of the materials and components used in the borrower's manufacturing activities are verifiably manufactured within the United States.

At the same time that he and Mandel were advancing the Made in America Bonds idea, Lind authored an equally compelling paper proposing a new "manufacturing credit system."[22]

This proposal would readily counter the reluctance of the nation's commercial banks to finance small and medium-sized manufacturers by having the federal government create a dozen or so regional manufacturing credit banks. This system would be modeled both on the Reconstruction Finance Corporation (RFC), created in 1932 to provide financial aid to railroads, financial institutions and businesses, and on the now nearly 100-year-old farm credit system with its five existing Farm Credit and Home Loan banks. With the manufacturing sector facing even more rebuilding and reconstruction than during a traditional recovery, the common distinction between short-term relief and long-term reform has largely collapsed, which is why some clone of the RFC and the farm credit system for the manufacturing sector is appropriate now. As Lind writes, "if the RFC hadn't been abolished, we'd already be having an entirely different conversation."[23]

Each new regional manufacturing credit bank would be cooperatively owned by banks and other credit institutions located in its geographic region. Complementing these banks would be a single new federally chartered government-sponsored enterprise, which Lind cleverly suggests be called the "National Manufacturing Loan Marketing Association" (or "Mannie Mac"). Mannie Mac would be charged with creating the secondary market necessary for this low-interest loan program to function on a day-to-day basis in the financial marketplace.

The seed money to fund the new regional manufacturing credit banks could be provided in one of three ways: either directly or indirectly by the federal government; each individual bank, structured as its own government-sponsored enterprise, could be allowed to issue its own bonds and use the proceeds to build reserves; or, if the first two alternatives are difficult to accomplish for political reasons, the banks could be funded indirectly by means of state and local municipal bonds that receive favorable federal tax treatment.

R&D AND INVESTMENT TAX CREDITS

Side by side with the Made in America Bonds program and the new manufacturing credit system, and equally central to any strategy for industrial revitalization, must be a permanent R&D tax credit and an investment tax credit directly linked to jobs.

Investment tax credits and R&D tax credits function as financing tools in their own right. They are used for rehabilitating and renovating existing manufacturing facilities, providing incentives for the large-scale purchase of new equipment and jump-starting new technologies and process development. They would pump billions of dollars into modernizing America's plants, retooling its factories and maintaining the country's global competitiveness.

As Jonathan Browning, CEO of Volkswagen Group of America, has written: "When you combine the high-tech sector that is a global strength for the U.S. with a strong manufacturing sector, you have the opportunity to strongly drive knowledge development and value creation within the economy, and be very competitive on a global basis."[24]

As it is, however, the American manufacturing sector as a whole continues to operate significantly below its potential. In the manufacturing sector and the durable goods manufacturing sub-sector, capacity utilization in 2012 remained at record lows going back to the 1960s, when capacity utilization was first measured. Yet at the same time, there is significant demand for both green- and high-tech manufactured products such as wind turbines, photovoltaic cells, advanced batteries for electric cars, light rail and high-speed rail products and, at some point soon, a national smart grid. The fact that the country simultaneously faces an underutilized domestic manufacturing sector and demand for green and high-tech manufactured products that could be produced in the United States provides it with an extraordinary opportunity.

Unfortunately, there are two major obstacles to taking advantage of this opportunity. On the one hand, there are the country's stagnating R&D efforts. On the other, there is a lack of financial means to purchase new equipment and retool existing American manufacturers, which could then manufacture the innovative green-and high-technology products that the nation needs. Investment tax credits and similar investment incentives — especially permanent R&D tax credits — in many ways afford the most immediate and productive access to capital and would be an important contributor to overcoming these obstacles.

The Task Force on Jobs identified three investment incentives that should co-exist with traditional investment tax credits and be made part of any overall access-to-capital initiative. They are:

- First, extend and expand the Treasury's 1603 Cash Grant Program for manufacturing-centric renewable energy production. This program converts non-refundable tax credits for renewable energy production into cash grants. Previously, renewable energy-related companies were able to take advantage of tax credits, even if they had no tax appetite, by entering into tax equity partnerships with entities like financial institutions. Because the financial crisis has dramatically shrunk the tax equity market, however, renewable energy companies are now denied this tax credit advantage and have seen their business models suffer as a result. Extending the 1603 Program until the tax equity market recovers will help create jobs and avoid further job losses in the renewable energy industry.

- Second, extend the Advanced Manufacturing Tax Credit (Section 48c) of ARRA in order to prompt further investments. ARRA authorized up to $2.3 billion in tax credits for investments in qualified advanced energy projects at manufacturing facilities, such as energy storage, electricity transmission and energy conservation technologies.

- Third, expand the Loan Guarantee Program of Title 17 of the Energy Policy Act of 2005 to include "energy-efficiency" investments. Right now, this program provides federal loan guarantees for the construction of energy-related facilities that use new or significantly improved technologies that are non-commercial and have high technological risk. Broadening Title 17 to include energy-efficiency investments would help spur this market and create many new industrial building jobs.

In addition, and as an underlying principle, it is vital that the federal budget process adopt a scoring methodology that views R&D and other development costs as "investments" and not as expenses. Although R&D costs have not been analyzed this way, the costs of the National Institutes of Health (NIH) have been. Research by University of Chicago economists Kevin Murphy and Robert Topel indicates that improvements in health from 1970 to 2000, many of them driven by NIH grants, have added a staggering $3.2 trillion a year to U.S. national wealth. The amount is 100 times greater than the entire current NIH federal budget of $31 billion a year.[25] Clearly, similarly high-benefit figures could be determined for government R&D and other development costs in the non-health sectors of the economy, especially in manufacturing.

TAX REFORM

The third leg of this chapter's conceptual three-legged stool is the imperative for fundamental corporate tax reform that both changes the provisions of the tax code that discourage American manufacturers from expanding domestically and eliminates the incentives that encourage them to close plants in the United States and shift jobs to countries like China. Right now, the corporate tax code provides incentives for companies to invest overseas, which is a sure sign that the U.S. economy is now working better for multinational corporations than for domestic manufacturers and working Americans.

Repeating a demand he made during his 2008 campaign for the presidency, President Obama, in his 2012 State of the Union speech, said: "It's time to stop rewarding businesses that ship jobs overseas, and start rewarding companies that create jobs right here in America."[26]

As it is, however, since 2009 at least 10 large U.S. public companies have moved their incorporation address abroad or announced plans to do so, including six in late 2011 and early 2012. According to a *Wall Street Journal* analysis of company filings and statements, this is up from just a handful of companies from 2004 through 2008. Recent moves include those of the risk manager AON Corp. to the U.K., the manufacturer Eaton Corp. to Ireland, oil firms Ensco International and Rowan Cos. to the U.K. and a spinoff of Sara Lee Corp. called D.E. Master Blenders 1753 to the Netherlands.[27]

The answer to the President's demand comes in two parts, each of which would significantly improve the financing prospects of the manufacturing sector, especially when it comes to bank financing.

The first part is simply to reduce the corporate tax rate from 35 percent to between 25 and 28 percent while getting rid of virtually all of the corporate "tax expenditures" that have nothing to do with retaining existing jobs and creating new ones. Today, the United States stands almost alone with one of the highest corporate income tax rates in the world, inspiring large-scale tax evasion while generating surprisingly little revenue.

The second part is to offset the significant tax disadvantages faced by American corporations on account of the value-added tax (VAT) used by most foreign trading partners, including all of the largest partners, but not by the United States. A value-added tax is a consumption tax, much like a sales tax. However, because a VAT is collected at each stage of the production of a product, it avoids the problem of "cascading" sales taxes on top of sales taxes.

Right now, the United States relies exclusively on an income tax to raise revenue from its corporations. In contrast, in order to attract overseas investment and retain domestic production, its foreign competitors use a much lower corporate income tax combined with a VAT. And because the VAT is refunded on exports and charged on imports (while income tax is not), the result is net higher, and usually much higher, taxes on U.S.-made products sold both at home and abroad. This acts as another incentive for American manufacturers to move production out of the United States and play games with shell corporations. In the process, both the American manufacturing sector and American workers lose.[28]

Influential figures on the right, in the center and on the center-left have concluded that a modest, sensitively framed VAT that reduces corporate income taxes and/or payroll taxes has the potential to make the American tax system much friendlier (and fairer) to those enterprises that can most effectively resuscitate the ailing economy and broken manufacturing sector. It could also become a principal means of reducing the federal deficit. An exhaustive study by Eric Toder and Joseph Rosenberg for the Urban-Brookings Tax Policy Center and the New America Foundation clearly shows how.[29]

A NATIONAL INFRASTRUCTURE BANK

These proposed solutions to the current crisis in access to capital notwithstanding, all of the nation's manufacturers, from the largest multinationals to medium-sized manufacturers and to the smallest of the SMEs, would greatly benefit by participating in the large-scale rebuilding and upgrading of the country's very dilapidated and inadequate infrastructure.

After years of underinvesting in public infrastructure, America now faces a massive infrastructure deficit that is impeding economic growth and undermining the economy's efficiency.[30] Even the infrastructure necessary for information technology is lagging. Fears about the reliability of U.S.

energy, water and transportation systems are deterring investment in many parts of the country and interfering with new, business investment and job creation.

The answer to this challenge and opportunity is a new, large National Infrastructure Bank with the following characteristics:

- The new National Infrastructure Bank should be an independent financial institution owned by the government, rather than an arm of an existing agency, and it needs to be very large-scale in its capitalization (at least $1 trillion). According to the American Society of Civil Engineers, America needs to spend $1 trillion or so over the next several years just to meet its core infrastructure needs.[31] These long-term investments in infrastructure would create jobs, trigger growth in all economic sectors — especially in the manufacturing sector — spark private investment and stimulate the economy. According to the non-partisan Congressional Budget Office, every dollar of infrastructure spending generates an estimated $1.60 increase in GDP, and each one billion dollars of spending on infrastructure creates at least 25,000 new permanent jobs. Some critical transportation and energy projects have even larger job-creation effects, with up to 40,000 new permanent jobs created per $1 billion.

- The scope of the National Infrastructure Bank should be proportional to its capitalization, and it should be able to fund a broad range of infrastructure projects beyond traditional roads, rails and runways. It should be able to make and guarantee loans, leverage private capital, sell or issue general-purpose bonds to raise funds for lending and investment, and sell specific project bonds when necessary. The bank, consistent with the AAA credit rating that it could be expected to have, would likely be able to finance up to 10 dollars of infrastructure investment for each dollar of equity capitalization.

- A soft federal guarantee, equal to about one-tenth of the bank's total capitalization, should be its equity-capital base. Because of the relatively large amount of leverage above this equity base — which would be on the order of nine times the amount of the soft federal guarantee — this federal support of the bank would likely not need to be "scored," and thus would not be an addition to the federal deficit.

- The primary source of the bank's leverage should be the large state and municipal pension plans, with a target-rate real return of, say, 3 percent per annum.

- Governance of the bank should be by an independent, non-partisan board of executives who are expert in matters related to infrastructure, along with labor leaders and public policymakers.

- Projects in the states and local governments whose pension plans participate in capitalization of the bank should have preference over those put forward by states and local governments that elect not to participate.

- As with the Made in America Bonds program, the bank should fund projects that adhere to strict "buy domestic" (or Made in America) requirements, consistent with the United States' international trade agreements. Requirements in the Defense Authorization Bill of 2012 that the Pentagon buy solar panels from U.S. manufacturers provide the right model for these bank-related requirements.

- Finally, as a complement to the bank, there should be a temporary, limited federal guarantee program for the bonds of those state and local governments whose creditworthiness for infrastructure projects has been excessively negatively impacted by the Recession and whose projects are, therefore, not immediately appropriate for the bank, which, however, would assume them eventually.

TRADE WITH CHINA

Under normal circumstances, this chapter would end immediately above. But these are not at all normal times, and they won't be until the United States fundamentally reforms its trading relationship with China. The trade imbalance with China is as much a capital formation/constraint issue for the American manufacturing sector as are the sector's currently depleted balance sheets and faltering income statements.

At least as long ago as December 2007, when the current Recession officially began, several of us were writing that, without some immediate and dramatic changes to U.S. trade and economic policies and practices, America's Great Recession would prove to be China's "Great Opportunity."

Ever since, American companies have further cut their payrolls and capital spending, driving additional business to China, while China continues to increase the global competitiveness of its own manufacturers.

On February 3, 2010, President Obama told the Democratic Policy Committee of the Senate that one of the international challenges the United States has to address is currency rates, and specifically how the United States can make sure that its goods are not artificially inflated in price at the same time that foreign goods are artificially deflated in price.

Chinese manipulation of its currency, the renminbi, is certainly the most visible "symbol" of China's mercantilist practices, being that it is obviously undervalued at present on the order of 25 to 30 percent. However, it really is only the tip of China's mercantilist iceberg. Granted, it is a very big tip, but then China's unfair trade practices are a very big iceberg.

Much has been written about how China has unfairly gained trade advantages through its abysmally low direct-labor costs, lack of meaningful environmental and labor standards, and currency manipulation. All of that is valid. Less appreciated, however, are the variety and the magnitude of the other measures China uses to game the system. These other so-called "trade advantages," which will allow China to dominate certain industries for years to come, include regulations to block non-Chinese firms from selling their products to Chinese government agencies; technical standards that prevent, or at least significantly hinder, the Chinese government and Chinese businesses from buying non-Chinese goods; and rules that force Western companies to give up technological secrets in exchange for access to China's markets.

Right now, fully 90 percent of the cost differential between an average good manufactured in China and a similar good manufactured in the United States is accounted for by various Chinese subsidies, most of them illegal under the World Trade Organization (WTO). Only about 10 percent of the difference is due to the differences in wages — which, of course, is contrary to popular belief.[32]

The necessary United States responses to China's unfair trade practices and demands are pretty simple:

1.   The United States should not let its recent focus on growing its exports "come at the expense of ensuring a fair playing field for our manufacturers."[33] This means focusing on America's net exports position with China — that is, its trade balance — rather than on simply growing gross exports to China.[34]

2.   If the evidence is there, then the next required "Semiannual Report on International Economic and Exchange Rate Policies" from the Treasury Department needs to designate China as a currency manipulator. Current law requires the administration to determine whether U.S. trading partners are deliberately undervaluing their currencies. However, the last time any Secretary of the Treasury labeled a country a currency manipulator was July 1994, when China was so cited, even though the evidence is strong that there has in fact been currency manipulation by China in every semi-annual period since.

3.   The U.S. government needs to go after all of China's other illegal subsidies, while also putting a quick halt to China's persistent theft of America's hard-gained, valuable intellectual property, which zaps America's economy almost as much as do China's adverse currency moves.

4.   Americans need to demand that the U.S. government not enter into a bilateral investment treaty with China until China makes WTO-compliant its Indigenous Innovation Production Accreditation program (IIPA). In the interim, the Office of the U.S. Trade Representative should bring a Section 301 case against that program.[35] The IIPA, which was launched on November 15, 2009, limits all Chinese central and provincial government procurement to companies that have "indigenous" — that is, Chinese — "innovation." It is far more restrictive than any other buy-domestic program in the world, and its adverse impacts are felt across all industries that seek to export to China, but especially in computers and consumer electronics, green technologies, autos, aviation and specialty materials.

5.   Congress needs to pass a bill similar to the Reciprocal Market Access Act of 2011 (HR−1749), bipartisan legislation sponsored in the House by Reps. Louise Slaughter (D-N.Y.) and Walter Jones (R-N.C.). In the Senate, the bill (S−1711) was sponsored by Sens.

Sherrod Brown (D-Ohio) and Kay Hagan (D-N.C.). Such legislation would immediately eliminate the distinction that exists between traditional tariff barriers and the much-larger and increasingly significant non-tariff barriers that prevent fair market access by American suppliers.[36]

6. The United States must establish stronger review procedures for any planned investments by China in U.S. ports, the transportation industry, natural resources, financial markets, advanced technology products manufacturing and items deemed by the Defense Department to be "militarily critical." Before a controlling or influencing investment is made, a "national security impact statement" that considers the investment's defense, security and infrastructure implications should be prepared jointly by the Departments of Commerce and Defense for the Congress and the administration.

7. Finally, advocates of U.S. manufacturing need to demand that the Department of Commerce "use the trade enforcement authorities and tools it has readily available to defend American manufacturers and workers against unfairly subsidized imports."[37] At the same time, trade enforcement should be moved from the U.S. Trade Representative's office to a fully enabled and funded office in the Justice Department. Trade negotiation and the enforcement of agreements are distinct activities requiring very different skills, and enforcement best belongs with "enforcers," not with those who negotiated the trade agreements.

CONCLUSION

After decades in which manufacturing in America was neglected or seen as a sector doomed to be replaced by other industries, there is growing recognition of the importance of manufacturing in a flourishing economy. At the same time, there is greater acknowledgment that globalization has not taken the form of a borderless world in which countries pay no attention to the location of strategic industries. "Industrial policy" is still denounced by many American politicians and economists, but the consensus in favor of a do-nothing approach has been shaken by the examples of the successful industrial policies of export power-houses like China and Germany.

One promising sign is the determination of many in Congress to act to support America's industrial base. In late 2012, the House of Representatives passed legislation calling for the United States to have a National Manufacturing Strategy (HR—5865). The American Manufacturing Competitiveness Act of 2012, introduced by Rep. Daniel Lipinski (D-Ill.) and 44 co-sponsors, would direct the President to submit a National Manufacturing Competitiveness Strategy to Congress every four years; establish a Manufacturing Competitiveness Board[38] to "advise the President on issues affecting the Nation's manufacturing sector"; and, in preparing each annual budget, include information regarding that budget's consistency with the goals and recommendations included in the latest Strategy. Unfortunately, the Obama administration did not make this a priority and the Senate failed to act on the bill.

Right now, the United States is, unfortunately, tolerating very selfish, short-sighted behaviors that are hurting the middle class and its workers, creating large and unsustainable trade imbalances and crippling its economic vitality and national security. These behaviors have been tolerated mostly because too many leaders in Washington are overly deferential to the interests of multinational corporations and financial institutions, which currently wield undue influence on them.

All Americans must work to change this in order to put the country on a healthier, growing economic path. An excellent place to start is with economic policy initiatives of the sort discussed in this chapter, all of which are aimed at bolstering the critically important but underappreciated manufacturing sector in the United States.

1. This chapter and its author owe a debt of gratitude to Michael Lind of the New America Foundation, whose writings have guided and informed discussions about the issues covered for many years, and to Alan Platt of the U.S. Economy and Smart Globalization Initiative of the New America Foundation and of Johns Hopkins School of Advanced International Studies (SAIS).

2. "A Reality Check on American Manufacturing," *Bloomberg Businessweek,* September 10-16, 2012.

3. In writing this chapter, I have benefited greatly from the writings and speeches of Senators Sherrod Brown (D-Ohio), Debbie Stabenow (D-Mich.) and Sheldon Whitehouse (D-R.I.) and from the work of the U.S. Economy and Smart Globalization Initiative.

4. "Made in America" special advertising section, *Bloomberg Businessweek,* September 10-16, 2012.

5. John Hofmeister, "The U.S. Needs an Industrial Policy," *Wall Street Journal,* February 8, 2010.

6. U.S. Bureau of Economic Analysis, Input/Output Accounts (Industry-by-Industry Total Requirements after Redefinitions), Sector Level Chart, 2010, cited in Michael Lind and Joshua Freedman, "Value Added: America's Manufacturing Future" Washington, D.C., The New America Foundation, 2012.

7. Ross C. DeVol, Perry Wong, Armen Bedroussian, Candice Flor Hynek and David Rice, "Manufacturing 2.0: A More Prosperous California," Milken Institute, June 2009.

8. Michael Mandel and Diana G. Carew, "Manufacturing in the App Economy: How Many Jobs Should We Aim For?" Progressive Policy Institute, May 2012.

9. Ibid.

10. Table B-1 et al. of the August 2012 BLS Employment News Release, http://www.bls.gov/news.release/pdf/empsit.pdf.

11. Kerwin Kofi Charles, Erik Hurst and Matthew Notowidigdo, "Manufacturing Busts, Housing Booms, and Declining Employment: A Structural Explanation," University of Chicago Harris School of Public Policy, Booth School of Business and NBER, August 2012. http://faculty.chicagobooth.edu/matthew.notowidigdo/research/charles_hurst_noto_manufacturing.pdf.

12. Ibid.

13. Jesse Eisinger referencing Steven M. Davidoff, "Distortion in Tax Code Makes Debt More Attractive to Banks," *New York Times DealBook,* September 19, 2012.

14. Saumya Vaishampayan, "Businesses Are Sweet Spot for Banks," *Wall Street Journal,* September 13, 2012.

15. Jose de Luna-Martinez and Carlos Leonardo Vicente, "Global Survey of Development Banks," The World Bank – Policy Research Working Paper 5969, February 2012.

16. Ibid.

17. Ibid.

18. Ibid.

19. Isabella Massa, "Export Finance Activities by the Chinese Government," Briefing Paper, Directorate-General for External Policies of the Union (Belgium: European Parliament, 2011).

20. Michael Lind and Daniel Mandel, "Made in America Bonds," New America Foundation, March 22, 2010.

21. Ibid.

22. Michael Lind, "The Manufacturing Credit System," New America Foundation, March 22, 2011.

23. Ibid.

24. "Made in America" special advertising section, *Bloomberg Businessweek,* September 10-16, 2012.

25. Michael Milken, "Investing in Science, Reaping Rewards," *Wall Street Journal,* September 6, 2012.

26. http://www.whitehouse.gov/the-press-office/2012/01/24/remarks-president-state-union-address.

27. John D. McKinnon and Scott Thurm, "U.S. Firms Move Abroad to Cut Taxes," *Wall Street Journal,* August 28, 2012.

28. Leo Hindery, Jr. and Michael Lind, "America needs a VAT," *Los Angeles Times,* May 24, 2010.

29. Eric Toder and Joseph Rosenberg, "Effects of Imposing a Value-Added Tax to Replace Payroll Taxes or Corporate Taxes," Urban-Brookings Tax Policy Center and the Economic Growth Program of the New America Foundation, March 18, 2010.

30. "Report Card for America's Infrastructure," American Society of Civil Engineers, http://www.infrastructurereportcard.org/.

31. Ibid.

32. Leo Hindery, Jr., "China: Continued Abusive Trade and Now A 'Blue Water Navy,'" *Huffington Post,* January 10, 2012.

33. August 4, 2010, letter to President Barack Obama by Senators Sherrod Brown (D-Ohio), Olympia Snowe (R-Maine), Charles Schumer (D-N.Y.), Debbie Stabenow (D-Mich.), Jim Bunning (R-Ky.), Arlen Specter (D-Pa.), Susan Collins (R-Maine), Ron Wyden (D-Ore.), Benjamin Cardin (D-Md.), Robert Casey, Jr. (D-Pa.) and Carl Levin (D-Mich.).

34. Leo Hindery, Jr., "U.S. – China: How Long China's Doormat?" *Huffington Post,* August 24, 2010.

35. Because China is still not a member of the WTO Government Procurement Code, a Section 301 action is the only remedy currently available.

36. Leo Hindery, Jr., "China Trade: A 'Target Rich Environment,'" *Huffington Post,* March 20, 2012.

37. Supra fn 41.

38. HR–5865, Section 4.

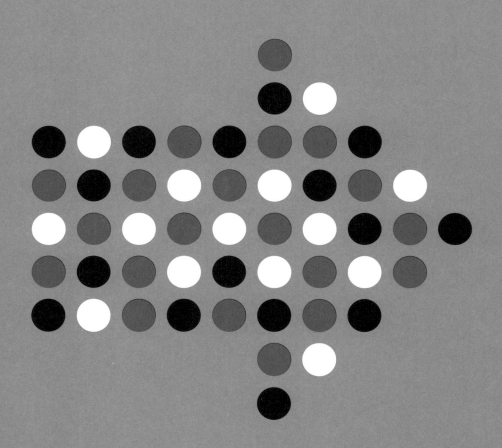

CHAPTER 3

Reshoring: Turning a Trend Into a Torrent

A Strategy for a Strong U.S. Economy

Harry Moser
Reshoring Initiative

There are two possible strategies that can be pursued to reduce the United States' trade deficit enough to increase the nation's GDP by several percentage points. The choice is between exporting more and importing less.

Public discussion has been limited almost entirely to the first option: President Obama, most economic policymakers and many commentators have placed great emphasis on boosting exports. But they are misguided.

Instead of simply relying on a strategy of increasing exports, increasing domestic production by bringing back to the United States the manufacture of products that Americans consume would simultaneously displace imports and increase the range of goods that can be exported. Increasing the amount of manufacturing taking place in the United States would be easier, have a much higher payback and reduce the trade deficit more quickly.

The reason: Exporting is far more easily said than done. Every country competing with the United States protects its home market. All are focusing their resources on producing high-tech products — the same products that are often viewed as the only hope for U.S. exports. As a consequence, it is getting harder by the day for American producers to dominate high-tech markets around the world. For example, American-made products are, on average, 35 percent more expensive in the Chinese market than equivalent products made in that country. But in the U.S. market, the same U.S.-made products have almost a 10 percent average total-cost advantage, a figure based on 2009 data for Chinese wages, which have been rising since.

In fact, although America's exports have grown by 40 percent since President Obama started his "Export Initiative" in 2009, imports have grown even more — by 42 percent, and from a larger base. The best efforts of the administration have failed to lower the trade deficit in goods, which instead skyrocketed by $230 billion on an annual basis to $736 billion in 2012. Clearly, the strategy is not working.

FIGURE 1: *U.S. Imports Substantially Exceed U.S. Exports – Trade Data for 2012*

CATEGORY	GOODS	SERVICES	TOTAL
U.S. Exports	$1,564	$630	$2,194
U.S. Imports	$2,299	$435	$2,734
U.S. Net Exports	-$735	$196	-$539

Figures in billions[1]

For a number of reasons, reducing imports through reshoring[2] — bringing back to the United States production that had been sent abroad — is the best strategy for shrinking and even entirely eliminating America's trade deficit.

Why?

1. Since the United States imports 47 percent more than it exports, the trade deficit responds more to a given percentage reduction in imports than to an increase in exports.

2. U.S. companies are much more competitive in the American market, where imports bear "hidden" logistical and other costs, than they are in offshore markets where U.S. products have to bear those costs.

3. U.S. companies already know the American market. They derive an inherent advantage from understanding the nation's language and its legal, measurement and regulatory-compliance systems.

4. Selling more products overseas requires a company to increase fixed costs throughout an entire enterprise, especially those costs incurred on the ground in foreign countries. By selling more domestically, American companies can take advantage of assets already in place.

5. Reshoring eliminates for companies both the hurdles of foreign non-tariff barriers and cultural bias among foreign consumers, who may favor the products of their nation's domestic firms.

6. Operating in the U.S. market all but eliminates a variety of risks, such as losing sales due to foreign-government policy changes or regulatory and financial favoritism for domestic companies; changes in currency exchange rates; political instability; and lack of legal protection when product designs are stolen, pirated or counterfeited.

These advantages alone make American manufacturers competitive at home in a broad range of product categories, while foreign tariffs and duties, exchange rates, value-added taxes (VAT) on imports and many other restrictions keep U.S. exports from being price-competitive abroad. And U.S. manufacturers have room to grow at home, since the U.S. market in some of these products is now dominated by imports.

Moreover, small and medium-sized enterprises, America's main source of job creation, are more able to compete in the domestic market than in crowded markets overseas. According to the 2008 U.S. Census, 45 percent of the nation's manufacturing jobs are in firms with fewer than 500 employees. Many manufacturers with fewer than 200 employees — a class that accounts for around 25 percent of all U.S. manufacturing jobs — work under contract to make parts and components for other companies. These smaller companies, which are generally not effective at exporting, sell their output to domestic original equipment manufacturers (OEMs). When OEMs bring back work from offshore, contract manufacturers will supply the components and tooling that is purchased by large companies for this increase in domestic production. The jobs created at these smaller contract manufacturers will represent at least as many jobs as those reshored by OEMs; making them just as important if not as visible to the public.

The United States has further reason to favor reshoring versus exporting, even if the same number of jobs could ultimately be achieved by increasing exports alone. By broadening instead of narrowing the country's industrial base, reshoring leads to improved defense readiness and the strengthening of domestic industrial "ecosystems." Reshoring generates more jobs for less sophisticated workers. And it provides for a faster economic impact and reduces the severity of recessions since there is less inventory to slash when the economy begins to soften.

Fortunately, industries that left the United States over the past decade — including those that sought to take advantage of low-cost labor in China and elsewhere offshore — are reconsidering their financial justifications for doing so. Some are already starting to return, prompted by changes in wage rates abroad, the rising value of foreign currencies relative to the dollar, the difference between U.S. and foreign energy prices, increasing preference among U.S. consumers for domestic products and the adoption at home of lean-manufacturing processes, automation and quality standards.

The tide that is just now turning back in favor of the United States may herald a trend that would have great potential to revive the nation's economy. The return of manufacturing to U.S. shores would potentially eliminate the trade deficit, adding up to eight million new jobs commanding high-enough wages to generate significant tax revenue and lower the unemployment rate by four percentage points. What's more, a consequent reduction in the federal budget deficit and alleviation of the societal stress caused by income inequality would go a long way to solving many of America's economic and social problems.

But even if encouraging reshoring is the quickest and most cost-effective way to achieve these goals, reshoring won't happen on its own. A great deal of work will be required to make the United States an attractive place for investment, and every interested party — industry, government, educational institutions and consumers throughout the country — must be engaged. It must become a top national priority. Together, we can create a reshoring torrent that will restore to our children and grand-children confidence in the American dream.

BACKGROUND: TRENDS IN OFFSHORING[3]

Over the past decade, the United States has lost about six million manu-facturing jobs, a significant number of them to offshoring.[4] Globalization is commonly characterized by economists, politicians and the media as a "win-win process" based on David Ricardo's theory of comparative advantage. However, an analysis by David Autor, a professor of economics at the Massachusetts Institute of Technology (MIT), suggests that the United States has not been benefiting, and that costs accruing from job losses — increased unemployment payments among them — are about equal to the benefits of the lower prices for imported goods.[5]

The offshoring trend resulted from a complex set of circumstances that has led to a deterioration of U.S. competitiveness. Some of the factors could not be controlled, such as low wages and a lack of regulation in developing countries that actively recruited foreign investment and provided companies with strategic growth markets. But some factors that encouraged offshoring could have been controlled, and there are a lot of them: America's poor basic education system; its weak skills-training programs; its high corporate-tax rates; its lack of a VAT that can be rebated to exporters and charged to importers; companies' simplistic sourcing decisions; and their underinvestment in automation technology, quality systems and lean-management and -production techniques. Plus, email and teleconferencing have enabled efficient communication between the United States and factory managers abroad. The efficiency of sending product designs and manufacturing-process specifications to foreign factories via the Internet, coupled with the explosion of cheap container shipping, strengthened the case for offshoring.

In some cases, sending production offshore was the result of good business decisions, but in many other cases the business decisions have proved to be wrong.

BUSINESSES' SHORTSIGHTED FOCUS ON LOW WAGES AND PRICES

The chief error that many companies made when they offshored production was focusing exclusively on low labor rates and product prices. They threw themselves at "low-cost opportunities" and engaged in wage arbitrage without considering the total cost. A survey of manufacturers conducted by Archstone Consulting found that the majority of U.S. manufacturers do not accurately compare costs. "Sixty percent of manufacturers, when calculating costs, use rudimentary tools [that] ignore 20 percent or more of the total cost," according to Archstone.[6] Nor did companies consider other factors that could overcome large wage differentials. Peter Nolan of the University of Cambridge commented that there existed "a 'herd' mentality to participate in the 'Chinese miracle.'"[7]

Put another way, production decisions were based more on what the boss wanted to hear and the potential for better stock valuations than on rationality or careful analysis.[8] By not recognizing all of the additional costs associated with shifting production to a foreign location, it was easy to justify an offshoring bonus for the price variance achieved. It was harder to earn a bonus by calculating total costs associated with offshoring and then going throughout an enterprise implementing an effective program that arduously but relentlessly tackled inefficiencies and waste. Offshoring production was easier.

Excessive focus on low offshore wages and prices dovetailed with American manufacturers' insufficient or late adoption of lean, Theory of Constraints, Quick Response Manufacturing, Six Sigma and other process-improvement systems. Investment in automation technologies was insufficient or late as well. Companies chose the simple solution of offshoring, rather than the hard work associated with achieving quality and efficiencies in the Unites States.

A LACK OF MANUFACTURING SKILLS TRAINING

The negative image of manufacturing employment among young workers has not helped the sector either. The United States had been so wealthy for so long that young people and their parents started to make career decisions based more on immediate enjoyment than on probable lifetime income. This led to low levels of enrollment in vocational-training programs. Without much demand, those programs withered. Now there is a nationwide failure to train enough skilled manufacturing professionals to meet the current high level of demand from industry.[9]

The quality of recruiting and training a skilled manufacturing work-force has become the most important controllable factor influencing U.S. offshoring and reshoring trends.

Manufacturing jobs are based upon a foundation of math and physics and require mastery of sophisticated information technologies, software programs and machinery. Today's skilled technical worker is tomorrow's company leader. In many factories, most workers are positioned in front of a computer screen and use high-tech software programs. Manufacturing is no longer primarily a low-skill job.

Almost all the major U.S. manufacturing trade associations have proposed strategies to revive U.S. manufacturing.[10] Often their most important recommendation is to improve skills-training programs aimed at a new generation of manufacturing workers. Companies, especially those making high-value, complex products, are moving production to where a concentration of skilled workers and manufacturing-production engineers can be found.

Meanwhile, federal, state and local governments have funded and promoted university education while consistently neglecting the vocational institutions required to train a competitively skilled industrial workforce. A training system that is focused on manufacturing skills would provide individuals with the foundation they need for further education in engineering. Such a system would complete a virtuous economic cycle: Highly skilled workers earning good wages producing products that are now made offshore would provide the tax base needed to fund an educational system to train new workers for increasingly technical jobs.

CONSUMERS DON'T CARE

American consumers have mimicked companies' behavior, basing their purchasing decisions primarily on price, with no regard to where products were manufactured. Priding themselves on buying the lowest-priced products, they do not sufficiently consider the extent to which low prices reflect low-product quality. Moreover, many Americans still do not associate purchasing products made offshore with weakening the national economy and threatening their own jobs. In most other countries, consumers choose domestically made products over imports. They know how important it is to keep their local industries healthy by consuming local products.

GOVERNMENT PRIORITIES ARE MISALIGNED

On the political front, the federal government has sacrificed America's economic strength for diplomatic objectives by providing unbalanced trade preferences and advantages to other countries. This is the case with Washington's relationship with China and China's leverage in addressing the nuclear threat posed by North Korea. U.S. trade policy toward developing countries is aimed more at helping alleviate poverty and developing democratic institutions than it is at safeguarding American industries and jobs. The United States has long accepted the status of the dollar as the world's reserve currency, which helps keep interest rates low but has raised the value of the dollar by 10 to 15 percent, decreasing U.S.-made products' competitiveness in global markets. The result: Low interest rates enabled the housing bubble, and the high value of the U.S. dollar eliminated millions of middle-class manufacturing jobs that were required for homeowners to pay their mortgages.

High corporate tax rates and burdensome federal regulations in the United States further reduce its attractiveness as a place to manufacture. Meanwhile, other countries continue to offer incentives and subsidies to attract manufacturing. While other countries were repeatedly creating and implementing five- and 10-year strategic plans for their manufacturing industries and backing those plans with resources, the United States was doing nothing, assuming the free market would resolve all of its economic problems. What's more, many foreign nations have created an uneven playing field by manipulating their currencies in such a way as to drive the dollar's value up. Global rules regarding currency manipulation are not being enforced.[11] All these factors contribute to lowering prices for foreign imports and raising prices for U.S. exports.

Finally, the United States is the target market for exports from all foreign countries and companies. The U.S. market is huge, stable and rich. That one language is spoken throughout its large territory makes selling to a sizable population easy. America's high-value currency and minimal or non-existent tariff barriers make it even more attractive to exporters, as does the fact that there is neither a VAT nor a national manufacturing strategy. America's consumers want low prices and don't care where a product is made, while its manufacturers and retailers are obsessed with low prices and short-term profits. What's more, the country has a corporate culture made up of senior managers and MBAs focused on bonuses that are based on the kinds of marginal improvements generated both by laying off workers and by closing plants and shifting them off-shore. Why wouldn't any company located outside the United States focus all its attention on selling into this bonanza of a market? What's not to love?

THE ROLE OF OFFSHORING IN MANUFACTURING'S DECLINE

One-third of U.S. manufacturing jobs have disappeared since 2001, a loss that many observers attribute almost entirely to an increase in manufacturing productivity. But a growing number of economists argue that the effect of productivity gains on job losses has been dramatically overstated. They believe that the decline of U.S. manufacturing can instead be directly linked to offshoring by American companies and a corresponding surge of imports. "Government statistics significantly overstate the [positive] change in U.S. manufacturing output, and most economists and pundits do not extend their analysis beyond one macro-level number (change in real manufacturing value-added relative to GDP)," according to Robert Atkinson, president of the Information Technology and Innovation Foundation. "But the conventional wisdom that U.S. manufacturing job loss is simply a result of productivity-driven restructuring (akin to how U.S. agriculture lost jobs but is still healthy) is wrong, or at least not the whole story. . . . The loss of U.S. manufacturing jobs is a function of slow growth in output (and, in most sectors, actual loss of output) caused by a steep increase in the manufactured goods trade deficit."[12]

WHAT HAS CHANGED TO CAUSE THE RESHORING TREND?

Within the complexity of current global supply chains there are three main drivers for the increasing shift from offshoring to reshoring. First, costs of offshore production and shipping are rising. Second, companies are experiencing supply risks, painfully demonstrated by such events as the earthquake and tsunami that hit Japan and massive floods in Thailand. Third, companies are starting to analyze the total cost of offshore production and are learning that low foreign wages and purchase-price savings are increasingly offset by dozens of hidden costs.[13]

RISING WAGES AND CURRENCIES

Costs for raw materials such as steel, copper, plastics and oil are about the same worldwide. The overwhelming basis for developing national competitive advantage in manufacturing is in wage differentials, adjusted for productivity differences. In the United States, total employee compensation costs (including wages, benefits and social insurance costs at all levels of the supply chain) equal 50 percent or more of total manufacturing cost. But as wages rise in a developing country, the contribution of labor costs to total manufacturing cost approaches the U.S. level. With little to no recent growth in U.S. wages and a lower-valued dollar, the total costs of U.S. and offshore manufacturing are gradually moving toward parity.

For example, Chinese wages have been rising at an average of 15 percent per year, while China's currency, the renminbi, has been rising in value against the dollar by about 4 percent per year (FIGURE 2).[14]

This combination has been increasing China's hourly labor costs by about 18 percent per year in dollars,[16] and implies a doubling of Chinese workers' wages about every four years. In the case that China's economy remains stable and maintains medium to high single-digit growth rates, wages there are predicted to continue rising rapidly. As a result of the one-child policy that went into effect in 1979, China's working-age population today has 120 million people aged 20 to 24, that age group is expected to contract by more than 20 percent in the next decade.[17]

FIGURE 2[15]

MANUFACTURING WAGES: U.S. VS. CHINA
2002-2010 ACTUAL AND 2011-2015 EST.

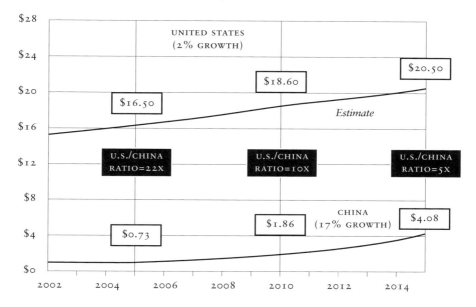

At the same time, the real income of Chinese citizens is rising at about 5 percent per year, causing a steep increase in domestic demand for goods and services. And with many children leaving home to work in factories and live in cities, more services have to be provided for a growing elderly population. This shift in population balance illustrates that demand for labor will continue to rise rapidly as the supply of labor falls, reinforcing the trend of rapid wage growth.

But the financial impact on U.S.-based corporations that shifted production to China extends beyond higher wage rates. Consider the example of Scoville Manufacturing Co., which brought its button production back from China to Georgia because each year 20 to 25 percent of the company's Chinese workforce failed to return from annual holiday. For Scoville, the loss of workforce knowledge and the costs to retrain new employees proved to be huge.

While the efficiency of the Internet in transmitting product and production data led to an acceleration of offshoring, the same technology is also driving offshore wage growth as employees in developing countries are able to compare their living and workplace standards to those doing similar jobs in developed countries. They are also using social networking to exchange plans for organized protests.

China controls the value of its currency to achieve its economic goals, making China's currency a complicated issue. By recycling hundreds of billions of U.S. dollars from its trade surplus through the purchase of U.S. government debt, China continues to drive up the value of the dollar versus the renminbi. China is caught between conflicting forces: It is in China's interest both to let the renminbi's value rise in order to control inflation and to keep it low in order to maintain its competitiveness in world markets. The future of the renminbi is less predictable than that of wage rates, but it seems likely that a failure to allow the renminbi to reach its true market value will result in bitter trade conflicts with the United States and other countries that suffer because of China's artificially low currency. A proper exchange rate for the renminbi would be about ¥3 per dollar versus the spring 2013 level of around ¥6.2.

HIDDEN COSTS REVEALED

As companies realize that total hidden costs are larger than they had previously assumed and that the benefits of labor arbitrage are smaller than they were a few years ago, they are increasingly deciding to bring production and sourcing closer to home. An analysis of 114 companies that reshored production to the United States through September 2012 found 20 reasons for doing so:

FIGURE 3: *Distribution of Reasons for Reshoring*[18]

REASON	NUMBER OF CASES CITED
Higher foreign wages and currency values	54
Low foreign quality leading to high warranty costs and rework	41
Delivery times are too long	38
Freight costs are rising	32
Travel costs and travel time are prohibitive, as is performing onsite audits of foreign factories	27
Inventory costs are too high	25
Total costs are rising	20
Intellectual property is being stolen or is at risk of being lost to foreign competitors	20
Communications are difficult	14
Image and brand are impacted as customers are starting to prefer U.S.-made products	12
Loss of customer responsiveness	9
Growing need for expensive emergency air freight	9
Difficulty of innovation and product differentiation	6
Natural disaster risks are rising	4
Prices are higher	4
Growing interest in sustainable manufacturing processes and supply chains	4
A growing burden on staff	3
Product liability costs are difficult to collect from offshore suppliers	2
Growing security risks to personnel	1
Higher regulatory compliance costs	1

Companies bringing work back to the United States have felt the pain associated with offshoring. As profits suffer, they become less willing to put up with the hassles of frequently calling Asia at three in the morning and dealing with the logistical challenges caused by delays. They are tired of political corruption and the personal risk of violence. As the chart on the previous page shows, a combination of reduced profits and difficult logistics is the reason most companies cite for reshoring their production.

U.S. companies are only beginning to understand the hidden costs associated with offshoring. A new tool called the Total Cost of Ownership (TCO) Estimator, devised by the Reshoring Initiative,[19] is making it possible for firms to calculate all costs associated with sourcing parts, components and finished products from different locations. When comparing costs in developing countries to those in the United States, raw material costs are about equal, but almost all others save for wages are higher in developing countries. Placing a real value on shipping, time to market, travel, risk of the loss of intellectual property, increased inventory and struggles with foreign languages and cultural barriers can tip the scales in favor of producing at home. Total-cost analysis can identify more than two dozen hidden relevant costs, each of which represents up to 2 percent of a product's final total cost. Savings from lowering or eliminating these costs can offset some or even all of a 30 to 50 percent advantage in purchase price enjoyed by products made in China.

When companies understand the true costs of offshoring, they offshore less and reshore more. Data from companies using the Reshoring Initiative's total-cost analysis program suggest that about 25 percent of the production that has gone overseas might come back to the United States if companies considered factors other than purchase price or landed cost in making sourcing decisions. Reshoring this 25 percent would generate at least 500,000 new manufacturing jobs. Reshoring the remaining 75 percent will require a continuation of offshore wage inflation, increased competitiveness by American manufacturers and government action on multiple fronts, as described later in this chapter.

SUGGESTED CORPORATE PRIORITIES FOR OBTAINING THE LARGEST SHORT- AND LONG-TERM PAYBACK ON INVESTMENT ARE:

1. Keep existing domestic manufacturing sources. Think twice before offshoring any more U.S. production.

2. Shift outsourced production back to the United States. Minimal effort — no write-offs.

3. Repurpose an offshore facility to serve the offshore market. Incrementally invest domestically to serve the U.S. market and gradually bring production closer to the customer.

4. Shut down the offshore facility and build a new domestic facility. This is a tough decision for most companies.

NEARSHORING

Bringing work not all the way back to the U.S., but to a country that is close by (most commonly Mexico), is also increasingly popular. Nearshoring to Mexico offers companies labor rates similar to those of China along with lower hidden costs. Some of the nearshore countries have their own problems, including an insufficiently skilled workforce, poor availability of financing for equipment and high rates of crime and corruption. Still, analysis sometimes points to nearshoring as the best option, and it is one that can help revitalize U.S. manufacturing by providing opportunities for nearby American suppliers. Priorities and logic regarding sourcing location decisions are listed in FIGURE 4.

FIGURE 4: *Priorities for Reshoring and Nearshoring Destinations*

PRIORITY	RESHORING DESTINATION	BENEFITS FOR THE UNITED STATES
1ST	United States	More jobs, better sustainability, higher-quality products.
2ND	Partnering with another nearshore country. For example, a company places more labor-intensive work in Mexico and more skill-intensive work in the United States.	Better to be part of the winning team than all of a losing one.
3RD	All in the nearshore country	Components, tools, consulting and materials are more likely to be supplied from the United States than if the work stays in Asia. Having regional production stabilizes the U.S. supply-chain ecosystem, helping to retain related production, assembly and engineering. The enriched nearshore country will become a stronger market for U.S. parts, components and finished products.
4TH	All offshore	Very little U.S. content or incremental exports.

QUANTIFIABLE PROGRESS — RESHORING IS HAPPENING

For the first time, data is becoming available on actual reshoring trends. According to a Reshoring Initiative analysis, about 80,000 manufacturing jobs have been announced due to reshoring since early 2010. Reshoring therefore accounts for as much as 16 percent of the approximately 500,000 manufacturing jobs added in the U.S. economy from the January 2010 low through May 2013.[20] Calculations using a conservative 1.0 multiplier indicate that the trend has generated approximately 160,000 total jobs in the United States.

Reshoring has definitely made a good start, but offshoring is still happening. The two trends are roughly in balance.

Published surveys confirm the reshoring trend. Of large companies surveyed by the MIT Forum for Supply Chain Innovation, 34 percent were "considering bringing manufacturing back to the U.S."[21] In another survey, conducted by the Boston Consulting Group in 2012, nearly half of the respondents from companies with sales greater than $10 billion said they were considering reshoring production.[22] And 40 percent of surveyed contract manufacturers had reshored some work during the first four months of 2012, according to MFG.com.[23] Based on the strength of the trend, the National Institute of Standards and Technology's Manufacturing Extension Partnership program included reshoring as one of the top five manufacturing trends of 2012.[24]

A specific impetus for reshoring — consumer attitudes — is highlighted in a survey conducted by the Alliance for American Manufacturing (AAM). The percentage of U.S. consumers who view products made in America "very favorably" increased from 58 percent in 2010 to 78 percent in 2012.[25] U.S. consumers have become more enthusiastic about the quality of American-made products, most notably automobiles. Repeated recalls of low-quality and dangerous products from China have alerted consumers to the added risks of imports. Overall, two-thirds of product recalls are imports, and Chinese products are recalled twice as often as U.S.-made products.[26] At least three other consumer surveys confirm AAM's findings.

This high level of recalls is due partly to the fact that demand for inexpensive products leads manufacturers to cut corners. In some countries, working conditions in factories are sorely inadequate, with few health or safety regulations and inspectors who can be "persuaded" to produce favorable inspection reports. Poor working conditions result in the production of inferior and potentially harmful products. Factory employees and managers are often not properly trained due to high turnover rates. Lack of regulation is also a problem, frequently leading to severely polluted water and air as well as to the frequent use of banned chemicals.[27]

Production is more likely to take place in a developed country's market if it requires advanced automation technologies, a small but skilled workforce, meeting rigorous regulatory requirements, continuous product innovation for fast-changing markets, high shipping costs and small batch sizes. Naturally, production that was best done locally was the least likely to leave the United States: think products like medical devices, durable goods, special machines and large tooling. Labor-intensive manufacturing will be the last to return.

The bulk of the current reshoring trend is taking place in mechanical and electrical products, and the South and Midwest are benefiting the most. There are not many factories returning to the Northeastern states. Details are in FIGURES 5, 6 AND 7.[28]

FIGURE 5: *Reshored Cases by Industry*[29]

INDUSTRY	NUMBER OF NEWS ARTICLES
Electrical Equipment, Appliances and Components	37
Transportation Equipment	28
Miscellaneous Industries	22
Machinery	19
Fabricated Metal Parts	12
Plastics and Rubber	12
Computers and Electronics	11
Furniture	11
Clothing and Textiles	4
Food and Beverages	3
Primary Metal	2
Chemicals	1
Oil and Gas	1

FIGURE 6: *Countries from Which Production Was Reshored*[30]

COUNTRY	NUMBER OF NEWS ARTICLES
China	79
Mexico	18
Japan	10
India	6
Taiwan	5
Philippines	3
Canada, Germany and Malaysia	2 EACH
Brazil, El Salvador, Indonesia, Singapore and UK	1 EACH

FIGURE 7: *Regions and States That Have Reshored Production*

U.S. REGIONS	STATES MENTIONED	RESHORED COMPANIES	
		NUMBER	PERCENT
South	Florida, North Carolina, Georgia, Kentucky, Tennessee, Virginia, Maryland, South Carolina, Texas, Oklahoma, West Virginia	31	40
Midwest	Indiana, Ohio, Michigan, Illinois, Missouri, Minnesota, Kansas	29	37
West	California, Washington, Idaho, Oregon	14	18
Northeast	New York, Pennsylvania, New Hampshire	6	5

Top States: Calif., 11; Ohio, 8; N.C., 7; Ill., 5; and Texas, Mich., Tenn., Ga. and Ky., 4 each.

GET LEAN

While embracing lean management and production methods to reduce waste, increase value to customers and become more globally competitive, many companies have ignored the advice of W. Edwards Deming, the famed interpreter of lean's precursor, the Toyota Production System. In his seminal book *Out of the Crisis*, Deming enshrined as his "4th Key Principle" — the recommendation that companies "end the practice of awarding business on the basis of a price tag. Instead, minimize total cost." James Womack, founder of the Lean Enterprise Institute, and other leaders of the lean movement have made similar exhortations. Womack encourages companies to use "lean math" to calculate the actual cost of offshoring production and services.

FIGURE 8[31] shows how offshoring increases each of the "Seven Wastes" addressed in Toyota's program.

FIGURE 8: *Offshoring's Impediments to the Lean Journey*

SEVEN TOYOTA "WASTES"	HOW OFFSHORING CONTRIBUTES TO WASTE
Over-Production	Large batches are required to fill shipping containers.
Waiting	Delivery times are uncertain due to delays at ports and customs. Too much "awake time" at odd hours of the night is required for live discussions and troubleshooting between remote locations.
Transport	There are 6,000 miles of transit. Container ships return to Asia either half-full or empty, requiring inbound charges to cover the return trip. The high cost of oil requires ships to travel more slowly. There are additional costs for emergency airfreight if orders are wrong, incomplete or of poor quality.
Over-Processing	Additional time is spent packing and unpacking, as well as dealing with customs paperwork and complying with additional regulations.
Inventory	With inventory in transit, there is less possibility to see and count what is available or required (i.e., no visual controls). More "safety" stock is needed. Delivery times and quality are uncertain.
Motion	Additional labor is needed to deal with inventory that is being moved. Workers loading and unloading are at increased risk of repetitive-motion injuries. There are additional costs, among them injury-compensation insurance or payments.
Defects	The defect rate for imports is much higher than for the same items from local sources whose processes can be easily monitored. With offshore sources, there is a need for extra inspection of materials and tolerances. Poor quality leads to unhappy customers and real potential for permanent loss of business.

EXAMPLES OF RESHORING SUCCESSES

FIGURE 9 shows reshoring cases that demonstrate the breadth of industries and companies that are bringing production back to the United States, along with their reasons for doing so.[32]

FIGURE 9: *Nine Reshoring Cases Demonstrate the Breadth of the Industries Involved*

WRIGHT ENGINEERED PLASTICS

PRODUCT	REASONS PRODUCTION RESHORED	FROM	TO
Plastic injection molding for medical and telecom customers	High transportation costs Rising foreign wages Quality issues	China	Santa Rosa, Calif.

GENERAL ELECTRIC

PRODUCT	REASONS PRODUCTION RESHORED	FROM	TO
Water heaters	State of Kentucky provided tax incentives High-tech appliance models redesigned Lean production processes adopted in the U.S. Ease of design and innovation with manufacturing and engineering working together Collaboration with workers and unions cut U.S. unit cost enough to reduce the retail price by about 20 percent versus the China-sourced product Total cost of ownership: Chinese costs are 30 percent below American costs based on "ex-works" price but are higher than American when considering inventory and delivery issues	China	Louisville, Ky.

FREEMAN SCHWABE MACHINERY

PRODUCT	REASONS PRODUCTION RESHORED	FROM	TO
Hydraulic die-cutting presses	Restoring the company's long-term "Made in USA" heritage Warranty costs reduced by 90 percent Ability for the company to control its own destiny Improved speed to market Rebuild employee skills and morale	Taiwan	Cincinnati, Ohio

FORD MOTOR COMPANY

PRODUCT	REASONS PRODUCTION RESHORED	FROM	TO
Hybrid transmission components, battery packs and steel forgings	Quality issues	India, Mexico, Japan	Ohio, Mich.

BAILEY HYDROPOWER

PRODUCT	REASONS PRODUCTION RESHORED	FROM	TO
Hydraulic cylinders	Slow delivery Quality issues	India	West Knoxville, Tenn.

KAREN KANE

PRODUCT	REASONS PRODUCTION RESHORED	FROM	TO
Women's apparel	Quality issues Rising labor costs Nimble domestic companies are better able to capitalize on fashion trends More sophisticated manufacturing techniques mean U.S. production is no longer prohibitively expensive	China	Los Angeles, Calif.

MOREY CORP.

PRODUCT	REASONS PRODUCTION RESHORED	FROM	TO
Circuit boards	Quality issues Inventory cut by 94 percent	China	Woodbridge, Ill.

ACE CLEARWATER ENTERPRISES

PRODUCT	REASONS PRODUCTION RESHORED	FROM	TO
Welded assemblies for aerospace and energy	Quality issues Customers are willing to pay more for high precision and quality	Hungary	Torrance, Calif.

NCR

PRODUCT	REASONS PRODUCTION RESHORED	FROM	TO
ATMs	Slow response time from foreign contract suppliers, especially from the lower tiers Rising labor costs Innovation: silos eliminated by having manufacturing near engineering and customers	China, India, Brazil	Columbus, Ga.

INCREASED VISIBILITY OF COMPANIES RESHORING PRODUCTION

If reshoring is to grow quickly, visibility of the trend will be critical. Many companies will not reconsider their offshoring practices unless they see that others are reshoring. More important, industrial companies will have difficulty attracting a sufficiently skilled manufacturing workforce unless the wider public believes that the country is truly entering a new economic era in which manufacturing will provide the foundation for economic growth and employment.

TOTAL COST OF OWNERSHIP: UNIVERSAL APPLICABILITY AND IMPACT OF TOTAL-COST ANALYSIS

Although the primary users of the Reshoring Initiative's TCO software are U.S. companies, the economic benefit of producing near the customer and the cost calculation used to assess the benefits of local production can be applied to any country or region.

The impact of using total-cost analysis instead of price for sourcing decisions is demonstrated by a statistical analysis of user calculations. FIGURE 10 aggregates the results for 27 recent cases comparing sourcing in China versus the United States.

FIGURE 10: *Summary of 27 Cases Where Total Cost of Ownership Was Used to Analyze China Versus the United States for Sourcing Location*

COST COMPARISON BASIS	U.S. RELATIVE TO CHINA, AVERAGE	PERCENT OF CASES WHERE U.S. SUPPLIERS HAVE THE ADVANTAGE
Price	U.S. suppliers are 69 percent higher on the basis of price	15 percent
Total Cost of Ownership	U.S. is 4 percent lower on the basis of TCO	56 percent

Using a TCO analysis changes the sourcing decision in 41 percent of the 27 cases studied. Since the database is small, a conservative estimate is that about 25 percent of the work that has already been offshored to China would return to the United States if companies used TCO instead of price to make sourcing decisions. Ongoing research will refine that estimate. Yet, many manufacturing companies still make sourcing decisions based only on price. Others make these decisions based on landed cost, which could also include freight, duty and packaging. Total cost is much more comprehensive. It includes all of these costs as well as the hidden costs that are often overlooked, such as costs affecting cash flow, predictable future costs (such as scrap, emergency air freight and obsolete inventory), opportunity costs (such as lost orders due to long delivery times, low quality and the lack of a "Made in America" label) and the estimated costs of various long-term risks (such as natural disasters and the loss of intellectual property). The list of relevant costs of producing a product offshore is long and changes with specific products and companies. Many of the costs in individual categories are relatively small. Most cannot be found in financial statements or be easily quantified by accountants. As a result, many companies make sourcing decisions based on the most obvious factors, which are easy to measure but do not provide a complete cost picture.

Recent supply-chain shocks due to natural disasters and political instability, along with higher wages and transportation prices, have caused cost savings from offshoring to diminish. Accenture has found that many legitimate cost factors that it believes "should compose any best-practice total-cost model, have traditionally been ignored," such as packaging, customer responsiveness, quality, inventory and broker fees.[33] In a 2011 report on reshoring, Boston Consulting Group (BCG) emphasized that companies "should undertake a rigorous, product-by-product analysis of their global supply networks that fully accounts for total costs, rather than just factory wages."[34] BCG predicts that for products to be sold in the United States, total-cost parity between products sourced in China and those made in the southeast U.S. will occur by 2015 for a broad range of "tipping point" industries: computers and electronics, appliances, electrical equipment, machinery, furniture, plastics and rubber, fabricated metals and transportation goods.

BCG recommends that companies adopt total-cost analysis immediately so as to not fall behind competitors. Preparing for the shift toward reshoring in coming years is one thing, the company argues, but getting a jump on reshoring ahead of the curve is an even better decision.

THE TOTAL COST OF OWNERSHIP ESTIMATOR TOOL

The Reshoring Initiative's TCO Estimator software program guides companies through a comprehensive system for recognizing and adding all costs associated with offshoring and reshoring. The relevant cost factors must be fully captured in order to provide a complete picture of total cost. To determine a single cost value for a part, component or finished product, the user assigns a value — price, delivery time, intellectual property loss, risk or weight — to each factor that is relevant to the specific case. The user then repeats the process, substituting from other vendors. In this way, it is possible to readily and objectively compare the total cost for the same product from multiple suppliers, whether they are based locally or offshore. The following list is a guide to the kinds of costs calculated using TCO, beginning with easily quantified "hard-cash" costs and progressing to more subjective though equally important measures:

1. **Cost of Goods Sold or Landed Cost.** This includes price, packaging, duty and freight.

2. **Other "Hard" Costs.** These are costs that have an immediate effect on cash flow:

    A. Carrying cost for in-transit products. Foreign and local suppliers often are paid on different schedules. For example, Chinese suppliers often require payment prior to shipment and, typically, four to six weeks prior to U.S. receipt of the goods. U.S.-based suppliers typically are paid two to three months after the shipment date, which essentially is the same as the receipt date. For goods purchased from offshore sources, the customer's cash often will be tied up for three to four months longer than with a domestic source.

    B. Carrying cost of inventory on site. The amount of onsite inventory will be dramatically higher for products shipped via ocean freight than for shipments from a local, just-in-time supplier. Total inventory is typically two to six times higher with offshore sourcing.

    C. Prototype cost. Many companies prefer to source prototypes locally so their engineers and marketing organizations can work closely with suppliers and customers during product development. Local suppliers tend to charge less for the prototype if they also receive the production order.

    D. End-of-life or obsolete inventory. When demand dries up or a product is updated or replaced, a company must deal with obsolete inventory. When parts and components or even the finished product come from offshore, the amount of obsolete inventory that is en route or on order is higher than it would be with a local source of production. Companies that source offshore have to carry and dispose of more obsolete inventory.

E.   Travel costs. The costs of ongoing auditing and problem-solving requiring foreign factory visits and oversight are often overlooked, yet they can have a sizeable impact on a product's total cost.

3.   **Potential Risk-Related Costs.** The impact on costs of high-frequency risks such as emergency airfreight, scrap and rework can be calculated based on past experience with an existing supplier. New products or new suppliers will require estimates. Other risks increase from over-seas sourcing, such as a foreign government's shutting down a local factory, labor unrest, environmental compliance issues and bad press generated by illegitimate suppliers or sub-suppliers. These tend to have a low probability but could be devastating and should also be considered.

A.   Rework. Costs that occur when rework is required can be especially high for custom products such as molds and dies. If an American-made mold is defective, the moldmaker does the rework. But for an Asian mold that is defective, the cost and time involved in shipping the mold back to Asia for rework makes doing so prohibitive, meaning that a domestic moldmaker will have to be hired and paid to fix the Asian mold or make a new one.

B.   Quality. Companies say it is hard to get a supplier in a develop-ing country to replace defective parts or pay for replacements. In addition to the cost of lost production and warranty-related payouts when a product fails, quality problems are costly in other, less tangible ways, such as lost profits due to declining market share, permanent loss of customers or negative impact on brand image.

C.   Product liability. How do suppliers compare in their ability and willingness to pay product-liability claims? It can be difficult to sue a foreign company for damages, and even harder to collect.

D.   Intellectual-property risk. Approximately 5 to 7 percent of world trade consists of counterfeit goods, according to the International Anti-Counterfeiting Coalition.[35] By providing a foreign contract manufacturer with a computer-aided product design, companies are, in many cases, giving away their most important asset and sowing the seeds of their own destruction.

E.   Opportunity cost. What is the cost of lost orders and lost customers when an offshore supplier can't respond quickly enough to changes in quantity or product specifications demanded by the market? Causes for extended offshore response times include shipping times of four to six weeks versus a few hours or days, a strong supplier preference for container-sized shipments, and difficulties involved in agreeing to new product specifications.

F.   Brand image. At a time when developed nations continue to experience economic instability and millions of people are concerned about their jobs, consumers increasingly are buying locally made goods as a way to improve the economic and job prospects in their communities. A foreign country-of-origin label can negatively impact sales and brand image.

G.   Economic stability of the supplier. It is much easier to find accurate information about the stability of a supplier located in the home market than it is for a supplier located in a developing country.

H.   Political stability of the source country. It is not difficult to rate the stability of countries that are already in chaos. But it is much harder to correctly assess countries that are making good economic progress but whose populations are destabilized because of either changing consumer expectations or issues related to government corruption, pollution and workforce abuse.

4.   Strategic Cost Considerations. The following are just two examples of how sourcing decisions can affect product strategy and value:

    A.   Impact on innovation. Separating manufacturing from engineering degrades the innovative effectiveness of both a company and its home country, according to Harvard Business School professors Gary Pisano and Willy Shih.[36] Similarly, Harvard professor Michael Porter has long promoted the economic advantages associated with innovation that results from industry "clusters" — having suppliers, research universities, manufacturers and others involved in product development and production located in close geographic proximity.

    B.   Product differentiation and mass customization. Many companies in developed economies are shifting their focus from commodities to differentiated products through "mass customization," the production of distinctly different products that conform to the specific desires of individuals in a large market but at costs approaching those of mass production. It is easier and less costly to make the move to mass customization with tightly clustered supply chains. But these supply chains need to be close to the individual customers buying custom products.

5.   Environmental costs. Finally, for each product sourced, a company should measure: the "cleanliness" of the electricity generation at each production location; pollution from its manufacturing process; the carbon footprint of its shipping operations; the amount of obsolete inventory that has to be disposed of; and other factors that affect the environmental impact of an extended global supply chain. Once the "green" impact has been quantified for each production source, the next step is to apply a dollar value to that impact.

With its ability to calculate and compare all of the costs listed above, the TCO Estimator is a unique analytical tool for the up-to-$1 million "buy" decisions. It produces an ideal list of costs to consider for the $10 million "buy" decision or the $25 million to $100 million "make" decision that includes the construction of a new in-house production facility.

In addition to calculating the total cost for each source, the TCO Estimator provides visual graphics of the data. In a typical example, shown in FIGURE 11, total costs are graphed for a part sourced from a U.S. company versus from a China-based manufacturer. The current total cost for each part is shown in "Year Zero." The future total cost is then forecast based on the user's expectations for wage inflation in each country and for the changing value of the offshore country's currency. In this example, the assumptions are that wages in China are increasing at 10 percent per year versus 2 percent per year in the United States, and that China's currency is appreciating at 5 percent per year against the dollar. The Chinese total wage cost, expressed in dollars, is thus about 15 percent higher in each subsequent year. An increase in the dollar-wage cost of 1.0 percent in either country produces a 0.3 percent increase in the product's total cost.

FIGURE 11: *A Typical Total Cost Output Example*

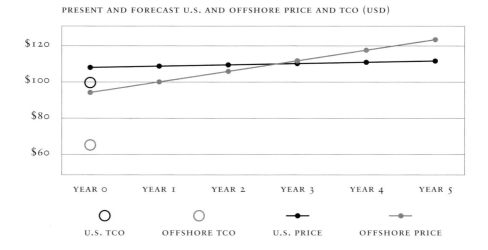

PRESENT AND FORECAST U.S. AND OFFSHORE PRICE AND TCO (USD)

Another chart shows users how total costs accumulate for each source, starting with firm numbers such as price, duty, freight and packaging and then adding increasingly subjective costs. The intent is to make sure that company accountants accept at least the firm cost numbers.

USER EXPERIENCE WITH TOTAL COST OF OWNERSHIP

Companies using the TCO software are changing their sourcing plans. "We are actively using the TCO tool for our new-product sourcing, and we have made multiple decisions not to send some parts offshore," said Steven Wiegers, supply chain manager at Hubbardton Forge, a high-end lighting fixture manufacturer in Castleton, Vt. "We are also in the process of educating the organization about total cost. Our supply-chain team is starting to understand it, but we also need our plant-control and engineering teams to feel comfortable with it. And we have discovered it will force us to review our process for how we cost our product."

In Northern California, the local Manufacturing Extension Partnership center, Manex, worked with a $50 million glass company that was planning to move its production from the San Francisco Bay Area to Mexico. Manex used TCO software and found that while direct-labor differences between the locations were significant, indirect and secondary costs — warranty, travel, logistics, transportation, third-party subcontracting fees, worker safety and other factors — were substantially higher in Mexico than the firm had estimated. As a result, the company decided to build a newer and larger facility in the East Bay and to adopt lean-manufacturing techniques to reduce costs. It also achieved cost savings because of lower real-estate prices for industrial space. It was even able to add a second shift and improve employee morale.

DETAILED COST COMPARISON FOR CHINESE PRODUCTION

The statistical distribution of costs among the 27 TCO cost elements changes by country and industry. The distribution for Chinese-sourced products is shown at the cost element level in FIGURE 12 and at the cost category level in FIGURE 13.

FIGURE 12: *Item Level Cost Distribution for 27 Chinese TCO Case Studies*[37]

COST ITEM	PERCENTAGE OF TCO
Price of product from the source	54.5
Routine air freight, excluding local transportation costs	8.1
Routine surface freight, excluding local transportation costs	5.7
Freight fees that are fixed — not based on a product's price	4.5
End-of-life/obsolete inventory costs	3.8
Emergency air-freight costs	3.6
Travel and audit fees	3.2
Purchasing department cost, excluding travel	2.4
Carrying cost for inventory	1.8
Import duties	1.8
Rework and costs due to poor quality	1.4
Travel and start-up expenses	1.3
Packaging for shipping	1.3
Intellectual-property-loss risk	1
Picking and placing into local inventory	0.8
Economic stability of foreign suppliers	0.8
Carrying cost for in-transit offshored product if paid before shipment	0.7
Political stability of supplier country	0.7
Opportunity costs (lost orders and customers due to long delivery times, poor quality, etc.)	0.7
Product liability non-recovery risks due to difficulty of getting Chinese supplier to accept tort responsibility	0.5

COST ITEM	PERCENTAGE OF TCO
Negative impact on innovation	0.4
Shipping fees that are based on a product's price	0.4
Freight insurance	0.3
Negative impact on product differentiation	0.2
Prototyping costs	0.1

FIGURE 13: *Category Level Cost Distribution for 27 Chinese TCO Case Studies*[38]

COST CATEGORY	PERCENTAGE OF TOTAL COST
Cost of Goods Sold or Landed Cost	74.0
Other "Hard" Costs	16.7
Potential Risk-Related Costs	8.7
Strategic Costs	0.6

TOTAL-COST ANALYSIS HELPS JUSTIFY INVESTMENTS INTENDED TO IMPROVE CORPORATE COMPETITIVENESS

When companies complete a total-cost analysis and make decisions based on a small TCO gap instead of a large price gap, they can then often justify making investments in their domestic facilities around lean process improvements, automation and training. These investments further reduce or eliminate the total-cost gap with foreign production while improving product quality, delivery schedules and time to market.

PLANS FOR ESTIMATING "EXTERNAL" COSTS

Estimating total cost is currently focused only at the company level, with measures of current and future profits and losses. But reshoring has much wider domestic economic impacts that are not estimated. The next version of TCO software will include a tool that will allow companies to estimate the macroeconomic impacts of reshoring or offshoring on U.S. employment, safety-net expenses and taxes paid to governments.

Government procurement and contracting offices should be required to use a total-cost estimating tool for the products they are purchasing. Had they done so in the case of the San Francisco-Oakland Bay Bridge project, they would have determined that outsourcing steel production and fabrication to China cost the United States an estimated 3,000 jobs, the tax revenues that went with them and the resulting increase in government expenditures for unemployment benefits. The Reshoring Initiative will encourage companies to measure and promote to the public and to their customers the benefits their reshoring decisions bring to the U.S. economy, the environment and the workforce.

RESHORING VERSUS OTHER MEANS OF STIMULATING THE U.S. ECONOMY

Reshoring offers a way to stimulate economic growth and increase tax revenues without new government expenditures. Past measures for boosting demand — lowering taxes under the Republicans, increasing federal spending under the Democrats — have not been without success but have proven insufficient to counteract the impact of the country's huge trade deficit. The result has been massive budget deficits and reduced economic growth. In contrast, reshoring expands the economy, requires no increases in government expenditures and thereby reduces the federal budget deficit.

Many politicians and economists claim that the United States can generate wealth by shifting to a post-industrial economy based on research and services. But they have failed to recognize not only that every country in the world is maximizing investment in innovation in order to compete economically, but also that innovation is dependent on a tight coupling of manufacturing with product design, engineering and marketing. The United States has never had a monopoly on good ideas or technology, especially production technology — but now, as manufacturing has been allowed to leave the country, much of the engineering know-how upon which innovation is based has left with it. Reshoring, then, can play an important role not only in speeding up the current recovery, but also in providing the nation with long-term economic strength built on new technological capabilities.

TURNING A TREND INTO A TORRENT

The Reshoring Initiative's forecast of reshoring combines some concepts from others with its own analysis to create four cumulative reshoring scenarios, summarized in FIGURE 14. The full impact of each scenario would be achieved within a few years of the scenario's occurring.

FIGURE 14: *Potential Impact of Reshoring: Four Cumulative Job Scenarios*

SCENARIO DESCRIPTION	SOURCE OF THE SCENARIO	CUMULATIVE NUMBER OF MANUFACTURING JOBS RESHORED	TOTAL CUMULATIVE NUMBER OF U.S. JOBS CREATED ASSUMING A 1.0 MULTIPLIER
Companies use total-cost analysis tools in sourcing decisions	Reshoring Initiative	500,000	1,000,000
By 2015, if Chinese wage trends continue	BCG	1,000,000	2,000,000
Adoption of better U.S. training; increased process improvements and automation; competitive corporate-tax rates	Federal government's Advanced Manufacturing Partnership	2,000,000	4,000,000
End of foreign currency manipulation	Almost all manufacturing groups	3,000,000	6,000,000

CALL TO ACTION

FIGURE 15 identifies actions that many segments of society can take to strengthen U.S. manufacturing and drive the reshoring trend. Some of the changes have a high impact but are difficult to achieve. Others are more realistically attainable. We have indicated the feasibility and the impact/cost ratio from a national viewpoint, then devised a priority ranking based on the first two factors. The highest priority goes to actions that have the best combination of feasibility, cost and impact. The highest-priority items are listed first. Ratings are High, Medium and Low.

FIGURE 15: *Behavioral Change*

CONSUMERS

PRESENT BEHAVIOR	DESIRED BEHAVIOR
Driven by lowest prices	Seek products that are made in America
Not discriminating about where products are made and show little concern about product durability	Be willing to pay slightly more for better quality and durability

Feasibility: Low   *Impact/Cost Ratio:* High   *Priority:* High

ORIGINAL EQUIPMENT MANUFACTURERS

PRESENT BEHAVIOR	DESIRED BEHAVIOR
Sixty percent have decided to offshore based on price or other simple measures	Consistently use total-cost analysis tools
	Base the bonuses of supply-chain managers and others on total-cost savings, not on price
	Calculate and report societal impacts of sourcing decisions

Feasibility: Medium   *Impact/Cost Ratio:* High   *Priority:* High

ALL MANUFACTURERS

PRESENT BEHAVIOR	DESIRED BEHAVIOR
Improving quality and cost Underinvesting domestically vs. in China and much of Europe Training programs are generally poor	Apply lean techniques, automation, Theory of Constraints, Quick Response Manufacturing and other techniques to close the cost gap between U.S. and offshore production Start apprentice training programs Report cases of reshoring to the media and the public in order to build momentum, to both promote own firm's competitiveness and product attributes and to demonstrate to the public that manufacturing is coming back and is thus a good career choice

Feasibility: Medium   *Impact/Cost Ratio:* High   *Priority:* High

COMMUNITY COLLEGES

PRESENT BEHAVIOR	DESIRED BEHAVIOR
Have dropped manufacturing training programs	Emphasize the importance of manufacturing careers Offer a variety of manufacturing-career preparation courses Offer credentials such as those provided by the National Institute for Metalworking Skills Provide tools for comparing the return on investment of obtaining a associate's degree in a technical field vs. a liberal-arts bachelor's degree, adjusted for the student's academic preparation and socio-economic background

Feasibility: High   *Impact/Cost Ratio:* Medium   *Priority:* High

U.S. GOVERNMENT

PRESENT BEHAVIOR	DESIRED BEHAVIOR
Overly focused on exporting, but starting to appreciate reshoring	Fight currency manipulation
	Make highest priority providing the workforce needed for the nation to be globally competitive
Too focused on four-year university education, but starting to understand the importance of vocational training	Show the benefits of training as well as of education
Not focused enough on training to fill the jobs that compete with imports	Exert leadership in motivating companies to use total-cost analysis tools
	Identify important industries and product segments necessary for a strong industrial ecosystem that the U.S. lacks, and put in place policies to attract those industries to the United States

Feasibility: Medium   *Impact/Cost Ratio:* High   *Priority:* High

RESHORING INITIATIVE

PRESENT BEHAVIOR	DESIRED BEHAVIOR
Very visible in the factory-level manufacturing community and among contract manufacturers, economic developers and government	Convince and assist all players to adopt TCO
	Identify and pursue industries/product categories that are:
	1) large (with respect to $/year)
Not effective enough with OEMs	2) at the "tipping point"
Largely focused on mechanical industry	Obtain a "poster-child" large OEM that reshores and serves as a model for others
	Broaden base to be more involved in electrical and electronics, furniture, appliances, apparel and other industries.
	Expand total-cost analysis to cover IT, call centers and other services

Feasibility: Low   *Impact/Cost Ratio:* High   *Priority:* High

BRICK-AND-MORTAR RETAILERS

PRESENT BEHAVIOR	DESIRED BEHAVIOR
Too high a priority on lowest-cost products	Source based on total costs Make it easier for consumers to find American-made products and understand the quality differential

Feasibility: Low   *Impact/Cost Ratio:* High   *Priority:* Medium

ONLINE RETAILERS

PRESENT BEHAVIOR	DESIRED BEHAVIOR
A number of small retailers promoting American-made products Too high a priority on lowest-cost products	Take advantage of dramatically lower overhead to offer better quality, American-made products at the price of offshore-made products that are stocked by brick-and-mortar retailers Use total cost analysis as a sales tool to convince customers of the benefits of buying domestically from them

Feasibility: Low   *Impact/Cost Ratio:* High   *Priority:* Medium

CONTRACT MANUFACTURERS

PRESENT BEHAVIOR	DESIRED BEHAVIOR
Generally provide good quality but have a slower response, higher prices and poor training	Respond fast enough to preserve the natural advantage that flows from proximity to the OEM customer Use the Manufacturing Extension Partnership program and other resources to improve operations

Feasibility: Medium   *Impact/Cost Ratio:* Medium   *Priority:* Medium

K-12 EDUCATION SYSTEMS

PRESENT BEHAVIOR	DESIRED BEHAVIOR
Overall a poor system, especially for the lower socio-economic groups, for whom manufacturing was the best route to the middle class Guidance counselors primarily guide students to college rather than to vocations that would provide them with a career appropriate to their aptitudes and abilities	Dramatically improve student performance in technical fields and in preparation for careers in manufacturing Make clear to students the importance of manufacturing and the desirability of manufacturing careers Provide the tools for students to compare the career and pay benefits provided by a career as a skilled manufacturing professional compared to the probable outcome of attending a four-year college

Feasibility: Low   *Impact/Cost Ratio:* High   *Priority:* Medium

POLITICAL LEADERS

PRESENT BEHAVIOR	DESIRED BEHAVIOR
Talking about manufacturing much more than in the past	Promote manufacturing as good for the country and the source of a better career for many citizens Propose legislation to strengthen American manufacturing Promote total-cost analysis and actively encourage companies to use it Insist that government agencies use total-cost analysis for sourcing decisions Insist that government contractors use total-cost analysis for purchasing decisions

Feasibility: Low   *Impact/Cost Ratio:* High   *Priority:* Medium

HIGHER EDUCATION

PRESENT BEHAVIOR	DESIRED BEHAVIOR
Just get the desired number of students enrolled Majors selected by students are not important	More focus on engineering, especially manufacturing and industrial engineering

Feasibility: Low   *Impact/Cost Ratio:* Medium   *Priority:* Medium

EMPLOYEES OF MANUFACTURING COMPANIES

PRESENT BEHAVIOR	DESIRED BEHAVIOR
Too accepting of sourcing decisions made by "MBAs" who don't understand total cost Too often not sufficiently motivated	Urge company to source based on total cost instead of price Help company become more competitive Promote the joys of a manufacturing career

Feasibility: Low   *Impact/Cost Ratio:* Medium   *Priority:* Low

WALL STREET

PRESENT BEHAVIOR	DESIRED BEHAVIOR
Rewards companies for offshoring and job cuts	Ask companies about their use of total-cost analysis instead of price variance for sourcing decisions and bonuses Invest in companies that will benefit from reshoring

Feasibility: Low   *Impact/Cost Ratio:* Medium   *Priority:* Medium

VENTURE CAPITAL

PRESENT BEHAVIOR	DESIRED BEHAVIOR
Routinely insists that start-ups get prototypes made in the United States and produce products in Asia	Help start-ups use total-cost analysis to make better sourcing decisions

Feasibility: Low   *Impact/Cost Ratio:* Low   *Priority:* Low

STATE ECONOMIC DEVELOPMENT ORGANIZATIONS

PRESENT BEHAVIOR	DESIRED BEHAVIOR
Tend to focus on competing with each other for factories that will be sited or are already located somewhere in the U.S.	Focus on helping companies decide not to offshore Focus on persuading companies that have shifted offshore to sourcing parts and components from local companies

Feasibility: Medium   *Impact/Cost Ratio:* Low   *Priority:* Low

UNIONS

PRESENT BEHAVIOR	DESIRED BEHAVIOR
Some unions are providing lean consulting to help their employers succeed Some training workers and their leaders in the use of total-cost analysis	Provide total-cost analysis training and promotion to union leadership Create conditions (cooperation, training, use of lean, acceptance of automation, support of competitive tax structures) so that unionized industrial companies become the most profitable ways to supply the North American market Recognize that the union is stronger and its members' jobs are more secure if the company sources its components from domestic producers, even if they are non-union suppliers, than if the components are supplied from overseas producers Encourage union members to promote the consumption of U.S.-made products and not just union-made products

Feasibility: Medium   *Impact/Cost Ratio:* Low   *Priority:* Low

RECOMMENDATION

To attract more smart young people into industry, leaders of the Reshoring Initiative have met with officials from the Department of Labor and recommended that they start collecting and distributing data on the incomes of skilled workers who do not hold college degrees. The Bureau of Labor Statistics currently publishes data on average incomes of workers sorted by degree level: no high school; high school; Associate's; Bachelor's; Graduate; and Ph.D. The Department of Labor should include income for workers who have completed an apprenticeship, hold three or more skilled-training certificates such as those from the National Institute for Metalworking Skills or have achieved equivalent forms of advanced manufacturing training. The goal is to show that upward income mobility correlates not only to formal education, but also to skills training as measured by apprenticeships and certificates, which the government already enables through numerous training and vocational grant programs. The Department of Labor has responded positively to this suggestion.

CONCLUSION

Reshoring is becoming a significant trend. The economic basis for the trend will grow as wages increase in developing nations and if energy prices remain low in the United States. Reshoring is superior both to federal programs aimed at encouraging more exports and to the adoption of classic supply-or-demand economic-policy strategies. It is the most cost- and time-efficient way to strengthen U.S. manufacturing while growing GDP, employment and government revenue. It is the single most important trend that can be promoted to improve income equality and rebuild the U.S. defense-industrial base. But the United States must create the conditions to generate a wave of reshoring, and it must do so while it remains the world's largest market for most products — and thus the most desired manufacturing site for either U.S.- or foreign-owned firms wishing to sell into it.

We have outlined and prioritized a broad range of actions for 17 national economic segments that we believe would accelerate reshoring. The lowest-cost, highest-payback, fastest-action item is increasing corporations' use of total-cost analysis to find the production that it is in their interest to reshore now. Government, state and local leaders and corporate employees can help by encouraging companies to reevaluate their offshoring decisions and find opportunities for increased profitability and economic and job stability by reshoring. In addition, widespread promotion of reshoring successes can raise consumer, retail and corporate recognition of improved U.S. competitiveness. Placing additional value on buying U.S.-made goods can help accelerate the trend. All Americans in their roles as consumers, manufacturers, retailers, educators and government leaders can contribute to the revitalization of U.S. manufacturing. The reshoring trend now under way can be turned into a torrent that will restore three million American manufacturing jobs.

ACKNOWLEDGEMENTS

The Reshoring Initiative has 47 sponsors made up of manufacturing-technology providers, trade associations, economic development organizations, Manufacturing Extension Partnership centers and others. Doug Woods, President of The Association for Manufacturing Technology, was the first to provide active support. The National Tooling and Machining Association, the Precision Metalforming Association and the Association for Manufacturing Excellence, quickly followed as did 43 other companies and groups. The manufacturing-industry media have widely reported the work being done by the Reshoring Initiative. The Obama administration increased the Initiative's credibility by including the Initiative in the 2012 Insourcing Forum, held January 11, 2012, at the White House. Rep. Frank Wolf (R-Va.), chairman of the House Appropriations subcommittee on Commerce, Justice, Science and Related Agencies, included a requirement[39] in the fiscal year 2012 budget for the Commerce Department to promote total cost of ownership. All of these organizations and people — and many more — continue to provide the support and encouragement necessary to sustain and grow the Reshoring Initiative and reshoring.

1.   U.S. Census Bureau, Foreign Trade Division. http: www.census.gov/foreign-trade/statistics/historical/gands.pdf.

2.   Reshoring is also referred to as "backshoring," "onshoring" and "insourcing."

3.   The term "offshoring" refers to the practice of transferring production out of a company's home market, either to a facility under its ownership or to those of a contracted firm. "Outsourcing" refers to the practice of contracting an outside company for work, no matter where the contractor is located. "Offshore outsourcing" means contracting work with an outside company located abroad. "Sourcing" means procuring materials, components or equipment from a source that is most often an outside company, but the term can also be used to refer to company-owned sources.

4.   The U.S. government measures imports, exports and domestic production. But, historically, offshoring has not been extensively measured. Offshoring reduces domestic production and replaces it with imports. When production has gone down, there has been no way to determine which jobs are lost due to offshoring and which to reduced domestic or export demand. When imports have gone up, there has been no way to determine whether that growth was caused by offshoring or increased domestic consumption. Solid numbers on the growing U.S. trade deficit are available and are generally used as a proxy for the jobs lost to offshoring. The trade deficit in both goods and services at this writing is about $600 billion per year. To balance that deficit by reducing imports would create about three million manufacturing jobs, each generating an average of around $170,000 in annual sales. This number is generally consistent with estimates of Boston Consulting Group (BCG), Information Technology & Innovation Foundation (ITIF) and others.

5.   David Autor, *The China Syndrome: Local Labor Market Effects of Import Competition in the United States,* May 2012, http://economics.mit.edu/files/6613.

6.   James Benes, "Made in the USA: Returning Home," *American Machinist,* July 16, 2009, http://americanmachinist.com/shop-opeations/made-usa-returning-home.

7.   Peter Nolan. "System Fragility, Industrial Policy and China's International Relations, with Special Reference to Strategic Industries," prepared for the U.S.-China Economic and Security Review Commission, September 2003.

8.   Stone and Associates, *Competing Against Manufacturing in Low-Cost Regions: Focus on China,* March 2004, page 12, http://www.stone-assoc.com/uploads/CompetingAgainstChina-LowCostRgns-FinalReportMEP3-30-04.pdf.

9.   Countries like Germany, Switzerland and Austria never lost sight of the fact that vocational training for their workforces needed to be well-funded in order to keep industry from moving jobs offshore. Highly evolved and well-supported apprenticeship programs remain the most important factor in these countries' continued technical, industrial and commercial success.

10. Trade groups that have recently produced manufacturing strategy documents include the Association for Manufacturing Excellence, the National Association of Manufacturers, the Association for Manufacturing Technology, the Society of Manufacturing Engineers and the Information Technology Innovation Foundation.

11. Ro Khanna. *Entrepreneurial Nation: Why Manufacturing is Still Key to America's Future,* McGrawHill, 2012.

12. Robert Atkinson, Luke Stewart, Scott Andes and Stephen Ezell, *Worse Than the Great Depression: What Experts Are Missing About American Manufacturing Decline,* ITIF, March 2012.

13. Costs can include increased instability during recessions. At the macro level, long supply chains can exacerbate recessions. A company sourcing from offshore typically has two to six times more inventory in house, en route or on order than if it were sourcing domestically. When demand falls, there is a surge of inventory, which simply sits rather than generating revenue. Without a just-in-time production system, it takes much longer for this inventory to be cleared, further slowing economic recovery. Companies with high levels of inventory are the first to cut production, an action that then cascades through the supply chain and aggravates a slowdown.

14. Russell Flannery, "China Faces Years Of Double-Digit Wage Increases, Currency Appreciation," *Forbes,* March 18, 2011, http://www.forbes.com/sites/russellflannery/2011/03/18/china-faces-years-of-double-digit-wage-increases-currency-appreciation/.

15.   Mark Perry, "Wage Gap With China Continues to Shrink, Which Will Mean More Manufacturing Production in U.S.," *AEI Ideas,* November 12, 2011, http://www.aei-ideas.org/2011/11/wage-gap-with-china-continues-to-shrink-which-will-mean-more-manufacturing-production-in-u-s/.

16.   Harold Sirkin, Michael Zinser, Douglas Hohner and Justin Rose, *U.S. Manufacturing Nears the Tipping Point,* The Boston Consulting Group, March 22, 2012, http://www.bcg.com/expertise_impact/Capabilities/Operations/Manufacturing/PublicationDetails.aspx?id=tcm:12-100662&mid=tcm:12-100616.

17.   Dexter Roberts, "The End of China's One-Child Policy?" *Bloomberg Businessweek,* April 19, 2012, http://www.businessweek.com/articles/2012-04-19/the-end-of-chinas-one-child-policy.

18.   Reshoring Initiative Library, September 16, 2012, http://www.reshorenow.org/resources/library.cfm.

19.   The Reshoring Initiative (www.reshorenow.org) is a nonprofit organization created to help companies bring manufacturing back to the United States. The organization provides its TCO software free online to assist companies in accurately comparing the costs of offshoring and reshoring. The tool is also being used by suppliers, unions and economic development agencies to demonstrate the benefits of reshoring production. The Initiative also hosts an online Reshoring Library for research and a Case Studies feature that documents additional cases of reshoring. The reshoring trend data in this chapter is derived from TCO user calculations and from the cases in the Library. The Initiative presents on how and why to reshore at over 100 manufacturing or public policy events per year. The author of this chapter is the founder of the Reshoring Initiative.

20.   Reshoring Initiative from a tabulation of jobs listed in 430 Reshoring Library articles, 90 percent published since January 2010.

21.   "MIT Supply Chain Forum and Supply Chain Digest 2012 U.S. Reshoring Survey," May 2012 to September 2012. 156 U.S. companies with sales over $1 billion responded; http://dev22.geckodesigns.com/system/files/mit_forum_2012_annual_u_s__reshoring_report_final1.pdf.

22.   BCG Press Release, "More Than One-Third of Large Manufacturers Are Considering Reshoring from China to the U.S.," April 20, 2012, http://www.bcg.com/media/PressReleaseDetails.aspx?id=tcm:12-104216.

23.   "Job Shop Health and Capacity Report," *MFG.com,* April 2012, http://www.mfg.com/sites/default/files/files/American%20Job%20Shop%20Survey%20April%202012.pdf.

24.   Roger Kilmer, "The Top Five Manufacturing Trends of 2012," NIST MEP Manufacturing Innovation Blog, December 28, 2012, http://nistmep.blogs.govdelivery.com/2012/12/28/the-top-five-manufacturing-trends-of-2012/.

25.   The Mellman Group, "Findings From A National Survey, Focus Groups, And Dial Tests of Likely 2012 Voters," for the Alliance for American Manufacturing, http://americanmanufacturing.org/files/Slide%20Deck.ppsx.

26.   Joseph Farah, "Chinese Products Choke, Burn, Drown, Drop, Trap Americans," *WorldNetDaily,* June 6, 2007, http://www.wnd.com/2007/06/41966/.

27.   U.S. Consumer Product Safety Commission, quoted in "Defective Products Galore…What's Up With China?" *Total Injury,* http://www.totalinjury.com/news/articles/consumer-awareness/china-product-recalls.aspx.

28.   Totals for the three charts differ because some articles provide only partial information and because some counts are based on the number of articles and others on the number of companies.

29.   As measured by the number of news articles in the national media. Reshoring Initiative Library sample of 114 articles on real cases, September 12, 2012.

30.   Reshoring Initiative Library sample of 114 articles on real cases, September 12, 2012.

31.   Taiichi Ohno, *Toyota Production System: Beyond Large-Scale Production,* Productivity Press, 1988.

32.   Links to articles on each of these cases can be found at www.reshorenow.org/book/table.

33. Mike Heilala and John Ferreira, *Manufacturing's Secret Shift — Gaining Competitive Advantage by Getting Closer to the Customer,* Accenture, March 23, 2011, http://www.accenture.com/ SiteCollectionDocuments/PDF/Accenture_Manufacturings_Secret_Shift.pdf.

34. The Boston Consulting Group, *Made in America Again: Manufacturing Is Expected to Return to America as China's Rising Labor Costs Erase Most Savings from Offshoring,* May 5, 2011, http://www.bcg.com/media/PressReleaseDetails.aspx?id=tcm:12-75973.

35. International AntiCounterfeiting Coalition, "About Counterfeiting" fact sheet, http://www.iacc.org/ about-counterfeiting/.

36. Roger Thompson, "Why Manufacturing Matters," *Working Knowledge* newsletter, Harvard Business School, March 28, 2011.

37. From analysis of TCO Estimator data for 27 most recent cases of China versus U.S. sourcing as of September 15, 2012.

38. From analysis of TCO Estimator data for 27 most recent cases of China versus U.S. sourcing as of September 15, 2012.

39. An online calculator that firms may use to determine "hidden costs" of offshore manufacturing was included in the Commerce Department's 2012 budget by the House Appropriations subcommittee on Commerce, Justice and Science, chaired by Congressman Frank Wolf (R-Va.). It is in the Commerce, Justice, Science and Related Agencies Appropriations Bill for FY 2012, on page 42, "Repatriation initiative," http://thomas.loc.gov/cgi-bin/cpquery/R?cp112:FLD010:@1%28hr169%29. The Commerce Department has responded with a range of actions, including promoting reshoring, and the Reshoring Initiative's Total Cost of Ownership analysis tool has been placed on three federal government websites:
1) http://nist.gov/mep/reshoring.cfm
2) http://business.usa.gov/program/reshoring-initiative
3) http://www.manufacturing.gov/other_orgs.html
The Commerce Department has launched a major website called Access Costs Everywhere (ACE) with extensive data helpful for calculating the cost of offshore production. http://acetool.commerce.gov/.

CHAPTER 4

The Role
Of Innovation

Challenges and Opportunities

Sridhar Kota
Innovation

The term "innovation" denotes a process whereby a promising idea or an emerging technology is transformed into a practical solution — a marketable product, process or business model — at a scale sufficient to meet some societal need. Technological innovation is distinctly different from both scientific discovery and engineering invention. A critical step that follows a discovery or an invention, the translational step, is the key that enables product realization and wealth creation. A successful innovation process reduces technical and market risks and enables scale-up to manufacturing.

Teasing out the components of this process, the U.S. National Academies provided a much broader definition in a recent report: "Innovation commonly consists of being first to acquire new knowledge through leading-edge research; being first to apply that knowledge to create sought-after products and services, often through world-class engineering; and being first to introduce those products and services into the marketplace through extraordinary entrepreneurship."[1]

The United States still leads the world in two of these three stages of innovation, often being "first to acquire" and "first to introduce," but it has been steadily lagging in applying the knowledge that its creative minds generate. Being "best in the world" in scientific discoveries is important, but it is not sufficient in itself to keep any nation viable in today's global economy. Investments in science produce indispensable knowledge, but it is by applying that knowledge through rigorous engineering and development that people and nations produce wealth, thereby achieving economic strength and national security.

Consider who ultimately capitalized on the basic research investments made by a variety of U.S. federal agencies (FIGURE 1) that led to the development of MP3 technologies.[2] The MP3 device "itself is innovative, but it built upon a broad platform of component technologies, each derived from fundamental studies in physical science, mathematics and engineering," according to the White House Domestic Policy Council. While this statement is correct, the reality is that the subsequent development and manufacturing of component technologies, and thus the creation not only of wealth and jobs but also of the foundation for the next generation of innovations, took place abroad. The development and commercialization of the device's signal-compression technology were picked up by Germany's Fraunhofer Institute for Applied Research. The supply chains that support the manufacture of the hard drive, lithium-ion battery, LCD display and DRAM cache are all based in Asia. The jobs designing and making these hugely popular and technically complex products are there, too.

That the United States has fallen behind in the application function can be seen in its trade deficits in the high-tech sector. Its trade balance in advanced technology products (ATP),[3] which have long been a bastion of American ingenuity, fell into the red for the first time in 2002 (FIGURE 2), when it came in at a negative $16.5 billion, and worsened over 10 years of deficits to reach negative $91.5 billion for 2012.[4]

This is not due to a lack of national investment: In total dollars, the federal research and development (R & D) budget for Science and Technology was nearly $140 billion in 2011, and the country has invested well over $2 trillion in the past 20 years. Private-sector R & D investments, mostly in product development through incremental innovation, were upwards of $250 billion. The United States' total R & D investment of nearly $400 billion was twice that of its nearest competitor. Yet by 2011, the U.S.'s ATP-goods deficit exceeded the total net foreign earnings from the intellectual-property royalties and fees, including franchise fees, booked by all "U.S.-incorporated" companies, from Apple and Intel to Starbucks and McDonald's.[5] The claim that the country can prosper by simply creating technologies here and then letting them be manufactured "over there" is misguided. That path is neither economically sustainable nor governmentally justifiable, and it erodes confidence in America's future.

At this point, the United States has lost ground or is on the verge of losing ground to global competitors in many economically important advanced-technology industries that got their start in America:[6] Among them are flat-panel displays, lithium-ion batteries, solar cells and nanotechnology. Unless cultural and political awareness of engineering's importance to the U.S. economy increases, several strengths upon which its comparative advantage has traditionally been based — its ability to produce high-technology goods, its highly skilled workforce and its high productivity — will continue to diminish.

FIGURE I: *Research Funded by DOD, NSF, NIH, DOE and NIST that Contributed to the Breakthrough Technologies Embedded in MP3 Devices*

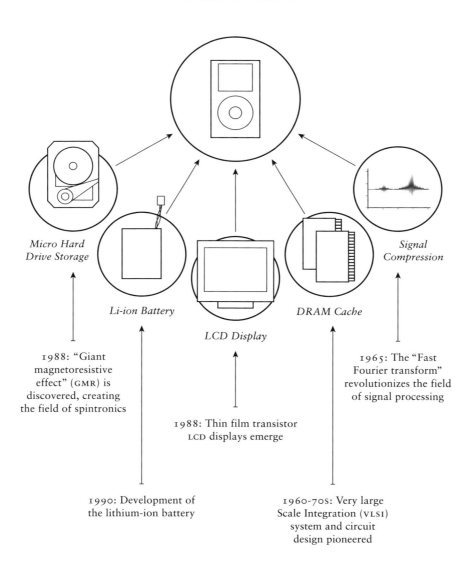

IMPACT OF BASIC RESEARCH
ON INNOVATION

Micro Hard Drive Storage

Li-ion Battery

LCD Display

DRAM Cache

Signal Compression

1988: "Giant magnetoresistive effect" (GMR) is discovered, creating the field of spintronics

1988: Thin film transistor LCD displays emerge

1965: The "Fast Fourier transform" revolutionizes the field of signal processing

1990: Development of the lithium-ion battery

1960-70s: Very large Scale Integration (VLSI) system and circuit design pioneered

FIGURE 2: *U.S. Trade Deficit in Advanced Technology Products*

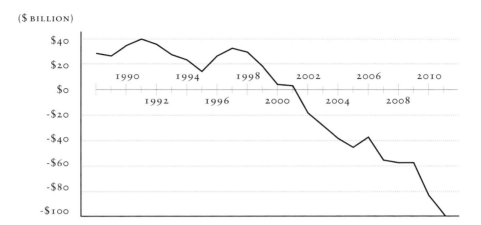

THE MISSING MIDDLE:
THE APPLICATION OF RESEARCH RESULTS

The implications of this weakening go well beyond the accounts-receivable column. Companies choose to expand or set up new manufacturing facilities based on many factors, among which are taxes and trade regulations, as well as access to capital, markets and a skilled workforce. But two additional factors that are often overlooked matter even more: engineering know-how and the presence of supply chains. Many electronics products, the Amazon Kindle and Apple iPhone being good examples, can no longer be made in the United States, primarily because their supply chains are now rooted in Asia. A similar erosion of U.S. supply chains in defense-critical technologies or products would be strategically dangerous.

The fact is that, in high-technology industries, manufacturing and R&D are closely knit. Ample evidence shows that combining the two is key to fueling real innovation, and that the co-location of R&D and manufacturing facilities adds value to each. Promising ideas must be matured through translational R&D if they are to end up in products that meet performance goals and are at the same time cost-effective, reliable and safe. Only a small

FIGURE 3: *Innovation and Manufacturing: Intricately Linked*

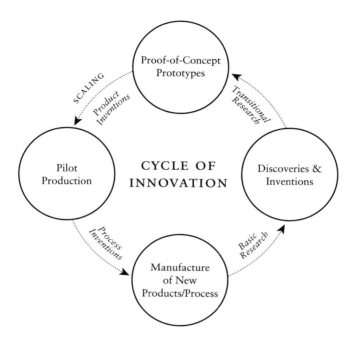

fraction of discoveries and first-generation inventions prove worthy of scaling up, and it is during scale-up and initial manufacturing that many improvements in design and efficiency are made that can then feed back to follow-on cycles of innovation. It is for this reason that the failure to manufacture each generation of advanced-technology products places at risk the ability to innovate the next generation of products (FIGURE 3). This has been well understood in industry for almost a decade but has been little recognized by the political establishment.

Declining expertise leads to the abandonment of facilities and infrastructure, which in turn has a negative impact not only on the skilled workforce and supply chains but on the whole culture of innovation. The offshoring of cutting-edge manufacturing is inevitably followed by the offshoring of R & D, something that over the past two decades has brought with it a significant change in the scope of corporate R & D in the United States.

Increasingly, in the interest of staying competitive in the moment, private-sector R & D has become focused on the immediate goal of turning out current products more quickly and more cheaply. The majority of America's industrial R & D is now essentially just D — and short-term, product-development D at that.

All the while, the bulk of federal R & D investment has remained focused exclusively on the R, the basic research that has no direct or clear relation to the industrial D except in a few sectors like pharmaceuticals and electronics, and even in these two sectors the United States runs large trade deficits. The result has been a gap — "the missing middle" of translational R & D — between the United States' cutting-edge science and its ability to create new companies and sell new products. Put another way, America excels in science, finance and marketing but is falling behind in the kind of engineering that drives innovative growth.

TRANSLATIONAL RESEARCH

The United States is by far the world's largest R & D performer: Its total of $400 billion in 2009 accounted for nearly 31 percent of global R & D spending. R & D performed by businesses in the United States came to an estimated $275 billion, about 71 percent of all U.S. R & D that year, while federal R & D accounted for approximately $125 billion.

While at first glance the portfolio represented in FIGURE 4 may appear fairly balanced, in reality it reveals a gaping hole in the American innovation pipeline: Translational R & D, which is necessary to mature nascent technologies and to assure their manufacturing readiness, goes largely unfunded. The federal government's R & D investments are primarily in basic research, and industry's are primarily in applied R & D, or perhaps no more than D, being focused as they are on incremental innovations aimed at making existing products better. There is very little connecting federal research and industrial development in most technology sectors.

Basic scientific research has traditionally been considered a "public good" and its funding, therefore, the responsibility of government. But while science is the ultimate source of most technological innovation, it does not by itself turn out the products and services that generate wealth. Creation of the Internet, for example, involved little or no new basic

FIGURE 4: *U.S. Investments in Research and Development Activities*

TOTAL U.S. R&D (2009) $400 BILLION

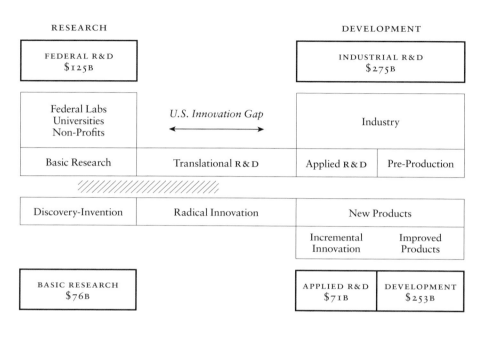

///// SBIR/STTR PHASE 1 & 2: ~$2.5B

science, but it did require significant investments in precompetitive applied research, or translational research, directed at such enabling technologies as communication protocols and networking infrastructure. These were investments that the private sector did not make because their time horizons were too long and their payoffs too difficult for any one company to capture. Now that the Bell Labs of yesteryear have disappeared and the scope of corporate R & D has narrowed significantly, the U.S. government has a major role to play in supporting translational research, which alone can ensure that the fruits of federally funded basic research are transitioned to homegrown products.

It is impossible to know in advance which specific investments in basic research will lead to useful discoveries. It is equally difficult to predict which useful discoveries will result in scalable, safe, reliable and cost-effective technologies without the intermediate step that translational research represents. For this reason, the lack of investment in translational research by federal and private sources over the past 20 years has created a significant innovation gap in the United States, the results of which are expressed in lackluster economic growth.

THE LABOR-COST MYTH

Low-cost labor is not the reason that the United States is losing its market share in high-technology products, whose labor content tends, in any event, to be quite low. The case of Germany's vibrant manufacturing sector puts this into perspective. Labor costs in Germany are almost 33 percent higher than those in the United States; in addition, although German companies pay marginal corporate tax rates that are slightly lower than those of their U.S. competitors, they pay nearly 25 percent more for energy (FIGURE 5). Yet in 2011 the difference in the two nations' trade balances in goods reached almost $1 trillion: The United States had a deficit in goods of $738 billion, Germany a surplus of over $200 billion. Another potentially crucial difference: Even though the U.S. federal government invests six times as much in R & D as Germany does, it invests less than one-third as much in industrial technologies. Seen in this light, the U.S. deficit in advanced-technology products suggests that the benefits of government R & D investments are trickling down to neither American industry nor American taxpayers in the form of high-wage manufacturing jobs.

FIGURE 5: *Various Inputs and Economic Output of German and U.S. Manufacturing Sectors*

		U.S.	GERMANY
Trade Balance ($B) (2011)	GOODS	-738	+214
	SERVICES	+178	-30
	NET	-560	+184
Manufacturing as % GDP (2010)		13	21
Hourly Compensation of Manufacturing Workers (2011)		$35.53	$47.38
Govt. Research Budget in Billions of Dollars (2011)		164	26
Investment in Industrial Production and Technology (as Percent of Total R & D Spending)		0.963 (0.6%)	3.3 (12.7%)
As Percent of Nondefense R & D		1.2%	13.5%
Share (%) of Business R & D Expenditures on Manufacturing		69.6	90.0
R & D as % GDP		2.68	2.53
Raw Cost Index of Manufacturers		$0.47	$0.52
Statutory Corporate Tax Rates (2012)		39.1	30.2
Social Insurance Expenditures and Other Labor Taxes (% of Compensation)		33	42
Industrial Pollution Abatement and Control Expenditures (% of Value Added)		6.2	6.0
End-User Industry Energy Costs (Index U.S. = 100)		100.0	124.7

THE CHANGING FACE OF U.S. MANUFACTURING

Over the past two decades, while the U.S. manufacturing sector has been struggling through a period of major change and downsizing, other nations' industrial production and exports have surged. In the 1990s, shedding low-cost, labor-intensive production was taken on as a major challenge in the United States, whose economic future was assumed to be in technology-intensive, high-productivity, high-skilled manufacturing. But manufacturing's contribution to U.S. GDP has simply continued along the downward trajectory that has taken it from above 25 percent through the 1950s and 1960s to 17 percent in 1990 and down to its current 11.5 percent. The nation's manufacturing employment has declined as well, from a peak of 19.5 million manufacturing payroll jobs in 1979 to fewer than 12 million in 2012.

The picture is notably different in two other developed countries, Germany and Japan. Although the levels of manufacturing employment in both have declined significantly and steadily since the 1970s, Germany's seems to have leveled off at 20 percent[7] of its workforce and Japan's at 16.8 percent,[8] and the manufacturing sectors of both have remained healthy throughout the recent worldwide economic downturn. These two countries can be expected to continue thriving in the advanced-manufacturing sector. At the same time, emerging economies that have fully embraced lower-tech manufacturing will be working harder to move up the value chain. To contend for leadership in advanced-technology products, the United States must invest in industrial infrastructure; in basic, translational and applied research; and in a highly trained workforce at all levels, from skilled production labor to high-quality graduate engineers.

Maintaining a strong research infrastructure is central to competing in high-technology products because there is ample evidence to suggest that real innovations come about when R&D and advanced manufacturing are co-located. But since U.S.-based manufacturing firms' rate of investment in R&D in the period 1999-2007 was three times as high outside the United States as it was at home,[9] it is evident that much of that co-location is sited overseas. Once U.S. corporations had begun offshoring lower-tech manufacturing — the production of toys and shoes, for example — higher-value-added activities like engineering design and development also started moving abroad.[10] R & D then followed. The same occurred in high-tech manufacturing, starting in 2001 with semiconductors and other electronic components and systems.

Thirty years ago, innovations would take root in the United States first. Years would pass before a product became a commodity item, at which point foreign companies might start by producing its components and then, a few years down the road, go on to make the entire product. In the cases of machine tools, robots, MRI machines, computers and LCDs, several years went by before U.S. manufacturers uprooted their domestic operations and reestablished them overseas. As years passed, however, the time it took to relocate manufacturing began to shrink: The migration time for LCD manufacturing was much shorter than that for MRI machines. It became the norm that the United States would play the role of technology inventor and that the manufacturing would subsequently move to other countries.

There is no shortage of examples, both past and present, indicating that whoever fails to manufacture a given generation of advanced-technology products loses the ability to innovate the next generation:

Lithium-ion batteries: The United States' loss of leadership in the consumer-electronics device industry led to its loss of leadership in lithium-ion batteries. Sony bought lithium-ion battery technology from the United States in the early '90s and has diligently improved it to meet the demands of the personal-computer industry. Having abandoned the lead it had in lithium-ion batteries 30 years ago, the United States must now work hard to regain a foothold in the multi-billion-dollar automotive lithium-ion battery industry.

Electronic displays: In the 1980s, U.S. companies started offshoring the assembly of printed-circuit boards to China, South Korea and Taiwan. As those countries gained technical know-how and moved up the value chain to engineering design, development and systems integration, they began manufacturing entire personal computers. Today, virtually all Windows-based PCs and notebooks are designed and manufactured in Asia. With the Kindle, what had been invented in the United States was never manufactured at home. Massachusetts-based E-ink, developer of the electronic ink that changes the appearance of screens without illuminating them, had to go to Taiwan to find an LCD manufacturer for its invention, since none are left in the United States. This supplier, Primeview, then purchased E-ink and moved its operations to Taiwan to bring it closer to the rest of the supply chain needed to manufacture each new version of the Kindle. And because the infrastructure, manufacturing expertise and supply chains for LCD/LED technology are all located in Asia, next-generation flexible displays — expected to become another multi-billion-dollar industry — are unlikely to be manufactured in America either. The supply chain won't be in the United States, and neither will any of the jobs.

Solar cells: Silicon Valley's Applied Materials, the world's leading manufacturer of equipment for making solar cells, recently constructed the world's largest private solar R&D facility in China to leverage proximity to the world's largest solar-manufacturing hubs. In view of such trends, the chances are good that soon the United States will no longer be manufacturing next-generation solar cells.

Nanotechnology: Lux Research in a 2010 report benchmarked various countries on their nanotechnology activity and technology-development strength. Germany, Japan, South Korea, Taiwan and the United States all ranked high in nanotechnology activity — but the United States ranked lowest of the five in technology-development strength and has been falling farther behind ever since. It is also important to note that U.S. technology-development strength moved in the wrong direction between 2007 and 2009 (FIGURE 6).

FIGURE 6: *Ranking the Nations on Nanotech: Hidden Havens and False Threats*
Source: Lux Research Report, August 2010

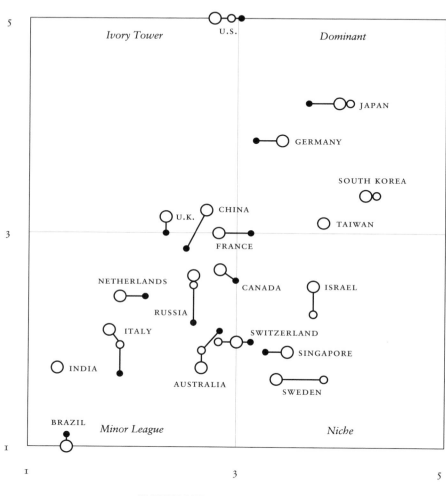

TECHNOLOGY DEVELOPMENT STRENGTH

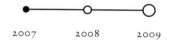

2007   2008   2009

As supply chains take root in faraway lands, it becomes more difficult not only to manufacture advanced-technology products at home, but also to innovate. Even when a marketable product has been successfully created in the United States, supply chains need to be nearby if manufacturing — the step where the most wealth creation occurs — is to take place domestically. And innovation will necessarily join manufacturing in moving to where supply chains exist. Examples like E-ink provide evidence that the "invent here, manufacture there" model is no longer economically sustainable — if it was, in fact, ever valid at all — and expose a big gap in America's innovation pipeline. By any strict definition, the United States has not done significant technological innovation for a long time. It continues to excel in scientific discoveries and in some engineering inventions, but not in the transition of inventions into products that society wants. It is important for the country to recognize this fundamental change before it is too late.

THE LABOR-PRODUCTIVITY MYTH

The U.S. has lost nearly 6 million manufacturing jobs over the last decade, 3.4 million of them vanishing in the years 2000-07, before the Great Recession began. Many attribute the job losses to an increase in labor productivity, but this claim is erroneous. As Stephen Ezell and Robert Atkinson[11] have demonstrated, 15 of the 19 manufacturing sectors that account for 79 percent of America's manufacturing GDP experienced contractions in output between 2000 and 2009. That the decline was primarily an effect of offshoring, not of productivity gains, has been documented by other economic researchers, including Gregory Tassey[12] of the National Institute of Standards and Technology (NIST); Susan Houseman[13] of the Upjohn Institute; and, later, Susan Helper,[14] who provides a clear explanation for the origin of the mistaken belief that productivity gains were behind the drastic job cuts of the past decade (FIGURE 7).

FIGURE 7: *Productivity and Employment Change in U.S Manufacturing Over the Past Two Decades*

Source: Houseman (see fn 13)

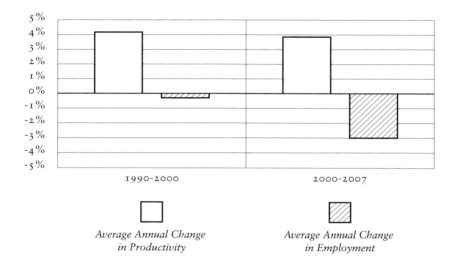

1990-2000

2000-2007

Average Annual Change
in Productivity

Average Annual Change
in Employment

Contributing to this misperception is the fact that U.S. government statistics on labor productivity, which are reported by the Bureau of Labor Statistics (BLS), overstate manufacturing productivity for three primary reasons:

1. Computer-industry statistics confound manufacturing productivity with product performance. According to BLS, annual productivity growth in the computer and electronics sector averaged about 27 percent. This change resulted far more from an improvement in the performance of computer chips, which continued to be produced on the same production lines by more or less the same number of employees, than from the same quantity of goods being produced by less labor. The notion that the latter was responsible is clearly misguided.

2. Imported inputs are not included when domestic labor productivity is computed. Value added is measured as "sales minus the cost of materials," but there are no data comparing the costs of inputs imported from different places.

3. Although the goods produced by temporary workers are counted as manufacturing output, the temporary workers themselves are not counted as manufacturing workers in the official statistics.

When corrections are made for these three sources of flawed calculation, U.S. manufacturing's annual productivity growth comes out at 2.3 percent in the period 1997-2007, not at 5.4 percent as reported by BLS. Even so, at 2.3 percent, productivity growth in manufacturing was higher than the 1.8 percent posted by the private sector as a whole.

THE PROFILE OF AMERICAN ENGINEERING IS TOO LOW

In light of the National Academies' definition of innovation as in part the application of knowledge, "often through world-class engineering," any attempt to revitalize America's manufacturing — and its transition of promising ideas into marketable products or processes — must go hand in hand with revitalizing the U.S. system of engineering education and engineering research.

"Engineering is not science, and confusing the two keeps us from solving the problems of the world," the engineering professor and author Henry Petroski has lamented on more than one occasion.[15] Yet, many engineering researchers become uncomfortable whenever a clear distinction is drawn between engineering and science, and some of them would argue that, nowadays, "engineering science" is the best term to describe what they do. But science attempts to understand and explain the world through experimentation and analysis, while engineering is about synthesis: Scientific discoveries may provide the foundation for engineering's creations, but these creations involve practical products and processes. Still, many in the engineering field, including agencies that fund its work, have come to regard publication in respected journals — especially scientific journals — as a worthy final outcome of engineering research.

In a departure from America's history of significant engineering efforts and outcomes, the vast majority of current U.S. research programs explicitly emphasize the scientific aspects of a problem, showing a purely analytical bent. The most prestigious of the country's granting agencies, the National Science Foundation (NSF), employs the same yardstick to measure the "intellectual merit" and "broader impacts of research" in engineering as it does to evaluate science. The seemingly innocuous generalization of science to include engineering has had real consequences in the past three decades:[16] It has nourished science, discovery and publication at the expense of engineering, invention and innovation.

One of the outcomes is that the dissemination of knowledge is held in higher regard than the application of knowledge. Publication is the true currency of science disciplines, as evidenced by academia's "publish or perish" model. In contrast, when engineering development, which takes place through the application of knowledge, is the goal, dissemination becomes less important. It can even be counterproductive before a product is at least partially developed and the intellectual property involved is protected. Engineering professionals must strive for innovation whose impact extends far beyond the academy to society at large. It is important, therefore, that influential institutions like NSF recognize that basic research in engineering does not have to be removed from reality, and that appropriate metrics for real engineering outcomes be established.

How a government allocates its resources is both a reflection of and an influence on the prevailing mindset. To illustrate, of the total U.S. federal research investment in science and engineering for 2008, approximately one-seventh (FIGURE 8) was allocated to engineering development and six-sevenths to various scientific fields. Although the acronym identifying its "STEM Education" effort stands for "Science, Technology, Engineering and Mathematics," NSF spends only $15 million annually on engineering education, barely more than 1 percent of the $1.4 billion it directs to education in science and mathematics (FIGURE 9). Federal research expenditures for 2011 were 8.1 percent above their 2001 level, with more of the gains going to life sciences than to other disciplines. Engineering, whose research expenditures went down 4.3 percent in 2011, was the only field that saw a decrease that year.[17] The Defense Department (DOD) still accounts for nearly one-third of federal investment in engineering, but there has been a steep decline in DOD's support for engineering, which fell 26 percent between 2001 and 2010. The important question here is not how much more the nation should be investing in engineering versus science, but how it can allocate available resources to ensure that the benefits of the science it funds come back to taxpayers as a return on investment.

FIGURE 8: *Federal Investments in Basic and Applied Research in Engineering: A Small Fraction of the Total Investment in Sciences*

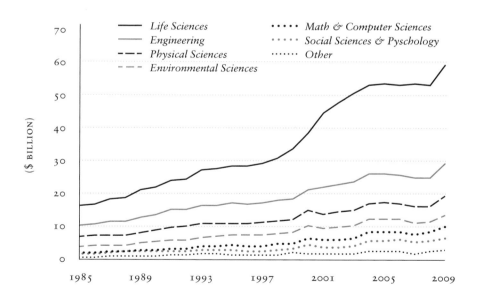

FIGURE 9: *Comparison of Federal Investments in Science*
Education vs. Engineering Education (in millions of dollars)

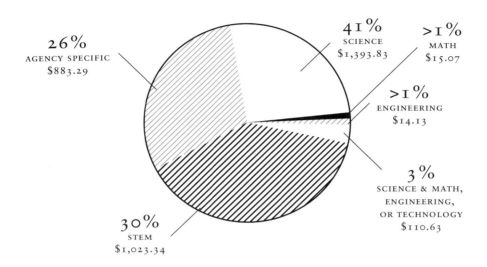

41%
SCIENCE
$1,393.83

>1%
MATH
$15.07

>1%
ENGINEERING
$14.13

3%
SCIENCE & MATH,
ENGINEERING,
OR TECHNOLOGY
$110.63

26%
AGENCY SPECIFIC
$883.29

30%
STEM
$1,023.34

FIGURE 10: *Decline in Federal Funding of Engineering Research*

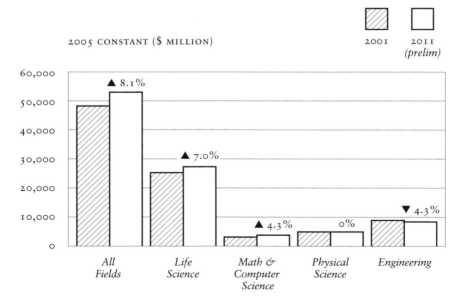

2005 CONSTANT ($ MILLION)

2001   2011
         (prelim)

▲ 8.1%

▲ 7.0%

▲ 4.3%

0%

▼ 4.3%

60,000

50,000

40,000

30,000

20,000

10,000

0

*All
Fields*

*Life
Science*

*Math &
Computer
Science*

*Physical
Science*

Engineering

Countries like Germany, Japan, South Korea, China and Taiwan, meanwhile, revere engineering, and their governments are leveraging scientific breakthroughs made in the United States to their own advantage by sharing development risks to help get products using those breakthroughs ready for eventual production by private firms.

NATIONAL TECHNOLOGICAL INFRASTRUCTURE I: EDUCATION

Considering that the federal government devotes so little of its STEM funding to engineering, it is hardly surprising that the current K-12 STEM curriculum emphasizes courses in math and science aimed at those bound for four-year colleges while treating as an afterthought "technology" courses that prepare students to go into the trades directly out of high school. What's more, since they have been educated to place value on analysis and mathematical rigor, modern generations of U.S. engineers tend to think of engineering not as a creative, synthetic field but as an applied-mathematics discipline. According to the U.S. Department of Education, 5.3 percent of all bachelor's degrees awarded in 2009 in the United States were in engineering. Internationally, the corresponding figure was 18.4 percent.

In Germany, 58 percent of upper-secondary students were enrolled in a vocational or technical training program in 2008. As apprentices, young German workers divide their time between the classroom and hands-on training, receiving a modest stipend from their employers, and even though there is no guarantee that students will stay on permanently, employers are willing to devote significant funding to apprenticeship programs. The electronics giant Siemens spends more than $200 million per year on these training programs, in which over 10,000 young workers participate. In 2012, as a means to address the aging of its workforce, one of its U.S. subsidiaries, Siemens Energy Inc., launched an apprentice-ship program at its Charlotte, N.C., gas-turbine plant for local high school students. The company is investing $165,000 to train each apprentice, and all will have jobs waiting for them when they are done.

Challenge-based, hands-on learning can get students excited about careers in engineering, but because engineering is portrayed as a discipline reserved for the mathematically gifted, creative minds are frequently scared off.

The United States needs a revitalized engineering culture that makes explicit the connection between theory and design, thereby providing experiences that can inspire future generations to pursue engineering and manufacturing careers.

To this end, the recent emergence of the "Maker Movement" is having a phenomenal influence on American youth. *Maker Faires* bring together science, art, crafts, engineering and music in fun, energized and exciting public forums. They inspire people of all ages to roll up their sleeves and embrace a do-it-yourself spirit. Making and tinkering is only the first step, of course. Making is not the same as manufacturing, just as tinkering is not engineering.

The number of programs that specifically target students has been increasing. A few examples:

Project Lead The Way has been highly successful in bringing hands-on engineering education to high schools across the nation, involving over 400,000 students in all 50 states.

FIRST Robotics is an outstanding example of an extracurricular program that has inspired thousands of middle school and high-school students to pursue careers in science and engineering.

Innovation 101, a program of the educational nonprofit The Henry Ford in Dearborn, Mich., promotes a culture of innovation by engaging students at all grade levels in hands-on activities that are contextual, experiential, challenging and fun.

The Society of Manufacturing Engineers has developed new programs, including computer-integrated manufacturing projects that are intended to inspire youth.

STIHL, a manufacturer of handheld outdoor power equipment, last year launched a week-long summer camp in Hampton Roads, Va., that features tours, lectures and manufacturing demonstrations for high school students. Student groups competed on design/build projects, gaining understanding of what it takes to make a product, grow a business and learn about robotics and automation.

These and other such programs need to be brought into the mainstream — into every classroom in every school at all grade levels. Only a new pipe-line of talented engineers can keep America at the forefront of innovation.

To encourage its employees, who are already in the manufacturing world, to transform their creative ideas into physical prototypes, Ford Motor Company has invested in TechShop facilities. The Detroit TechShop is a 17,000-square-foot facility stocked with $750,000 worth of laser cutters, 3D printers and CNC machine tools, and staffed with "Dream Consultants" whose job it is to help users fabricate pretty much anything. Ford employees are free to take advantage of the space day or night for projects related to their work or for personal projects.

NATIONAL TECHNOLOGICAL INFRASTRUCTURE II: RESEARCH

Other countries have recognized the connection between R&D networks, manufacturing and economic growth, and they have developed policies that promote advanced-manufacturing R&D at home. Germany's Fraunhofer Institutes[18] and the U.K.'s Innovative Manufacturing Research Centers[19] are specific manufacturing-R&D efforts. Other examples of how nations have included manufacturing R&D as part of a larger scheme to keep innovation within their borders include:

- the European Commission's Competitiveness and Innovation Framework;[20]

- China's 2006 policy package, which includes significant measures to support innovation,[21] and its subsequent development of four industry-research strategic alliances;

- Singapore's investment in public-private research parks such as Biopolis and Fusionopolis;

- Taiwan's Industrial Technology Research Institute; and

- Japan's prioritization of science-industry relations and cluster policies, including Technopolis.

FIGURE 11: *Role of Public and Private Entities in Maturing Emerging Technologies and Their Manufacturing Readiness*

GLOBAL MODELS FOR TECHNOLOGY DEVELOPMENT
(SUCCESSFUL MODELS IN OTHER COUNTRIES)

UNIVERSITIES, FEDERAL LABS			GERMAN FRAUNHOFER INSTITUTES, TAIWAN'S INDUSTRIAL TECH RESEARCH INST.					INDUSTRIAL R&D
1	2	3	4	5	6	7	8	9
TECHNOLOGY AND MANUFACTURING READINESS LEVELS								

That America's competitor nations have taken such actions makes the case for similar investment here compelling, since the United States no longer has private-sector research laboratories like Xerox PARC or Bell Labs, both of which contributed so much to the nation's prosperity. Beginning in Thomas Edison's time, American research institutions united knowledge, skills, resources, infrastructure and leadership, providing a full-service technology-development and commercialization model for the modern age. The scientific discoveries at Bell Labs that led to such inventions as the transistor, the laser, solar cells and satellite communications showed what scientists and engineers can do when they work together: transform scientific breakthroughs — the 1 percent "inspiration" of Edison's formula for "genius" — into the engineering solutions that arose thanks to the formula's 99 percent "perspiration." In a June 2011 report[22] to President Obama titled "Ensuring American Leadership in Advanced Manufacturing," the President's Council of Advisors on Science and Technology (PCAST) identified this gap in the U.S. innovation cycle and recommended that the government invest in pre-competitive applied research, i.e., translational R&D. The idea was to establish institutions modeled after Bell Labs and the Fraunhofer Institutes. This led to the establishment of a national network of Manufacturing Innovation Institutes, announced by President Obama[23] in March 2012.

To be sure, the technology innovation pursued by large corporations today is critical to America's remaining globally competitive, but that's in the short run. If new industries are to be created, "radical" technological innovation — innovation that leverages scientific breakthroughs — is needed. The value of "patient capital" and of the resources associated with the Bell Labs of the past is, however, no longer evident to most U.S. corporate managers. The average time investors on Wall Street hold a stock has dropped, dwindling from eight years in the 1960s to only four months in 2012.[24] Although the federal government continues to invest in basic research, which in turn continues generating new ideas and scientific breakthroughs just as it did when the big corporate research institutions were there to develop them, it is now other nations that are picking up the results, capitalizing on U.S. discoveries and inventions and creating value for themselves. Losing those private-sector facilities has significantly impaired America's innovation ecosystem, impairing its ability to transition good science into U.S.-based manufacturing. If the United States proves unable to find the 21st-century equivalent of those legendary hotbeds of creative industry, it may concede forever its lead in innovation and prosperity.[25]

It is generally acknowledged that the United States has the world's best higher education, since American universities still dominate the global top-100 list. But if America stands on the top rung of the academic ladder, that ladder may well be leaning against the wrong wall.[26] This is because current university rankings are not based on *outcomes* but are instead structured mostly on *inputs* such as standardized test scores, acceptance rates, research expenditures, reputation and alumni donations.

A more useful ranking system would be based on such outcomes as teaching effectiveness, the number of new businesses or industries created and societal impacts on health, national security and energy. It is perfectly conceivable that at least the top 10 to 20 U.S. universities could retain their high ranking even according to such outcome-based criteria. But the vast majority of U.S. universities are mainly driven by how to improve their standing in the annual *U.S. News and World Report* ranking because a high ranking there brings prestige, which attracts students, faculty members and new funding, both public and private. Even though the federal government measures research outcomes in terms of publications, citations and patents, the taxpayers who fund the research are likely to treat those measures as only intermediate outputs at best.

GERMANY'S FRAUNHOFER INSTITUTES FOR APPLIED RESEARCH

A cornerstone of Germany's innovation ecosystem is the Fraunhofer Institutes for Applied Research. Established in 1949 as part of the West German government's effort to rebuild Germany's pre-war research infrastructure,[27] the non-profit Fraunhofer-Gesellschaft is one of the world's largest and most successful applied-technology organizations. Fraunhofer's 80 research institutes and centers, 60 located in Germany and the rest abroad, employ some 20,000 scientists and engineers and train 4,000 Ph.D and master's students annually. Fraunhofer's $2.6 billion annual budget comes from Germany's federal and state governments, manufacturing clients and publicly funded research projects that it wins on a competitive basis from the German government and the European Union. The most closely comparable program in the United States, the NIST Manufacturing Extension Partnership (MEP), has a budget of $125 million, 15 percent of Fraunhofer's budget.

The Fraunhofer Institutes' mission is to act as a "technology bridge" connecting basic research and German industry.[28] Although Fraunhofer researchers publish scientific papers and secure patents, having filed 685 patent applications in 2009 alone, their primary mission is to disseminate and commercialize technology. Most of the organization's remarkable range of applied-research programs — which span microsystems, life sciences, communications, energy, new materials and security — focus on collaborating with German manufacturers to pursue clearly identified market opportunities.

Fraunhofer is growing quickly. Between 2007 and 2012, it added 6,000 researchers to its payroll and its overall budget increased by 29 percent. The institute has helped grow Germany's economy through an export boom. In 2011, German exports increased by 8.2 percent, helping deliver a 3.0 percent increase in GDP and driving the country's unemployment rate to its lowest level in 20 years. "We at Fraunhofer have clear research results," says its president, Hans-Jörg Bullinger. "We have a worldwide recognized model of research and application."

The 60 installations Fraunhofer runs in Germany collaborate closely with manufacturers in 16 different industry clusters. Fraunhofer Institutes offer a broad portfolio of services to 5,000 corporate clients, nearly a third of which are small and medium-sized enterprises. The diversity of its funding sources enables Fraunhofer to use different approaches to commercializing technology, one of which is helping develop specific technologies for companies. For example, Schott Solar contracted with Fraunhofer to develop technology for absorber tubes used in solar receivers that are being exported out of Schott's factory in Albuquerque, N.M.

Recent Fraunhofer lab inventions for industry include touch-controlled organic light-emitting diode lighting, artificial animal tissue for drug testing, lightweight bicycle-seat posts, new steel-cutting techniques for car manufacturers, micro-helicopters and ultra-efficient gem-cutting tools.[29] Fraunhofer earned several hundred million euros from licensing its signal-compression technology for MP3 players, which has been one of its most lucrative lab successes.[30]

In its 2012 annual report, Fraunhofer uses a quote attributed to Charles Darwin to motivate its German manufacturing forces: "It is not the strongest of the species, nor the most intelligent that survives. It is the one that is the fastest and most adaptable to change."

GOVERNMENT'S ROLE IN THE U.S. INNOVATION ECOSYSTEM

Fortunately, the federal government has a history of fostering innovation in ways other than simply funding basic research. For over a century, the federal government has played an essential role in bringing emerging technologies to market. In cases from aircraft, semiconductors and computers to the Internet and GPS, it is the federal government that has set the wheels in motion to transition promising technologies into products with societal benefits. Though it is fashionable to say that "government should not pick winners and losers" but rather "get out of the way," the U.S. government has historically enabled the creation of new high-technology industries by underwriting not only basic research but also applied research, development, demonstration and early procurement.

To choose a single but highly significant example, America's aircraft industry did not spring spontaneously out of the ground the day after Orville Wright took the Flyer airborne at Kitty Hawk. A dozen years after that 1903 maiden flight, the United States was lagging behind other nations in aviation. Then, in 1915, the federal government launched the nation's first aviation initiative, establishing the National Advisory Committee for Aeronautics to conduct the research and development needed to advance the standards, design and development of engines and airfoils. After producing only 411 aircraft by 1916, American companies churned out more than 12,000 in a nine-month period bridging 1917 and 1918 to support the war effort.

To be sure, it is the genius of individual entrepreneurs and dedicated scientists and engineers that creates the initial spark for new industries, but it sometimes takes the federal government to fund early, high-risk R&D in order to overcome hesitance, and occasionally even opposition, on the part of established firms. When the U.S. Air Force and the Pentagon's Defense Advanced Research Projects Agency (DARPA) approached AT&T and IBM about getting involved in applied research and demonstration of nascent ideas in networking communications research, the firms were less than enthusiastic for a number of reasons, one being their belief that a major success might threaten their business. So it was DARPA itself that invested in the packet-switching concept of computer pioneer Paul Baran in the early 1960s, and then in the 1969 demonstration of ARPANET, a forerunner of the Internet of today. Without government's investment in R&D the Internet revolution would not have occurred.

Government procurement has also had a significant impact on accelerating innovation in electronics by lowering the risk of emerging technologies so that they could be scaled in a cost-effective manner. The U.S. Air Force and the National Aeronautics and Space Administration (NASA) bought almost every microchip produced by private firms during the 1960s, which led to the creation of production lines capable of putting out large quantities of chips quickly and cheaply. Within a span of a few years, the price dropped by 98 percent, from $1,000 per unit to about $20 per unit.

By co-investing in pre-competitive R&D to mature emerging technologies both through public-private partnerships and through a coordinated, strategic approach to procurement, government has aided as well as encouraged U.S. firms to fill in the gap between basic research and advanced manufacturing.

Developing and assessing the scalability, reliability and cost-effectiveness of promising early-stage technologies requires both patience and capital. The federal government, in its role as funder of public goods, should invest in promising "platform" or generic technologies that can enable the development of a large variety of products further downstream. The private sector chronically underinvests in such "pre-competitive" technologies, daunted by market, financial and technological risks and by the fact that a single firm, or even an entire industry, can seldom reap a large enough share of the benefit to justify such an investment. Rather than going it alone and absorbing all the costs, however, government can engage industry in public-private partnerships structured as consortia that can enable maturation of emerging technologies and their manufacturing readiness, enhancing U.S. manufacturing competitiveness.

When the U.S. semiconductor industry lost a considerable portion of its market share to Japan in the 1980s, 14 U.S.-based semiconductor manufacturers came together with the federal government to form the Semiconductor Manufacturing Technology (Sematech) consortium. With total federal funding of $500 million for its first five years — a lot of money at the time — Sematech focused on conducting translational R&D in the field of advanced semiconductor manufacturing. It was instrumental in America's regaining its competitiveness.

Today the United States has significant opportunities to capture the fruits of its investments in basic research in areas like nanotechnology, flexible electronics, photonics, lightweight structures, next-generation robotics, IT-enabled smart manufacturing and biofuels. Basic research shows, for example, that electronic circuits can be printed roll-to-roll on flexible substrates. But there are numerous research and technology challenges that must be addressed — material degradation, encapsulation, feature size and resolution, to name a few — before flexible printed electronics can become practical. This is an example of an excellent occasion for pooling private and government investment, as large-scale roll-to-roll manufacturing of electronics, once matured, would create a platform to launch entirely new products across multiple sectors, including inexpensive flexible solar cells, displays, lighting, smart bandages, sensors and flexible batteries.

If the United States is to build an "industrial commons" and promote innovation-based manufacturing at home, it may take both government and private-sector participation in infrastructure investments like those needed to nurture the knowledge base, acquire the skills and build the equipment that provides the foundation for roll-to-roll platform technology. This is but one small example of the potential that exists to revive the American economy.

NATIONAL SECURITY IMPLICATIONS

It would have been worse had the Kindle been a defense-critical item. A recent investigation by the Senate Armed Services Committee (SASC) revealed a "flood of counterfeit electronic parts coming into the Defense Department's supply system."[31] The committee's final report, released in May 2012, outlined more than 1,800 cases of suspected counterfeits involving more than 1 million parts for use in some of the country's "most important military systems."

When committee staff started digging into the question, they found all types of shady Chinese suppliers, including, for example, Hong Dark Electronic Trade of Shenzhen, a company that sold 84,000 counterfeit electronic parts into the Pentagon's supply chain. Senate investigators found that the military version of the Boeing 737 commercial airliner, the Poseidon P8-A aircraft, was riddled with illegal Chinese electronic parts supplied to Boeing by BAE Systems, Honeywell, L3 Communications Systems and Rockwell Collins. The same fake parts may be on the commercial Boeing jetliner, but the SASC staff couldn't say for sure. It's not clear how many of the parts cited in the report could be manufactured in the United States.

CORPORATE R&D

Today, only 4 percent of private-sector R&D in the United States is targeted at basic research; as noted above, most R&D spending by industrial companies is on applied research and is devoted almost entirely to product development and incremental process innovation.[32] U.S. manufacturing sectors that devote large percentages of their sales to R&D are communication equipment (14.7 percent), pharmaceuticals (12.7 percent) and semiconductor equipment (12 percent). R&D-intensive industries typically have R & D-to-sales ratios greater than 3 percent. But the United States has slipped behind Japan, South Korea and Germany in its share of R & D-intensive industries.

FIGURE 12: *Percentage of Manufacturing Sector with 3 Percent or Greater R&D Intensity*

SHARE OF MANUFACTURING INDUSTRY

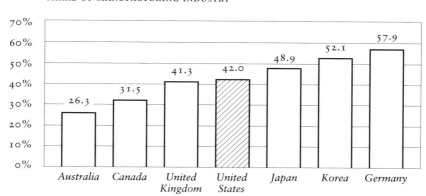

Companies' investments in R & D often create spillover benefits, many of which go to other companies, especially if they are clustered in regional high-tech centers of excellence. However, spillover benefits of U.S. public investment in science, advanced tools and new technologies are now being reaped more than ever by non-U.S. entities. China is the leading exporter of advanced-technology products to the United States, surpassing all of Europe combined, yet not a single publicly traded Chinese company is on the list of the world's top 100 R & D spenders.

Of the 57 major global telecommunications R & D announcements in 2011, more than 60 percent came from Asia, compared to 9 percent from the United States. Intel, which has invested approximately $1 billion in research in India, in 2008 unveiled the first microprocessor designed entirely in that country, which was also the first 45-nanometer chip to be designed outside the United States. Because U.S.-based manufacturing firms' offshore R & D investments grew more than three times as fast as their domestic R & D investments between 1999 and 2007, the prospects for a robust period of growth for the U.S. economy have been further diminished.

GLOBALIZATION OF UNIVERSITY R & D

The same trends hold true for universities. In recent years, U.S. universities looking for new ways to grow have established satellite campuses in other countries. As of 2010, 38 American universities had 65 branches in 34 countries[33] whose most popular programs are in the sciences, engineering and business. But the trend of attracting additional hefty tuition dollars from foreign students has gone beyond educational missions. A growing number of research universities in the United States have established overseas satellite research labs — some far more advanced than those at the home institutions — lured by massive investments by host countries eager to capture the "secret sauce" of American innovation. As host countries spend lavishly on scaling American inventions into commercial products, the knowledge, skills and infrastructure needed for the next generation of innovation begin to take root, raising more questions about the benefits U.S. taxpayers are gaining from the investments they are making in academic research.

INTELLECTUAL PROPERTY AND TECHNOLOGY COMMERCIALIZATION

The Association of University Technology Managers reports that from 2005 to 2009 its university members received $142 billion in federally funded R & D and presented over 85,000 invention disclosures. More than 53,000 patent applications based on those disclosures were submitted to the U.S. Patent and Trademark Office, with only 15,000 being granted a U.S. patent. That represents less than an 18 percent return on the total number of disclosures. During that five-year period, there were only 3,781 licenses executed with the private sector and 2,532 companies that spun out of these same universities. Considering the funding commitment, American taxpayers are not getting much of a return on their investment in university research.

FIGURE 13: *Invention Disclosures, Patent Applications, Licenses and Start-Ups*
Resulting from Research Conducted at U.S. Universities and Federal Labs.

AGGREGATE INVENTION DISCLOSURES, PATENT APPLICATIONS,
PATENTS ISSUED, LICENSES AND START-UPS (U.S. UNIVERSITIES)

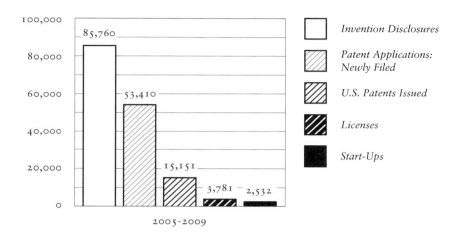

AGGREGATE INVENTION DISCLOSURES, PATENT APPLICATIONS,
PATENTS ISSUED AND LICENSES (FEDERAL LABS)

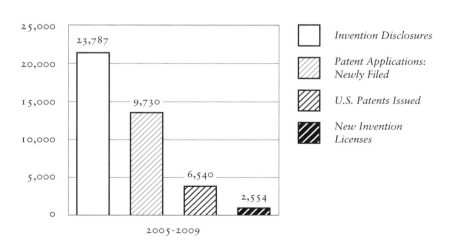

Nearly three decades after the passage of the Bayh-Dole Act, which promotes academic technology transfer, it has finally been widely recognized that university research rarely results in the creation of billion-dollar industries right out of the gate; further investments in technology maturation are needed. Many university technology-transfer offices across the nation are making aggressive efforts to license their intellectual property to private entities. But most of the technologies are not ready for prime time, as it requires years of design, development and testing to take an invention and turn it into a product that can be produced cost-effectively at scale. Universities commonly engage interested parties in complex legal agreements only to discover a few years later that all the effort had yielded little in the way of a practical product and the accompanying royalties they had hoped for. A new model is needed for commercializing university R & D that simplifies licensing agreements and provides companies with a grace period on paying royalties on technologies developed with federal funding. Also under this new model, products based on technology developed by universities with U.S.-government funds should be required to be produced in the United States.

REGAINING AMERICA'S COMPARATIVE ADVANTAGE

Innovation-driven manufacturing, the United States' traditional comparative advantage, relies on advanced technologies conceived and developed by top-flight scientists and engineers and subsequently manufactured with high productivity by a skilled workforce. It is by closing the innovation gap — the "missing middle" between research and entrepreneurship, where practical know-how fuels application — that America can regain its comparative advantage. This means focusing on the engineering required to convert scientific knowledge into new products, processes and industries that are rooted in the United States and that alone can eliminate the trade deficit in advanced-technology products.

As noted by Ralph Gomory, former director of research at IBM and president emeritus of the Alfred P. Sloan Foundation, goods production is indispensable for a healthy national economy. "Balancing trade on ideas and R & D simply cannot be done," he has written. "It is really wrong to think that you can scale up R & D to be big enough so we can trade it for the huge quantities of things we need but don't make in this country."[34] What will be required is an investment in translational research, accompanied by a new generation of engineers and skilled workers who are passionate about creating and working with new products and processes.

INSPIRING FUTURE ENGINEERS AND SKILLED WORKERS

While U.S. high schools commonly require students to dissect a frog, hardly any require students to disassemble a power tool. No matter their age, giving students the skills to take things like power tools or kitchen appliances apart can engage them in design, materials, manufacturing and safety challenges by tapping into the curiosity and creativity that many children naturally have. In the past, talented mechanics and passionate engineers grew up repairing farm machinery or fixing their own car, but today fewer kids are growing up on farms, and it takes a high-end computer and a trained technician to diagnose, let alone repair, an automobile. It is, therefore, critical that K-12 students be provided with opportunities to see how things work, why they don't always work the first time and how they can be improved and perfected. It is simply impossible to get that experience, and to be inspired by it, any way other than through practice.

America needs to attract to engineering those students who are passionate about innovation, invention and entrepreneurship, and those who dream of devices that can change the world for the better. Just 4 percent of U.S. high-school graduates pursue engineering, compared to 10 percent in Canada, 15 percent in Germany and 25 percent in China. Only when the United States starts to generate a new pipeline of talented engineers and skilled production workers will the country regain its position at the forefront of innovation and high-tech manufacturing.

OBAMA ADMINISTRATION INITIATIVES IN ADVANCED MANUFACTURING

President Obama has publicly recognized the vital importance of manufacturing to America's economic future on several occasions, one of them being the announcement of the Advanced Manufacturing Partnership[35] in 2011. Manufacturing is the lead-off topic in "Blueprint for An America Built To Last,"[36] a White House document that encapsulates points made by the President in his 2012 State of the Union address. The administration, to its credit, is supporting a number of initiatives[37] promoting advanced manufacturing, technology transition, entrepreneurship and access to development capital. Among them are:

- An Advanced Manufacturing Partnership with a $1 billion proposed investment to establish a national network of Institutes for Manufacturing Innovation,[38] an idea put forward in PCAST's June 2011 report on advanced manufacturing.[39] These institutes will be public-private partnerships aimed at maturing technologies and manufacturing readiness, with each addressing pre-competitive applied research and encouraging the establishment of shared facilities. The institutes are modeled after Germany's Fraunhofer Institutes and will focus on product and process innovation. This is an important step in the right direction, coming after Washington had ignored the manufacturing sector for over a decade. A $35 million pilot institute specializing in additive manufacturing was created in Youngstown, Ohio, in August 2012;

- Investment in new Manufacturing Demonstration Facilities by the Advanced Manufacturing Office in the Office of Energy Efficiency & Renewable Energy at the Department of Energy (DOE);

- Investment by DARPA in new manufacturing initiatives aimed at reducing product-development time and cost (the latter by a factor of five);

- The National Robotics Initiative,[40] a multi-agency initiative funded by NASA, NSF, the National Institutes of Health and the Department of Agriculture whose goal is to develop a new generation of robots to work alongside humans.;

- Proof-of-concept centers, funded by NSF, to be located throughout the country with the aim of promoting translational research, entrepreneurship and the innovation ecosystem at American universities;

- NSF's Innovation Corps, a public-private partnership providing help from successful entrepreneurs and business leaders, in addition to funding, to researchers with the aim of transitioning ideas from basic research to the marketplace;

- The Economic Development Administration's i6-Challenge Grants, which have established over a dozen regional innovation clusters and proof-of-concept centers to promote technology-based economic development;

- More than 150 challenges inspired by X-Prize competitions, through which more than 40 federal agencies are seeking out citizen-innovators to solve societal challenges ranging from advancing vehicle designs to combating Type-2 diabetes and forecasting solar activity; and

- The Right Skills Now[41] program, whose goals include training 500,000 workers over five years in much-needed manufacturing skills like computer numerical control machining and welding. The endeavor is a partnership of the Obama administration's Jobs Council, the National Association of Manufacturers' Manufacturing Institute, the National Institute for Metalworking Skills and the Society of Manufacturing Engineers.

In addition, the Obama administration has pledged resources[42] and attention to enhancing the competitiveness of the country's small and medium-sized manufacturers (SMMs) by providing easy access to 21st-century digital design and manufacturing tools. America's nearly 300,000 SMMs form the backbone of its industrial economy, contributing more that 50 percent of the nation's manufacturing GDP and employment. SMMs provide the core supply-chain infrastructure that is critical to developing and scaling new technologies and manufacturing processes, and they are less likely than large manufacturers to move their operations offshore.

COORDINATED AND STRATEGIC INVESTMENTS IN U.S. MANUFACTURING R&D

Given the significance of the manufacturing sector to its economy and national security, it is critical that the United States establish a permanent office to develop and implement policies aimed at ensuring coordination of investments with the private sector. In 2010, the White House Office of Science and Technology Policy established an interagency Committee on Advanced Manufacturing under the auspices of the National Science and Technology Council, which released a report[43] in 2012 outlining a national strategy for advanced manufacturing. Aside from this recent effort, there is no formal coordination of manufacturing investment across the federal government, spending is widely diffused across agencies and even the definition of "manufacturing research" varies from program to program and agency to agency. Federal R&D investments in such areas as agriculture, defense, energy and health care are at least administered separately by agencies that are dedicated to those sectors – although no formal mechanisms are in place to coordinate and leverage the different agencies' research findings. Because manufacturing cuts across multiple sectors, from chemicals and energy to medical and transportation equipment, it is difficult to identify research synergies and to avoid duplicative activities. Yet because technological breakthroughs spill across multiple fields of manufacturing, coordination of R&D investment that could benefit manufacturing is all the more compelling.

In the current budget climate, it is especially important to leverage the resources and unique strengths of the many agencies whose activities may have a bearing on manufacturing in order to reduce overall costs and to ensure a pipeline for innovation.[44] In addition, a coordinated approach is essential to ensuring that a breakthrough emerging from one agency is handed over to the agency or agencies best suited to carrying it to the next phase of development. It was in spite of a lack of coordination across federal agencies that NSF-funded research eventually led to the development and commercialization of MRI machines, rapid-prototyping machines and Google.[45]

As an alternative, a non-mission-oriented agency like NSF might want to coordinate with the NIST and perhaps with a relevant mission agency like NASA, DOE or DOD on the development path for a scientific breakthrough arising from one of its grants. If the technology continued to show promise for scaling, early adoption might then be coordinated with a government procurement office. Only through a strategic and coordinated approach to R & D investment can the nation fully reap the benefits of its investment in basic research.

A PROPOSED NATIONAL INNOVATION FOUNDATION

Real innovation requires a marathon relay in which federal agencies hand off their best outcomes to one another while progressing toward the same finish line — rather than engaging in a 100-meter sprint in different directions. The United States needs a whole-government approach that leverages the strengths and missions of different agencies to ensure that the development of promising discoveries and inventions made here is not left to chance or passively allowed to take root elsewhere. America needs to innovate — not just invent — at home, aided by the collective focus of multiple government agencies on creating conditions that will help anchor the manufacturing of each successive "next big thing." This requires creation of a new agency, the National Innovation Foundation (NIF).

One way to create a NIF without increasing federal expenditures would be by consolidating various existing programs.[46] For instance, NSF's Engineering Directorate could serve to advance the basic-research component of advanced-manufacturing R & D entirely through open-solicitation and extramural research. The translational research component of a NIF — which would support public-private partnerships dedicated to pre-competitive R & D — could be created by melding appropriate elements of NIST, DOE's Advanced Manufacturing Office and some elements of the DOD Research & Engineering Enterprise, including the Manufacturing and Industrial Base Policy Office. A NIF should also include the Commerce Department's Trade Adjustment Assistance for Firms program and the Manufacturing Extension Partnership (MEP) Technical Assistance Program at NIST.[47]

FIGURE 14: *Establishing a National Innovation Foundation by Merging Various Existing Uncoordinated Federal Programs in Advanced Manufacturing.*

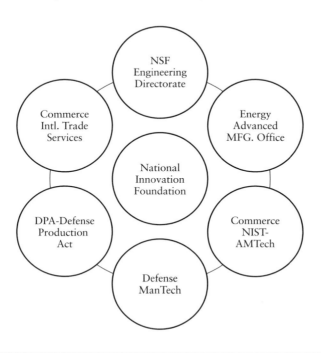

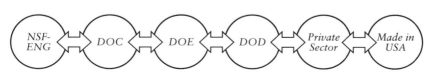

Basic Research	Precompetitive Translational R&D by NIF	Pre-Production/ Early Procurement	Scaling/ Manufacting
		Applied R&D by Mission Agencies & Private Sector	

Scientific Discovery	Engineering Inventions	Radical Innovation	Incremental Innovations	New Products/ Processes

The NIF should align its funding and programs under a strategic framework designed to advance specific goals, such as:

1. Enhancing the competitiveness of SMMs by democratizing the use of shared facilities, computational tools and access to emerging technologies;

2. Closing the innovation gap between basic science and manufacturing through a network of National Manufacturing Innovation Institutes[48] (as proposed in the Obama administration's budget for the fiscal year 2013);

3. Supporting translational research by transitioning to the marketplace scientific breakthroughs made by other agencies, including NSF, DOE, DOD, NASA and the Department of Agriculture;

4. Supporting engineering education at the K-12, community-college and university levels;

5. Establishing and disseminating best practices in product and process development[49] to the defense and non-defense industrial bases;

6. Accelerating innovation by supporting early adoption of emerging technologies for government procurement, both defense and non-defense;

7. Providing trade assistance to all industry sectors and ensuring a level playing field for U.S. manufacturers; and

8. Leveraging early procurement of emerging technologies by the DOD to accelerate innovation and to promote the development of advanced civilian technologies.

LEVERAGING GOVERNMENT PROCUREMENT

DOD purchases more than $200 billion in manufactured goods every year. There are about 30,000 American SMMs engaged in the U.S. defense supply chain, plus another 10,000 foreign suppliers, but DOD needs to make a concerted effort to expand its pool of domestic suppliers.[50]

DARPA, which is DOD's premier research agency, has funded many technological breakthroughs, the Internet and GPS among them.

No one familiar with DARPA should be surprised that it has developed other new technologies since, but it is not as clear how many of these inventions have been transitioned to the military services. Stronger coordination between emerging technologies and defense needs is necessary to transition and scale new advanced-technology products. It would be particularly troublesome, and perhaps strategically dangerous, if products based on technologies painstakingly developed with DARPA funding ended up being manufactured in other countries.[51]

Although ensuring economic security and manufacturing-job growth at home is understandably not its focus, the Pentagon could make a significant impact both on these and on U.S. technological innovation as well by linking technology development to defense procurement. This is not a new idea by any means; DOD has done it before to prop up the aircraft and semiconductor industries, among others. But there remains no formal coordination between the technology-development process and procurement needs.

CHALLENGES AND OPPORTUNITIES GOING FORWARD

Challenge 1: Legislation That Helps Anchor Advanced Manufacturing in the United States

Establishing a network of National Manufacturing Innovation Institutes along with a NIF as described above would be an important first step. But while such efforts could bridge the gap between basic research and manufacturing via coordinated technology development, there is still no guarantee that actual manufacturing of new products and processes resulting from new technologies would take root in America. Without legislation that strongly encourages domestic manufacturing while discouraging offshore manufacturing, U.S. investments in science will not benefit the nation's economic and national security.

Smart legislation offering concrete incentives for establishing new domestic manufacturing facilities and equally concrete disincentives to locating overseas could go far toward ensuring U.S. taxpayers a return on the extensive investments they have made in technology development.

Among the incentives that might be used to help anchor manufacturing in the United States are loan guarantees and a policy of early adoption by the public sector of technologies matured through federally funded programs and public-private partnerships. In cases where firms prefer to manufacture outside the country, they could do so only if they returned to U.S. taxpayers a certain percentage of the profits gained from the offshore manufacture of systems or components employing government-funded technologies or their derivatives.

Challenge 2: Revitalizing American Ingenuity with a Focus on Rebuilding an Engineering Economy

To regain its comparative advantage in high-technology products and rebuild the highly productive and highly skilled workforce that turned them out, America must rebrand engineering, promote the "E" in STEM education at the K-12 level, restore the balance between theory and practice in higher-level engineering education and establish a single, strong voice for engineering in the sphere of public policy.

Rebranding Engineering — It is critically important to reestablish engineering as a creative discipline that contributes huge value to American society. Universities, primary and secondary schools, the private sector and federal agencies should all promote the marvels of engineering culture through easy-to-understand media so as to engage and inspire citizens of all ages.

Promoting Early Engineering Education — Stellar programs like FIRST Robotics and Project Lead The Way, along with the Maker Faires, can play a major role in transforming engineering into something that is engaging and inspiring to kids. It is important to mainstream such activities by including engineering courses in K-12 education. In addition, the private sector should offer manufacturing internships to high-school students and paid apprenticeships to students in community and four-year colleges. Doing this would inspire youth toward more broad-based careers in engineering and serve as a recruitment tool for sponsoring companies. Since many students exposed to engineering through summer camps subsequently consider a career in engineering, engineering societies and universities should actively engage in administering and scaling up such camp experiences.

Striking a Balance Between Theory and Practice — The private sector, nonprofit foundations, universities and other organizations have outstanding programs in place to promote innovation and entrepreneurship and to nurture a pipeline of skilled workers at all levels. Their best practices must be embraced and scaled up to make them effective nationwide. Among these programs' sponsors are:

- The Deshpande Center for Technological Innovation at MIT, which has awarded grants since 2002 to fund proof-of-concept exploration and validation for emerging technologies. Successful projects from the center have attracted hundreds of millions of dollars in additional investment;

- Stanford University, the University of California at Berkeley, Georgia Tech, the University of Michigan and other schools, which have launched successful programs dovetailing hands-on projects with courses in preparing business plans and entrepreneurship;

- Olin College, which focuses on engineering as a creative discipline and prepares students to be innovators. Twenty-five percent of its graduates are now involved in start-up entrepreneurial enterprises; and

- Kettering University in Flint, Mich., which has had nearly 100 years of experience balancing classroom learning with industrial internships for all of its engineering graduates. With over 600 industrial relationships, Kettering rotates about 1,000 engineering students to industry every semester.

More universities should focus on restoring the balance between theory and practice and on promoting hands-on engineering and entrepreneurship projects that keep that balance.

Public Policy — Public policy significantly impacts everyday life and economic well-being because it sets societal goals and determines the resources that will be allocated to achieving them. For more than a century, the U.S. federal government has played an instrumental role not only in seeding and developing technologies, but also in bringing them to market. From railroad and aerospace development to computers, the Internet and GPS, public investments have provided critical support for basic and applied research. The government has helped establish shared facilities for conducting cutting-edge research and has served as an early adopter of new technologies so as to help the private sector hone manufacturing processes before entering commercial markets.

It is therefore important for the engineering community to educate the public at large and policy makers in particular about the significance of engineering in technology development and the urgency of investing in the intellectual and physical infrastructure America needs to regain its comparative advantage. Unfortunately, there is no single voice representing the field of engineering, a discipline that has a crucial role to play in closing the nation's innovation gap. Instead, there are 32 different engineering societies, each representing a specific sub-discipline. Although the American Society of Mechanical Engineers has a long track record of leadership in public policy, it is important for the engineering community at large to present a unified, strong and effective voice[52] that can influence public policy and engage the public imagination.

CONCLUSION

Being the world's best in scientific discovery is still vital to America's success, but it is no longer sufficient for maintaining competitiveness in the global economy. The United States must close its innovation gap by:

- investing in translational research in a strategic and coordinated way through a new National Innovation Foundation;

- implementing policies that help anchor manufacturing of advanced-technology products at home; and

- focusing on research and education in real-world engineering.

It is critically important that both policy makers and citizens understand the importance of investing in engineering to confront the challenges that face the nation. The United States' economy must remain vibrant, diverse and flexible in a world that continues to challenge it to be great, helpful and strong. A new, engineering-friendly economy that values both research and development can become the basis for American prosperity. And Americans need to rediscover the value of their birthright as pioneers and inventors of the future, as the world is in need of both.

1.   *Rising Above the Gathering Storm, Revisited: Rapidly Approaching Category 5*, The National Academies Press, Washington, D.C., 2010.

2.   White House Domestic Policy Council and Office of Science and Technology Policy, *American Competitiveness Initiative — Leading the World in Innovation*, February 2006.

3.   The U.S. Census Bureau explains its definition of Advanced Technology Products as follows: "About 500 of some 22,000 commodity classification codes used in reporting U.S. merchandise trade are identified as 'advanced technology' codes and they meet the following criteria:

   • The code contains products whose technology is from a recognized high technology field (e.g. biotechnology).
   • These products represent leading edge technology in that field.
   • Such products constitute a significant part of all items covered in the selected classification code.

   "This product and commodity-based measure of advanced technology differs from broader NAICS industry-based measures which include all goods produced by a particular industry group, regardless of the level of technology embodied in the goods. ATP classifications are assigned by the Foreign Trade Division of the U.S. Census Bureau." https://www.census.gov/foreign-trade/reference/definitions/index.html.

4.   United States Census Bureau, "Trade in Goods with Advance [sic] Technology Products," http://www.census.gov/foreign-trade/balance/c0007.html#1989.

5.   Charles McMillion, "'Made In The World' Data Initiative Is A Made-Up Hoax," *Manufacturing & Technology News*, October 21, 2011.

6.   Gary Pisano and Willy Shih, "Restoring American Competitiveness," *Harvard Business Review*, July-August 2009.

7.   Federal Reserve Bank of St. Louis, "Percent of Employment in Manufacturing in Germany," June 8, 2012, http://research.stlouisfed.org/fred2/series/DEUPEFANA.

8.   Federal Reserve Bank of St. Louis, "Percent of Employment in Manufacturing in Japan," June 8, 2012, http://research.stlouisfed.org/fred2/series/JPNPEFANA.

9.   The manufacturing sector still accounts for two-thirds of America's R&D, employing about 64 percent of its scientists and engineers.

10. Gary Pisano and Willy Shih, *Producing Prosperity: Why America Needs a Manufacturing Renaissance*, Harvard Business Review Press, 2012.

11. Stephen Ezell and Robert Atkinson, "The Case for a National Manufacturing Strategy," The Information Technology and Innovation Foundation, Washington, D.C., April 2011.

12. Gregory Tassey, "Beyond the business cycle: The need for a technology-based growth strategy," *Science and Public Policy*, December 19, 2012.

13. Susan Houseman "Offshoring and Import Price Measurement," February 2011 (http://research.upjohn.org/jrnlarticles/152/); Houseman, Paul Lengermann, Christopher Kurz, Benjamin Mandel, "Offshoring Bias in U.S. Manufacturing," 2011 (http://research.upjohn.org/jrnlarticles/155/) and "The Debate Over the State of U.S. Manufacturing: How the Computer Industry Affects the Numbers and Perceptions," 2012 (http://research.upjohn.org/empl_research/vol19/iss3/1/).

14. Susan Helper, Timothy Krueger, Howard Wial, "Why Does Manufacturing Matter? Which Manufacturing Matters? – A policy Framework," Brookings Metropolitan Policy Program Report, February 2012.

15. Henry Petroski, *The Essential Engineer: Why Science Alone Will Not Solve Our Global Problems*, Knopf, 2010.

16. In fact, the National Science Foundation's Engineering Directorate showcases "engineering discoveries" but not engineering inventions. Many engineering-research organizations and programs have even added the word "science" to their titles to garner prestige. Purpose-driven engineering R&D, the culture of engineering, and even the term "engineering" are slowly disappearing from the U.S. science and technology lexicon.

17. Stephen Merrill, "A Perpetual Imbalance – Federal Funding of Physical Sciences and Engineering Research," *Issues in Science and Technology*, Winter 2013.

18. http://www.fraunhofer.de/EN/institutes/index.jsp.

19. http://www.epsrc.ac.uk/ResearchFunding/Programmes/BetterExploitation/IMRCs/default.htm.

20. http://europa.eu/scadplus/leg/en/lvb/n26104.htm.

21. OECD Reviews of Innovation Policy: China (2009) http://www.oecd.org/document/44/0,3343, en_2649_34273_41204780_1_1_1,00.html.

22. "Report to the President on Ensuring American Leadership in Advanced Manufacturing," Executive Office of the President, President's Council of Advisors on Science and Technology, June 2011, http://www.whitehouse.gov/sites/default/files/microsites/ostp/pcast-advanced-manufacturing-june2011.pdf.

23. http://www.whitehouse.gov/the-press-office/2012/03/09/president-obama-announce-new-efforts-support-manufacturing-innovation-en.

24. Jesse Eisenger, "Challenging the Long-Held Belief in 'Shareholder Value,'" *New York Times*, July 27, 2012, quoting Lynn Stout's book *The Shareholder Value Myth: How Putting Shareholders First Harms Investors, Corporations and the Public*, Barrett-Koehler Publishers, May 2012.

25. It should be noted, however, that "radical" or "disruptive" innovation did not cease in the United States with the demise of the big corporate laboratory. Rather, it has become the province of the startup company. Typically the outgrowth of basic research, disruptive technologies can be risky technically, require a good deal of time and resources to develop and often ultimately fail to make it into a lucrative market. Although larger firms typically shy away from initial investment in disruptive technologies because of the risk involved and the possibility that they will be unable to capture all the benefits for themselves, they often get access to game-changing technologies by acquiring the startups that developed them. Still, a large firm may need to invest significantly to insert an acquired technology into its products or processes before it can bring them to the marketplace.

26. From a pure research and scientific discovery point of view, the U.S. is still ahead of most (if not all) other countries.

27. For a history of the organization, see *60 Years of Fraunhofer-Gesellschaft*, Munich: Fraunhofer-Gesellschaft, 2009. The publication can be accessed at http://www.germaninnovation.org/shared/content/documents/60YearsofFraunhoferGesellschaft.pdf.

28. Presentation by Roland Schindler, executive director of Fraunhofer, in *Meeting Global Challenges: U.S.-German Innovation Policy*.

29. Explanations of these are examples are found in the Fraunhofer-Gesellschaft 2009 annual report.

30. Mary Bellis, "The History of MP3," *About.com,* (http://inventors.about.com/od/mstartinventions/a/MPThree.htm).

31. Senate Armed Services Committee, "Inquiry Into Counterfeit Electronic Parts in the Department of Defense Supply Chain," May 21, 2012, http://www.armed-services.senate.gov/Publications/Counterfeit%20Electronic%20Parts.pdf.

32. Clayton Christensen, *The Innovator's Dilemma: When New Technologies Cause Great Firms to Fail,* Harvard Business Review Press, 1997.

33. Andrew Hacker and Claudia Dreifus, "The Trouble with Going Global," *Newsweek.com*, Sept. 20, 2010.

34. Ralph Gomory, "The Innovation Delusion," *Huffington Post*, March 1, 2010, http://www.huffingtonpost.com/ralph-gomory/the-innovation-delusion_b_480794.html.

35. http://www.whitehouse.gov/the-press-office/2011/06/24/president-obama-launches-advanced-manufacturing-partnership.

36. http://www.whitehouse.gov/sites/default/files/blueprint_for_an_america_built_to_last.pdf.

37. http://www.whitehouse.gov/blog/2012/04/30/made-america-helping-revitalize-us-manufacturing.

38. http://www.whitehouse.gov/sites/default/files/microsites/ostp/adv_man_press_release_final.pdf.
     http://www.whitehouse.gov/the-press-office/2011/06/24/president-obama-launches-advanced-manufacturing-partnershipXXX.

39. See fn 22, supra.

40. http://www.whitehouse.gov/blog/2011/06/24/developing-next-generation-robots.

41. http://www.whitehouse.gov/the-press-office/2011/06/08/president-obama-and-skills-americas-future-partners-announce-initiatives.

42. http://www.whitehouse.gov/blog/2012/02/15/progress-report-modeling-simulation-economy.

43. http://www.whitehouse.gov/sites/default/files/microsites/ostp/iam_advancedmanufacturing_strategicplan_2012.pdf.

44. Additionally, budget strains make establishing a clear correlation between research outcomes and the creation of private-sector jobs in the United States essential to justifying continued funding of federal agencies and labs.

45. Identifying cross-sector applications is generally up to the individual investigator, who must then have the motivation and entrepreneurial spirit to push development. That most programs shy away from funding translational R&D makes success particularly elusive.

46. Robert Atkinson of the Information Technology Innovation Foundation and Howard Wial of Brookings Institution proposed the formation of a National Innovation Foundation within the Department of Commerce to catalyze industry-university partnerships that would promote technology commercialization and entrepreneurship.

47. MEP attempts to enhance competitiveness of SMMs by helping them implement established best practices such as lean manufacturing but is not typically involved in the process of technological innovation.

48. http://www.manufacturingnews.com/news/national-network-for-manufacturing-innovation-228112.html.

49. This would go far beyond the scope of what MEP does with lean-manufacturing principles and Six Sigma.

50. http://www.whitehouse.gov/blog/2011/12/21/tech-initiatives-build-it-here-sell-it-everywhere.
     http://www.manufacturing.net/articles/2012/11/transforming-the-relationship-between-manufacturers-and-the-dod.

51. Besides, even a commodity product such as a printed-circuit board or something as mundane as a fastener could be designed and manufactured to bring down an aircraft or disable a tank. Such commercial off-the-shelf items are not considered high tech, but trusted sources are critical to the defense supply chain.

52. In this, it could look to the American Association for the Advancement of Science as an example.

CHAPTER 5

Energy Manufacturing: The Linchpin For America's Future

Carl Pope
Energy

INTRODUCTION

"I shot Solyndra, but I didn't shoot no 'conomy.
I shot Solyndra, but I swear it was in self-defense."

That paraphrase of the late Bob Marley's famous lyric has been the defense of the fossil-fuel lobby and its conservative allies since they began plotting to turn a lynch mob loose on whichever company became the first to default on a federal energy loan guarantee — and, thereby, on a burgeoning revival of American energy manufacturing. "We of course want clean-energy manufacturing in the U.S.," the Big Carbon posse swears. "We simply don't want the federal government to pick winners and losers."

That is not the truth. Fossil-fuel interests want to stop clean energy because it interferes with their monopoly profits. Conservatives want to stop clean energy because those same fossil-fuel interests finance their campaigns. Koch Industries Inc. and its allies have managed to kill some key federal programs that aimed to level the financial playing field for clean-energy manufacturing in the United States. They continue these efforts, complaining that not even a "No More Solyndras Act" pending in Congress would bring a halt to renewable-energy-manufacturing projects in the pipeline.[1] In the first of the three Presidential debates held in October 2012, one of the significant moments was Republican nominee Mitt Romney's attack on President Obama's support for clean-energy manufacturing. In the second debate Romney declared, "I will fight for oil, coal and natural gas."

The United States is in the midst of an enormous political struggle between incumbent fossil-fuel-energy monopolies left over from the 1930s and an innovative, disruptive set of clean-energy technologies coming out of the space program of the 1970s and the Internet of the 1980s.

It is fair to say that America's destiny depends on getting on the right side of history: the side of energy innovation. This is not only vital for the global climate, it's also the key to both national security and economic recovery. But the United States is not united on this issue, not by a long shot.

Fortunately, the odds are that even the successful destruction of the Department of Energy (DOE) loan-guarantee and finance programs for clean energy would not stop American manufacturers. Manufacturing is coming back, and it's going to be driven by clean energy. The underlying economics of innovation are just too good, and the public desire for a new way of powering the economy is too strong.

THE DILEMMA:
IT'S NOT WAGES — IT'S EVERYTHING ELSE

I began my personal journey into energy manufacturing at the headquarters of Bloom Energy, a Silicon Valley start-up that produces a solid-oxide fuel cell called the Bloom Box. Fuel-agnostic in that they can utilize biomass or natural gas, Bloom Boxes are radically cleaner than conventional electricity generators because they don't burn their fuel, they convert it to power chemically. But their main advantage is reliability. Twenty percent of America's power is currently backed up with stand-by generators because of users' fears that the electrical grid is not sufficiently reliable.

The Bloom Box, comprising thousands of small fuel cells, is the perfect power source for a data center, hospital or any other facility for which blackouts are simply not an option.

After a tour of Bloom Energy, I sat down with company CEO K.R. Sridhar. A former NASA scientist whose job there was to convert solar energy into biomass and water on Mars, Sridhar decided to run those processes in reverse and use them to produce clean energy back on Earth. He started our conversation by commenting, "I'd love to make this product in America. But I'm afraid I won't be able to."

"Wages?" I sadly asked.

His dark eyebrows arched as if I were clueless. "Wages have nothing to do with it. The total wage burden in a fab [semiconductor fabrication factory] is 10 percent. When I move a fab to Asia, I might lose 10 percent of my product just in theft."

I was startled. "So what is it?"

"Everything else: taxes, infrastructure, workforce training, permits, healthcare. The last company that proposed a fab on Long Island went to Taiwan because they were told that in a drought their water supply would be in the queue after the golf courses. Have you read Andy Grove's piece?"[2]

In a commentary published in *Bloomberg Businessweek*, former Intel CEO Andy Grove notes that the U.S. economy will not survive if high-tech outsources its manufacturing to China. "What kind of society are we going to have if it consists of highly paid people doing high-value-added work — and masses of unemployed?" Grove asks.

Right off the bat, I learned why the hollowing out of the American economy and the loss of manufacturing preeminence — the most important economic story of our era — ought to carry the tag line, "It's not wages, stupid."

WHY THE U.S. ENERGY MANUFACTURING SECTOR STAGNATED — AND WHAT'S CHANGING

It's a stark fact that in 2001, when a cell-phone call from San Francisco to Mumbai involved no equipment or technology more than a decade old, my office in the United States was powered by electrons generated by a Khrushchev-era nuclear power plant, transmitted through mechanical switches dating to the Truman administration and then largely turned into waste heat by light bulbs whose basic design hadn't changed since tungsten became the filament of Edison's choice in 1906.

The energy sector has long lagged behind the rest of the U.S. economy in innovation. It's not that energy and related sectors somehow failed to attract creative minds — think Edison, Ford and the Wright brothers. Many of the great names in innovation pioneered one or another of today's key energy technologies. And at the upstream end of energy — resource extraction — innovation roars along at a stunning pace: Whatever the wisdom and prudence of drilling for oil two miles beneath the Gulf of Mexico, the technology BP deployed was absolutely cutting edge. Similarly, the shale-gas revolution that has transformed America's natural-gas landscape is driven by radically new technologies that enable drillers to track for 10 miles a very thin layer of hydrocarbon-bearing shale, such as the Bakken formation in North Dakota, which is never more than 140 feet thick.

Henry Ford envisioned powering the economy with the sun. It took a while, but in the last 20 years American engineering and science have made both wind and solar power the electricity sources whose prices are falling the fastest, to the point that wind turbines are now cheaper than new coal power by a large margin.

So the problems don't lie with inventors, scientists or engineers, or with the fundamental difficulty of the science of energy innovation. Except on the extreme frontiers, such as fusion, energy lends itself to being reinvented every bit as much as Alexander Graham Bell's telephone, William Shockley's transistor or Watson and Crick's twisted helix, which led to the modern biotech industry.

The reason that change in the energy sector has been so sluggish lies not in the laboratory, but in the influence of an archaic legislative and regulatory framework combined with that of the financial community, which together shape the intersection between energy producers and consumers. The United States holds onto policy and financial approaches to energy that emerged in the 1920s, when both electrification and automobiles first swept the nation. In 1920, fuels were abundant, pollution seemed costless and information was scarce and expensive. The United States was a newly industrializing, fossil-fuel powerhouse — much like Venezuela is today.

The major risk then facing energy producers was volatility, and the major concern of consumers was reliability. Electricity by its nature could not be stored, and demand fluctuated whenever a light went on or off. Wildcatting was the dominant form of searching for crude, and boom-and-bust cycles swept through each new oil patch.

Electrons and oil were excruciatingly dependent on the networks that connected customers. Transmission lines and highways were more expensive than electrons or gasoline. Both lent themselves to some form of monopoly. So the great regulatory bargains were struck, but only after more rough-and-tumble free-market approaches had been tried. The volatility of oil prices in Texas led to the gradual expansion of the powers of the Texas Railroad Commission, culminating in its 1927 regulations limiting production. And the collapse of Samuel Insull's utility empire led to the passage of the Federal Power Act. Reining in market forces was accepted as the price of diminishing the volatility of energy prices and increasing the reliability of energy supplies.

Electric companies would either be publicly owned or would be granted geographic monopolies. In both cases, the major job was to recover the cost of building the power plants and transmission grid that generated power from water or coal and enabled it to reach homes or factories. Fuel costs were passed on to customers as they fluctuated, but competition was ruled out for fear of creating too much risk. The generating companies took responsibility for reliability and, in exchange, were protected from market competition.

The new petroleum-based transportation technologies got an even bigger public subsidy. The roads themselves were planned, built and maintained by government, a sharp contrast to the 19th century railroads. Drivers paid for some of this through fuel taxes, but mostly the first generation of roads was paid for like schools — with general revenues. The oil industry was protected from competition by the creation of the Standard Oil cartel and, when antitrust action broke that apart, by the regulatory umbrella erected by the Texas Railroad Commission, as well as by highly favorable federal tax structures.

Because neither electricity nor transportation was structured as an open, competitive market, the major players — utilities and oil companies — had no trouble raising capital — and energy was, and is, very capital intensive. But this combination of sheltering cartel producers under an umbrella of government protection with granting them access to exceptionally cheap capital turned out to have an unintended and, ultimately, almost-lethal side effect: Innovation was frozen out of power and roads, the down-stream core of the energy sector.

Before 1920 both electric and steam-powered cars were viewed as highly competitive, but once the government built the roads, the oil and automobile industries entered into an effective partnership. Other forms of fuel vanished from the nation's publicly built roads, and the pipelines and service stations erected to provide fuel where and when drivers needed it were under the control of companies whose main assets, in addition to their reserves of petroleum, resided in their ability to explore for and refine it.

Similarly, the power companies were compensated in their rate bases for the value of their power plants and transmission lines, not for the efficiency or cost of the services they provided. So, today, half of America's coal-fired power plants are more than 30 years old, and some have been operating since Warren Harding was president.

The result has been that America's energy policies and regulatory structures, coming out of the 1920s and 1930s, locked its energy sector into a set of technologies appropriate for an era of cheap fuel and cost-free pollution. These policies have been utterly unsuited to the economy as it has matured; as abundant, cheap oil and coal have been exhausted; as pollution has become a significant and, with climate change, an existential threat; and as information technology has become the economy's dominant driver.

As solar and wind-based technologies became the cutting-edge sources for the production of electricity, and as other energy-efficient technologies were developed for transportation, America's energy sector allowed those technologies to be deployed and dominated by foreign competitors: advanced vehicles by the Japanese, wind by the Europeans and solar by the Chinese.

Energy isn't like most highly competitive industries, General Electric CEO Jeffrey Immelt has observed. It's sluggish. "We still," he has said, "sell some products in the energy sector that sold 25 years ago."[3]

WHY NIXON AND CARTER FAILED TO CHANGE THIS — AND WHY SILICON VALLEY CAN SUCCEED

Largely because of security issues and the economic impact of importing oil, American presidents have periodically tried to break out of the energy policy they inherited from the 1920s with its bias in favor of incumbent technologies and companies and its resistance to innovation.

Richard Nixon tried to do this in the wake of the first energy embargo and crisis, and Jimmy Carter made it the centerpiece of his term after the Iranian oil shock. In both cases, incremental and isolated policies were put in place. Nixon saw to the establishment of auto fuel-economy standards that for a number of years did drive down America's dependence on imported oil. Carter secured investment in research and technology, which led eventually to the wind and solar revolutions.

But neither president ultimately transformed the overall pace of innovation in the energy sector. Both left in place the regulatory structures that created and defended energy cartels, and neither created any incentive structure for ongoing, permanent acceleration of the turnover of energy capital stocks and infrastructure.

Starting in 1980, however, other previously stultified sectors of the economy entered a drastic innovation cycle, most spectacularly telecommunications with the abolition of the Bell System monopoly. So too did information processing with the emergence of the Internet, and biotechnology in the aftermath of the development of recombinant DNA technology. Innovation cycles emerged from a combination of technology developed by the federal government with new, decentralized financing structures grounded in venture capital and initial public offerings.

With the emergence of concern about climate change and sustainability, the high-tech community looked around and identified energy as the new opportunity — as big as telecommunications, information processing and biotech combined. The energy sector was stagnant: Its monopoly structures made AT&T look nimble. And the basic science for the disruptive technologies needed to displace the fossil-fuel incumbents had already been developed, thanks in part to the legacy left by Nixon and Carter.

High tech became clean tech. Silicon Valley powerhouses like venture capitalist Vinod Khosla shifted their investment focus to biofuels and other substitutes for fossil energy. Companies like Google, whose core competence had nothing to do with electricity but which were large consumers of it, set up projects aimed at transforming energy by making renewable power cheaper than coal (RE<C). New investment firms and units within existing private-equity players began developing technologies and business models designed to disrupt the monopolies enjoyed by energy companies.

The early clean-tech investors were right about some things. Energy was big, it was stagnant and it was vulnerable to disruption by new technologies. But they underestimated two challenges: energy was very capital intensive, and U.S. capital markets had not been structured to meet the needs of an innovative energy sector. Most important, the energy incumbents were not about to give their monopoly position up without a fight. Inside the halls of Congress and state public service commissions, the fossil-fuel cartels held much higher cards than Silicon Valley had been able to draw.

The collapse of capital markets in 2008 made it far more difficult for Clean Tech to challenge Big Carbon, and the challenge might have become overwhelmingly difficult had not events in the larger world begun making the emergence of a new energy model unavoidable. Yes, driving that inevitability is climate change, but even more so is the force that drove Nixon to play the role of transportation disrupter back in 1973: the price of oil.

WHAT IT TAKES TO MAKE IT IN AMERICA

It's a common mistake to think of manufacturing as somehow separate from innovation upstream and markets downstream. As a couple of recent U.S. examples show, the energy supply chain is an integrated one, and manufacturing rests on strong support for both innovation and open markets.

Applied Materials: The Tragedy of the Road Not Taken

Applied Materials is a Silicon Valley manufacturing powerhouse. But it doesn't specialize in making microprocessors, silicon chips and solar cells — it makes the factories that produce all of those high-tech products. With the Great Recession and the 2008 election of President Obama, Mike Splinter, Applied's CEO, saw an opportunity. In the winter of 2008, a lot of comparisons of the country's current predicament to what it faced at the advent of the New Deal were floating around, and Splinter saw a modern opening to do what Franklin Roosevelt had done with the federal power projects from Grand Coulee Dam to the Tennessee Valley Authority and the rural electric cooperatives.

Splinter identified a series of federal properties that had been contaminated with toxic waste, mostly the result of the government's own investments in nuclear energy. These nuclear weapons reservations were no longer needed for their original purposes but could not be used for homes and businesses. They were either a liability or, as Splinter saw it, a hidden asset. Because these facilities had used so much electricity, each of these properties was located on federal transmission lines. Splinter proposed to the Obama transition team that the government lease these reservations as solar farms and purchase the power they generated for the various government facilities and co-ops that buy power from Uncle Sam.

Splinter in turn would build at each nuclear reservation a factory to manufacture solar panels for that location. That would give his factories initial customers. The American economy would get not only the solar power, but also the solar manufacturing capacity and, when the federal solar farms were finished, the solar-cell factories could sell their production to private power projects.

The key was combining the access to wasteland, good electrical transmission facilities and an agreement by federal power administrations to buy the power. Such an arrangement would have made it possible for Applied Materials to raise the capital needed to build the solar-panel manufacturing plants.

The idea never gained traction within the short-handed Obama transition team. It's not clear why. But while the Obama administration was trying to get going, another player was already in gear. The government of China had decided to gain a worldwide monopoly in photovoltaic technology, and it was eventually to commit about $30 billion in cheap capital, plus low-cost land and other incentives, to bring companies like Applied and their technological capacity to its shores. Splinter went looking for customers and finance, and he found them in Beijing.

Today, Applied has relocated most of its manufacturing and much of its engineering capability to Asia because Asia is where the markets and finance are.

In and Out of Duluth? Growing Supply Chains

In 2008, I picked up a good news/bad news story in the local paper in Duluth, Minn. The good news was that the major growth in revenue for the Port of Duluth was coming from importing wind turbines. The port was also doing a brisk business exporting taconite iron ore to places where those wind turbines were made. The bad news was that instead of the taconite being made into steel for wind turbines in steel mills in Chicago, Gary, Detroit, Cleveland, Erie and Buffalo — all ports the freighters pass — it was going to China. The other bad news was that the turbines themselves were being imported from Europe.

But in the summer of 2012, while I was in Brazil, some much better news appeared: Brazil was importing hundreds of wind-turbine blades on freighters from Duluth. Demand for wind power on America's Great Plains had grown so much that Denmark-based LM Wind Power had built a turbine-blade factory in Grand Forks, N.D., and the nearby port of Duluth on the westernmost point of Lake Superior was exporting not only taconite, but turbine blades. The fact that the Grand Forks blades have found an export market is proof again that manufacturing follows markets and that if the United States keeps building demand for energy-innovation products, the country can build a mighty manufacturing economy to serve those markets.

Indeed, in the five years since I was in Duluth, the share of the U.S. wind supply chain that is domestic has doubled — from 25 percent to more than 50 percent.[4]

Both the Applied Materials story and the LM Wind Power turbine-manufacturing plant illustrate a basic and important principle: Manufacturing follows markets. As Intel founder Andy Grove eloquently wrote in his seminal article "How to Create an American Job Before It's Too Late,"[5] innovation follows manufacturing. The two go together as a package.

Here the United States has some natural advantages and some disadvantages. A laid-off steelworker in Canton, Ohio, told me in 2006 that if the United States was going to rely on wind power, then it was going to make it here, because here — offshore on Lake Erie — was where the wind blew. Indeed, the wind-energy manufacturing supply chain has grown right along with the market.

Similarly, the sun in California or New Mexico is not going to be outsourced to Shanghai or Frankfurt. And, in the last few years, the United States has gained a unique competitive edge in its supply of unconventional shale gas.

On the other hand, the biggest chunk of the U.S. energy bill is for oil. And here, in spite of new sources like the Bakken, the country is poorly positioned. It uses about 20 percent of the world's oil and holds only 3 to 4 percent of its reserves. So anything the United States can do to reduce its reliance on oil is going to help its position for energy manufacturing leadership because the country can do better in every other fuel source.

Again with apologies to a talented singer, this time Tina Turner, let's consider this question:

WHAT'S OIL GOT TO DO WITH IT?
WHAT'S OIL BUT A SECOND-HAND DISTRACTION?

The slogan "energy independence" brings out the worst in American politics. Presidents since Nixon have insincerely promised to achieve it and have then done nothing. The oil companies proclaim, falsely, that they can achieve it by having the government give them more subsidies and free rein to drill on public lands while polluting the air and water. "Free market" advocates like the Cato Institute correctly point out that oil prices are set at the global level and that the question of how much oil the United States produces versus how much it imports has little to do with those prices. But they leave unmentioned the reality that what does drive prices is the demand for oil, over which the United States exercises real leverage.

The worst habit of all, however, is focusing on barrels of oil rather than on billions of dollars. In 2003, the United States imported 9.1 million barrels of oil a day at a cost of $29 per barrel. In 2011, imports of oil were down to 8.9 million barrels per day, only a 3 percent decline, but the average price was $111 a barrel. Was the country making progress towards energy independence as the import bill soared from $96 billion to $360 billion?

Surely not. The difference between the two numbers — $264 billion — is two-and-a-half times the full cost of the Bush tax cuts. This comes to more than half of the total U.S. trade deficit and would pay for almost half of the country's military budget, even leaving aside the fact that another quarter of the military budget is devoted to protecting the supply of this imported oil.

The price of oil was not so volatile in the past. Before October 2003 prices stayed comfortably below $30 per barrel, and increases in global demand caused them to creep — not leap — upward. But in October 2003 global demand rose above 80 million barrels a day, and producers of cheap Persian Gulf oil reached their peak capacity. With that, prices took off almost vertically with demand. An increase of even 1 million barrels per day in global demand jumps the price of oil a full $7 to 11. Global consumption has now gone from 80 million to 90 million barrels per day, with a rise in the price of a barrel from $30 to $110 or even higher. In July 2008 oil was at one point selling at an absurd $145 per barrel.

And every time the price of oil goes above $90, the global economy begins to splutter.

The problem of expensive oil can't be solved by exploring for more oil. New and affordable sources like the Bakken are good for the economy, but there are not enough of them to bring down the price. Reserves like the Canadian tar sands, the remote Arctic or the ultra-deep ocean may be abundant, but they make economic sense only as long as oil is above $80 — precisely the level the U.S. economy cannot afford. Importing oil from Canada may seem safer than relying on the Persian Gulf or Africa, but the economic drain on the U.S. economy is identical.

As for the security risk, well, if someone blew up an oil pipeline in the depths of an Alberta or Alaska winter, hundreds of miles of crude oil would turn into the world's longest ChapStick, as Amory Lovins has pointed out. Based on how long it took to cap the BP blowout in the Gulf of Mexico in 2010, it appears the U.S. could clear the Straits of Hormuz and defeat the Iranian navy much faster than it could restore an Arctic pipeline.

Building an All-American Transportation System

There is a solution to the price of oil. It is to be found on the factory floor, not in the oil field. It lies in building an all-American transportation system, rather than continuing to rely on oil. If the world simply keeps demand for oil down below 85 million barrels per day, global needs can be met by pumping cheap reserves like those in the Middle East or the Bakken shale. Prices will drop accordingly. And as the world's largest consumer of oil, the United States can do a lot to reduce demand for oil while manufacturing the new transportation technologies that the rest of the world will need to curb its own oil addiction.

Start with railroads. The American freight rail system is the best in the world and the most efficient. Rail freight now gets 415 ton miles to the gallon, which represents two-and-a-half times the fuel efficiency of a diesel truck. So if the United States can shift only 10 percent of its current truck traffic onto rail, it will save 250,000 barrels of oil a day.[6]

If rail is cheaper and if shippers prefer it, why do they use trucks instead? Well, a potato grower in Maine might be delighted to ship his spuds to Washington, D.C., by rail, but he can get them only as far as Boston's North Station on a train. Then — whoops! — they must be off-loaded onto a truck and carried through the streets of Boston to South Station, as there is no freight rail link across the city. So the potatoes go all the way by truck, using more expensive imported oil.

In Missouri, work has just begun to eliminate another major rail bottle-neck, the Osage River Bridge.[7] But scores of similar projects remain on the drawing boards.

Imagine the orders that would pour into American manufacturers if U.S. railroads entered an era of massive investment, eliminating bottlenecks like the Boston gap, grade-separating overloaded corridors like the Elgin, Joliet and Eastern around Chicago and updating infrastructure like the Osage River Bridge. Not only would the steel and cement for the expansions and upgrades revitalize American factories, but also the increased volume of rail traffic would mean orders for locomotives, freight cars and switching equipment. If the country took the next step and electrified the rail system to reduce its dependence on diesel fuel, enormous orders for wires, pylons, transformers and substations would fatten the order books of American manufacturers and position them to supply global markets.

Nor is freight the only opportunity the United States has to electrify trans-portation and thereby drive down the volume of oil the country imports and, with it, the high price of imported oil — which is an economic drag itself. A new generation of Americans is making it clear that it wants a much richer menu of personal transportation choices than simply which brand of SUV to buy. San Diego, Denver and Salt Lake City have found that providing urban light rail is the key to reducing traffic congestion and increasing property values. Again, if the United States is a reliable market for the makers of light-rail vehicles and systems, then that is exactly where they will be manufactured.

How to Finance Transportation Innovation

The key policy intervention regards the cost of capital. Investments in freight or passenger rail are good business choices if there is access to capital. For the last four years, the federal government has been deadlocked over how to finance basic improvements in transportation infrastructure that business, labor and both political parties all agree are desperately needed. The federal gasoline tax isn't large enough anymore to pay for even the roads that are needed, much less rail and other alternatives. Conservatives don't want to increase the tax because they dislike taxes and their financial backers in the oil industry are none too keen. The Obama administration has estimated a need of an additional $50 billion a year for 10 years to bring the country's roads, bridges, transit and rail up to international standards.[8]

A possible solution to this gridlock sneaked into the 2012 short-term federal highway bill. Called "America Fast Forward," it emerged from Los Angeles, where voters approved a 30-year sales tax to fund new transit systems. Los Angeles wanted to build the transit system in a decade rather than in dribs and drabs because, right now, materials and labor are cheap and the jobs are needed. So why wait?

Los Angeles can't borrow money affordably. So the city devised the idea of selling bonds to the federal government, which can borrow very cheaply — currently, at zero interest rates. The city would pledge the sales tax revenues to repay the loans. The decisions about the transit projects are all made locally and the money is approved by local taxpayers, which pleased conservatives; Los Angeles gets access to cheap finance, which pleases its citizens and businesses; the transit gets built, which liberals and environmentalists applaud; and Los Angeles gets a new transit system, which reduces the country's use of oil not in 30 years, but in 10.

It's an all-around win-win. But America Fast Forward does not need to be limited to transit. A similar mechanism can be used to finance investments in upgrading the network of natural-gas pipelines, which are badly in need of maintenance and investment. The costs of the explosion in 2011 in San Bruno, Calif., for instance, have been estimated at $183 million, with eight lives lost.[9] Cities could use funds to place utility wires underground, eliminating blackouts like the one in June 2012 that left 20,000 PEPCO customers in the Washington, D.C., area without power for more than four days in 100-degree heat.

These kinds of federal-state-city partnerships for transportation go all the way back to the first national highways and canals, built in the 1830s.

But if anyone is still dubious about the appropriateness of a big federal role in infrastructure that gets the country off imported oil, think about it this way: If the price of oil were to decline back to $30 per barrel, the decrease in federal oil costs alone — $350 billion over 10 years — would pay for most of the needed investments in the nation's transportation infrastructure at the level sought by the Obama administration.

Similar creative solutions to the problem of access to capital could also accelerate the purchase of new, all-American, non-petroleum-powered vehicles. Right now, a natural-gas-powered long-haul truck pays for itself in about five years. That shows how much cheaper natural gas is than diesel. In urban fleets, trucks powered by electricity can save enough money on fuel purchases to pay for the additional expense in only three years.

But the up-front costs are a major barrier for most consumers, whose cost of borrowing is very high. Here an innovation can be borrowed once again from the highly innovative successors to Alexander Graham Bell. I recently "bought" a spiffy smartphone for the absurdly low price of $150. Its real price is north of $500, and I would never have paid that amount, but Motorola and AT&T know that. So I'm not buying the phone outright. I'm making a down payment on it and paying the rest off via the somewhat elevated service rate I've committed to under my mandatory two-year contract. Voila!

Now imagine that a small bakery in San Francisco with three or four delivery trucks would like to switch to new electric vehicles but can't afford their purchase price, which is $20,000 above that of a comparable diesel-powered vehicle. What if they could buy an electric truck for the same price as the diesel in exchange for signing a fuel contract that fixes their electricity fuel bill at the equivalent of $2.50 per gallon — more than they would pay for the electric power on the market but still much less than they are currently paying for diesel? In effect, they'd be paying off the difference between the two vehicles' prices over time through the fuel rate they'd committed to, while still cutting their overall fuel cost. That is the marketing strategy that has put cell phones into the hands of hundreds of millions of people. The same thing is needed for energy.

NOT ALL ELECTRONS ARE CREATED EQUAL

In the electricity sector, the true economics of innovation are almost completely obscured by the dominance of monopoly transmission and, in many states, generation systems that treat electrons as a commodity. This system conveniently ignores the critically different value of a peak, summer-afternoon electron coming off a rooftop in Queens (or saved by replacing an inefficient air conditioner beneath the roof) and a 2 a.m. electron coming off a remote hydro facility in Quebec.

The manufacturing opportunity in electricity comes from breaking away from this old, centralized-monopoly model and taking advantage of new technologies that can deliver the electrons that are really needed when they are needed and at a much better price.

The Lessons of Enron

In the spring of 2001, California's newly deregulated electricity market ran off the rails. For reasons the public had a hard time grasping, the state was suddenly running out of power and was threatened with massive blackouts. The result: Northern California's biggest utility operator, PG&E, went $9 billion in debt and filed for bankruptcy.

But as neither the state's demand for electricity nor its stock of generating units had changed significantly, the fact that the world's seventh-largest economy teetered for months on the brink of catastrophe was simply inexplicable. Power prices went up eightfold. Consumers rallied and reduced demand enough to avoid the looming summer blackouts, but an explanation was slow in coming.

Eventually, a major factor turned out to be the sluggish, outmoded electro-mechanical switches that handled the state's transmission system. Enron, the "new age" energy trading company, had realized that in California's deregulated electricity market it could game the sluggish response time of the grid both by threatening to flood it with demand or by taking power plants offline, and then getting paid for withdrawing power purchases or deferring power withdrawals it never really intended to make.

The vulnerability stemming from the outmoded technology of the grid was not unknown. Ever since the New York City blackout of 1965, electrical utility experts like former Electric Power Research Institute (EPRI) President and CEO Kurt Yeager had been decrying the lack of grid modernization.[10]

But until the Enron scandal broke, no one had realized that there was an actual business model behind making money off backwardness. In response, Yeager went on to lead the Galvin Electricity Initiative, dedicated to the principle that modernizing America's grid is an enormous economic opportunity and an essential national mission because, as he posited in the subtitle of a 2008 book, *How the Microgrid Revolution Will Unleash Cleaner, Greener and More Abundant Energy.*[11]

Yet, today, the enormous economic savings that could be booked from making the U.S. grid more reliable and decentralized — along with the phenomenal manufacturing opportunity that replacing outmoded grid technology would provide — remain largely unrealized. The reason: Utilities, which continue as the central players in business models designed in the 1930s, have now become powerful incumbent opponents of modernization.

The job orders are awaiting the moment the country pushes the start button. Public officials like Sen. Harry Reid (D-Nev.) and the head of the Federal Energy Regulation Commission, Jon Wellinghoff, have been clearing away the underbrush obstructing transmission modernization.[12] They say bluntly that traditional power suppliers need to be "restructured to unbundle their service" and to "think in non-traditional terms, where utilities are a different animal."

Unleashing information on energy and prices "allows consumers to use their energy smartly," according to Wellinghoff. "The first step is to give consumers access to the real costs of delivered energy so that they're not in the dark."

New private-sector models like the dedicated 65-kilovolt transmission system for renewable-energy projects proposed by Clean Line Energy Partners are attracting investors by figuring out how to overcome the regulatory barriers. The United States really has no choice but to modernize its grid. Doing so would create an entirely new manufacturing sector to go with it.

But it won't be easy.

You don't have to leave California to find the evidence. PG & E, back from bankruptcy, is fighting a determined rear-guard action against the threat of distributed renewable power, particularly rooftop solar. After initially embracing rooftop solar initiatives, PG & E evidently concluded that they posed a serious threat to its monopoly model. In collaboration with other utilities in the state, PG & E began offering a series of regulatory proposals, carefully couched as solar friendly — just minor adjustments, mind you — but clearly intended to kill much of the momentum behind PG & E customers' deciding to provide their own power at their own cost. The hand-to-hand combat between the utility's advocacy of centralized electricity monopolies and the solar industry's push for a distributed model has been waged in a Marin County ballot measure (PG & E lost), the state legislature (the utility won), the California Public Utilities Commission (mixed results) and even a mammoth statewide ballot measure (the utilities lost).

In spite of the overall success of efforts by advocates of distributed solar to prevent PG & E from strangling the rooftop model, it is still the case that a great many common-sense applications of rooftop electricity remain illegal. For instance, a factory with facilities on two sides of a street may not electrify both buildings by placing solar generation equipment on only one of them. Investors who are trying to create larger markets face the continued threat of hitting various ceilings on the number of utility customers who can "net" meter their excess electricity back into the grid.

Since it is rooftop solar that powered the tremendous success of Germany in building its solar market, solar manufacturers in the United States badly need their customers to be released from the monopoly-utility model. As Yeager points out, this is also key for manufacturing businesses that want reliable power. Once again, incumbents' resistance to change is cramping the North American manufacturing market for energy innovation.

But at this point, PG&E's goal can only be to delay. Every time the voters of California have been asked to choose, they've opted for innovation and for breaking PG&E's monopoly. Indeed, so unpopular are many public utilities — from PG&E to PEPCO — over issues like blackouts and natural-gas explosions that clean-energy advocates have an enormous tailwind helping them break open the electricity sector.

The opportunity to rebuild not only the national grid, but also the generating units that feed it, is growing.

WILL WE MESS UP A BONANZA? THE NATURAL GAS BOOM

It's hardly news that novel technologies for exploiting seemingly abundant unconventional shale-gas reserves have created an enormous opportunity for energy-dependent American industries. Natural-gas prices in 2012, below $3 per thousand cubic feet at the wellhead, were unsustainably low. Companies are pumping at that price only to extract the oil that is associated with the gas or to comply with lease requirements. Liquefied natural gas (LNG) terminals built to bring gas into American markets are now petitioning regulators for permission to become gas export facilities.

But the United States is at risk of squandering this opportunity. Shale gas poses three challenges: It must be produced responsibly, used widely and priced fairly. Failure approaches on all three fronts.

Why is this important? Because if the United States gets it right, it will dramatically reduce both electricity and process-heating costs for American industry; return to the country's petrochemical industries the big competitive edge over the Middle East, Russia and the like that they lost in the 1980s; enable the U.S. to kick the curse of coal in the utility sector; set the stage for the use of natural gas in transportation; and slash oil imports. Plus, the upstream manufacturing impact of gas drilling and exploration for supply chains in steel pipe, for example, is already taking up some of the slack caused by the mismanagement of the equally exciting American wind opportunity.

Why is the United States blowing this? Most of the controversy has been about whether shale gas can be produced at an acceptable environmental cost. While drilling proceeds in most places, in New York State, one of the early sites of the leasing boom, it has been delayed, perhaps indefinitely; in New Jersey and Pennsylvania, public opposition has seriously slowed development.

Let's dispose first of the issue of "fracking," because it's not the central issue — for either side. Most of the risks of natural-gas drilling — methane blowouts, discharge of polluted water, disruption of communities and air pollution — are just as likely to result from drilling a conventional natural-gas well as from drilling one using hydrofracking. Both advocates and opponents of drilling use "fracking" as shorthand; advocates because they are pretty confident fracking itself is not a problem, and opponents because it sounds new and scary.

But drilling requires strong oversight, regulation and enforcement. Communities need to be involved. And not all locations where there might be geologic gas are appropriate for the kind of industrial development gas drilling brings.

The gas industry, foolishly, has resisted these common-sense principles. It knows that sloppy operators can create problems, but it doesn't want to concede that controlling them demands firm oversight of everyone, including responsible companies. It knows that state regulation alone won't work, because some states will always be inexperienced or corrupt; some gas companies avoid certain states because of regulatory shoddiness. The industry hasn't even been able to accept the basic notion that its service companies — Halliburton and others — need to disclose the ingredients in their fracking fluids. Gas companies vociferously argue that Environmental Protection Agency (EPA) regulation of the fracking compounds going into a well is totally unacceptable — even though when those same fluids come out of the well, the industry typically disposes of them in an EPA-regulated facility.

The 70 to 90 percent of well operators that are adhering to best practices when they drill are running regulatory interference for the 10 to 30 percent that are irresponsible and cause most of the problems. This has turned the conversation into one pitting local forces that want no drilling — often for legitimate reasons — against companies seeking no uniform regulation. Caught in the middle is the great majority of the public, which thinks the country needs the gas but ought to do it right.

This battle over safe drilling has almost drowned out a more important conversation: how to use the gas that is produced. Home and industrial heating uses are not controversial. Electrical utilities are moving rapidly to substitute gas for coal for simple economic reasons. Evidence suggests that the United States could meet these two priority needs and still have a substantial surplus of domestic gas. That leaves three potential courses of action:

- back out oil as a chemical feedstock;

- substitute gas — compressed natural gas (CNG), LNG, or methanol — for oil in transportation; and

- export LNG to foreign countries.

From an overall economic perspective, the clear loser among these choices is the last. Exporting would minimize the number of manufacturing jobs in the United States — so it ought to be a last resort. Using natural gas as a chemical feedstock is one of the biggest manufacturing opportunities the United States has. And so the country shouldn't squander it to help fatten the balance sheets of oil and gas producers.

The potential use of natural gas in the transportation sector is a matter of great uncertainty. There's far too little analysis available that considers which of the natural gas options — LNG, CNG or methanol — is the most promising. Until it is clear which road should be taken, building the necessary equipment and distribution infrastructure will be hampered.

But the enormous transportation opportunity strongly suggests being cautious about exporting. Why should the United States take a domestic fossil fuel with a low carbon footprint and waste its advantage by liquefying and shipping it to Asia, then import high-carbon foreign oil for vehicles that could have run on natural gas?

As for getting the price right, the problem is that if the controversies about drilling standards are not solved and the priorities for using the gas are not determined, then it will be impossible to create long-term market expectations with stable contracts. The resulting volatility would inevitably mean higher prices.

THE ELECTRIC CHALLENGE — SELLING CARS LIKE CELL PHONES

One of the fallouts of the Solyndra ambush was that the Obama administration decided to stop providing loan guarantees for advanced-vehicle manufacturing projects. This was, to put it bluntly, an act of cowardice taken to avoid congressional challenge. The result was that a whole series of efforts at automotive innovation went down the tubes because the government pullout sent a signal to private investors that innovative vehicles were a bad investment.

Some, like Bright Automotive, had such major corporate players as Alcoa investing in modernizing the inadequate technology behind a typical urban delivery vehicle like the Ford Econoline. Others, like Next Autoworks, were trying to combine good — though not cutting-edge — fuel-efficiency technology with new business models to make inexpensive, efficient cars. Next Autoworks had substantial private investment and an offer of $67 million from the state of Louisiana.[13] But the business model depended on getting a DOE loan guarantee — and when those were pulled, Next took its business to Turkey.

The slowdown in auto innovation is further exacerbated by the slow sales pace of the two leading-edge, mainstream electric vehicles — GM's plug-in Volt and Nissan's Leaf. Neither has taken off in the marketplace, even when gasoline was above $4 a gallon. That's not surprising. Auto buyers are very sensitive to purchase price yet relatively unmoved by future fuel costs, because they don't know what oil will cost tomorrow and they don't know whether they will own a car long enough to recoup its up-front costs.

This is neither a new nor an unusual dilemma. But it is damaging for manufacturers who need cash flow to pay for turning over old technology and assembly lines. If customers won't buy innovative vehicles when they are new — and hence expensive — who pays for the innovation?

Let's go back to the business model taken from cell phones, under which I could buy a Leaf or a Volt for the same price as an equivalent internal-combustion vehicle — in the case of the Volt, a Chevy Cruz. At the same time, I would sign a five-year fuel contract under which GM would provide my car with a smart card good for an unlimited amount of electricity at a fixed monthly charge that would be large enough to offset the discount I got upon purchase of the vehicle. When I plugged into my home charger — or one on the road — the smart card would bill the power I used to GM.

Right now, this wouldn't be a great deal for the customer because the Volt's savings in gasoline take more than five years to pay for themselves. But then neither is my "$150" cellphone. Both business models leverage the fact that as a customer I am overly aware of purchase price and not tuned enough into operating bills. Again, that's how innovation happened in the phone business — so why not cars?

I ran this question by a senior GM official. He cocked his head, looked at me and said, "You realize our industry hasn't yet figured out how to sell a car for a fixed price? Can you imagine your idea working when you are still haggling with the dealer? "

So accelerating innovation, which is the key to restoring energy manufacturing, isn't just a matter of technology or policy, it's also a matter of innovative business models and culture. Americans did it with smartphones. Why not electric vehicles?

ADAM SMITH WAS RIGHT: MONOPOLIES FIGHT BACK

In spite of the fact that in both the electricity and transportation sectors innovation offers enormous manufacturing promise, innovation also threatens to disrupt incumbent monopolies, whether electrical utilities or oil companies. And when they see their assets about to be outmoded and stranded, monopolies fight back.

Take the "Solyndra Syndrome": a political frame-up intended by the fossil-fuel monopoly and the political Right to ensure that government doesn't partner with business to accelerate the restoration of America's energy-manufacturing leadership. Stripped of the rhetoric and deceit, Solyndra may have been a mistake, but it wasn't a scandal. To encourage the construction of manufacturing facilities for new energy technologies in the United States, the Obama administration decided to take a tiny leaf out of China's forests of successful industrial development practices and, incidentally, copy the exact idea that conservatives put forward during the Bush administration when advocating for nuclear power: federal loan guarantees.

The purpose of loan guarantees is to get private investors to put up the capital for expensive projects that would be good for the country if they succeeded but that private capital sees as too risky to undertake on its own. As part of the Stimulus Package, the Obama administration got Congress to authorize it to make $16 billion in federal loan guarantees for clean energy.[14] Most of the money went to solar or wind-power plants — projects that are low risk, as long as the technology works, because they sign long-term power purchase agreements with utilities for the electrons they generate. But Obama and his secretary of Energy, Steven Chu, wanted to encourage manufacturing. They had watched the Europeans gain control of wind technology by providing capital for wind manufacturers, and the Chinese were doing the same with solar. Obama wanted to compete, and he knew that — as Dow Chemical CEO Andrew Liveris says — companies can't compete with countries.[15]

Elevated risk is the essence of investment in a new manufacturing technology. Imagine there are three plausible ways to make rooftop solar power cheaper and three companies are pursuing them. Even if all three technologies end up working, one is likely to be cheaper than both the others, so that two of the three companies will fail.

Private investors will refuse to back any of the three because the risk of losing money is way too high. As a result, in a purely private market, none of the factories get built in the United States, while the Chinese build all three. One works, and the Chinese own the future of solar manufacturing.

The loan-guarantee program was a well-designed solution to this problem. It turned out that Solyndra's circular thin-film technology wasn't the winner — even though it worked. And perhaps Solyndra was not a well-run company, so that, had it investigated more fully, DOE might not have extended the $535 million in loan guarantees.

Overall, DOE has done a very good job. Congress budgeted it to put at risk $2.5 billion, or 15 percent of its total $16 billion loan-guarantee portfolio, and it is on track, in fact, to lose only about $1 billion. How many government programs come in 60 percent under budget and are called scandals for doing so?

Focus-Grouping an Assassination

How did this happen? I can tell the story because I watched the drive-by shooting that became the Solyndra scandal in its test-drive phase in the spring of 2011 — at a News Corporation/*Wall Street Journal* conference on environmental economics called ECO:nomics.

By March of 2011 the Fossil Right had very quietly completed an extensive set of research and strategic projects aimed at discrediting clean energy, as well as climate protection, by tying them to "big government" — specifically, the Obama administration's approach to energy innovation. As it brought renewable energy into disrepute, it would advance its anti-government message, which would also help fossil fuels.

But a test of the approach was needed. So during the 2011 ECO:nomics conference, while corporate executives argued for stronger federal policy support for manufacturing innovation and clean energy, *WSJ* editorial writers consistently pushed back with the following story line: Isn't government support of innovation too risky? Won't there be a public backlash when the first one of those investments goes sour? Will the American people tolerate the government's picking winners and losers?

None of the business executives bought the argument — whether, like Dow's Liveris, they were representing mainstream, old-line manufacturing companies or New Economy start-ups such as those funded by Ray Lane of Kleiner Perkins, a venture-capital firm.

Indeed, the anti-government bias that dominates the *Journal's* editorial page was slammed by speaker after speaker, beginning with Vinod

Khosla. Khosla went after what he called "incumbent capitalism," in which government policy and incentives are designed not to encourage competition and innovation but to protect entrenched interests, with the coal, oil, nuclear and utility monopolies being the most spectacular beneficiaries of this bias against innovation.

Liveris, the leader of a well-established incumbent company, then piled on. The Australian-born executive had a new book out called *Make It In America: The Case for Re-Inventing the Economy*, which argues for bringing the United States back as a manufacturing power. Liveris conceded that, for weird historical reasons, the term "industrial policy" is too politically toxic to use — but he then went on to advocate an industrial policy without using the actual words, just a wink. Challenged by the *Journal's* moderator on whether this wouldn't simply lead to the government's wasting money, Liveris responded by citing China and Germany today and Japan in the 1960s and '70s as models for the sort of government intervention that's essential for economic vibrancy.

"Around the world, countries are acting more and more like companies: competing aggressively against one another for business and progress and wealth," he said. "Governments are boosting business, creating a climate that attracts and rewards investment, spurs innovation and job creation, and appeals to companies that are less bound by national borders than ever before…"

Liveris was not the only incumbent CEO who called for massive restructuring of the American economy based on government support for innovation. DuPont's Ellen Kullman warned skeptics that customer interest in the sustainability and greenness of products soared from 2005 to 2008, and surprisingly did not fall back with the economic crisis. William Clay Ford, Executive Chairman of Ford Motor Co., envisioned a very different automobile market, driven by electric vehicles. Clean-tech entrepreneurs like Suzlon's Tulsi Tanti were blunt in predicting that unless the U.S. government provides stable policy signals for renewables, the supply chain will be driven overseas to an even greater extent than it has been to date.

The sharpest edge to the tension between business and the *Wall Street Journal's* pro-laissez-faire editorial policies came when *WSJ* editorial board member Kimberley Strassel repeated her oft-stated concern that if the federal government acted like a venture capitalist and supported research in a wide variety of important but risky innovations, the public would turn against the program because some innovations would fail to pan out. Ray Lane of Kleiner Perkins shot back: "The American people would be fine with it if you would write about what's really happening. It's the media, not the public, that is the problem."

No one in the audience knew it, but the Solyndra scandal was being primed — not with Solyndra itself in mind, but with the knowledge that the recipient of some federal loan guarantee would go bankrupt.

When business executives vigorously rejected the proposition that "federal support for innovation is a bad idea," the Right recalibrated. New messages were devised that were focused not on the technologies themselves, but on the argument that political favoritism and cronyism were involved. Since clean-tech entrepreneurs had, almost without exception, supported Obama, it was a good bet that whichever company became the first to call on its federal loan guarantees would have investors who had backed the president.

When Solyndra filed for Chapter 11 bankruptcy on September 1, 2011, the entire apparatus was ready to roll out. The messages had been researched, quietly tested in semi-public venues like ECO:nomics and disseminated to key parts of the fossil-fuel-defense echo chamber.

Indeed, in the week after the first of three presidential debates in October 2012, Republican campaign committees all over the country resumed attacking their opponents for having supported Solyndra.

Fragging the Marines

While the Solyndra counterassault was framed around "loan guarantees," "cronyism," and "winners and losers," that wasn't its core. The Fossil Right wanted to prevent the United States from accelerating its shift from fossil fuels to innovative energy by regaining its manufacturing leadership. No one was safe from its campaign — not even the U.S. Marines.

Dependence on oil has, since the Iranian oil crisis of 1979, been at the heart of the threat that young American men and women will die in combat. Oil kills American troops in two ways. First, the threat to U.S. import lifelines, and those of America's European allies, forces repeated intervention in the Persian Gulf. U.S. involvement in Kuwait was directly over oil security. The American troops needed in Saudi Arabia galvanized Osama bin Laden to his Jihad which, in turn, triggered U.S. involvement first in Afghanistan, then in Iraq and, finally, in Pakistan.

Once U.S. armed forces got to places like Afghanistan, getting them the diesel and gasoline to fight became a major source of casualties. By the time a gallon of diesel fuel reached a forward base near Kandahar, it might have cost $400.[16] Worse, the convoys carrying that diesel fuel made perfect targets for roadside bombs and other tools of asymmetric warfare, playing directly into the strength of the Afghan militant movement, the Taliban. One in every 24 fuel convoys led to a military fatality.[17] So, by 2012, over 3,000 American men and women had been killed while transporting fuel to the battlefield — 40 to 50 percent of all U.S. casualties.

And since fossil power wasn't very good in combat, a soldier or Marine in Afghanistan might be carrying seven types of batteries weighing a mobility-impeding 20 pounds.[18] It turned out that the 21st century high-tech battlefield on which the American military chooses to fight is no place for outmoded, 20th century energy sources.

Up to this challenge stepped a former Marine and governor of Mississippi, Obama's secretary of the Navy, Ray Mabus. In partnership with the rest of the Department of Defense (DOD), Mabus was determined to tackle both halves of the oil threat to his troops. The Pentagon would help wean America off what President Bush had called its "addiction to oil" by being an early market for innovative biofuels, efficient engines and renewable electricity.

DOD would deploy those energy innovations in ways that reduced the direct threat to troops once they were on the battlefield — whether it was from convoy ambushes or overloaded and unreliable battery-dependent weaponry.

Mabus and his colleagues set ambitious goals: By 2020, the Navy would reduce its oil dependence by 50 percent. Ingenious solar devices were created to take the battery weight out of a Marine's fighting gear. New generations of hybrid technologies and efficient engines were brought into the fleet. To help government contractors innovate, Mabus revived the Cold-War support mechanisms embodied in the Defense Production Act.

This effort paid off on the battlefield, according to an account of combat that took place in Afghanistan's Helmand province in autumn of 2010 and involved India Company from the 3rd Batallion, 5th Marine Regiment (3/5).[19] "Early on in the fighting, First Lieutenant Josef Patterson, India 3/5's second platoon commander, took a small force south. They established a patrol base, but for two months, the area remained so volatile that fuel convoys couldn't reach it. Without fuel or battery resupply, the team could have been left with no way to run generators or power radios or computers — a potentially crippling situation. As Patterson later explained, 'If I don't have [communication] with my troops and my higher-ups, I am lost.'

"But the soldiers of India 3/5 had another source of power: the sun. Specifically, they had a Ground-Renewable Expeditionary Energy System (GREENS): four portable modules that fold out into two large solar panels each, all connected to a power cell to store the energy overnight. Normally, a patrol carries enough batteries to last three or four days — 20 to 35 pounds for each grunt — and is dependent on frequent and dangerous resupplies. But with these packable solar panels, says Patterson, his patrol of 35 soldiers shed 700 pounds. 'We stayed out for three weeks and didn't need a battery resupply once," he said.

In short, Mabus treated oil dependence for what it was — a lethal threat to his Marines.

The Fossil Right didn't like it at all. Republicans in Congress launched legislation to cripple efforts by DOD to play the same role it had played in the Cold War — that of the catalyst of and reliable customer for American innovation and manufacturing leadership. When that legislation found no hearing in the U.S. Senate, House Republicans resorted to badgering, summoning Mabus to Capitol Hill to be lectured by Virginia Congressman Randy Forbes, who thought it necessary to enlighten Mabus that "you're not the secretary of Energy. You are the secretary of the Navy."[20]

But the Defense Department is not easily swayed when the lives of its troops are at stake. However hard Big Oil tries to maintain the dependence of American troops on oil and batteries, an entire generation of warriors is returning home with firsthand experience of the power of energy innovation. Their message will be difficult to drown with misleading 30-second spots.

The Myth of the Keystone Excel

Next to Solyndra, the Keystone Excel Pipeline has probably been the biggest effort by the fossil-fuel industry to keep America locked into a high-priced, outmoded energy future. Again, the facts are fairly straightforward. The Canadian province of Alberta has enormous reserves of a quasi-oil, tar sands bitumen. It can be turned into gasoline or diesel, but only at substantial cost and with resultant environmental damage. It is simultaneously the world's most expensive and dirtiest source of oil. When oil prices fall even to $90, new projects in Alberta get cancelled.

But this expensive oil sells at a discount in the American Midwest — a $20 per barrel discount — because it is landlocked and cannot reach more-lucrative European markets.

Canadian oil interests and the Koch brothers, who are major investors in Alberta, desperately want to gain access to high-priced European markets. Keystone Excel would give them that access by shipping tar sands bitumen across the Mississippi Valley to refineries in tax-free havens on the U.S. Gulf Coast. For Canadian producers, this is a triple win: They get more oil out of Alberta, they get access to pricey European diesel markets and they get to raise the prices they charge consumers in the American Midwest.

What's not to like? Nothing, if you are an Alberta oil producer. But if you are a refinery worker in the United States currently refining bitumen, or an industrial customer in the Midwest buying diesel, or a Texas homeowner downwind from a refinery, or a Nebraska farmer whose water supply would be threatened by a probable leak from the pipeline, then Keystone Excel is an All-American Loser.

Of course, it has been sold as a source of U.S. jobs and reliable oil. While not as many jobs will be created building the pipeline as Keystone claims, they will be real jobs. And the fact that those will be construction jobs does not diminish their value. As America enters an era in which it upgrades its entire energy infrastructure, many of the jobs will be "temporary" — after all, an apartment building needs to be modernized only once.

But what Keystone's backers do not include in their calculations is the result of raising oil prices in the Midwest by $20 a barrel or more. Nor do they concede the risk to those refineries in the Midwest that are currently cracking bitumen into gasoline and diesel. In fact, Keystone's overall effect would be to shift manufacturing jobs from the Midwest to Texas or upstream to Canada.

Yet this proposal has become a central feature of conservative energy policy, even though the oil the pipeline will transport is so expensive that it makes no economic sense unless one assumes that the world is condemned to a future of $90-plus oil. And that would be very bad news for American manufacturing.

The odds are that Keystone will be built. President Obama has already approved a pipeline segment that will get Canadian bitumen to refineries on the Gulf in smaller volumes. So oil prices in the Midwest are going up. That's a self-inflicted wound on American manufacturing. But what really matters is the long-term price of oil, and here we still, as outlined below, have lots of options.

THE PATHWAY FORWARD

While we can expect the incumbent fossil-fuel monopolies to fight hard against energy-manufacturing innovation because it has the potential to disrupt their existing assets, we've got some fairly good models for going forward — models that haven't yet been applied in Washington but that can and should be.

As I mentioned earlier, Dow CEO Andrew Liveris likes to say he is puzzled that he can't talk about industrial policy in polite company in the United States. Well, he actually can — as long as he is in a state capital talking about industrial policy for Michigan, Texas or Mississippi. Indeed, successful governors often talk about little else.

At the ECO:nomics conference where Liveris took on the Tea Party and the Anti-Federal-Support-for-Manufacturing clique, the final speaker was Haley Barbour, then governor of Mississippi and a former head of the Republican Party. Barbour delivered a passionate stemwinder of a speech urging companies to choose Mississippi for future investments because it understood how to help manufacturing. Here's the lead paragraph on economic development from Barbour's website, which gives you the flavor:

"In the four years before Haley Barbour became Governor, Mississippi lost a higher percentage of manufacturing jobs than any other state in the nation. Mississippi suffered a net loss of 49,700 of our highest-paying jobs — a 22-percent decline in manufacturing employment. Gov. Barbour made attracting high-skilled, high-paying jobs utilizing advanced materials a priority of his administration."[21]

State manufacturing policy — picking winners and losers — seems to be a specialty of Republican governors. Louisiana's Bobby Jindal was ready to help Next Motors when Obama's DOE backed out. Texas Gov. Rick Perry's website[22] and the platform for his 2012 presidential bid would have warmed Liveris's heart: "Aggressive Job Creation. Since July 2003, Texas has created more than 1 million net new jobs... The Texas Enterprise Fund, the largest job creation fund of its kind in the nation, began under Perry in 2003 and is generating more than 55,000 new jobs and $15 billion in capital investment for Texas."

Governors like Barbour, Jindal and Perry clearly have no difficulty with the concepts that states compete with other states and that state policy matters. Often what it takes to land a factory is some direct help from the public coffers. So why has it become conservative orthodoxy that for the federal government to do the same thing — and compete with Germany and China — is a new form of socialism?

THE REGULATORY CONUNDRUM —
A GRAND BARGAIN IS TO BE HAD

A major concern of energy manufacturing firms — and their customers, companies like wind and solar developers — is the gnarly, convoluted and far-too-slow process for getting permits in the United States. Clean-tech innovators routinely tell me, "I don't mind high standards, but I can't stand slow permits. It's killing us." Venture capitalist Ray Lane says that one of the big advantages in China is that "if we are building a four-story factory and finish the first floor, we start shipping product — here we wait a year for a final inspection."

America's environmental standards are, in some areas, pathetically weak. America's permitting processes are, in some cases, pathetically complicated and slow. How did the United States ever manage to get the worst of both worlds — weak standards and enormously expensive bureaucracy?

There could be a grand bargain: cut permitting time, probably by four-fifths, and give communities and the environment much less air and water pollution, health risk, noise, disruption and climate risk. Getting there will require an understanding of the present gridlock. Here is a look at examples of how to break it:

After 42 years of personal participation, observation and perhaps some culpability — from the moment of original sin, the passage of the Clean Air Act of 1970 — I am compelled to say that the country's dilemma is neither inadvertent nor unavoidable. There were powerful interests in the business community that preferred weak regulations even at the price of slow permitting — incumbent companies that owned old facilities with outmoded and dirty technology. They didn't want to be forced to modernize, and as environmental regulation evolved, it didn't make them: They were "grandfathered."

For example, in 1977 Congress proposed to require that all power plants, regardless of when they were built or what they burned, meet basic pollution-control standards. The coal industry and its allies among the utilities, led by the Southern Company, argued that they were about to shut down their fleet of old coal clunkers anyway, and that pollution controls would be a silly expense for assets that were about to be retired.

Congress believed them, and it even gave the Southern Company a loop-hole that allowed it to grandfather — thereby exempting from pollution controls — coal power plants that came on line as many as 12 years after the law was passed.

At the same time, to satisfy pressure from citizens that they be enabled to stop new but dirty facilities, politicians layered in multiple opportunities for the organized to prevent new projects from obtaining approval. (Unorganized communities still get stuck with pollution. It may take longer for that hazardous-waste dump to get a permit, but it still gets one and it is still dirty. Similarly, natural-gas drilling is banned in New York but poorly regulated in West Virginia.)

So dirty, old facilities were allowed to go on forever, like vampires, but regulatory procedure made it hard for new projects — clean or dirty — to get a decision. And still, when dirty, new projects did come along, they could count on eventually being able to identify a poorly organized or just plain poor community and to roll it, since the underlying substantive requirements for permits were simply too weak, however many hearings had to be held.

A new approach is needed in which every facility would get cleaned up as technology improved, but every facility would also face a predictable set of standards it would have to meet to get a permit in the first place. If the initial permit didn't condemn a community to a polluting facility in perpetuity, resistance would be lower; and if investors could get answers quickly, they could apply the money saved on procedural obligations to achieving higher environmental standards.

Is my concept of a grand bargain just wishful thinking? I don't think so — because on a case-by-case basis I've seen it work. In 1984, a shuttered General Motors assembly plant in Fremont, Calif., was reopened by a partnership of Toyota and GM, New United Motor Manufacturing Inc. (NUMMI). Its purpose was to allow Toyota to learn the American market and to allow GM to learn how Toyota innovated.

Toyota brought an attitude toward environmental compliance that was very different from that of most U.S. firms. When during the renovation a major crack was discovered in the paint bay — one that had leaked

large volumes of toxic fluids into the ground underneath the plant —
Toyota officials called not their lawyers but EPA as a first recourse.
Toyota built a partnership with the Fremont community, a process
I watched as an occasional informal adviser and kibitzer.

Ten years later, NUMMI officials contacted me. They wanted to open
a truck assembly line, one that would be the biggest new source of air
pollution permitted in the San Francisco area for decades. They were
anxious about regulatory delay and wanted my thoughts. I told them I
thought their "open-kimono" approach to the community had worked
and would work again this time. "Just bring people in," I counseled.
NUMMI did, and the plant was permitted in record time with no
citizen opposition.

High standards do yield quick answers. But there are forces on both
sides favoring sluggishness and delay — and real leadership will require
acknowledging that.

SOME QUESTIONS:
HOW TO KNOW IF OUR LEADERS ARE SERIOUS

Although the last presidential election was ugly, at least it was one in which
manufacturing got more attention than it had in recent years. But neither
candidate demonstrated a real commitment to doing what it will take to
bring back U.S. manufacturing, even in the energy sector, where the case
seems clearest.

So, as a guide forward, I'd like to close with three questions we ought
to ask our leaders when they tell Americans they want economic recovery,
jobs, energy innovation or a manufacturing revival.

1. *Where Are Your Big, Concrete Ideas?*

For the past two years, the U.S. government has done essentially nothing
if it required any level of collaboration between the two political parties
or the two houses of Congress. Anyone who proposes federal policy
initiatives to help accelerate an energy manufacturing revival will be

told, repeatedly, "That's too big an idea for Washington." Even T. Boone Pickens's modest tax incentives for natural-gas trucks have gone nowhere in this climate.

So, while both Barack Obama and Mitt Romney (earlier joined by Rick Santorum and Rick Perry) talked urgently about manufacturing and jobs, neither offered programs and policies that would really help.

For example, Romney's "energy independence for North America by 2020" plank depends on so much Canadian tar sands and very expensive, remote Arctic drilling that it signals a permanent commitment to $4-per-gallon gasoline and $100-per-barrel oil. Dollars sent to import oil from Alberta are lost to American manufacturing just as surely as dollars sent to Norway. Obama's plank hangs together better, but it is too modest, calling only for halving oil imports by 2020, something that is close to accomplished already.

America's leaders need to be pressed for some big ideas, ideas that will really jump-start energy innovation and energy manufacturing in the United States — and now.

2. *Where Will You Play Your Chips in Doha?*

Any government has only so many chips to play at a given poker table. A key table for energy manufacturing is trade, and how the next administration plays its trade chips is crucial. There's no doubt in anyone's mind that when German Chancellor Angela Merkel sends her representatives to the Doha Round of World Trade Organization negotiations, the interests of Germany's small and medium-sized manufacturing enterprises are first and foremost on her mind. And it is inconceivable that the Chinese negotiators would give away access to the U.S. market for Chinese manufactured goods in exchange for some favor to Chinese banks seeking to invest in America.

But since 1992, U.S. trade negotiators of both parties have consistently put manufacturing below the interests of banks, investors, agribusiness and extractive industries. Any serious manufacturing revival will require this to change.

Both Romney and Obama supported various trade agreements that fail to put manufacturing on a level playing field with finance — agreements that allow Asian competitors, for example, to keep U.S. autos out of their markets. A new start is needed in the White House, one that takes its playbook from Merkel, not JP Morgan Chase CEO Jamie Dimon.

3. Do They Blame the Voters Or the Chinese Wage?

The biggest threat to a revival of energy manufacturing is a combination of a lack of political ambition, as reflected in both Obama's and Romney's energy-independence planks, with the sense that the American public isn't serious in demanding a manufacturing revival, or that U.S.-based firms can't compete because of the low level of Chinese wages.

Ironically, if there is a bipartisan consensus on any issue, it is on the urgency of a manufacturing revival. The public has overwhelmingly voiced its support for the government's adopting a manufacturing policy that puts Americans to work.[23] In recent polls, two-thirds of Republicans, Independents and Democrats alike agreed that other sectors could not replace manufacturing as a source of economic strength, and similar majorities favored a national manufacturing policy.[24]

I would argue that the main reason politicians have gotten away with selling manufacturing short is that the media have persuaded the public — and, indeed, many of America's leaders — that it is wages that drove manufacturing overseas.

The success of high-wage countries like Denmark and Germany in dominating wind manufacturing is one very strong piece of contrary evidence, but it doesn't get much publicity. And most Americans believe that it was wages at U.S. auto plants — rather than legacy pensions and healthcare costs — that burdened the Big Three, when in fact their hourly assembly-line wages differed by only a tiny amount from those in Tokyo or Stuttgart.

China did not obtain its dominance of the solar industry with cheap labor. It provided its solar companies with free land and cheap capital, probably about $30 billion worth. It then began providing reliable markets with feed-in tariffs. Andy Splinter didn't shift so much of Applied Materials' operation to Asia for low labor costs. He wanted a government that understood how to support a start-up industry. Beijing did. Washington doesn't (Although, under Republican Gov. Haley Barbour, Mississippi did).

America's leaders need to lead. That means educating the American people, and themselves. That means setting ambitious, not puny, goals. That means aligning the efforts of the federal government as a whole, not piece by piece.

So far, they haven't. They need to be held accountable not for their rhetoric, but for their results. The next time a politician says, "Now, I like clean energy as much as anyone," remember, this is code for, "I've been rewarded for helping to slow it down."

The energy sector is too big to be sluggish and too important to remain in the last century. Energy innovation is too central to America's manufacturing future to be sacrificed for the interests of the financial and extractive economies of the past.

EPILOGUE I: BACK TO DULUTH

As Congress got ready to delay yet again renewing the basic tax credits on which the wind industry has relied, the LM Wind Power manufacturing facility in North Dakota was threatened with being shuttered. On October 2, 2012, LM Wind Power announced that it would build a new wind-turbine factory in Brazil.[25] Once again, the United States stands to lose manufacturing and exports because it has not secured a reliable domestic policy and adequate demand.

EPILOGUE II: BACK TO BLOOM ENERGY

K.R. Sridhar and Bloom Energy will get to manufacture in the United States after all. Bloom's first factory will be built in Delaware. In exchange, in a move that Haley Barbour or Rick Perry would appreciate, the state of Delaware agreed to count electricity from fuel cells as "renewable" even if the fuel cell in question happens to be powered with cheap, non-renewable natural gas.

But Delaware is being sued — by the legal arm of the Delaware Tea Party, the Caesar Rodney Institute. The legal argument: "unconstitutional cronyism." No one quite knows what this means — it's a brand new legal theory. But it sounds evil. The idea seems to suggest that government can never help business in any way. (Hamilton would be amused, Madison appalled.)

That the Tea Party is against a typical state economic-development tactic, even deployed on behalf of a fossil fuel, because it is innovative, tells you how far the Right has embedded itself in the energy past.

So Bloom Energy has one more challenge to overcome before Sridhar's dream — energy innovation for electricity taken from the Mars Mission to the United States — comes true. But I'm confident. He'll get there. And so will America.

1. The No More Solyndras Act (HR — 6213) was introduced in the House of Representatives by Rep. Fred Upton (R-Mich.) on July 26, 2012. It passed the House on September 14, 2012, by a vote of 245 to 161, with 223 aye votes from Republicans and 22 aye votes from Democrats (four Republicans and 157 Democrats voted against the measure).

2. Andrew Grove, "How America Can Create Jobs," *Bloomberg Businessweek,* July 1, 2012, http://www.businessweek.com/magazine/content/10_28/b4186048358596.htm.

3. Jeffrey Immelt, General Electric CEO, before the MIT Energy 2.0 Conference, March 7, 2007, https://mitei.mit.edu/news/video/energy-20-morning-keynote.

4. American Wind Energy Association, http://www.awea.org/issues/supply_chain/index.cfm.

5. Andrew Grove, *ibid.*

6. http://www.merkley.senate.gov/imo/media/doc/Senator%20Merkley%20-%20America%20Over%20 a%20Barrel%200614101.pdf.

7. U.S. Department of Transportation, "Osaga River Rail Bridge will ease freight bottleneck, roadway congestion," March 30, 2012, http://www.fastlane.dot.gov/2012/03/osage-river-rail-bridge-eases-congested-bottleneck.html#.UIRYQ46q7a4.

8. http://www.infrastructurereportcard.org/sites/default/files/RC2009_exsummary.pdf.

9. *Wall Street Journal,* "PG&E Second Quarter Down On San Bruno Pipeline Costs," August 7, 2012, http://online.wsj.com/article/BT-CO-20120807-712768.html.

10. *Wired Magazine,* "Girding Up for the Power Grid," June 14, 2001, http://www.wired.com/techbiz/media/news/2001/06/44516?currentPage=all.

11. Kurt Yeager and Robert Galvin (former Motorola CEO), *Perfect Power: How the Microgrid Revolution Will Unleash Cleaner, Greener and More Abundant Energy,* Greentechmedia, 2008.

12. "Greentechgrid, A Day in the Life of the Grid With Jon Wellinghoff, FERC Chairman," March 2, 2012, http://www.greentechmedia.com/articles/read/A-Day-in-the-Life-of-the-Grid-with-Jon-Wellinghoff-Chairman-of-FERC.

13. "Next Autoworks: The Curse of the Solyndra DOE Loan Guarantee," Greentechmedia, November 25, 2011, http://www.greentechmedia.com/articles/read/Next-Autoworks-The-Curse-of-the-DOE-Loan-Guarantee.

14. *Bloomberg Businessweek,* "New Clean-Energy Loan Guarantees Planned by Obama Administration," April 5, 2012, http://www.businessweek.com/news/2012-04-05/new-clean-energy-loan-guarantees-planned-by-obama-administration.

15. http://globalpublicsquare.blogs.cnn.com/2012/01/29/zakaria-does-america-need-an-industrial-policy/.

16. "Blood and Oil," *Sierra Club Magazine,* July/August, 2011, http://www.sierraclub.org/sierra/201107/blood-and-oil.aspx.

17. Ibid.

18. Sandra Erwin, "Army, Marines Face Uphill Battle to Lighten Troops' Battery Load," *National Defense,* National Defense Industrial Association, May 2011, http://www.nationaldefensemagazine.org/archive/2011/May/Pages/ArmyMarinesFaceUphillBattleToLightenTroops'BatteryLoad.aspx.

19. David Roberts, *Outside Magazine,* "The Marines Go Renewable," November 9, 2011, http://www.outsideonline.com/outdoor-adventure/natural-intelligence/Natural-Intelligence-Charge.html?page=all.

20. Sandra Erwin, "Amid Political Backlash, Pentagon Pushes Forward With Green Energy," *National Defense,* National Defense Industrial Association, April, 2012, http://www.nationaldefensemagazine.org/archive/2012/April/Pages/AmidPoliticalBacklash,PentagonPushesForwardWithGreenEnergy.aspx.

21. Gov. Haley Barbour, http://www.governorbarbour.com/about/.

22. "Gov. Perry on Economic Development in Texas," http://www.rickperry.org/issues/economic-development.

23. "Voters See Manufacturing as the Irreplaceable Core of a Strong Economy," survey taken by Mark Mellman, CEO of The Mellman Group, and Whit Ayres, President of North Star Opinion Research, for the Alliance for American Manufacturing, July 16, 2012, http://www.americanmanufacturing.org/press-releases/voters-see-manufacturing-"irreplaceable-core-strong-economy".

24. http://americanmanufacturing.org/blog/voters-see-manufacturing-%E2%80%9Cirreplaceable-core-strong-economy%E2%80%9D.

25. "LM Wind Power Announces Expansion in Brazil," LM Wind Power, October 2, 2012, http://www.lmwindpower.com/Media/Media-Kit/Press-Releases/2012/10/Brazil.

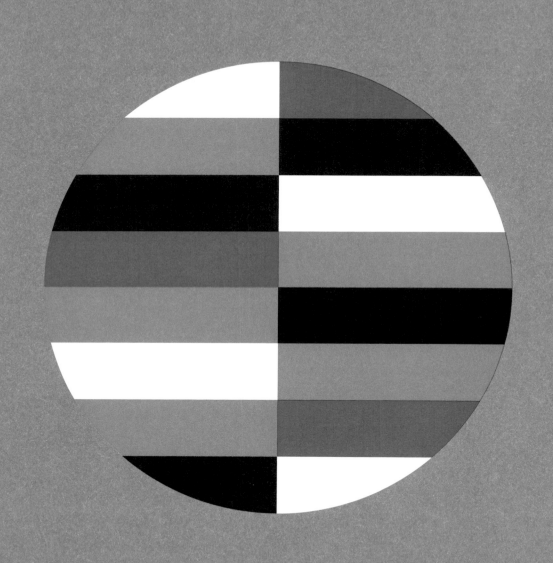

CHAPTER 6

Why Strengthening the Enforcement Provisions Of the WTO is Important For American Manufacturing

Eric Garfinkel
Trade Enforcement

The World Trade Organization (WTO) and its predecessor, the General Agreement on Tariffs and Trade (GATT), can be credited with reducing barriers to trade in goods and services and with reinforcing protection for intellectual property rights. Trade liberalization through the WTO system has helped drive global economic growth. But trade liberalization cannot continue to progress without effective enforcement of WTO rules.

When the WTO was created, the United States abandoned unilateral trade retaliation against other nations to ensure reciprocal access to their markets. The United States agreed to pursue trade conflicts through the WTO's dispute-settlement system. However, the WTO dispute system is suffering from procedural and substantive flaws, many of which have become apparent in recent years as the United States has begun to use the system more frequently. The filing of more WTO cases in recent years is commendable, but the quality of outcome — that is, the timeliness and commercial significance of WTO rulings — is what really matters to American manufacturing businesses and workers. It is vital that the full benefits of the WTO materialize, especially at this critical time.

The fact that damages are not awarded by the WTO for past harm to the complaining member's interests means there are no consequences for countries that break the rules. Lengthy timeframes for adjudication lead to rulings that arrive well after harm has become irreparable. And the WTO's evidentiary requirements can be easily frustrated if a government hides discriminatory practices and injurious subsidies from public view.

In this chapter, I argue that a stronger, more credible WTO enforcement system with shorter timeframes for adjudication, proactive evidence collection by the WTO and retroactive and provisional remedies is essential to maintaining the reciprocity upon which trade concessions are made by WTO members.

The economic and political case for trade liberalization depends heavily on the enforcement of rules that limit the ability of governments to tilt the playing field in favor of their own industries and workers. This chapter argues that the United States should help restore the credibility of the WTO by working with like-minded countries to improve and strengthen the WTO enforcement system.

I begin by answering questions that are on the minds of many Americans when it comes to U.S. trade policy, in particular how the WTO, an obscure but powerful international organization based in Geneva, directly affects the interests of American industries and their workers. In the form of a conversation, I explain how WTO rules operate and what happens when a WTO member challenges another member's trade practices through the dispute-settlement process. The chapter separates trade-policy rhetoric from reality, underscoring the practical legal and policy challenges of WTO trade enforcement. It concludes with a series of policy recommendations that, if implemented, will enhance the effectiveness of WTO enforcement proceedings.

Isn't more trade good for everybody?

One's view of liberalized trade depends on where one sits. More trade has been good for some but harmful to others.

Trade liberalization is the central theme of U.S. trade policy and the WTO system, which Americans played a central role in creating. The pursuit of trade liberalization is grounded in the theory of comparative advantage: the idea that a country should export the products it is most efficient at making, while importing goods and services that other countries are better at producing. According to the theory of comparative advantage, liberalized trade increases the wealth of every country that participates in the open trading system.

The system creates winners and losers, however. Among the winners are consumers, who have more choices at lower prices. Other winners include companies that can access foreign markets through exports or through direct investments to produce goods and services abroad. In contrast, companies and workers that face direct import competition are often harmed. Workers in growing export businesses may win, but workers in plants that are closing their doors due to imports or outward investment lose.

Economists recognize that there are winners and losers from liberalized trade, and when they speak about the benefit of trade liberalization, they are speaking of national economies considered as a whole. They base their case on the idea that, overall, the gains of winners outweigh the losses of losers.

However, concern has been growing among American economists over losers from trade, whom they place in a category they describe as "distributional consequences." In the United States, the distributional consequences have become more widespread in recent years, especially as the Internet has eliminated barriers to the cross-border delivery of services. The jobs that are threatened now extend beyond basic manufacturing industries. Trade, outward investment and technological change are eliminating U.S. jobs in the high-tech-products category, as well as highly skilled service-sector positions in computer programming, medical record-keeping, accounting, and legal and architectural services, among others.

Economists generally favor the use of more generous unemployment and training programs for workers displaced by free-trade policies. Though inadequate, such programs can have the benefit of helping those negatively affected by imports, but they do not address trade-distorting practices used by many countries, which can be the root cause of the harm. As discussed below, improved enforcement of WTO rules to address such practices is essential to maintain support for further liberalization of global trade.

One of the original U.S. objectives under the GATT was to lock in trade-liberalizing commitments in order to reduce protectionist pressures from powerful American industries that had to compete against imports. Today, the political dynamic has shifted. Import-competing industries in the United States are relatively less powerful, and the WTO system has overwhelming support from global industries with a strong interest in an open and stable trading system. There is now a bias in the U.S. Congress in favor of trade liberalization, but insufficient attention is being paid to addressing the distributional consequences arising from it.

But wouldn't you agree that if the government adequately addresses the negative effects of trade through unemployment and retraining programs, trade liberalization should continue to drive U.S. trade policy because of its overall benefit to the national economy?

Not completely. The U.S. government needs to be vigilant about making sure all countries play by the rules. When governments distort the terms of competition by discriminating against imports or subsidizing produc-tion, true comparative advantage based on the highest-quality products at the best price no longer exists. Shortcomings in the WTO dispute system impede the enforcement of global trading rules and thus limit America's ability to ensure a level playing field.

Then do U.S. trade laws that operate independently of the WTO provide a level playing field for American businesses, workers and farmers?

U.S. law is fairly limited when it comes to unfair trade. Three primary avenues exist for addressing unfairly traded imports: the antidumping law, the countervailing-duty law and Section 337 of the Tariff Act of 1930. I won't go into too much detail, but the U.S. government can only do so much on its own. To address most foreign unfair-trading practices, the federal government must get authorization from the WTO.

Private parties can petition the U.S. government to investigate dumped or subsidized imports. If the U.S. Commerce Department finds that an imported product is dumped or subsidized, and the International Trade Commission (ITC) finds that a U.S. industry producing that product is materially injured or threatened with material injury by those imports, additional import duties are assessed to offset the dumping or subsidies.

From a policy perspective, there is legitimate concern over whether the antidumping and countervailing-duty remedies are truly accessible to most industries and whether these laws provide timely and cost-effective relief. Access to these provisions of U.S. law has been limited by an amendment to the WTO Antidumping (AD) Agreement that the United States accepted in 1995. WTO rules require a petition to be expressly supported by 25 percent of the domestic producers of the product at issue, and at least 50 percent of the domestic producers submitting an opinion on the case must be in favor of it. Historically, these cases have been filed by industries that are American-owned and produce the majority of their products in the United States. But the composition and structure of most industries have changed in recent years due to the growing mix of foreign- and domestically owned producers.

Many companies now import finished products as well as parts and components for their U.S. assembly lines. For most companies today, the decision on whether to support or fund a trade-remedy case is complicated. Growing legal expense involved in bringing a case to the government and importers' use of novel strategies to circumvent dumping and countervailing-duty orders often make the cost of filing a case greater than the prospective benefit.

Section 337 import cases are investigated by the ITC. The typical case targets such activities as infringing patents, copyrights or trademarks in a way that injures a U.S. industry. No remedy is granted if the ITC determines that it would not be in the public interest to vote in favor of the complaint, and all the agency's determinations are subject to presidential review and reversal on policy grounds. The remedy in Section 337 cases is typically an order banning the infringing product from importation.

It should be stressed that these cases deal only with import-related unfair practices and do not involve trade in third-country markets or in the markets of the exporting countries, and rarely do they compel a change in practices that damage the global competitive position of U.S. businesses. For that, American companies and industries need to convince the U.S. government to file a complaint on their behalf at the WTO.

What is the process for bringing a case to the WTO? Can a business or labor union file complaints?

Only governments can bring complaints to the WTO. To change foreign-government behavior that tilts the scale against U.S. manufacturers in global markets, American companies must persuade the U.S. government to file a complaint at the WTO. The Office of the United States Trade Representative (USTR) has done a commendable job in filing WTO cases and maintains a high standard for filings. If USTR feels that the evidence and legal arguments are insufficient to prevail before a WTO dispute-settlement panel, it will turn down a request to file a case, and for good reason: Losing a WTO case can, in a single stroke, eliminate any leverage the United States might have to induce compliance. Loss of a case can also destroy prospects for negotiating a clarification or improvement in a WTO rule in future trade rounds. The threat of a WTO case can often be more effective in achieving a desired outcome than actually litigating.

Why does the United States need to go to the WTO? Doesn't the country have the right to insist on reciprocity and take unilateral action against other countries if they don't open their markets to American goods and services?

Prior to 1995, Section 301 of the Trade Act of 1974 was a very effective tool used by the United States to force negotiations and, when necessary, to impose countermeasures in response to unjustified trade practices or violations of GATT rules. Section 301's wide berth of discretion was historically important because of serious deficiencies in the old GATT dispute-settlement system. Section 301 was extremely controversial globally and was the source of much diplomatic irritation. A threat from the United States to employ Section 301 often led to counterthreats from its trading partners.

Moreover, the old GATT dispute system was not useful in combating unfair trade. The GATT practice of consensus decision-making for disputes allowed the country that was target of a complaint to delay or block the dispute process at several phases of the case. Frustrated by the blocking tactics of the European Commission and Japan, among others, the United States began using Section 301 to take, or threaten to take, unilateral action against trade violations. The United States agreed to end its unilateral actions in exchange for the automatic and compulsory WTO dispute-settlement mechanism.

Under the WTO system, countries can no longer block or veto WTO dispute-settlement decisions that are rendered against them. Nor can WTO members make a determination that a violation of rules has occurred or that negotiated benefits have been impaired or nullified other than through the WTO dispute-settlement process. This means that taking unilateral action under Section 301 without first obtaining a WTO finding against another country would place the United States in violation of WTO rules.

Section 301 has stayed on the books as the principal mechanism through which private stakeholders can petition the U.S. government to bring a case to the WTO. But because WTO approval is required before sanctions can be imposed, Section 301 is far less useful than it had formerly been in pressuring other countries to open their markets.

Most countries pay little attention to threats by Congress of legislative action to impose countermeasures or otherwise retaliate in response to their unfair-trade practices. Additionally, tough talk by the President yields little change among foreign countries that pursue questionable or mercantilist trade practices. America's trading partners know that the U.S. government is committed to bringing its concerns to the WTO through the dispute-settlement system. As astute observers of the political process, these countries know that the biggest and most influential American companies and farm groups actively lobby for trade liberalization. They know that, as a result, the political balance in Congress has shifted decidedly in favor of trade policies that support the WTO and that the United States would likely not risk damage to the WTO by acting unilaterally.

What's to stop the United States from making a unilateral determination, notwithstanding its commitments to the WTO?

The way the system works, the United States marshals evidence and puts its best legal arguments before a WTO panel but is no longer the arbiter of whether a trade practice causes adverse effects, is discriminatory or otherwise violates global trade rules. Aside from the use of antidumping or countervailing-duty determinations or Section 337, if the United States made its own finding and imposed countermeasures against what it perceived as an unfair practice, it would be in violation of WTO rules. In response, the WTO member country accused could obtain authorization from the WTO to retaliate against American exporters by demanding concessions equivalent to the measures imposed when the United States acted without WTO authorization. You can see how easily a trade war could develop if countries retaliated against each other without going through the dispute-settlement process.

Politicians may threaten trade retaliation against other countries, but the reality is that the United States has to go to the WTO, spend the better part of two years providing proof that another country is violating the rules and get a ruling in its favor. Even if the United States does get a favorable ruling, it can't retaliate. The United States is obligated under WTO rules to allow the country in question as much as 15 months to implement the recommendations of the WTO Dispute Settlement Body before the WTO will grant authorization to retaliate. On top of that, remedies are available on a "prospective" basis only: Under WTO rules, there are no damages provided for past harm, and remedies are applied only from the expiration of the implementation period.

Much seems to rest on the integrity and effectiveness of the WTO dispute system. Who are the WTO officials that now determine U.S. trade policy?

If a dispute cannot be resolved through consultation between two countries, the complaining party can ask for the establishment of a dispute-settlement panel. The panel is charged with assessing the facts of the case and the applicability of WTO rules, and it makes findings and recommendations. The panel has three members who are generally former government officials, international trade professors or experts in trade matters. Panelists typically have other jobs or responsibilities, so they rely heavily on the WTO Secretariat's legal and economic team to assess market conditions and facts, analyze legal questions and draft the panel's decision.

An Appellate Body was created by WTO members to hear appeals of decisions made by panels. This body was created as an institutional guarantee that untenable panel decisions could be overturned. The role of the Appellate Body is limited under WTO rules to "issues of law covered by the panel report and legal interpretations developed by the panel." Hence the Appellate Body operates much like an appeals court in the United States, considering legal matters but not re-examining the facts. Appellate Body members are under an obligation to consider cases impartially and independently of their nationality.

The Appellate Body is composed of seven members, also former government officials, international trade professors or experts in trade matters, each named to a four-year term with the possibility of one four-year reappointment. Member countries nominate candidates, who may not be current officials of a member government, for appointment to the Appellate Body. The appointment process involves vetting by the WTO Director-General, as well as by the chairpersons of the WTO's Councils on Goods, Services and Intellectual Property Rights and of its Dispute Settlement Body. Composition of the Appellate Body is designed to be regionally representative of WTO membership. Historically, candidates from the United States and the European Union have each maintained seats on the Appellate Body.

How much discretion do the panels and Appellate Body members have? Must they follow the letter of the WTO rules as strict constructionists, or do they have leeway to interpret in a manner that furthers the WTO's mission of trade liberalization?

The WTO's "Dispute Settlement Understanding" specifically provides that the purpose of the system is to preserve the rights and obligations of signatories to the WTO agreements and to clarify existing provisions. The Dispute Settlement Body "cannot add to or diminish [WTO members'] rights and obligations."

As a practical matter, however, there really are no institutional limits on the Appellate Body's ability to advance the trade-liberalization agenda. The decisions may be criticized by the WTO membership, but absent a "negative consensus" — that is, a decision by all WTO members — to reject an Appellate Body report, the report must be adopted.

With the Doha Round of trade liberalization, which is charged with negotiating new rules, having been stalled for many years, the Appellate

Body has begun to legislate by filling gaps in the rules or altering rules' meanings. This, however, has begun to alter the balance of concessions carefully negotiated by the parties that created the WTO. One prominent example of gap-filling is a recent decision by the Appellate Body that establishes a new meaning of the term "public body" as used in the WTO's Subsidies and Countervailing Measures (SCM) Agreement.[1]

State-Owned Enterprises (SOEs) have historically been treated under U.S. trade law as "public bodies" because SOEs can easily be a conduit for government subsidies. The Appellate Body's decision in the case defines the term "public body" in ways that are neither found in the text of the SCM Agreement nor contemplated by the SCM Agreement's negotiators, and that will make it significantly more difficult for the United States and other WTO-member governments to adequately respond to subsidies provided through SOEs.

Another prominent example of the Appellate Body legislating occurred in the area of antidumping. In a decision that significantly weakened the ability of the United States to respond to targeted dumping by foreign producers, the Appellate Body determined that the longstanding and internationally recognized practice of disregarding negative antidumping margins, also known as zeroing, was inconsistent with the AD Agreement.[2]

In rendering this decision, the Appellate Body ignored the specific text of Article 17.6 of the AD Agreement requiring it to give deference to the interpretation of the domestic administering authorities — in the case of the United States, the Department of Commerce and the ITC — when there is more than one permissible interpretation of the Agreement's terms and provisions. Most disturbing was the fact that the Appellate Body rejected the zeroing methodology in the face of ample negotiating history establishing that parties were deadlocked on the issue of zeroing through-out the Uruguay Round and that the text of 17.6 was included in the AD Agreement, partially to ensure that the zeroing methodology would not later be found to be inconsistent with it.

*It looks like the judicial branch of the WTO has more
power than the members themselves. Can you give me
a brief overview of the basic rules of the WTO?*

WTO rules operate through a five-part framework.

The first part concerns tariffs. The WTO agreement establishes a maximum tariff level — known as a tariff "binding" — for each country and product. The GATT promoted trade liberalization through its stewardship of eight rounds of trade negotiations focused principally on tariff reductions. These negotiations succeeded in reducing tariffs among the industrialized nations from about 40 percent at the end of World War II to less than 5 percent today.

Tariff reductions are of little value if they can be circumvented through the use of non-tariff barriers such as quotas and other measures limiting the volume of imports. So the GATT framers added the second part to the framework by adopting rules prohibiting any restriction on imports or exports made through quotas, voluntary export restraints, import or export licenses or other measures.

The third part of the framework is the Most Favored Nation (MFN) principle. This is the obligation to offer imports from (and exports to) another WTO-member with a tariff treatment that is equal to the best available to any other country. There are exceptions to this rule for free-trade agreements, customs unions and developing countries.

But gradually reducing tariffs and generally prohibiting quantitative restrictions on imports didn't go far enough. Countries could reduce border restrictions in accordance with international law but effectively negate such reductions by imposing internal restrictions once the imports cleared customs. For this reason, the fourth part of the WTO framework concerns what is known as "non-discrimination." This principle is designed to prevent governments from impeding imports through the use of internal taxes, regulations and other measures once products cross the border and enter commerce.

When the GATT drafters sought a way to eliminate internal measures that restricted trade without intruding upon a government's ability to regulate health and safety, they settled on the principle of non-discrimination as a means to determine whether a government is regulating based on a legitimate concern or is simply being protectionist.

The "national-treatment" principle requires WTO-member nations to apply taxes and regulations to imports as they are applied to locally produced goods. This principle also applies to services under the General Agreement on Trade in Services and intellectual property under the Agreement on Trade Related Aspects of Intellectual Property Rights (TRIPs). The national-treatment rules are perhaps the most important rules in the system because it is through internal regulations that most governments intervene to help their producers. Transparency — being able to see inside government policymaking — is essential to enforcing the national-treatment rules.

The fifth part of the GATT framework concerns prohibited subsidies. The WTO bans subsidies that are intended to encourage exports, including those that encourage or require recipients to meet certain export targets. Similarly prohibited are subsidies designed to stimulate the use of domestic goods over imported goods. These kinds of subsidies are prohibited because they are specifically designed to distort international trade. Other types of subsidies are permitted under WTO rules unless a complaining country can show that the subsidies have an adverse effect on its interests.

To sum up, the five core principles of the WTO are: countries agree to bind their tariffs (i.e. not raise them); not to impose WTO quotas; not to discriminate against imports through internal regulations and taxes; to treat all WTO members alike; and not to use export subsidies or subsidies designed to encourage the use of domestic over imported goods.

Are there any exceptions to these principles, or are they absolute?

There are exceptions that allow countries to deviate from these general rules. Several fall under the category of what trade lawyers call "state-contingent protection," such as antidumping and countervailing duties, as mentioned earlier, and safeguards that could take the form of tariffs or quantitative import restrictions. All of these can be imposed without going to the WTO as long as countries provide such protection in accord with WTO standards.

Another category of exceptions is provided for in GATT Article XX, which under certain conditions allows WTO members to breach WTO rules to protect public morals; to protect human, animal or plant life or health; to secure compliance with laws and regulations; and for other reasons. We will look at this in depth a little later on.

You suggested earlier that the mere existence of rules covering trade is insufficient without a practical way of ensuring that WTO-member countries follow them. Can you explain?

Reciprocity drives negotiations, whether those negotiations concern tariffs, subsidies, intellectual property or market access for services. For example, when WTO members negotiate and commit to bind their tariffs at certain levels, their trading partners are considered to have paid for this commitment by offering reciprocal tariff commitments. In a sense, the WTO agreements establish reciprocal property rights that are protected from government interventions that would nullify them. If a WTO member provides protection or assistance to its industries, it can nullify or diminish the property rights that its industries' competitors have paid for through the reciprocal commitments. For instance, a country that uses government funding to build steel mills despite excess global steel capacity will further help reduce the world price for steel, discourage imports and dilute the value of market-access commitments it provided on steel.

As you can see, without an effective enforcement system, the commercial and political balance upon which market access and other trade commitments were based can be thrown out of alignment by subsequent actions of governments.

It is important to understand the true effectiveness of the WTO enforcement system. If what can be achieved through enforcement is overestimated, the United States risks entering into agreements whose true benefit — the level of market access received from other WTO members — is far less than the value of the concessions it has given other members. No enforcement mechanism is perfect, but the lack of rules covering many forms of trade-distorting behavior and the WTO's flawed system of enforcement through the Dispute Settlement Understanding have worked in many cases to the disadvantage of U.S. interests.

What precisely are the shortcomings of the WTO enforcement system?

The problems fall into four categories:

- A trade-distorting practice is harming a member country's interests, but there is no coverage of the practice under WTO rules.

- A WTO rule appears to generally apply to a trade-distorting practice, but, because of vagueness and ambiguity in the rule itself, it is uncertain how a WTO panel or the Appellate Body will decide the case. In such circumstances, the perceived risk associated with losing a case can tip the scales against filing one.

- A WTO rule applies to a trade-distorting practice, but the absence of transparency in the violator's system of government makes it difficult to gather evidence needed to successfully pursue a case.

- A WTO rule applies to a trade-distorting practice, but the three years it takes for the WTO to resolve a case and the fact that it provides for remedies only on "prospective" behavior, not on past practices, diminish the commercial utility of a WTO case.

What happens when there are no WTO rules that cover a trade-distorting practice?

When WTO rules do not apply to the specific behavior of concern, then it is no use initiating a dispute-settlement case. And since the WTO is the established international venue for addressing trade disputes, diplomacy that seeks to address trade distortions outside the WTO is far less productive. Where the WTO system fails to provide a remedy for a trade-distorting practice, the system actually works against the harmed party, since the harmed party cannot fashion its own trade-related remedy without violating the WTO's proscription of unilateral retaliation.

One example of the absence of rules covering trade-distorting practices concerns China's use of Value Added Tax (VAT) rebates. As noted by USTR in its 2012 National Trade Estimate Report on Foreign Trade Barriers, China sets VAT rebates at varying levels for products that are in the same chain of production, a departure from the VAT system of all other countries, under which the VAT is automatically rebated in full for all exports. Some manufacturers in China receive lower VAT rebates than others and therefore have less incentive to export their output. This practice increases domestic supply and lowers the price of many primary products, making downstream products less costly to produce.

According to USTR, China has also applied its VAT rebate policy to promote exports, and the lower export prices of downstream products created by these policies have injured higher-value-added steel, aluminum and soda ash producers around the world. Although China's discriminatory VAT rebate policy has a trade-distorting effect, the WTO has no explicit rules prohibiting it.

Labor policies are another area WTO rules fail to cover. While national governments retain the right to regulate labor conditions, some labor standards concern fundamental rights established under the United Nations' Universal Declaration of Human Rights, which all governments are obligated to uphold. These include freedom of association and the right to work for a fair wage in a safe environment. If a country ignores these standards, it distorts the terms of trade by enabling labor-intensive firms to reduce their costs and make their products more cost competitive with imports.

China's labor policies are often identified as an example of how the failure of a government to enforce labor laws can distort trade. In its 2012 National Trade Estimate Report on Foreign Trade Barriers, USTR stated that while China had adopted several new labor laws, it "does not appear to adhere to certain internationally recognized labor standards."

*Okay, tell me about the circumstances where WTO
rules appear to apply but, because of definitional
ambiguities, it is uncertain how a WTO panel or
the Appellate Body will decide a case.*

Let me give you two examples that have been the subject of the ongoing
U.S.-China economic dialogue: China's currency policy is the first, and
its failure to effectively enforce intellectual property rights is the second.

Lets start with currency. Many economists believe that the Chinese
currency is undervalued as a result of market intervention by the Chinese
government. Economists argue that the practice raises the price of U.S.
exports to China, reduces the price of Chinese exports to the United States,
diminishes U.S. export competitiveness, adversely affects job creation
in the United States and has had a negative impact on the willingness of
many developing countries to open their markets through multilateral
negotiations. On its face, China's currency policy appears to provide a
financial contribution and a benefit to Chinese exporters. However, because
of vagueness and ambiguity with regard to prior interpretations of the
term "contingent upon export performance" under the WTO's SCM, it
is uncertain whether a panel and, eventually, the Appellate Body would
find that China's currency policy is a prohibited export subsidy.

Another area where definitional vagueness weighs on the calculus of
a WTO case filing concerns the enforcement provisions of the TRIPs
Agreement. At the insistence of developing countries such as Brazil and
India, the enforcement provisions of TRIPs were drafted by broad legal
standards. Many of the rules are undefined and others are ambiguous.
For example, one TRIPs provision requires that procedures be available
that permit effective enforcement, but the term "effective" is left undefined.
This raises questions over how panels might test the agreement's effectiveness and what types of evidence might be required to prove that procedures
are "ineffective." The enforcement provisions are also watered down by
language stating that a WTO member is not required to devote more
resources to enforcing intellectual property rules than to other areas of law
enforcement. This leaves an opening for countries with weak intellectual
property enforcement to argue that resource constraints prevent them
from meeting their obligations.

Undefined terms and ambiguity may make it difficult for a WTO panel to find a violation of TRIPs enforcement provisions, something the United States learned in a WTO case it brought against China on intellectual property rights that was decided in 2009.

The United States won on several of the issues involved in the case but lost on its most important claim, which concerned China's failure to extend criminal sanctions to willful trademark counterfeiting on a commercial scale. Since TRIPs does not define the term "commercial scale," the panel was forced to conjure a meaning that focused on local market conditions that might vary by the product and the size of the market. According to the panel, the United States did not submit sufficient evidence on the local market conditions at issue and as a result lost on this very important claim.

Can you give me a few examples of where WTO rules apply to an illegal foreign-trade practice but a lack of transparency in the violator's system of government poses a challenge to gathering evidence needed to successfully pursue a case?

The difficulty of applying WTO rules to the behavior of governments in connection with their SOEs affords a good example of where a lack of transparency can undermine WTO claims.

State capitalism blends features of market liberalization with government control and with support and protection of industries that are deemed to be strategically important to a country's economic health. In support of its national champions, countries like India, Brazil and China provide an array of benefits, including preferential bank lending; tax, regulatory and purchasing privileges; discriminatory market access; and immunities often not available to privately owned companies. These privileges give SOEs and state-supported enterprises (SSEs) an edge in competing for global business opportunities and distort the terms of global trade.

With respect to the provision of subsidies, preferential access to capital and other financial support, in a WTO case the U.S. government would carry the burden of proving before a panel that the support received by a state-owned enterprise met the WTO definition of a subsidy. It would then have to prove that the subsidy had adversely affected U.S. interests.

But documenting and quantifying the nature and extent of the subsidy provided to an SOE can be challenging. Proving discrimination against U.S. imports in a WTO case is equally challenging, especially since SOEs are often managed by former government officials or executives with political ties. Governments can guide or encourage SOEs to buy from national suppliers without ever publishing a law or passing a regulation requiring them to do so.

Enforcing the WTO's rules on foreign-investment-related requirements could also be a challenge. It could be difficult to obtain evidence that proves a government has required foreign companies wishing to invest to transfer technology to local companies or research institutes. Investment requirements have been an important topic in the U.S.–China economic dialogue. When it joined the WTO in 2001, China agreed that it would not pressure foreign firms to transfer technology to Chinese partners in joint ventures as a condition for investment approval. Yet a 2012 report from the American Chamber of Commerce in China states that one-third of the responding companies said technology-transfer requirements were adversely impacting their business. China does not publish such requirements, but according to USTR's "2012 Report to Congress on China's WTO Compliance," companies report being pressured informally by the government ministries that serve as gatekeepers for new investment or plant expansion.

Can you explain how WTO's three-year dispute resolution timeframe and "prospective-only" trade remedies diminish the desire of companies facing unfair trade practices to press for the filing of WTO cases?

To understand this it is important to know how the WTO's dispute-settlement system works.

Suppose a WTO member discovers a foreign-country trade practice that it believes to violate WTO rules. The first step under the WTO system is to formally request consultations with the alleged offending country. The consultations must take place within 30 days. If the two countries cannot come to an agreement, then a WTO panel can be requested to rule on the dispute. However, the creation of a panel cannot be requested until 60 days after the request for consultations.

Once a panel is established, it takes on average another 18 months, including an appeal, for the case to be decided and formally adopted by the WTO membership. After the panel's report is adopted, which is now approximately 22 months removed from the consultation request, the dispute enters the implementation phase. The offending party then has 30 days to come forward with a plan for implementation and can generally obtain an additional 15 months to implement the panel's recommendations. In total, from consultation request through to successful implementation of a panel ruling, it typically takes approximately three years for the offending country to terminate or withdraw its trade-distorting practice.

If you couple this three-year timeframe with the fact that, as stated earlier, damages are awarded on a prospective basis, you can see why many companies or other stakeholders, such as labor unions, choose not to bring their complaints to their national governments. The remedy, if granted by the WTO, simply comes too late to provide meaningful redress for the harm caused to the injured stakeholder.

The system also allows countries to buy time for industrial policies to achieve their desired effect. It is not surprising that some countries violate WTO rules when necessary. There is no price to be paid for this strategy under the WTO system.

There are two other hurdles worth mentioning. One concerns what is known as the "moving target" problem and the other is the WTO's GATT Article XX "exceptions." We'll talk about the latter in detail below, so let's tackle the "moving target" issue first.

WTO disputes revolve around whether specific measures such as laws, regulations, policies or government practices are consistent with a member's commitments to the WTO. When a panel is formed, the complaining party must specify precisely which measures violate WTO obligations. This creates the potential for an offending party that wants to game the system to turn its policies or practices into a moving target that is hard to hit.

Just before or midway through a panel proceeding, a defending party can terminate the original illegal measure while substituting a different type of measure to achieve illegal policy objectives. Assuming the substitute measure was not part of the original complaint and is a different type of measure from the original, the panel typically would not be able to render findings on it. The complaining party would have to begin the entire process over again to attack the substitute measure, which, too, could change in mid-course.

What are the GATT Article XX "exceptions" and how do they work? It sounds like they could provide a large loophole for countries wanting to protect their industries.

The Article XX exceptions allow a member to impose a measure that violates any of the WTO's substantive rules if it deems that measure necessary to protect public morals; to protect human, animal or plant life or health; or to secure compliance with laws or regulations that are not inconsistent with WTO rules. Countries can also seek exceptions to WTO rules to conserve exhaustible natural resources if they do so in conjunction with domestic restrictions on production or consumption. There are several other exceptions under Article XX, but these are the ones most frequently invoked. The use of these exceptions is subject to a precise set of standards and conditions, including that the measure imposed not be applied in a manner that results in unjustifiable discrimination, arbitrary discrimination or a disguised restriction on international trade.

There have been more than a dozen cases challenging the use of these exceptions. In most of them the WTO dispute-settlement panels and the Appellate Body have found that the countries seeking to use the exceptions had failed to properly justify them. But that has not stopped countries from trying to use these defenses. If properly crafted in accordance with the guidelines set forth by the Appellate Body in recent cases, these exemptions can serve as major loopholes for escaping WTO obligations. For example, in a case pending in late 2012, China is seeking to justify its restraints on exports of rare-earth minerals as necessary to protect human or plant life or health, as well as to conserve exhaustible natural resources. China has invoked the public-morals exception to justify its system of reviewing the content of imported publications and audio-visual materials and of allowing only state-owned companies to import such items. China is not the only country that has utilized Article XX exceptions. The United States has invoked them in WTO disputes to justify a ban on tuna and shrimp caught using fishing methods that endangered dolphins and turtles, and to justify a ban on Internet gambling, among other examples.

The existence of these exceptions, whether justified or not, and the other shortcomings you mentioned must weigh on the litigation calculus for firms and governments facing trade problems.

Yes. When you combine the exceptions with the three-year timeframe for the resolution of disputes, vague or ambiguous rules, prospective-only remedies and the potential for moving-target practices, there are many good reasons not to take a case to the WTO. There is also reluctance to file cases where an opposing government controls all the levers, from investment approvals to business licenses, that can set a company up for success or virtually ensure its failure. The use of subsidies for new investment adds another disincentive to taking trade cases to the WTO.

With respect to China, my understanding is that its compliance record is, on balance, pretty good. Has China not made strides in deepening its integration into the trading system through economic and legal reforms?

When it comes right down to it, the WTO operates on a self-policing basis. Countries that have political and corporate support for complying with the rules-based WTO system keep protectionist pressures in check. In such countries, exporting interests act as a watchdog against WTO violations and oppose legislative or regulatory initiatives that are not consistent with WTO's approach to trade regulation. In contrast, if a country is committed to government intervention in certain industries, trade distortions can result.

It seems to me that the dispute system does not protect
U.S. commercial interests in a timely manner,
nor does the system induce compliance or provide
a reasonable deterrent against its being gamed.

Exactly. The WTO's system of enforcement does not sufficiently induce voluntary compliance with its trade rules. It is too easy for countries inclined to bend the rules, for example, to achieve industrial-policy objectives, to do so.

What is your conclusion?

The WTO system is not capable of delivering the compliance part of the trade-liberalization bargain when a member nation chooses to circumvent and game the system. This has implications for trade liberalization because countries around the world are losing confidence in the rules-compliance component of the WTO system. The Doha Round is stalled in part because of concerns that the benefits of any negotiated agreements will be undermined by trade practices that are too difficult to enforce, owing to ambiguous rules and evidentiary issues, and by dispute procedures that do not deliver results until well after commercial damage is done.

Where the WTO offers no solution, countries around the world — especially developing countries — are making unprecedented use of antidumping measures to respond to interventions by other governments that distort the terms of competition.

Without an effective enforcement system to induce compliance with commitments, the commercial and political balance upon which market-access and other WTO trade commitments have been made will not hold.

If the WTO is flawed when it comes to enforcement, why haven't we heard more about it?

In the private sector, businesses innovate by benchmarking results, by questioning methods and strategies and by challenging themselves to innovate. That does not typically happen in the development of U.S. trade policy. There is little incentive to assess performance, particularly with respect to the enforcement of trade agreements. Presidents from both parties put political gloss on their enforcement victories and downplay their defeats. Nor is there acknowledgement of the important cases that should be but have not been filed at the WTO because of the ineffectiveness of the dispute-settlement system. Presidents want to demonstrate that they have provided the level playing field that they promised for businesses, workers and farmers.

What changes in the WTO dispute system will induce compliance?

First, the United States should propose new WTO rules to make it easier for those lodging complaints to gather the evidence necessary to bring a case to the WTO. To this end, the WTO's country-level monitoring system needs to be expanded and better funded so that it is able to provide more information about every WTO member's trade practices. Transparency in governance must become a top priority.

Second, timely and comprehensive notification of subsidies should be made mandatory. There should be sanctions, and perhaps the suspension of a member's procedural rights, for failure to comply with notification obligations.

Third, to assist in evidence gathering, once a complainant has set forth a case, the WTO Secretariat should play a facilitating role in gathering evidence from the respondent. The Secretariat should have authority to conduct its own discovery as necessary to ease the investigative burden on complainants. This would be popular with developing countries that lack resources to investigate and prosecute cases on their own.

Fourth, the WTO should tighten up the dispute-settlement process so that findings and recommendations are rendered and adopted by the WTO Dispute Settlement Body in half the current time. This can be done by reducing the amount of time currently allowed under the Dispute Settlement Understanding for composing a panel, briefing the panel, preparing the panel report and adopting the panel's findings. Consideration should also be given to eliminating the requirement that there be interim reports from the panels. To work on a faster schedule, the WTO should add staff to assist in preparing panel reports and create a standing body of experts to serve as full-time panelists.

Fifth, to induce countries to comply with the rules and dispute-settlement decisions, consideration should be given to making remedies retroactive to the date a panel is established. This would mean that if the WTO ruled against a respondent, the complainant country would be entitled to trade compensation for the level of nullification or impairment (i.e. lost trade volume) that occurred from the date of the panel's establishment until the date the respondent complied with the DSB's recommendations. Currently, remedies are applied from the end of the reasonable period of time that is allowed for implementation.

Finally, consideration should be given to allowing a panel to authorize provisional remedies made effective during its proceedings on a case, as long as the complainant can demonstrate to the panel that the measures under investigation are causing irreparable injury to the complainant's trade interests. If irreparable injury is demonstrated, then the respondent would be required to take immediate steps to stop or offset any such damage on a provisional basis while the panel is considering the facts and evidence before it.

How do you work through the WTO to achieve those changes?

The United States needs to make fixing the WTO dispute-settlement system a priority. While attention is focused on new agreements like the Trans-Pacific Partnership and the Transatlantic Trade and Investment Partnership, the United States must devote resources to improving the WTO agreements, which are, by far, the most important trade agreements the United States has entered.

During the active phase of the now-stalled Doha Round, more than 80 WTO members participated in negotiations on reforming the dispute system. More than 40 proposals covering virtually all aspects of the dispute-settlement system were considered. Clearly, a consensus exists that the dispute system needs improvement. The United States should work with like-minded nations to incorporate the kind of improvements outlined above into a revised dispute-settlement system.

There is no reason for the reform of the dispute-settlement system to become a hostage of the stalled Doha Round agenda. Negotiations concerning the dispute-settlement system are specifically excluded from the round's mandate. This means that changes in the dispute-settlement system can be agreed upon outside of any broader Doha agreement. Dating back to the 1994 Marrakesh Ministerial meeting, there has been agreement among WTO members to conduct a complete and full review of the dispute-settlement rules and procedures and to make a decision on whether to continue, modify or terminate the system.

The time for reforming the WTO's dispute-settlement system is ripe. There are many nations around the world that are concerned about the ineffectiveness of the dispute-settlement system. The United States should draw on this sentiment and build a consensus for reforms that will induce all countries to play by WTO rules.

Reducing hurdles to filing cases should result in less, not more, litigation because more timely and potent remedies will induce voluntary compliance. This should be helpful to smaller developing countries that typically lack the resources to bring cases and are disadvantaged, when it comes to imposing sanctions that limit imports, by the modest size of their markets and the importance of trade to their economies.

What can be done to address trade-distorting practices that harm U.S. interests but are not covered under WTO rules, or to which WTO rules apply but, because of definitional ambiguities, it is uncertain how a WTO panel or the Appellate Body would decide a case?

Negotiating for more clarity in the terms and definitions of the substantive rules will be far more difficult than negotiating procedural changes in the dispute-settlement system. But, again, the path is to work with nations that share America's concerns. Even if the United States cannot obtain a rule change, putting a spotlight on the practices in question can deter a country from engaging in them.

1. *United States — Definitive Antidumping and Countervailing Duties, China*, WT/DS379/AB/R, 2011.

2. *United States — Laws, Regulations and Methodology for Calculating Dumping, Zeroing, EU*, WT/DS294/AB/R, 2006.

CHAPTER 7

A Manufacturing Renaissance for Whom?

Harold Meyerson
Workforce Empowerment

*Manufacturing may be returning to the United States,
but manufacturing jobs ain't what they used to be.
Increasing workers' power won't just make those jobs better.
It is the key to reviving American manufacturing.*

FLEXING LIKE YOU CAN'T BELIEVE

In February 2013, economic geographer Joel Kotkin authored a
Wall Street Journal op-ed column extolling the growing economy of
the American South. "Korean and Japanese firms are already swarming
into South Carolina, Alabama and Tennessee," Kotkin wrote. "What
the Boston Consulting Group calls a 'reallocation of global manufacturing'
is shifting production away from expensive East Asia and Europe and
towards these lower-cost locales."[1]

That Kotkin made this observation in passing doesn't negate the fact that
he was completely redefining the economic identity — or, at a minimum,
the economic self-image — of the United States. The first nation in human
history to have developed, during the decades following World War II,
a middle-class majority had somehow become a "lower-cost locale" when
compared not only to Europe, but to East Asia. Even more amazing, this
transformation, this outbreak of mass downward mobility, had somehow
become cause for celebration, at least among some business leaders and
economists. The United States was getting its manufacturing mojo back,

in this view, and if that required not just increasing productivity through the use of high-tech machinery but also slashing workers' wages and benefits, substituting contract workers for employees and resisting unions at every turn — well, so much the better.

To the extent that this "low-road" strategy for reviving manufacturing had a manifesto, it was, as Kotkin noted, a 2011 report from the Boston Consulting Group. "Reinvesting in the United States will accelerate as it becomes one of the cheapest locations for manufacturing in the developed world," proclaimed the report, titled "Made in America, Again." Wages in China's manufacturing export sector were rising steeply, the Group noted, even as they were stable or declining within the United States. While production wages in China were at just 3 percent of those in the United States in 2000, they had risen to 9 percent by 2010 and would continue rising, to reach 17 percent in 2015. Factoring in the far-higher American productivity levels, the cost of Chinese labor had risen from 23 percent of U.S. labor costs in 2000 to 31 percent in 2010 and would rise to 44 percent in 2015. With the price of energy decreasing in the United States and the expense of transportation to and from China climbing, the report concluded, it more than penciled out for those U.S.-based companies that had offshored to China over the previous decade to bring at least some of their production back home. "When all costs are taken into account, certain U.S. states, such as South Carolina, Alabama and Tennessee will turn out to be among the least expensive production sites in the industrialized world."[2]

In case those numbers weren't convincing enough, the report went one step further, making a comparison between manufacturing-wage trajectories in the Yangtse River Delta around Shanghai and those in Mississippi. Shanghai labor costs would rise to 69 percent of those in Mississippi, the report pointed out.[3]

The key to onshoring American manufacturing, the report argued, was an "increasingly flexible workforce willing to accept non-union wage levels and benefits." When I interviewed Hal Sirkin, the report's primary author, in May 2011, he was even more explicit, albeit within the confines of the "flexibility" euphemism. "With unemployment at 9 percent," he said, "the economy can flex in ways people wouldn't believe.

We'll be getting the work rules right, getting the wage scales right, so the U.S. can be competitive on a global scale."[4]

Is that what it takes to bring manufacturing back to America: reducing wages and benefits (if any) to Mississippi- or South Carolina-like levels? Paying workers not a $25 to $30 hourly rate, which once was the norm in American manufacturing and still is in a diminishing number of embattled plants, but the $10 to $18 hourly rate that is fast becoming the new norm? If that's the key to reviving U.S. industry, then one of the linchpins of the modern American economy — manufacturing jobs paying wages that create a modest level of mass prosperity and the purchasing power to sustain a robust domestic economy — is no more. Not the bottom but the middle will have fallen out of the American economy.

It doesn't have to be this way. Germany hosts a robust manufacturing sector, nearly twice the size of the U.S. manufacturing sector as a percentage of gross domestic product, that is globally competitive while providing its workers with higher wages and more generous benefits. Germany accomplishes this in part because the nation has a greater structural — indeed, existential — commitment to manufacturing, as embodied in its excellent vocational-education program and a banking system with an entire sector devoted to serving the needs of small and middle-sized manufacturers. But it also accomplishes this because German workers have more power than their U.S. counterparts. They use that power through workers' councils that consult with management, through representation on corporate boards and through their union, IG Metall, to preserve and create high-value-added work. Germany's global manufacturers — Siemens, BMW, Volkswagen, Daimler and the rest — have plants throughout the world just as American manufacturers do, but they keep their most highly skilled and remunerative jobs at home.

American workers lack the works councils, the corporate-board seats and most of the other institutions that their German counterparts enjoy as a matter of law. A dwindling number of U.S. manufacturing workers, however, still benefit from the presence of powerful unions — and, as is the case in Germany, so do their employers. Unions like the Machinists in aerospace or the Steelworkers at some of the largest steel manufacturers work jointly with management to increase productivity by upgrading the skills of the existing workforce and training its successors. They file suits to penalize the unfair labor practices of competitor nations such as China, suits that U.S.-based manufacturers with facilities in China don't file for fear of retaliation. And they still win their members the kind of pay and benefits that make for a modestly comfortable lifestyle, something that's increasingly out of reach for most workers within the 21st-century American economy.

Can the experience of the unionized Boeing machinists or the steelworkers at U.S. Steel or ArcelorMittal become a model for labor practices at other manufacturers? Can American manufacturers learn from their more successful German counterparts?

While the growing use of robotics and technology means that American factories aren't likely to restore the quantity of jobs that American manufacturing once generated, the quality of those jobs, along with the quality of the goods that workers doing them produce, can surely be improved. But that won't happen unless workers can wield more power on the job.

This chapter will chart the declining fortune of American manufacturing workers as they have lost that power and as they continue to lose power even though some manufacturing jobs have returned to the United States. It will then look at the successes that workers' organizations in Germany and the United States have had in bolstering their nations' manufacturing sectors and assess the possibilities of this high-road strategy's gaining more purchase within American manufacturing.

MANUFACTURING GOES SOUTH

No one questions that the productivity of the American manufacturing worker is rising. While some recent productivity metrics have been called into question, the issue has been whether they adequately measure the value of foreign-made inputs in U.S.-assembled products, not whether American workers' productivity is increasing.

"The average U.S. factory worker is responsible today for more than $180,000 of annual output, triple the $60,000 in 1972," Mark Perry, an economist at the University of Michigan, has written. "We're able to produce twice as much man-output today as in the 1970s, with about seven million fewer workers."[5]

In some industries, the increase in productivity has exceeded Perry's estimates. "Thirty years ago, it took 10 hours per worker to produce one ton of steel," John Surma, the CEO of U.S. Steel, said in 2011. "Today, it takes two hours."[6]

Of the seven million manufacturing jobs lost since 1970, fully five million were lost during the decade ending in 2010, or nearly one of every three manufacturing jobs in the United States. That's not because manufacturing productivity suddenly accelerated, however. In the 1990s, as U.S. manufacturing productivity increased by an annual rate of 4.1 percent, manufacturing employment declined by just 0.2 percent yearly. But from 2000 to 2007 U.S. manufacturing productivity's annual increase was 3.9 percent — slightly lower than in the preceding decade — while employment in manufacturing declined by 3 percent per year, a rate 15 times higher than the previous decade's.[7] The acceleration in job loss was chiefly due, at least before the financial collapse of 2008, to U.S. manufacturers offshoring their work, above all to China, with which the U.S. government established Permanent Normalized Trade Relations in 2000, during the Clinton administration.

The steep loss in manufacturing jobs and the ongoing rise in manufacturing-worker productivity could have resulted in higher wages for those workers who retained their jobs. That had been the pattern in the longshoring industry after containerization revolutionized the conditions of work on the docks beginning in the 1960s. Today, the 3,500 longshoremen at the port of New York-New Jersey load and unload far more cargo than their 35,000 predecessors did before containerization had substituted a single crane operator for teams of men working with slings and pulleys.[8]

When containerization was first inaugurated, the president of the West Coast longshoremen's union, the legendary Harry Bridges, agreed to drastic reductions in the size of the harbor workforce, but only on the condition that the workers let go would be compensated from the employers' increased revenues and that the workers who remained would share in the ongoing productivity gains. There are far fewer longshoremen today than there were half a century ago, but they have what are generally regarded as the highest-paying blue-collar jobs in the United States. "There may come a day when the entire port of San Francisco-Oakland is operated by one guy pushing some buttons," Bridges is sometimes quoted — perhaps apocryphally — as saying, "but he'll be a union member and the highest paid son-of-a-bitch in the world."[9]

No such wage increases have accompanied the last two decades' gains in manufacturing productivity. The reason for the difference is twofold: First, containerization, while hardly an overnight process, happened more abruptly than have the productivity increases in manufacturing — its fundamental transformation of the industry impelled the longshoremen to strike a grand bargain. Second and more crucially, unlike manufacturing jobs, longshoring jobs could not be relocated or, as the volume of international trade increased, interrupted by a strike or other event without imperiling the broader economy.

Dockworkers had two of the strongest unions in the nation, one on the West Coast, the other on the East and Gulf Coasts, and were able to retain their power. Workers in manufacturing plants who were no longer represented by the UAW, the Steelworkers or the Machinists — once among the strongest unions in the nation — could not hold onto their power. No matter how much more productive than their predecessors, over the past 20 years, workers on the lines at Ford and GM have not seen their incomes rise accordingly, if they rose at all.

That had not always been the case. The quarter-century from 1947 through 1972 was the one period in American history when unions had real power, claiming between one-third and one-quarter of the American workforce. Over those 25 years, productivity rose by 102 percent and median household income rose by an identical 102 percent.[10] The sector that contributed most to this widespread prosperity was manufacturing, which constituted more than a quarter of the gross domestic product through much of this period and was heavily unionized in the durable-goods sector. Workers in the auto, steel, aerospace and agricultural-implement industries won annual cost-of-living adjustments (COLAs) and productivity-based pay increases by virtue of their union contracts. These contracts had spillover effects that benefited non-union workers as well. Princeton economist Henry Farber calculated that workers in non-union workplaces within industries where 25 percent of the workforce was unionized had wages that were 7.5 percent higher than workers in non-unionized industries.[11]

But that was then. Wages that track productivity improvement and COLAs have long since vanished, done in by the shift of durable-goods manufacturing to the "right-to-work" states of the South, the rise of foreign-owned transplant factories in those states, the increase in manufactured imports and the offshoring of factories by U.S. manufacturers.

Workers' challenges were heightened by increasing employer resistance to the unionization of employees at newer workplaces. Firing a worker involved in a union organizing campaign is a violation of the National Labor Relations Act, but because the penalties it carries are inconsequential — reinstating the worker with back pay, minus anything she has earned since being fired — such violations have become routine. Harvard labor economist Richard Freeman has calculated that while one such worker in 200 was fired in 1950, nine in 200 were fired in 1990.[12]

As the economy, manufacturing and otherwise, expanded from the Northeast and Midwest into the right-to-work states of the South and Southwest, and as unionization of new workers proved increasingly difficult, the share of workers in unions declined. While just over one-third of all American employees were unionized in 1955, today that figure stands at a scant 11.3 percent, and in the private sector at just 6.6 percent. The rate of unionization in manufacturing is about twice that of the private sector overall, but that's still far too low to exert any upward pressure on wages and benefits. The United Auto Workers has seen its membership drop from 1.5 million in 1979 to 380,000 in 2013, with barely half working for auto manufacturers. While employment in manufacturing has risen by roughly 500,000 since December 2009, the number of unionized manufacturing workers actually declined by 4 percent between 2010 and early 2013.[13]

Today's auto workers are compelled to compete with non-union auto workers in Southern factories owned by European and Japanese companies. In their homelands, these companies work closely with unions and pay their workers as much as or more than the best-paid U.S. auto workers. When such companies move into the American South, however, they go native, not only paying their workers far less than they do in Europe or Japan but also foregoing the greater mutuality that characterizes their labor relations at home.

According to Tim Krieg, a former manager at Nissan's factory in Smyrna, Tenn., Nissan paid its plant workers an hourly wage of $26 in 2013, comparable to that which the Detroit Three pay their senior workers.[14] But, Krieg said, roughly 70 percent of the workers at the Smyrna plant aren't Nissan employees. Instead, they are workers under contract to employment-service companies that pay them between $14.50 and $18.50 per hour for the same work that Nissan's own employees perform. In 2012, the contract workers received year-end bonuses of $1,000; the Nissan employees got $3,000 bonuses. (The percentage of contingent or contract workers in manufacturing, like their percentage in the overall workforce, is not something that the government measures, but it is undoubtedly on the upswing. One 2004 academic survey concluded that while just 2.3 percent of manufacturing workers in 1989 were contingent, by 2004 the number had risen to 8.7 percent. Of course, employers very seldom offer benefits to contingent workers.[15])

Manufacturing's move south is nothing new. Clothing and textile plants began relocating to Dixie from the Northeast in the early 20th century. But it's only in recent decades that durable-goods factories have been opening there in considerable number, a process that has accelerated in recent years. Writing in the December 2012 *Atlantic*, Charles Fishman reported on the return of General Electric — which under Jack Welch's leadership in the 1980s and '90s had been the trailblazer for American companies moving their work offshore — to its almost-abandoned Appliance Park in Louisville, Ky. Employment at the plant had peaked at 19,600 in 1979, just before the Welch years began. By 2011, it had shrunk to 1,863. Today, the plant is hiring again, and employment has risen to 3,600 workers.[16] But while the most-senior workers are making as much as $32 an hour, those hired since 2005 have started at $13.50, and their wages will hit a ceiling at $18.19 per hour no matter how long they may work there. It was in order to keep the plant open at all that the union representing its workers felt it must agree to the two-tier system in 2005. Today, 70 percent of Appliance Park workers are paid at the lower tier.[17]

Unionized manufacturing workers in America still make more than their non-union counterparts: In 2012, their average weekly pay was $872, while non-union workers made $786.[18] But the union pay advantage is eroding in the face of the two-tier contracts that most manufacturing unions have been compelled to accept. Newer hires working under UAW contracts at the Detroit Three's auto plants have hourly wages that top out between $16 and $19, according to the Center for Automotive Research, while workers hired before the institution of the two-tier system can see their base pay rise to between $29 and $33 an hour.[19] At other plants, among them American Axle and Manufacturing in Three Rivers, Mich., UAW members have seen their wages reduced to $10 an hour — so low that full-time employees must rely on food stamps to feed their families and might actually do better working at the local Wal-Mart.[20]

It's not just economically beleaguered companies like the General Motors and Chrysler of 2008 that have imposed lower wages on their workers. In 2012, Caterpillar realized record profits and, according to a *Wall Street Journal* analysis, was one of the five companies whose stock price drove the Dow Jones Industrial Average to an all-time high in of the spring of 2013.[21] Yet, taking advantage of union weakness, Caterpillar in 2012 established a two-tier system at factories in Illinois and Indiana that now pay a starting wage of $11.30.[22]

The giant sucking sound that signals the decline in workers' wages may be coming from the South, but it no longer has to originate in Mexico. In recent years, incomes in the industrial Midwest have been dropping toward levels set in Alabama and Tennessee. According to Moody's Analytics, the employee hourly compensation gap between Midwestern and Southern workers, which was $7 in 2008, had shrunk to just $3.34 by the end of 2011.[23] Nationally, the Commerce Department's Employment Cost Index shows labor costs in manufacturing declined by 2.7 percent between 2005 and 2012, while for all civilian employees they declined by just 0.3 percent. The decline in manufacturing was thus nine times greater than the decline overall.[24]

An entire region, an entire sector of American workers, is downwardly mobile. And in the opinion of various economic strategists, among whom those at the Boston Consulting Group are merely the most forthright, this downward mobility is precisely what is required to spur the rebirth of the American manufacturing colossus.

But is the Mississippization of American workers really the one and only path to rebuilding a manufacturing sector? And what sort of economy — and nation — might emerge from such a transformation?

Other advanced economies have more robust manufacturing industries even though their labor costs are considerably higher than those in the United States. Australia, France, Germany, Italy, the Netherlands and Sweden all kept larger percentages of their manufacturing during the past decade than did the United States despite the fact that manufacturing workers in those countries make considerably more on average than their American counterparts.[25] The average German hourly compensation cost for manufacturing workers in 2011, according to the U.S. Bureau of Labor Statistics, was $47.38, one-third higher than the hourly average for American manufacturing workers, which was $35.53.[26] Yet Germany, though enmeshed in the same global economy that U.S. business leaders and economists insist requires slashing wages and benefits, has not been compelled to radically downsize manufacturing or slash wages. Its manufacturing workforce declined by just 6 percent in the first decade of the 21st century, to 21 percent of the German workforce, while the number of U.S. manufacturing workers fell by 28 percent, to 10 percent of the U.S. workforce.[27] Not only has Germany remained globally competitive, but it trails only China in the size of its trade surplus, while the trade deficit of the wage-slashing United States is the world's largest and continues to expand.

Demonstrably, cutting wages, curtailing benefits and suppressing unions are not the only way — and certainly not a socially beneficial way — to bolster manufacturing. For a more effective way, we must look to the Germans.

THE VIEW FROM FRANKFURT

More than in any other nation with an advanced economy, manufacturing remains the center of Germany's economy. Its financial sector is, by American and British standards, underdeveloped. Its retail sector has been constrained until recently by legislation restricting its hours of operation, and more generally by the parsimoniousness of German consumers. Its manufacturing sector, in contrast and by design, is the marvel of the world.

The success of German manufacturing is the result of many factors. Germany's use of the euro as its currency has held down the price of its products and helped secure the nation's place as the export superpower of the West. If Germany reverted to its previous national currency, the mark, its exports would cost much more than they do in euros. But the high-road course Germany has chosen in its manufacturing is just as responsible, if not more responsible, for its dominance of those world markets in which it participates. From its automobiles and machine tools to the high-end niche products that its small and mid-sized manufacturers (both encompassed by the German word *Mittelstand*) make and market, the way of the German manufacturer is to turn out the best product of its kind and have the world beat a path to its door. A Mittelstand factory in Saxony-Anhalt that I visited in late 2010 specializes in making axle-box housings for Chinese and European high-speed rail cars, as well as a range of precision measurement tools. "We are number one or two in the world in these," Thomas Hess, the plant manager, told me. "That's why we focus on these products."[28]

The German economy is an idiosyncratic mix of pre-corporate 18th-century localism and mid-20th-century social democracy, a combination that has given Germany the most competitive manufacturing sector of the 21st century. Germany's capitalism — unlike that of the United States and the United Kingdom — is stakeholder capitalism: The companies of its Mittelstand, which do the bulk of German manufacturing, are largely family owned and financed by hometown banks whose activities are restricted to counseling and lending to local enterprises. Its signature corporations — the auto, steel and chemical companies that are known the world over — are not merely unionized: They are compelled by law both to establish works councils where employees confer with managers over plant issues and to divide their corporate boards equally between management and employee representatives.

Neither Germany's Mittelstand nor its mega-corporations rely on equity markets for their capital to the extent American companies do; the reliance is small in the case of the giant corporations and non-existent in the case of the Mittelstand. The disfiguring aspects of the American form of shareholder capitalism — the focus on short-term profits often realized by reducing wages, the skimping on both research and development and worker training — are minimal, if not absent altogether. "The key to our success is not having shareholders," German entrepreneur Klaus Hubner, the owner of the Saxony-Anhalt factory, told me. "That enables us not to have short-term strategies, only long-term ones."[29]

Germany boasts the world's most effective vocational-education system, which provides young workers with a rigorous school and shop-floor apprenticeship. At Hubner's factory, new workers go through three-and-a half years of apprenticeship once they have completed their vocational education. After reaching journeyman status, they can attend four-year technical colleges and earn higher degrees, qualifying them for the highly demanding precision design and assembly work in which the factory engages. Hess also testified to the value of works councils, which, he said, "tell me things my managers aren't telling me. We were under pressure to deliver an order quickly, so workers came in for a last-minute Saturday session. My managers told me that everything went well; the works council told me that the managers had no plan for how to turn out Saturday's work. The council helps me refine or rethink new processes, like automating a kind of welding."

"Our workforce," said Hess, "is very stable and very skilled."

During the financial crisis of 2008 and its aftermath, Hubner's company, like most German manufacturers, kept its workers on part-time through the nation's *Kurzarbeit* — literally, "short-work" — program, under which government funding maintains the pay levels of workers whose companies have cut their hours back. Twenty percent of his workers, Hess said, were enrolled in the program. None of them left the company — and when orders for axle-box housings for China's rail program took off, the company was able to expand production quickly, having retained virtually all of its employees.[30] (The equally successful Swedish version of Kurzarbeit wasn't mandated by law but emerged from negotiations between the nation's powerful union movement and its employer association.[31])

One key to the Mittelstand companies' success is the funding they receive from local banks — chiefly, co-op banks and savings banks. Germany has 430 savings banks, each restricted to doing business solely in its locality and nominally controlled by a municipal board, though managed by professionals. Created in the 18th century to provide funding to local craftsmen and merchants, the savings banks are the institutions in which most Germans deposit their savings. The banks are forbidden from participating in capital markets, and as Germans tend to rent rather than buy homes, their primary business is to advise and fund local businesses. "We have to concentrate on the real economy," said Peter Steinpass, the chief economist for the National Association of Savings Banks.[32]

Workers at the larger Mittelstand companies tend to be unionized, though unions are less common in firms with 50 employees or less. Roughly half of German workers are covered by collective bargaining contracts; in the manufacturing sector the rate of coverage is well more than 50 percent, while hardly any of the nation's service or retail workers are covered.[33] Germany's foremost manufacturing union is IG Metall, which represents workers in the auto, steel, machinery and appliance industries. The organization boasts 2.3 million members in a nation with one-fourth the population of the United States.

"Our goal is to retain high-value-added manufacturing in Germany," Martin Allespach, IG Metall's Director of Industry Policy, said at the union's Frankfurt headquarters. "Our orientation is for German manufacturing to do things better, not cheaper. During the financial crisis, we brought in 200 experts in logistics to improve our employers' logistics abilities. We focus on industrial policy at our regional and national headquarters." The union has won agreements from automakers that research and development on electric cars will be done in Germany, not abroad.[34]

In addition, some of the nation's most celebrated products — for instance, the Porsche, which is sold in 120 nations — are manufactured almost entirely in Germany.[35]

When the downturn came, IG Metall helped the German economy rebound by coming up with a cash-for-clunkers program, which German industry quickly adopted. More broadly, it uses its co-equal representation on corporate boards and its voice in works councils to diminish the economic inequality that is often the consequence of contemporary capitalism. The union got Audi and BMW to eliminate the lower pay levels for contract workers, and its representatives on corporate boards have insisted on linking executive pay not to short-term profits but to long-term metrics of company success.[36]

The union also succeeded in getting Siemens and several other major companies to guarantee they would maintain the size of their German workforce — in return for which it has moderated its wage demands for most of the last decade and placed renewed emphasis on the ongoing skills development of German workers.[37] It has retained workers' standing and a high level of social cohesion in Germany's economy while at the same time making the economy more vibrant and competitive.

A more different and successful alternative to the American model of manufacturing is hard to imagine. As U.S. Steel CEO John Surma once ruefully said, "Germany is socialistic, it's green and it's kicking our ass by any capitalistic measure."[38]

UNIONS AND AMERICAN MANUFACTURING

In recent years, a selective remorse has overtaken many within America's business elite. Offshoring manufacturing, they have concluded, was not the panacea they had hoped for. As Willy Shih and Gary Pisano argued in an influential *Harvard Business Review* article in 2009, the flight of manufacturing weakened American research and development and the nation's capacity for technological innovation.[39] The erosion of American manufacturing diminished American power and prosperity. Soon, such corporate leaders as General Electric's Jeffrey Immelt were publicizing their companies' efforts to bring some of their manufacturing back to the United States.

This remorse at the flight of manufacturing fails to recognize that, in dismissing the dire predictions of America's labor movement and promoting such policies as normalization of trade relations with China, the American financial and corporate sectors brought about just what the unions had foreseen: the destruction of much of the United States' industrial core and the diminution of its middle class. Perhaps the strongest argument to be made for strengthening America's manufacturing unions is that they have been, and remain, the only institution in American society committed to preserving, expanding and upgrading of the nation's manufacturing sector. For only if manufacturing is nurtured in this way will it be able to pay wages that can support the kind of working-class prosperity that America once enjoyed and that Germany enjoys even now.[40]

That unions are not only suited, but uniquely suited, to advocating for American manufacturing is clear from the actions they have taken against Chinese business practices that violate international trade law. Seeking to preserve the U.S. tire-manufacturing industry against an onslaught of underpriced Chinese tires, the United Steelworkers filed a complaint with the U.S. government that led to sanctions against the Chinese imports. Though there are several prominent U.S.-based tire companies, none joined with the Steelworkers in the action because all had factories in China and feared retaliation from the Chinese government if they signed the complaint.

As U.S. corporations continue to roam the globe — their rhetoric about coming home notwithstanding — and as American unions continue to weaken, the day is approaching when there will be no institutional advocate for either American manufacturing or a domestic industrial policy. While public-opinion polling makes clear that a decisive majority of Americans favors bolstering American manufacturing and opposes the kind of free-trade agreements the nation has entered into, there are no significant U.S. institutions other than unions that bring this majority's perspective into the political discourse and, specifically, the debate around industrial and trade policies.

Take away America's unions — which are dwindling every day — and the prospects for American manufacturing dim perceptibly. In an age of globalization, the strength of a nation's union movement, and of its manufacturing unions particularly, is a key determinant of the strength, even of the existence, of that nation's manufacturing sector. This is an incontestable point, as is powerfully illustrated by the example of Germany and the contrasting example of the United States.

Unions can do more to help manufacturing than ensure its existence. American unions have long provided the training and apprenticeships that have set quality and other standards in a range of industries, the building trades most prominently. Contractors and construction companies have long relied on the training programs of such unions as the carpenters', the plumbers' and the operating engineers' to turn out the workers they have needed. But such programs haven't been limited to the trades. One of the most innovative training centers is the Las Vegas Culinary Academy, a project of that city's mammoth hotel-employees' local, funded by the hotel-casinos in an agreement that is part of the union's contract with them. The Academy offers courses and certification in hotel-related jobs ranging from fry-cook to sommelier, the latter entailing a 46-week course.[41]

Some of America's leading manufacturing companies have long benefited from extensive training programs that they have jointly developed and administered with their unions. Like their German counterparts, the U.S. corporate managers and union leaders who have put these programs together have recognized that their companies' prospects depend on maintaining and continually improving their products and manufacturing processes. And like the best German companies, the companies involved in these endeavors exhibit a "we're all in this together" mentality. This recognizes a mutuality of interest between workers and managers that implies a level of respect for workers' organizations that is otherwise increasingly absent from contemporary American labor relations.

I witnessed one such program, and its consequences, when in late 2011 I toured the massive, 3,300-acre Burns Harbor, Ind., mill of the world's largest steelmaker, ArcelorMittal. Located 14 miles east of Gary, the plant was built by Bethlehem Steel in the early 1960s and went through a succession of owners during the steel industry's restructuring. It has emerged as a model of efficient, high-tech production, in large part by virtue of collaboration between its management and union, in this case Local 6787 of the United Steelworkers.[42]

When Larry Fabina, the ArcelorMittal manager who guided me through the Burns Harbor plant, first started work there in 1974, "they gave me a shovel and put me to work," he said. Today, every new hire is given a three-week course in all aspects of the factory's production processes and an additional week on its safety procedures. The school — its curriculum devised and taught jointly by the company and the local — also offers a wide range of courses in the many specialized skills required to run the plant. In one classroom, workers were dismantling air-pressure valves as part of a 37-week course that would allow them to become electrical technicians. In another, an electrical engineer was teaching employees to reprogram the computers that customize temperatures, flow rates and pressure levels for the plant's many and varied kinds of steel.[43]

An integrated mill like Burns Harbor has to run around the clock. Were it to grind to a halt, restarting it and firing up its giant furnaces could take weeks, even months. The plant requires workers who can fix things on the fly — these days, chiefly through adjustments entered on computers. In earlier times, Pete Trinidad, a local union official, said, "the steelworker's job was 80 percent back, 20 percent brain. Now it's the reverse."[44]

Trinidad's ratios aren't hype, something made clear by a tour of the plant's hot-strip mill, a building nearly a mile long that yearly customizes four million tons of steel to its many clients' specifications. The steel-shaping process may at first glance look old-school. Slabs of steel, each ten inches thick, are melted down in furnaces heated to more than 2,000 degrees. Glowing a bright, molten yellow, they then are transported at speeds up to 40 mph down a series of sluices and conveyor belts, during which they are strengthened and reshaped to anywhere from 26 to 76 inches in width and as little as 0.03 of an inch in thickness. They are then cooled and coiled. Seventy percent of this coiled steel ends up in cars made by General Motors, Nissan, Chrysler, Honda, Toyota and Mercedes-Benz.

The role of labor in the steelmaking process has changed. While 18 workers are assigned to each shift in the hot-strip mill, hardly any are on the factory floor. Instead, they're working in monitoring booths positioned along catwalks on the walls of the mill, high above the molten steel racing down the center of the floor. The booths are filled with computer monitors that register each ingot's heat, tensile strength and thickness, as well as whether it is being conformed to the programmed specifications and whether the lasers and robotic tools that are shaping the steel are performing correctly. In one such booth, Frank Munoz, a 42-year employee at the mill, tells me, "We can see all the properties of the steel as it flows. I can tell if something is wrong, and if needs be, get in touch with the guys at the furnace or the techs" — mechanical technicians who can re-program the specifications.[45]

Munoz learned his current trade — which has little in common with the production job he was hired for at the end of the 1960s — in the plant's school, where every one of the plant's 3,400 production workers and 600 engineers and managers takes at least one course a year. The plant's workforce has been downsized from its peak of 6,600 workers in the 1980s because many of the steelworkers' old tasks have been taken over by machines. Reflecting that increase in productivity, today's new hires have a starting wage of $19.56 and are not confined to a second tier of lower pay as they accumulate skills and seniority. With premiums and overtime, says Madhu Ranade, the plant's general manager, workers can make up to $73,000 a year. "You can earn a middle-class lifestyle working here," Ranade says, "and you don't have to take out student loans."[46]

The local union has made concessions to maintain this standard of living: It has agreed to consolidate some previously separate jobs into a single job classification, even though in some instances that has meant reducing the plant's workforce. "We have fewer jobs," local union official Trinidad said, "but they're more secure and better-paying jobs."

Much like German manufacturers, ArcelorMittal has a range of joint programs with local colleges and offers paid internships to college students who come to work at its Burns Harbor mill. As the plant faces ever-changing technological challenges, upskilling new and current workers is a priority for Ranade. New gas-mileage restrictions on cars require automakers to shift to lighter, stronger steels. At Burns Harbor, Ranade says, "we've worked with designers to identify how to take 30 to 70 pounds out of a new Chevrolet." That has required the company to upgrade its heat treatment for the ultra-high-strength steel that comes out of the hot-strip mill — a task that has benefited from the input not just of designers but of the Frank Munozes as well. "We expect a lot from these people as the industry is modernized," Ranade says.

Another company that has benefited from a joint labor-management apprenticeship and ongoing worker education is Boeing. Boeing's school has been around almost as long as the aircraft company itself: In 1935, Eleanor Roosevelt spoke at its first graduation ceremony.

Based in the Seattle area near Boeing's primary factory, the International Association of Machinists-Boeing Joint Apprenticeship Program offers two programs through which workers can acquire the skills for the most technically advanced non-professional jobs the company has. One is a four-year, 8,000-hour course combining classroom education and factory work; the other is a five-year, 10,000-hour course that is also a mix of classroom and plant. Of the 32,000 workers employed at Boeing's Puget Sound facilities, 1,000 have successfully completed one of the two courses, which together usually graduate roughly 40 workers a year. The highest job grade for course graduates pays nearly $40 an hour and, not surprisingly, the courses are deluged with applicants every year. In 2012, says Machinists official Connie Kelleher, nearly 8,000 applicants took a series of tests, with only the highest-scoring 100 admitted to the program. "The math test is rigorous," Kelleher explains.[47]

While the cost of the program is borne by Boeing, the curriculum is developed and the instruction conducted jointly by union and management. But as Boeing, like most manufacturers, has grown increasingly reliant on its supply chain of parts manufacturers, the union and officials of the state government have seen a need to upgrade the skills of industry workers in the area as well. In 2008, the state's Democratic legislature and Gov. Christine Gregoire, also a Democrat, together created the Aerospace Joint Apprenticeship Program for Boeing's suppliers in Washington state. Funded by the state and a one-time start-up grant from the U.S. Department of Labor, the program is run by the Machinists Union and a group of local employers. Currently, says Machinists official Jesse Cote, 86 companies participate in the program, which is training about 230 workers in courses similar to those that Boeing offers.[48]

The supply-chain apprenticeship program illustrates, again, the key role of labor in advocating for high-skilled domestic manufacturing. The travails of Boeing's 787 Dreamliner, the development of whose problematic battery the company offshored, has underscored the desirability, if not the necessity, of a manufacturing process that allows ongoing interaction between managers, designers, engineers, skilled machinists and assembly workers who are located near one another. The Joint Apprenticeship Program represents the union's attempt to create remunerative employment, upgrade worker skills and ensure quality control in a time of outsourcing. In a sense, it is a union-made version of the "industrial commons" that Pisano and Shih argue is essential if America is to retain the manufacturing and research prowess that has provided its economic edge. Whether anyone besides unions and unusually enlightened business-school professors has a genuine interest in creating such a commons remains to be seen.

MANUFACTURING WITHOUT UNIONS?

In the last couple of years, the human toll of America's abandonment of manufacturing has become apparent to the nation's elites. It was apparent to ordinary Americans well before then.

The metrics of that toll are now the stuff of everyday commentary: the income stagnation of American workers, the steep income declines of working-class males and the increasing disappearance of their jobs from the nation's labor force. The rate of labor-force participation for males aged 25 to 64 with no more than a high-school education was 97 percent in 1970. By 2011, it had shrunk to 76.7 percent.[49] With the decline in the number of working-class men with stable and adequate incomes has come a decline in working-class marriage rates and a rise in out-of-wedlock births.

Improving the fortunes of working-class Americans has been, and remains, the fundamental mission of the nation's unions. As unions have lost power during the past half-century, American workers have experienced a decline in their living standards and economic security. American manufacturing has shrunk as well, a casualty of the demands of a shareholder brand of capitalism that has been as indifferent to the national interests of the United States as it has to the welfare of working Americans. In opposition to the tenets of shareholder capitalism, unions stand for the idea of common purpose: of workers and managers cooperating to improve the prospects of their company, of workers sharing in the productivity gains their company realizes, of industrial policies that upgrade the economy not only of a place like Puget Sound but of the whole of the United States.

That's why a vibrant American manufacturing sector is unlikely to be reborn absent a vibrant American union movement. That's why American manufacturing needs American unions.

1. Joel Kotkin, "America's Red State Growth Corridors," *Wall Street Journal,* February 16, 2013.

2. Boston Consulting Group, "Made in America, Again," August, 2011.

3. When I wrote a *Washington Post* op-ed column on May 10, 2011, "China's Bad Economic News is Not Necessarily Good for the U.S." based on the preliminary draft of the Group's report, I questioned whether Americans really looked favorably on a future of Mississippi-level living standards. When the Group's final draft of the report was published three months later, the references to Mississippi had vanished; in their stead were references to South Carolina. I cite this to demonstrate the power of the press.

4. Hal Sirkin, interviewed by author, May 6, 2011.

5. Mark Perry, "The Truth About U.S. Manufacturing," *Wall Street Journal,* February 25, 2011.

6. John Surma, interviewed by author, March 24, 2011.

7. Susan Helper, Timothy Krueger and Howard Wial, "Does Manufacturing Matter? Which Manufacturing Matters?" The Brookings Institution, February 2012.

8. Steven Greenhouse, "Partial Deal with Union Averts a Strike at 14 Ports," *New York Times,* December 28, 2012.

9. Harold Meyerson, "Lessons from the Longshoremen," *Washington Post,* January 1, 2013.

10. U.S. Bureau of the Census, Current Population Reports, P60-203, *Measuring 50 Years of Economic Change Using the March Current Population Survey,* U.S. Government Printing Office, Washington, D.C., 1998.

11. Henry S. Farber, "Are Unions Still a Threat? Wages and the Decline of Unions, 1973-2001," Princeton University Working Paper, 2002.

12. Harold Meyerson, "If Labor Dies, What's Next?" *The American Prospect,* September-October 2012.

13. Jim Tankersley, "Manufacturing recovers, but unions are left behind," *Washington Post,* January 17, 2013 .

14. Tim Krieg, interviewed by author, March 10, 2013.

15. Matthew Dey, Susan Houseman and Anne Polivka, "Manufacturers' Outsourcing to Temporary Help Services," Upjohn Institute Working Paper No. 07-132, 2006.

16. Charles Fishman, "The Insourcing Boom," *The Atlantic,* December 2012.

17. Louis Uchitelle, "Factory Jobs Gain but Wages Retreat," *New York Times,* December 3, 2011.

18. Bureau of Labor Statistics, "Union Members – 2012," Table 4, January 23, 2013.

19. Center for Automotive Research, "2011 Detroit 3 – UAW Labor Contract Negotiations," November 29, 2011.

20. Richard McCormack, "Union Workers Are Classified Poor," *Manufacturing and Technology News,* July 27, 2012.

21. Steven Russolillo, "Five Stocks Handled the Heavy Lifting," *Wall Street Journal,* March 16, 2013.

22. Alejandra Cancino, "Pay in the New Era of Factory Jobs Falls Short," *Chicago Tribune,* October 3, 2012.

23. Conor Dougherty, "Midwest Closes a Cost Gap," *Wall Street Journal,* May 20, 2012.

24. David Wessel and James Hagerty, "Flat U.S. Wages Help Fuel Rebound in Manufacturing," *Wall Street Journal,* May 28, 2012.

25. Helper, Krueger and Wial, op. cit., p. 23.

26. Bureau of Labor Statistics, "International Comparisons of Hourly Compensation Costs in Manufacturing, 2011," December 19, 2012.

27. Helper, Krueger and Wial, op. cit., p. 26.

28. Thomas Hess, interviewed by author, November 17, 2010.

29. Klaus Hubner, interviewed by author, November 16, 2010.

30. Hess, op. cit.

31. Vera Glassner and Maarten Keune, "Collective Bargaining Responses to the Economic Crisis in Europe," European Trade Union Institute, 2010.

32. Peter Steinpass, interviewed by author, November 16, 2010.

33. Dierk Hirschel, chief economist, ver.di, interviewed by author, November 16, 2010.

34. Martin Allespach, interviewed by author, November 18, 2010.

35. Peter Marsh, "European Carmakers Eat German Dust," *Financial Times,* February 5, 2013.

36. Allespach, op. cit.

37. Dieter Scheitor, IG Metall representative on Siemens board of directors, interviewed by author, November 18, 2010.

38. Surma, op. cit.

39. Willy Shih and Gary Pisano, "Restoring American Competitiveness," *Harvard Business Review,* July 2009.

40. Harold Meyerson, "Save the Economy by Keeping Jobs at Home," *Washington Post,* December 15, 2010.

41. Harold Meyerson, "Las Vegas as a Workers' Paradise," *The American Prospect,* January 2004.

42. Harold Meyerson, "Back from China?" *The American Prospect,* December 2011.

43. Larry Fabina, interviewed by author, September 26, 2011.

44. Pete Trinidad, interviewed by author, September 26, 2011.

45. Frank Munoz, interviewed by author, September 26, 2011.

46. Madhu Ranade, interviewed by author, September 26, 2011.

47. Connie Kelleher, interviewed by author, February 13, 2013.

48. Jesse Cote, interviewed by author, February 13, 2013.

49. Jonathan Rauch, "The No Good, Very Bad Outlook for the Working-Class American Man," *National Journal,* December 5, 2012.

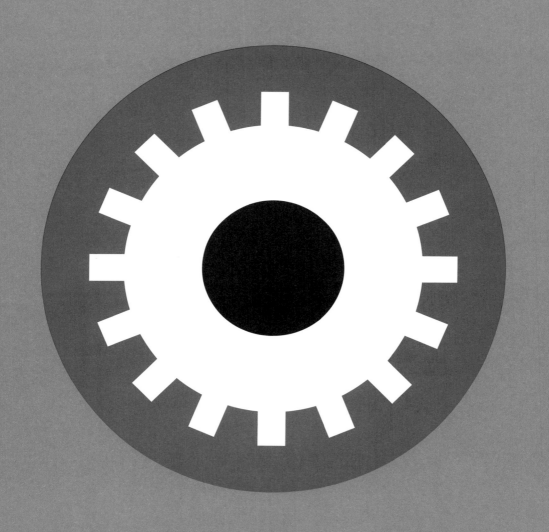

CHAPTER 8

Creating a Skilled Manufacturing Workforce

Stacey Jarrett Wagner
Training

Slater Mill, built in 1793 in Pawtucket, R.I., is considered the starting point of America's Industrial Revolution. When Slater substituted water power for human labor, manufacturing output, distribution and profits improved. The modern manufacturing business model was ignited. This business model still required human labor, but not in the same way as before. During this period, American manufacturers capitalized on recent discoveries, using new materials and energy sources to support improvements in farming, textiles, goods manufacture and everyday activities. This allowed farmers to grow more, tradesmen to produce more, and both groups to sell more. It also changed the nature of work, the routines of householders and businesspeople, and society in general.

The goods manufactured in America at that time served the domestic market, but they were also traded abroad and provided a platform for local, regional and national economic growth. From the 18th through the 20th century, America's industrial production index increased over 460 times.

Those centuries were marked by a sensibility that continues to guide manufacturing in the century now unfolding. Manufacturing has unfailingly put new ideas to work, from those early water-driven spindles to the nanoparticles used in "intrinsic healing" coatings today. Scientists, artists and backyard inventors continue to play a starring role in manufacturing innovation. At the shop-floor level, manufacturing employees are often playing an analogous role, identifying process innovations.

The manufacturing paradigm continues to shift away from labor-intensive activities toward knowledge-based and technological problem solving, and from commoditized to customized production. Likewise, manufacturing logistics have progressed from horse-drawn carts and tall ships, through phone calls and fax machines, to digital supplier networks and online shopping.

While the United States has long had international trading partners, its enterprises now instantaneously source goods, materials, employees, capital and ideas from around the world. American businesses have dealt with world trade since colonial times, but today's globalization — and the digital technology that supports it — are rapidly and radically reconfiguring America's workplaces and workforce demands.

THE MANUFACTURING WORKFORCE REQUIRES A NEW FOCUS

In the 1950s, American manufacturers employed more than one-third of the country's private-sector workforce; in absolute numbers, manufacturing employment peaked in 1979, at 19.5 million. But by September 2012, the U.S. manufacturing sector employed less than 10 percent of the country's workforce. Historically, nations have moved from low-wage, low-value manufacturing to higher-value-added production as a prescription for maintaining or improving the competitiveness of their manufacturing sector.[1] The United States is no exception: It must continue to create innovation-intensive workplaces to ensure a high standard of living for its citizens. As it does so, manufacturing jobs are changing and many may be lost, but higher-wage jobs and careers are also being created.

From the 1950s through the first decade of the new millennium, the manufacturing environment changed dramatically, and small and medium-sized American manufacturers often failed to keep pace. As the industrial cycle accelerated, companies sought an ever-bigger share of existing markets, which influenced the movement of operations in and out of the United States. Locally based manufacturers were eventually forced to choose either low-cost, labor-intensive production or high-tech, innovation-based production. The many companies that made no choice, preferring to wait, are now facing a critical dilemma: whether to move to a foreign location where cheap labor and a relaxed regulatory environment support the manufacture of commodity products, or to adopt an advanced manufacturing system at home. By reinvesting in America, both small and large manufacturers will be positioned to create millions of high-wage manufacturing jobs, as well as jobs in other sectors of the economy.[2] To ensure that this occurs, new tax, trade, technology and talent policies need to be adopted.[3]

Nostalgia for "old-time manufacturing" has afflicted many Americans, who pine for the days when a person with little education but a lot of strength of character could hold down a good job with a Michigan auto-maker, an Ohio parts-maker, an Alabama shipbuilder or a California avionics supplier. America's middle class was literally forged in the man-ufacturing sector. But as times have changed, manufacturing has changed with them, so that not only new skills, but also new combinations of skills, are required of a manufacturing employee. Today's requisite manufacturing skills are still being defined and certified, and they will continue to evolve over the next several decades into some of the following:

- Sense-making (for dealing with complex situations);

- Novel and adaptive thinking (for developing innovative ideas and problem-solving);

- Social intelligence (to understand how best to connect and work with people);

- Trans-disciplinary facility (to work across multiple disciplines);

- New-media literacy (to know how to use many forms of media to find, analyze and use information);

- Computational thinking (for deploying a systems approach to an enterprise or sector);

- Cognitive load management (to manage information overload);

- Design mindset (to create new forms that meet function);

- Cross-cultural competency (to ensure global fluency); and

- Virtual collaboration (to be able to partner with others not seen in the flesh).[4]

As these new skill combinations suggest, manufacturing employees will need to be adept at maneuvering within a high-tech, information-loaded, fast-paced, multidimensional, multinational framework whose inputs may be sourced from anywhere in the world. These inputs include personnel. If there are gaps in critical areas and functions, manufacturers can be expected to source employees who have the right skills from wherever they are located, regardless of country or region.

Offshore outsourcing, outdated education and training systems, and manufacturers who won't invest in training have been singled out as causes of America's current manufacturing-skills gap. Specifically, the last 20 years have so transformed the manufacturing workplace that it has become difficult to understand the skills or skill combinations that are necessary at any given moment or that might become necessary in future decades.

In the 1980s, few really understood the extent to which computers would change the workplace. Who knew that radio-frequency ID tags would revolutionize the supply chain to such an extent that any excess supplier capacity would be deemed a liability? Who could have predicted that atomic particles would be manipulated to create the high-capacity processors that are now taken for granted, or that the supply of rare-earth materials could restrict industrial growth around the world?

FIGURE 1: *Future Work Skills 2020*

DISRUPTIVE SHIFTS THAT WILL RESHAPE THE
WORKFORCE LANDSCAPE

EXTREME
LONGEVITY

*Increasing global lifespans
change the nature of careers
and learning*

COMPUTATIONAL
WORLD

*Massive increase in sensors
and processing power
make the world a
programmable system*

SUPERSTRUCTED
ORGANIZATIONS

*Social technologies drive new
forms of production and
value creation*

RISE OF SMART
MACHINES & SYSTEMS

*Workplace robotics nudge
human workers out of rote,
repetitive tasks*

NEW MEDIA
ECOLOGY

*New communication tools
require new media libraries
beyond text*

GLOBALLY-CONNECTED
WORLD

*Increased global intercon-
nectivity puts diversity and
adaptability at the center of
organizational operations*

KEY SKILLS NEEDED IN THE FUTURE WORKFORCE

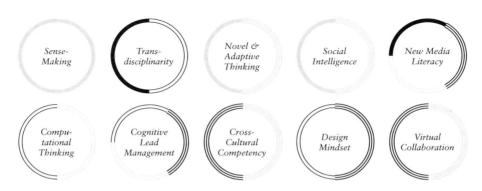

*Sense-
Making*

*Trans-
disciplinarity*

*Novel &
Adaptive
Thinking*

*Social
Intelligence*

*New Media
Literacy*

*Compu-
tational
Thinking*

*Cognitive
Lead
Management*

*Cross-
Cultural
Competency*

*Design
Mindset*

*Virtual
Collaboration*

Education and workforce development are the bedrock of 21st-century manufacturing. If this is not well understood, then America will lack the commitment to educate its current or future employees so that they can lead, or simply keep pace with global manufacturing or industrial and scientific innovation. It is critical that the pioneering nature of advanced manufacturing be understood nationally, for only then will the education needed by its workforce be made available.

Advanced manufacturing "is driven by advances in science and technology that occur in university or industrial laboratories, on factory and shop floors or at business schools," states a 2012 report from the Institute for Defense Analyses.[5] There is often debate over the exact definition of advanced manufacturing, but the concept is clear: Advanced manufacturing embraces technology and innovation as the platforms from which it creates products for consumer, commercial, military and scientific markets. Location plays only a minor role. Innovation, supply chains, production, distribution and customers may be geographically co-located within an "industrial commons" or spread across the world.[6]

At each stage of manufacturing, from concept to delivery, the business components — supply chain, modeling and simulation, production, distribution, sales and end use — can be contiguous, but they need not be. Design may take place in California, manufacturing in Florida, and supply-chain management in Montana, while customers can be located around the world or right next door. "Manufacturing" will become a mixture of technologies that are characterized by high levels of innovation and collaboration. In emerging techniques such as additive manufacturing, less manufacturing knowledge will be needed at the production stage than in the design stage, which will depend upon advanced materials science.[7] Automation will become a dominant force within the manufacturing environment, and employees will need to understand how to manage sophisticated robots and other automated technologies that are built upon information technology and advanced software.[8]

FIGURE 2: *Advanced Manufacturing Enterprise Concepts*

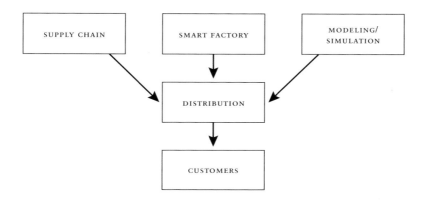

Source: Adapted from SMLC (2011)

Advanced manufacturing is fast becoming the dominant type of manufacturing in the United States, driven by the necessities of economics
and national security,[9] and the majority of manufacturing employees
will soon be working in its fluid, computational, adaptive, digital world.
New approaches to workforce development must therefore be initiated,
implemented and institutionalized so that America can — in fact, not in
rhetoric — build a pipeline of advanced manufacturing talent to fuel its
economic growth. But there exist today many small and medium-sized
manufacturers (SMEs) in America whose business models do not reflect
the accelerating transformation of production. As a result, the U.S. must
focus on its small manufacturing firms, which account for 98 percent
of the U.S. manufacturing base,[10] especially since SMEs create jobs
at a higher rate than large firms.[11]

Strategic management, acquisition, development and retention of talent
are the foundational components of a corporate workforce system. Large
companies, those with more than 500 employees, have strategically
managed their talent for decades, but small companies have often lacked
the wherewithal to manage their workers as part of their business systems.
In small manufacturing firms, managing production and sales has ranked

at the top of the "must do" list, while the "people side" has been managed in line with workforce regulations such as worker's compensation or seniority, and without the benefit of such human-capital-concepts as knowledge sharing and pay for performance. Small manufacturers think more about minimizing personnel costs and risks and less about creating value through strategic talent management. This needs to change.

Standardized technology-sharing infrastructure such as Tin Can (formerly SCORM[12]) and the proliferation of software applications have democratized the capture and distribution of information, making analytics newly accessible to small businesses. As the cost of investing in technology has decreased, more firms have been able to put technology to work in their operations. In the late 1980s, technology for capturing and managing firm-wide data on human resources and corporate training was taking its baby steps. It's now employed in all firms, from the neighborhood grocer to global businesses. Early human resource systems did little more than capture simple data, but today's systems can manage a firm's talent by using analytics to better understand how investments in human capital, from acquisition through training to retirement, affect an organization's performance, create value and reduce liabilities. These new processes will likely only be successful, however, in an organizational culture that values, and wishes to enhance, its workforce capacity.

Inside SMEs, a workforce initiative is rarely considered to be a "system" that is integrated with other business systems such as production, distribution or finance. But incorporating system processes such as workforce alignment and planning, recruitment, career development, management, retention and succession can mean the difference between managing workforce-development risks and rewards successfully and facing the unintended and costly consequences of hiring the wrong people, with the wrong skills, at the wrong time and for the wrong reasons.

The analytical tools for understanding workforce investments have never been better, but planning, analysis and evaluation of these investments among SMEs remains weak. A recent Boston College report describes how American manufacturers lag behind all other industries when it comes to planning for their workforces.[13] Data from this report show that manufacturers are woefully unprepared when it comes to understanding their employees' career plans, the changing demographic makeup of their companies' workforces, the demands of succession planning, what skills their firms currently possess, what skills their firms will need over time and what ability their supervisors have to anticipate and plan for staffing requirements.[14]

WHAT AMERICA MUST DO AND WHY

America is home to the "innovative solution," but in trying to fix the decades-old skills gap, it has created an overabundance of "solutions." Manufacturers can find useful workforce development partners in community colleges and technical schools; polytechnic institutes; career academies; science, technology, engineering and mathematics (STEM) magnet schools; manufacturing and science summer camps; First Robotics competitions; vocational clubs for high-schoolers such as SkillsUSA; non-profits that promote engineering education such as Project Lead the Way; skills certification providers like the Society of Manufacturing Engineers or the American Welding Society; awareness campaigns such as "Dream It. Do It."; and nationwide public-private technical assistance providers like the Hollings Manufacturing Extension Partnership.[15] The National Science Foundation's Advanced Technology Education (ATE) centers work with businesses, post-secondary schools and student outreach programs around the country to help revise curricula for advanced manufacturing professions, create a workforce supply for businesses and expand job opportunities for young people and adults. ATE centers in Washington and California are already teaching students about additive manufacturing and nanotechnology, and they will provide credentials in those disciplines. Generally, community colleges enroll about eight million students, many of whom attend specifically for workforce training.

In 2010, federal legislation was signed providing $2 billion over four years to fund the Community College and Career Training initiative with an eye toward workforce skills development.[16] More recent legislation gives military veterans grant funding for retraining opportunities and provides tax exemptions for employers who hire them. In 2012, the White House promoted legislation that would align credentials for military and civilian occupations.[17]

There appears to be no dearth of organizations, programs and initiatives that intend to re-create America's manufacturing workforce. So, what could possibly be missing in the effort to close the U.S. skills gap? Why do SMEs have a continuing problem finding skilled manufacturing employees?

The main problem is that along with disruptive technologies comes disruption in skill requirements. New requirements take some time to fully understand and to teach — once they are even identified. Because the manufacturing sector has changed so dramatically from the Baby Boom generation to the Millennial generation, the long lag that has taken place in updating formal education and training has had a considerable, detrimental effect on the manufacturing competitiveness of smaller U.S. companies. Unlike most large companies, SMEs don't have corporate trainers, corporate universities or chief learning officers to negotiate changing skill requirements.

The second but no less critical problem is that innovation, exporting, supply-chain management and sustainability used to be for "the big guys." These issues now shape the environment in which SMEs conduct business as well. Cost-reduction issues have already been pushed down to suppliers by the original equipment manufacturers (OEMs), and now small companies must move quickly beyond the general role of low-value, high-volume supplier. To do this, American SMEs must now use the technology, brainpower, capital financing and flexible business-process approaches that, for a long time, were not necessarily critical to their ongoing success. To stay on top in today's high-stakes business environment, SMEs have begun using technology to monitor inputs, outputs, throughputs and revenue. Everything from design and production through marketing and distribution is run or monitored by advanced software applications that can help evaluate the costs and value of business processes. It is critical for manufacturers to invest in these technologies, for without them they will not be able to compete either domestically or globally.

U.S. manufacturers cannot hope to grow without seeing the world as their marketplace and without embracing innovation and the development of new products and services that place them above low-value providers. Yet, to date SMEs' adoption of new technologies has been uneven not only across sectors and regions but also at the operations level, making it hard for states to provide large-scale education and training solutions.

To address these issues, SMEs need to adopt a set of workforce system standards that will allow them to analyze their workforce needs; calculate investments in programs, training and wages; and make decisions about what works best for their business based on their unique data. This means that SMEs, like their big-company brethren, must identify their short- and long-term business goals, the technology and processes needed to meet those goals, the skills that will make this work, the best source of those skills, how to attract those skills, the business value they place on those skills and how best to support their workforce investments.

Interestingly, in spite of the urgency felt by American manufacturers to find skilled employees, investment in corporate training has been rather static during the last decade.[18] Some of this can be attributed to the rapidly changing business environment and to a resulting uncertainty as to what kind of employees are needed, but it can also be attributed to a failure to integrate talent management with other business processes. Only 13 percent of the companies participating in the 2011 "State of Industry Report" by the American Society for Training and Development said that they integrate technologies and share data when it comes to talent management, while 70 percent acknowledged that they should.[19] Seventy-two percent said that they should use technology to better manage their talent, and 85 percent said that they should establish an organizational culture that supports talent management. But they don't do these things.

Another report, from the American Small Manufacturers Coalition, states that while almost 77 percent of manufacturers rate the importance of human-capital acquisition, development and retention as highly important to their business success, only 24 percent have a measurement system for reviewing the return on their workforce investments.[20]

For SMEs, employees have long been a fungible commodity that did not seem worth the "extra" investment. But that era is finished. Today's advanced manufacturing workplace requires employees with a multitude of advanced technical skills, as well as emotional intelligence, communication facility, talent in cognition and analysis, imagination, a capacity for systems thinking and creativity in problem solving. An internal system of standard management metrics and evaluative functions, integrated alongside other business systems, is critical to successful talent management.

HOW SMES CAN COMPETE
FOR HIGHLY-SKILLED EMPLOYEES

In today's workplaces three generations work side by side: the Baby Boomers, the Gen-Xers and the Millennials.[21] Each of these generational cohorts values specific attributes of their employers and specific benefits those employers offer. But Millennials are, and will continue to be, different from the other two groups. They have grown up in a world extraordinarily different from that of their parents and grandparents (who may still be young enough to work), and the expectations they have for their profes-sional lives align more substantially with their personal aspirations than the expectations of the two previous generations. Among the Millennials' expectations are:[22]

- that they will be offered international opportunities;

- that they will have access to excellent training and development programs;

- that their employer will have a solid reputation for ethical practices;

- that their employer's values will match their personal values;

- that the company they work for will have a reputation as an employer of the best people;

- that their employer will have a distinctive brand;

- that their employer will have an impeccable diversity and equal-opportunities record;

- that they will be afforded ample opportunity for career progress;

- that the wages and other financial incentives they are offered will be competitive; and

- that they will be offered good benefits packages.

Millennials are history's first "always connected" generation. They have grown up with digital technology and social media; in fact, they may be seen everywhere multi-tasking on hand-held devices. They are expected to become the U.S.'s most-educated generation.[23] They believe they are distinct from previous generations because of their use of technology, while Baby Boomers say their distinction is an intense work ethic. More Millennials than Baby Boomers say that most businesses should balance profit making and social justice and that they want to work for a company that mirrors their civic beliefs. If manufacturers are often heard to lament that younger workers don't understand the manufacturing opportunities available to them, perhaps the trouble lies in a failure by prospective employers to portray the career opportunities they have to offer so that they are in sync with Millennials' aspirations.

UNDERSTANDING THE VALUE OF ORGANIZATIONAL CULTURE IN A GLOBAL WORLD

As work life and personal life become ever more-tightly interwoven, it is important for manufacturers to understand how their operations attract and keep the right talent. Because individuals with talent will be able to work anywhere around the world, American manufacturers must create a work environment that encourages invention. Thus, SMEs must:

- promote effective collaboration, teamwork and access to knowledge sharing;
- nurture good communication among staff;
- eliminate barriers to staff performance;
- define jobs clearly and allow staff to do them well;
- engage in continuous improvement in their operations;
- demonstrate outstanding professional values at all times;
- plan on an annual basis for innovation and growth;
- match job profiles and staff skills;
- use job profiles to support innovation and growth goals;

- adopt human-resources policies that are fair and equitable;
- make a leadership program available to staff;
- assure that a succession plan is in place; and
- analyze the workforce's tangible and intangible value to the business.

Not only is it crucial to attract and retain the right talent, an organizational culture must support an environment of invention and creativity. It is not for nothing that the successful technology companies of Silicon Valley provide a stimulating work environment with flexible human resources policies that offer such benefits as continuing education, sabbaticals, skunk works and an attitude of fun.

UNDERSTANDING RESOURCES AND PARTNERSHIPS

In the interconnected world Americans now inhabit, SMEs will need to make better use of partnerships to gain access to existing resources and additional resources that may be created in the future to support them. The federal government's Manufacturing Extension Partnership (MEP) program, which is approaching its 25th year in operation, was instituted to act as a catalyst for strengthening American manufacturing and accelerating its ongoing transformation. In its early years, MEP focused on lean manufacturing and the production of quality products in the small manufacturing environment. Now it is driving growth through innovation, using five "Next Generation Strategies": continuous improvement, technology acceleration, supply-chain management, sustainability and workforce excellence.

All of these strategies require the use of outside resources to capitalize on change. The MEP centers partner with federal and state agencies, community and technical colleges, universities, governors' associations, think tanks, workforce investment boards, chambers of commerce and others, and they encourage SMEs to take advantage of the technical assistance they offer. Examples of partnership resources include skills certification through the National Association of Manufacturers' Skills Certification System and the National Governors Association Policy Academy; layoff aversion programs with local Workforce Investment Boards; and grant funding opportunities available from the Departments of Labor, Commerce, Energy, Transportation and Agriculture to develop models of regional advanced-manufacturing activities that focus on strengthening American manufacturing and encourage OEMs to "buy American."

CREATING A CORPORATE WORKFORCE SYSTEM

MEP is currently developing a talent-management tool to support the investments of small and medium-sized manufacturers in aligning workforce planning and development with specific business drivers. The overall system will include strategic planning and alignment, recruitment, retention, management and succession planning. MEP is creating this tool, to be piloted in 2013, with the intent that it will provide automated data analyses and analytical guidance for manufacturers in their workforce planning and implementation.[24]

But the MEP tool — or any technology, for that matter — will be only as good as its user. The nationwide network of MEP centers will therefore work with SMEs to help them not only understand how to put a corporate workforce system in place, but also to identify the kinds of questions they should put to themselves to ensure that the data they gather can shed light on their workforce-investment returns. An analytical method for understanding workforce risks and returns will raise the level of a SME's competitiveness from that of local operator to one of global business enterprise. While the MEP tool will not be the only one available in the talent-management marketplace, it will be specific to the small manufacturing environment. This tool and others like it will support American manufacturing competitiveness by helping small firms define their workforce challenges; identify data requirements; define a workforce analytics platform that is common and therefore easy to use; and enhance the firms' human-resources analytic capacity.

In a survey conducted by IBM during the recent recession, respondents were asked to rate the importance of human-capital challenges, as well as their organizations' effectiveness in addressing each. FIGURE 3 lists how businesspeople rated their challenges and plots the challenges' importance and the firms' effectiveness in meeting them.

The chart shows that keeping talent in the organization is the most important of the challenges in talent management and that the programs used to accomplish this were the most effective programs the firms engaged in, while strategies for reductions in force were the least important and ineffective. Additionally, firms said that aligning knowledge, skills and abilities with business strategies is very important, as is evaluating talent in support of business goals.[25]

FIGURE 3: *Reported Importance and Effectiveness of*
Strategic Human Capital Challenge

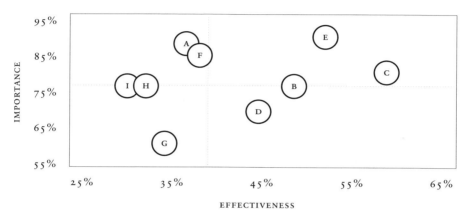

ITEM		GAP
A	Defining knowledge, skills and capability requirements for execution of business strategy	48%
B	Determining headcount and FTE capacity requirements by job assignments and locations	31%
C	Sourcing and recruiting individuals	22%
D	Developing training strategies	35%
E	Retaining valued talent within the organization	38%
F	Evaluating workforce performance	46%
G	Determining strategies for reduction in force, redeployment and retraining	24%
H	Understand collaboration and knowledge sharing	48%
I	Developing succession plans and career paths	49%

RECOMMENDATIONS TO ENSURE COMPETITIVE U.S. MANUFACTURING

The recommendations here are not necessarily specific to small and medium-sized manufacturers, but SMEs are at the heart of America's manufacturing growth and innovation, and they need support. Large manufacturing companies, while significant contributors to manufacturing employment, have more resources from which to draw as they attempt to improve their competitiveness. However, OEMs are closely linked to, and dependent on, the quality of the small firms in their supply chains. Thus, an increase in the ability of SMEs to compete will boost the entire U.S. manufacturing network as it continues contributing to America's economic growth.

- *Support the Proposed National Network of Manufacturing Institutes* (NNMI)

  President Obama announced a plan in 2012 to invest $1 billion to create a national network of up to 15 manufacturing innovation institutes around the country. These would serve as regional hubs of manufacturing excellence to make manufacturers more competitive and encourage investment in the United States. The proposed network has been endorsed by the federal government's Advanced Manufacturing Partnership (AMP) Steering Committee. The AMP's final recommendations outlined a set of actions designed to enable innovation, strengthen the U.S. workforce and accelerate investment in America. These institutes and the network should be quickly established.[26]

- *Promote Verified, Reliable and Standardized Skill Certifications to Create Reliability and Validity in the Recruitment Process*

  The country needs to ensure that nationally portable skill certifications are aligned to secondary and post-secondary programs of study and to industry-relevant training needed for employment in advanced manufacturing. And the alignment of military and civilian skill certifications must also be integrated into an agreed-upon certification taxonomy so that America's veterans can be placed in advanced-manufacturing jobs.

- *Expand the National Science Foundation's Advanced Technology Education (ATE) Centers and Connect Them to Education Providers*

  Expanded funding for the ATE program would support community colleges working in partnership with industry, economic development agencies, workforce investment boards, and secondary and tertiary educational institutions — with an eye toward advanced-manufacturing disciplines. The centers should be linked with STEM programs at all educational levels and with industry-Ph.D. fellows programs to increase the quality of research and education.

- *Invest in High-Quality Job Training Such As Apprenticeships and Internships*

  Companies, schools and training providers must ensure access to "real-world" manufacturing job experiences as part of the education process to demonstrate to prospective future employees the opportunities and excitement in advanced-manufacturing careers.

- *Support Initiatives That Help American Companies Make the Transition to Advanced Manufacturing*

  Expand resources at the national and state levels for the Manufacturing Extension Partnership. MEP programs have made a considerable impact by boosting the innovation, productivity and competitiveness levels of small American manufacturing firms. New efforts focused on helping manufacturers be more strategic in their management, acquisition and retention of talent include the development of an automated suite of tools.

- *Provide Business and Accounting Standards for Identifying and Capturing Both the Tangible and Intangible Effects of Workforce Investment*

  New accounting standards are needed to redefine "investments" and "expenses" as they pertain to the value and outcomes of workforce investment. Workforce "expenses" could be recalibrated as workforce investments and amortized, and workforce investment categories customer service, risk reduction and knowledge sharing.

1. Robert Atkinson, "Worse Than the Great Depression," Information Technology and Innovation Foundation (ITIF), March 2012, http://www.itif.org/publications/worse-great-depression-what-experts-are-missing-about-american-manufacturing-decline.

2. "Manufacturing continues to generate more economic activity per dollar of production than any other business sector in the country," *The Facts About Modern Manufacturing*, The Manufacturing Institute, 2009.

3. ITIF, Op cit.

4. "Future Work Skills 2020," Institute for the Future, 2011.

5. Stephanie Shipp, "Emerging Global Trends in Advanced Manufacturing," Institute for Defense Analyses, March 2012.

6. Gary Pisano and Willy Shih, "Restoring American Competitiveness," *Harvard Business Review*, July-August 2009. The resurgence of the U.S.'s "industrial commons" should be strongly encouraged for advanced manufacturing.

7. Mark Rice, President, Maritime Applied Physics Corp., "Presentation to the White House Symposium on Additive Manufacturing," August 20, 2012.

8. John Markoff, "Skilled Work Without the Worker," *The New York Times*, August 18, 2012.

9. ITIF, Op cit.

10. Small Business Administration, according to the Bureau of Labor Statistics and the Census Bureau, March 2, 2012, http://www.sba.gov/community/blogs/small-manufacturers-driving-job-creation-economic-growth.

11. Congressional Budget Office, "Small Firms, Employment and Federal Policy," March 2012.

12. The Sharable Content Object Reference Model (SCORM) integrates a set of related technical standards, specifications and guidelines designed to meet high-level requirements for accessible, interoperable, durable and reusable content and systems for computer-aided information distribution. For information, go to the Advanced Distributed Learning website, http://www.adlnet.gov/.

13. Sloan Center for Aging and Work, "Talent Pressures and the Aging Workforce," Boston College, 2009.

14. Ibid, figure 3.5, page 27.

15. The Hollings Manufacturing Extension Partnership is a federal grant program administered by the National Institute for Standards and Technology, an agency within the U.S. Department of Commerce.

16.   Health Care and Education Reconciliation Act of 2010.

17.   Hiring Heroes Act of 2011 (S-951, HR-1941). Read the report "Military Skills for America's Future: Leveraging Military Service and Experience to Put Veterans and Military Spouses Back to Work," The White House, May 31, 2012, http://www.whitehouse.gov/sites/default/files/docs/veterans_report_5-31-2012.pdf.

18.   American Society for Training and Development, "State of the Industry Report 2011."

19.   Ibid.

20.   American Small Manufacturers Coalition and the Manufacturing Performance Institute, "Next Generation Manufacturing Study Overview and Findings," June 2009.

21.   Baby Boomers were born between 1946 and 1964 and number 76 million; GenXers were born between 1965 and 1976 and number 51 million; Millennials were born between 1977 and 1998 and number 75 million.

22.   PricewaterhouseCoopers, "Millennials at Work: Reshaping the Workplace," Fall 2011. The list is not in rank order. Pew Research Center, "Millenials: Confident, Connected, Open To Change," 2010.

23.   Ibid.

24.   This technology is being created "in-house" with expert talent management technologists and manufacturing subject-matter experts.

25.   IBM, "Getting Smart About Your Workforce: Why Analytics Matter," IBM, 2009.

26.   A consortium of businesses, universities and community colleges from Ohio, West Virginia and Pennsylvania are co-investing with the federal government to create the National Additive Manufacturing Innovation Institute (NAMII) in Youngstown, Ohio. This new public-private institute for manufacturing innovation is the first institute in the NNMI. The site was selected through a competitive process led by the Department of Defense and includes $30 million in funding matched by $40 million from consortium members.

CHAPTER 9

The Future
Of Manufacturing

Irene Petrick
Technology Trends

This chapter is a story about the future of manufacturing based on
three predictions:

- that firms of all sizes will have increasing access to high-performance
  computing capabilities that will enable sophisticated modeling and
  simulation of both new products and production processes;

- that additive manufacturing will become commercially competitive
  across a wide range of industries and will support the use of multiple
  materials; and

- that new business models relying on information technology (IT)
  will reduce the administrative overload both of bidding and winning
  contracts and of delivering products and services.

If these predictions play out, it will favor localization of manufacturing
over today's more centralized, economies-of-scale production models
based most recently on offshore outsourcing. A fourth trend — a rise
in the number of hobbyists who become designers and producers of one-
off and small-lot products — will change the definition of "manufacturer"
and may, in fact, return manufacturing to the garage. An IT-driven
transformation in the manufacturing sector is inevitable.

INTRODUCTION

Technology has been revolutionizing industrial sectors for more than 200 years. We have seen the way mechanized production increased productivity during the Industrial Revolution when it replaced workers performing repetitive tasks. We have also experienced the way IT and computing have revolutionized the means by which production is planned, managed, accounted for, inventoried and even delivered. But the divide between the computing haves and have-nots has grown in the past decade, and nowhere has this been a more serious problem than in the manufacturing sector. A recent series of workshops conducted by the National Academy of Engineering highlights why this divide is so important, suggesting that adding value, and thus capturing a higher percentage of that value, means integrating innovation, design, manufacturing and service delivery. This will require a systems-wide view of the innovation-to-production process, and it may favor entrepreneurs. Kate Whitefoot and Steve Olson, authors of a report on the workshops' findings, believe that "there is no better time [than now] to be a talented entrepreneur who can take innovations and scale them rapidly, digitally and globally."[1]

In essence, this chapter presents a story based on predictions about the changes in store for the industrial supply chain, including changes in the relationship between larger original equipment manufacturers (OEMs) and their suppliers. This is also a story about the changing dynamics within current supply chains, where the traditional David-and-Goliath relationships are evolving. If these predictions are borne out, David may triumph over Goliath more frequently in the future, and at least will enjoy the luxury of increased self-determination.

THE POTENTIAL FOR A REVOLUTION
IN THE MANUFACTURING SECTOR

Strategic roadmapping[2] has been used successfully to help companies develop scenarios of the future, and the recent growth of *outside-in* thinking[3] emphasizes the importance of sensing and sense-making in the external environment for determining the critical forces that will be game changers. At the heart of this approach lies a need to capture the breezes of today that will turn into the gales of change for tomorrow. But it is rare that a single trend by itself is a disruptive force. Instead, it is the combination of multiple, often seemingly unrelated trends that presents truly disruptive future scenarios.

There are four trends that have the power to revolutionize the manufacturing sector. These four trends suggest that the current arrangement of tiered supply networks based on low-cost production and economies of scale is unlikely to dominate in the future. Instead, IT-driven design and production will favor local manufacturers and artisan-entrepreneurs (FIGURE 1).

FIGURE 1: *Four Trends With the Potential to Revolutionize the Manufacturing Industry*

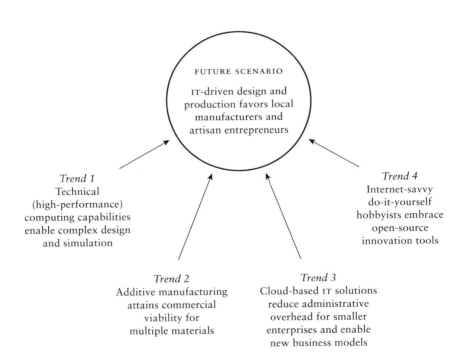

FUTURE SCENARIO

IT-driven design and production favors local manufacturers and artisan entrepreneurs

Trend 1
Technical
(high-performance)
computing capabilities
enable complex design
and simulation

Trend 4
Internet-savvy
do-it-yourself
hobbyists embrace
open-source
innovation tools

Trend 2
Additive manufacturing
attains commercial
viability for
multiple materials

Trend 3
Cloud-based IT solutions
reduce administrative
overhead for smaller
enterprises and enable
new business models

HIGH-PERFORMANCE COMPUTING CAPABILITIES TAKE SOPHISTICATED MODELING MAINSTREAM

The first trend is related to the increasing availability of high-performance computing capabilities beyond traditional research labs and large manufacturers. Many tools developed over the past two decades that support product-development innovation are well understood in the manufacturing environment, and their combination with automation technologies has transformed the factory floor. CAD/CAM, combined with the capabilities of computer-numerical controlled (CNC) machines, has boosted productivity and is commonplace in most manufacturing firms, regardless of size or sector.

Less well understood by the majority of companies are the tools that support testing, advanced analytics and simulation. Large companies such as Boeing have been designing, simulating and testing digitally for over two decades. The CATIA product-design software developed by Dassault Systemes enabled Boeing engineers and designers to see parts of enginesas solid images and then simulate the assembly of those parts on the screen, easily correcting misalignments and other fit or interference problems. But while the use of modeling and analytics has increased, it is still a relatively rare capability for the typical small or medium-sized enterprise (SME). A study of 232 manufacturers conducted in 2010 by the National Center for Manufacturing Sciences and Intersect360 Research found that 61 percent of companies with over 10,000 employees are using high-performance computing to model their designs digitally, yet only 8 percent of companies with under 100 employees are using this technology.[4] This same study found that the most significant barriers to adoption of high-performance modeling and simulation technologies were lack of internal expertise, the cost of software and, to a lesser extent, the cost of hardware.

To introduce SMEs to the potential of digital modeling and analytics, the National Digital Engineering and Manufacturing Consortium (NDEMC) was created in 2011 by the U.S. Department of Commerce's Economic Development Administration. NDEMC is a regional initiative focused on Midwestern manufacturers and includes partners such as John Deere, Lockheed Martin, General Electric and Proctor & Gamble.

There are currently 20 different ongoing projects in its portfolio that span alternative energy, medical devices, cooling systems and plastics.[5]

The consortium is already helping SMEs. Jeco Plastics is a small custom-mold manufacturer of large, complex and high-tolerance products for large OEMs in the automotive, aerospace, printing and defense industries. The company uses rotational molding and twin-sheet pressure-forming processes and employs materials ranging from commodity thermoplastic resins to highly complex resins with continuous unidirectional carbon fibers.

Recently, Jeco received a last-minute design change for a custom pallet that it was designing for a large German manufacturer. Jeco was able to access high-performance computing resources through NDEMC. Using the center's "ABAQUS" modeling and simulation tool developed by Dassault Systems, Jeco was able to analyze the needed design changes, resulting in a multi-year contract with estimated annual orders of $2.5 million. Under normal circumstances, these high-performance computing resources would have been beyond Jeco's reach due to budget constraints and a lack of modeling and simulation expertise.

Such successes should spawn similar efforts in other regions of the United States. Critical to these efforts will be access to hardware and software, combined with the expertise needed to develop and interpret the analytics and simulations they produce. To date, most manufacturing sectors, and particularly the SMEs within them, have failed to invest in these capabilities.

ADDITIVE MANUFACTURING COMES OF AGE

The second trend that will significantly influence the future of manufacturing is the increasing commercial viability of additive manufacturing, which is also known as "3D printing."[6] This process, involving the layer-by-layer creation of objects, has been used for rapid parts prototyping and small-run production in a variety of industries for more than two decades. But recent developments in its capabilities — the introduction of new machines and their declining costs — have begun to move additive manufacturing into more mainstream part production. Interestingly, low-capability and low-cost machines have begun to engage the interests of designers far beyond traditional manufacturers, a point to be addressed later in this chapter.

Rick Karlgaard, publisher of *Forbes* magazine, has speculated in his "Innovation Rules" column that "3D printing may be the transformative technology of the 2015-2025 timeframe."[7] Similarly, Terry Wohlers, a leading expert in the additive-manufacturing industry, believes that additive-manufacturing technology "could very well have a greater breadth of impact on manufacturing than any other technology in recent history."[8]

While additive manufacturing is, in fact, a digitally based trend in manufacturing that frequently relies on high-performance computing for sophisticated modeling, it deserves to be singled out as a key disruptor in its own right. Additive manufacturing uses computer-generated designs to create "build paths" that reproduce the digital model through consolidation of materials with an energy source. The process typically uses a laser or an electron beam that adds material as it is directed along the build path or can be scanned over a pre-placed layer of material. To date, additive manufacturing has been used with polymers, metals and ceramics.

The principal value of additive manufacturing lies in its potential to lower costs through reduced material usage and machining. Furthermore, the technology enables the design and creation of features that are extremely difficult to construct through traditional processes. From a customization and volume standpoint, additive manufacturing offers extreme flexibility for product differentiation, making it feasible to create highly complex one-off components and products.

In the realm of traditional manufacturing, additive manufacturing has long been used in rapid prototyping to create short-term molds or to develop mock-ups of parts, generally in some type of plastic form. These prototypes were considered precursors to the "real" parts design, which would be produced to tighter tolerances and in the actual final material, which was seldom plastic. But additive manufacturing has continued to move closer to that final production run in industry sectors such as healthcare, where dental and prosthetic devices are being produced with this process for final use, and has been migrating into higher-tolerance and complex materials industries, such as automotive and aerospace.

For example, in November 2012 GE Aviation bought Morris Technologies, a small, privately owned precision-engineering firm. Its specialty? Additive manufacturing. Morris will be developing parts for a range of jet engines, including the LEAP, which is being developed by DFM International. This engine is expected to enter service in commercial airlines in the coming years, and 4,000 units already have been ordered.[9] Morris begins with a digital description of the component and uses laser sintering to build it layer by layer. This process is capable of producing all types of metal parts, including those made of aerospace-grade titanium.

Currently, fused-deposition modeling is the most common additive-manufacturing technology available at the consumer level. This process, one of computer-controlled deposition of melted plastic, is found in recently introduced products for consumers and businesses like the Makerbot, RepRap and Solidoodle. Already, 3D printing has become cost competitive: MakerBot recently introduced a $2,199 3D printer, and costs continue to fall. Jeff Kowalski, CEO of Autodesk, a leading software maker for 3D modeling and printing, notes that the cost of 3D printers has dropped tenfold in five years, "essentially riding the Moore's Law curve, just as 2D printing started doing in the 1980s."[10]

Wohlers has reported that it took the additive-manufacturing industry 20 years to reach $1 billion in size. Sales of additive-manufacturing products and services are predicted to reach $3.7 billion worldwide by 2015 and to surpass $6.6 billion in 2019.[11]

CLOUD-BASED SOLUTIONS REDUCE COSTS, LEVEL THE PLAYING FIELD FOR SMES AND ENABLE NEW BUSINESS MODELS

The third trend that may disrupt current manufacturing-supply-chain practices is the increasing use of cloud-based solutions that can be accessed on an as-needed basis. Cloud computing is likely to enable SMEs to more effectively compete with larger companies because it reduces the cost of accessing sophisticated design, development and enterprise-related business tools. If this trend continues, SMEs will not be hobbled by the prohibitive cost of purchasing and maintaining comprehensive IT systems. The cloud effectively enables both internal decision making and new business models.

From a business-process innovation perspective, information technology improves internal decision making through software that provides support for enterprise resource planning (ERP), material requirements planning (MRP) and supply-chain-management logistics. These types of IT solutions help manufacturers develop a deeper understanding of the needs of their businesses, the flow of their work and the integration of the supplier network into a cohesive solution. While these solutions have typically been used successfully by large companies, SMEs will increasingly be able to take advantage of these enhancements.

In the future, many large-scale, legacy ERP systems will transition to cloud-based solutions. But these new solutions will require a different approach to IT management within the manufacturing environment by using a software-as-a-service (SaaS) deployment model for ERP implementations.

HIAWATHA RUBBER GOES CLOUD-BASED FOR ERP

Based in Minneapolis, Hiawatha Rubber is a family-owned designer and manufacturer of custom-molded rubber parts and assemblies for OEMs. Hiawatha recently replaced an aging, in-house ERP system with a cloud-based ERP solution from Plex Systems, an independent software vendor specializing in cloud-based manufacturing software. While their old system could provide basic information, it lacked the ability to provide the detailed, real-time and accurate financial and manufacturing information that company decision makers needed. This was particularly challenging when they were trying to integrate production data with costing and quality data.

Following a three-month implementation — about half the time it took to install the original in-house system — Hiawatha managers were able to see the value of real-time visibility. According to Tim Carlson, a company manufacturing manager, "the plant-floor employees now see upcoming jobs and where materials are located in real time, enabling them to make quicker and better decisions. Now when a customer calls for a rush order, we can tell them in minutes when their order will be ready, compared with several hours and a significant amount of manual effort when we had our previous system in place."[12]

The company's website proudly advertises this capability, saying: "Our extensive and sophisticated enterprise resource planning system lives in the cloud, giving us a platform that's typically only found at Fortune 500 companies."[13]

Just as the cloud has created new business models in retail, entertainment and journalism, it is doing so in manufacturing, with improved internal visibility, customer-relationship management and the extension of product sales into services. The cloud-based business model allows manufacturing franchises to compete locally and on a smaller scale using Internet-based tools. Drexel Metals is a good example of this emerging model, going beyond the Hiawatha Rubber example to focus on internal company business-process innovation.

DREXEL METALS ESTABLISHES A DISTRIBUTED MANUFACTURING NETWORK SUPPORTED BY WIKIS AND INTERNET TOOLS

In 1985, Drexel Metals was a steel supplier making everything from lighting fixtures to ceiling ribs for the construction industry. But its customers began asking for metal roofing products, where 80 percent of the market is dominated by traditional go-to-market factories selling pre-fabricated roof panels ready for installation. According to company President Brian Partyka, "a challenge with pre-fabricated metal roofing is that when you ship it, you're shipping unwieldy sections that require a lot of packaging to protect them during transport."[14]

Instead, Drexel Metals decided that the best way to get its product to both residential and commercial customers was through a network of specialty installers who could fabricate the "standing-seam" metal roofs onsite. This eliminated expensive shipping and also reduced the lead time necessary for contractors and installers. Now Drexel Metals sells one- to two-ton coiled metal rolls in 36 colors, and it offers installers the ability to buy or lease-to-buy a portable roll-forming machine that can transform these rolls into the specific standing-seam roof desired by the customer. But the company didn't stop there. As a way to support remote fabrication, Drexel developed cloud-based tools and services that enhance their customers' ability to plan for, bid and win sophisticated roofing jobs. In short, through a network of regional manufacturers, Drexel Metals now orchestrates a supply chain that runs from the steel manufacturer to the installed roof. The Drexel Metals Association of Regional Manufacturers provides these machine owners with everything they need to compete with the much larger, traditional, fixed-in-place manufacturers.

Drexel's distributed-manufacturing and -installation model relies heavily on the Internet to provide technical and engineering support. The members of its association are supported by a wiki — a website that allows its users to access, add to and edit its content — that contains more than 2,000 searchable documents describing everything about the product, its installation and the on-site forming of roof sections. In addition, cloud-based costing and bidding tools help potential installers estimate material needs and designs. The design support relies on images captured by Pictometry, a company that uses aerial images to provide precision measurements that are fed to installers via the cloud.

Today, Drexel Metals supports its customers with an anywhere-anytime access strategy that leverages mobile technology. In addition to its wiki, it has a YouTube channel and a LinkedIn group, and it also communicates via Facebook and Twitter. The result of this approach has been phenomenal growth. Revenue went from $24.2 million in 2008 to $51.3 million in 2011, with a three-year overall growth figure of 112 percent. In 2012, Drexel Metals reached number 2,260 on the *Inc. Magazine* 5000 and number 67 on the publication's list of the top 100 manufacturing companies.[15] Similar growth awaits other traditional manufacturers that decide to embrace the cloud.

THE HOBBYIST BECOMES THE PRODUCER

The fourth trend that will influence the future of manufacturing is the rise of IT-savvy Internet hobbyists who are using open-source software tools to design and innovate. As the design and development tools simultaneously become more sophisticated and easier to use, the capabilities that are currently restricted to high-end designers will migrate to less-experienced users, increasing their potential to translate their ideas into realistic and producible products. The decreasing costs and increasing capabilities of additive manufacturing will enable the hobbyists of the future to successfully compete against more-established traditional manufacturers. Chris Anderson, former editor-in-chief of *Wired Magazine*, has termed these hobbyists "makers" and argues that those who own the production technology get to determine what is produced.[16] As these makers grow in number, it is not unthinkable that manufacturing could return to the garage.

Wohlers Associates' most recent statistics support expectations for the rise of the artisan-entrepreneur, as they indicate that recent growth in sales of personal additive-manufacturing systems has been explosive (SEE FIGURE 2). Moreover, Wohlers notes that these systems do not appear to be going to professional or industrial buyers.

FIGURE 2: *Sales of Personal Additive-Manufacturing and 3D-Printing Systems*

Source: Data from Wohlers Report 2012

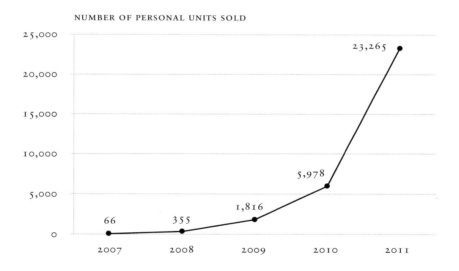

NUMBER OF PERSONAL UNITS SOLD

In January 2005, *Make Magazine* launched with a goal of encouraging do-it-yourself projects' being undertaken by hobbyists and other small-scale producers. The magazine appears both in print and online, where it hosts blogs and other forums where do-it-yourselfers can communicate with each other.

But it is not just hobbyists and do-it-yourselfers with additive-manufacturing capabilities that are involved in this transformation. For example, Shapeways — a 3D-printing services start-up company that spun out of the Royal Phillips Electronics lifestyle incubator program — is changing the meanings of "producer" and "consumer." Using Shapeways' website, clients can upload product specifications that the company feeds into a 3D printer, which then produces the desired device. In 2011, Shapeways shipped nearly 750,000 parts. Materials choices range from plastic and stainless steel to silver and ceramics, and the company is continuously expanding, most recently opening a 3D-printing-services factory in Queens, N.Y.

SUPPLY-CHAIN DISRUPTION

Before the Industrial Revolution, production of goods was done by local artisans and craftsmen relying primarily on locally available materials and selling to local customers. With the introduction of mechanization, production became increasingly centralized in factories, where machines replaced people, taking over many repetitive tasks. Factories grew larger as more people moved from rural areas to cities and as capital became more available. Modern transportation and information systems extended centralized production by enabling distributed material sourcing from low-cost suppliers. These modern transportation and information systems also enabled efficient distributed delivery (FIGURE 3). For over 200 years competitive advantage came from economies of scale and scope.

Joseph Pine, author and co-founder of Strategic Horizons LLP, envisioned markets of one, where individuals could set the specifications and purchase exactly what they wanted.[17] While manufacturers to date have not been able to achieve such mass customization, the Internet has created the expectation of individualized and customized experiences, and online tools that let consumers select various product features have become increasingly sophisticated. Today consumers — and industrial customers as well — demand an increasing level of customization, creating an opportunity for those companies that can service the "long tail" — those micro-manufacturers who will make one-off products on an as-needed or as-requested basis.

This is particularly true of the younger, Internet-savvy consumers who listen to playlists of their own choosing, wear clothes and shoes that are

FIGURE 3: *Manufacturing Comes Full-Circle*

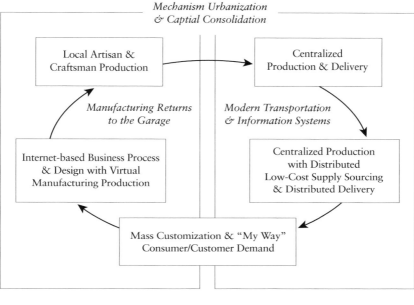

COMPETITIVE ADVANTAGE THROUGH
FLEXIBILITY & AGILITY

COMPETITIVE ADVANTAGE THROUGH
ECONOMIES OF SCALE & SCOPE

designed with their unique feature choices and receive news alerts, shopping alerts and other customized information feeds based on settings they have established on their mobile phones.

In short, society is going from a producer-centric model to a consumer/customer-centric model. When this new form of consumption is combined with advances in additive-manufacturing capabilities, markets of one will be achieved. In this future, artisan-entrepreneurs will use cloud-based design tools to transform ideas into products that can be produced and delivered at the point of demand. Manufacturing truly can go back to the garage in a cost-effective way in a world where the new competitive advantage will come from flexibility and agility. In this future, the same capital-intensive equipment, factories and distribution systems that were once barriers to entry will become barriers to change. FIGURE 4 summarizes the challenges and enablers in this new future, where mass customization and "My Way" consumer/customer demand will be met through virtual-manufacturing environments that displace supply chains as we know them today.

FIGURE 4: *Virtual Manufacturing Environments Displace Traditional Supply Chains for Customized & Localized Manufacturing & Delivery*

MASS CUSTOMIZATION & "MY WAY" CONSUMER/CUSTOMER DEMAND

DESIGN CHALLENGES	BUSINESS PROCESS CHALLENGES	PRODUCTION CHALLENGES
• Modeling	• Order Taking	• Material Sourcing
• Simulation	• Costing & Bidding	• One-off Manufacturing
• Testing	• Tracking	• Material Handling
	• Delivery	• Scaling

ENABLERS	ENABLERS	ENABLERS
• High-Performance Computing	• Cloud Computing	• Additive Manufacturing
• Broadband Access	• Software as a Service	

Supply chains will change in at least four ways:

1. Product innovation and manufacturing innovation will become tightly coupled;

2. Decentralized production and distribution will become localized to the assembler or consumer location;

3. Artisan-manufacturers producing customized products will compete successfully with established OEMs; and

4. Current logistics practices that emphasize efficient transfer of materials within the factory and between companies along the supply chain will become obsolete in many sectors.

Exactly when will this occur? It depends on development of an underlying infrastructure for additive manufacturing that can enable high-quality, high-tolerance production of complex materials at an affordable price. This infrastructure must include such things as design guidelines, economic models and metrics to assess and predict resultant microstructures and their effects on the products' properties and characteristics. A recent Atlantic Council Strategic Foresight Report describes how additive manufacturing is advancing simultaneously at the high end and at the low end. The report notes that, "While these two technical streams will continue to develop separately — with seemingly opposing end goals — we can expect to see a convergence, in the form of a small-scale direct metal 3D printer."[18]

CONCLUSION

Ultimately, if these predictions prove correct, there will be a transition from supply chains to supplier ecosystems, a localization of suppliers who are moving up the value chain closer to the consumer, and a renaissance of artisan manufacturing where individual firms armed with new technologies are truly able to deliver the mass customization that Joseph Pine predicted more than two decades ago. Centralized mass-production operations will continue to exist, but their dominance and growth will no longer be a foregone conclusion.

In this future, IT expertise will be essential for manufacturers to compete successfully — both locally and globally. Broadband communication and the ability to access high-performance computing will be a critical skillset in designing and creating new products in the evolving supplier ecosystems. And this same IT expertise, when combined with emerging additive manufacturing, will enable the long tail.

Unfortunately, this future will come at a price. Manufacturers with an installed base of capital equipment, large-scale factories and extensive long-term contracts with existing suppliers will find themselves up against very agile and flexible smaller competitors. Having an extensive installed base will go from being a competitive advantage to being a competitive disadvantage. Instead of being a barrier to entry, a significant installed base will become a barrier to change.

But the beauty of this future is that design can happen anywhere, innovation can happen anywhere and production can happen anywhere. The current wage-rate differentials between developed and developing nations become less important. Instead, access to consumers and key producers becomes the force that dictates where desired production sites are located.

In this future, innovators and designers have a key advantage. Understanding what the consumer wants and needs, designing the corresponding product and then enabling its production anywhere in the world where there is adequate additive-manufacturing capability fractures the current view of the supply chain.

1.   Kate Whitefoot and Steve Olson, "*Making Value: Integrating Manufacturing, Design and Innovation to Thrive in the Changing Global Economy,*" National Academy of Engineering, 2012.

2.   Irene Petrick and Russ Martinelli, "Driving Disruptive Innovation — Problem Finding and Strategy Setting in an Uncertain World," *Research-Technology Management*, November-December 2012, pages 49-57.

3.   George Day and Christine Moorman, "*Strategy from the Outside In: Profiting from Customer Value,*" McGraw-Hill, New York, N.Y., 2010.

4.   Michael Feldman, "The HPC Gap in U.S. Manufacturing," *HPC Wire*, http://www.hpcwire.com/hpcwire/2011-02-24/the_hpc_gap_in_us_manufacturing.html, February 24, 2011.

5.   John Kirkley, "NDEMC Update: Program to Bring HPC Advanced Manufacturing Technology to Midwestern Companies Now Underway," *Digital Manufacturing Report*, 2012, http://www.digitalmanufacturingreport.com/dmr/2012-11-19/ndemc_update:_program_to_bring_hpc_advanced_manufacturing_technology_to_midwestern_companies_now_underway.html.

6.   The terms *3D printing* and *additive manufacturing* are often used interchangeably. Additive manufacturing has been used to describe the layer-by-layer joining of materials based on 3D digital models. Recently the popular press has referred to this as "3D printing," a term that is gaining acceptance. Currently, *additive manufacturing* is used to describe high-end production in such areas as aerospace and automotive using industrial systems, which typically cost between $5,000 and $25,000 (but can top out at $1 million or more), while *3D printing* refers to production on machines costing below $5,000. The distinction between the two is unlikely to continue into the future, however, as the capabilities at the high end and the low end converge over time.

7.   Rick Karlgaard, "3D Printing Will Revive American Manufacturing," *Forbes*, 2011, http://www.forbes.com/sites/richkarlgaard/2011/06/23/3d-printing-will-revive-american-manufacturing/.

8.   Terry Wohlers, *Wohlers Report 2012. "Additive Manufacturing and 3D Printing State of the Industry, 2012,"* Wohlers Associates, Inc., Fort Collins, Colo. The quote is from page 14 of this report.

9.   *The Economist,* 2012, "GE Is So Stoked About 3D Printing, They're Using it to Make Parts for Jet Engines," Business Insider, http://www.businessinsider.com/ge-buys-3d-printing-company-to-make-parts-for-jet-engines-2012-11.

10.   Jeff Kowalski, "*The USA Could See a Self-Sustaining Future…*" Forbes.com Video Network, http://video.forbes.com/fvn/future-tech/autodesk-on-3d-printing, 2011.

11.   Terry Wohlers, *The Wohlers Report 2012*, page 131.

12.   Baker Tilly, "Success in the Cloud: Manufacturers are switching to cloud computing systems
        to achieve improved business performance," http://www.bakertilly.com/Manufacturers-
        Switching-to-Cloud-Computing.

13.   HiawathaRubber website, http://www.hiawatharubber.com/#!/capabilities/
        data-systems-cloud-computing/.

14.   Brian Partyka, personal conversation, 2012.

15.   *Inc. Magazine*, 2012, http://www.inc.com/profile/drexel-metals.

16.   Chris Anderson, *Makers — The New Industrial Revolution*, Crown Publishing, New York, N.Y., 2012.

17.   Joseph Pine, *Mass Customization — The New Frontier in Business Competition*, Harvard Business
        School Press, Cambridge, Mass., 1993.

18.   Thomas Campbell, Christopher Williams, Olga Ivanova and Banning Garrett, "Could 3D
        Printing Change the World? Technologies, Potential, and Implications of Additive Manufacturing,"
        Atlantic Council Strategic Foresight Initiative, 2011.

CHAPTER 10

The Blueprint for ReMaking America

Scott Paul

LEFT FOR DEAD

Five years ago, American manufacturing was left for dead. It had dominated global industry for more than a century, but now the end seemed near.

It's not like America wasn't manufacturing. We were. Lots of stuff. But consumers had a hard time finding American-made items like clothes, toys and electronics. Empty parking lots and padlocks defined places formerly occupied by hundreds of cars and animated by three shifts of hard work. And the news was all about layoffs, bankruptcies and outsourcing instead of innovation, expansion and investment.

By some economic measures, the United States still led the world in manufacturing five years ago. But the picture on the ground was grim. The 2000s were the worst decade for American manufacturing since the advent of the industrial era. With 1,276 manufacturing jobs lost on average every day, 5.5 million vanished over the course of the decade. Those 10 years saw the closure of 55,000 factories, large and small, which comes out to 17 each and every day. Manufacturing output declined in 13 of 19 industries. Capacity utilization reached a record low. The United States' trade deficit in manufactured goods over the course of the decade totaled nearly $4.5 trillion. The National Science Board reported that high-tech industries shed 28 percent of their manufacturing jobs in the United States while corporations created research and development jobs overseas at an "unprecedented rate."

Pay in the top four occupations in the United States — office clerks, retail salespersons, cashiers and food servers/preparers — averaged less than half of the U.S. median household income, anywhere from $7,000 to $16,000 below what is needed to afford the median rent. Even worse, jobs in three of those categories pay below the poverty limit for a family of four. That these are the nation's leading occupations hardly suggests it has a highly functioning economy, manufacturing or no manufacturing.

The public was down on manufacturing, too.

Poverty. Dirty. Depressing. Gone. These are some of the most common words I heard used in focus groups at the end of the last decade to describe the manufacturing sector. If pink slips and padlocks define your industry, you don't need an expert to tell you that you are in trouble.

At one point, young Americans preferred jobs in fast food to jobs in a factory.

But who could blame them? Fast-food jobs were not being shipped overseas. Many of these youngsters' parents had been laid off from a factory. And if they lived in a factory town, these kids saw the American Dream — good schools, plentiful jobs, a safe community — replaced by drugs, crime and ruin, as the fabric of these communities was torn apart by unemployment. Broken men, broken families, decaying cities. When the rest of America peeked in to see how bad things were, it quickly looked away.

The purveyors of conventional wisdom offered all sorts of salves to make Americans feel better about all of this. Here are a few:

- *America should design; the developing world should produce.* But that's just a surrender, considering that high-wage Germany still had 23 percent of its economy in manufacturing. Or that we were losing out on key innovations because of the co-location necessary to optimize competitiveness.

- *Cheap imports are great for our economy*, a slogan ignoring the fact that buying power is severely limited, even at Wal-Mart, when one doesn't have a job.

- *Outsourcing is a good thing*, which fails to take into account that a day may come when America can't supply its own troops.

- *Trade deficits don't matter.* Except that they, too, have to be financed somehow. So far, this obligation has cost Americans their jobs and their wealth.

- *Productivity and automation have been the sole culprits in job loss, which is fine, because that represents progress.* Except that productivity growth in each prior decade was not accompanied by substantial job loss.

- *The creative class should ascend*, which is one of the reasons why Americans have fantastic, otherworldly video games to play at home and 70,000 structurally deficient bridges in the real world over which they attempt to drive every day. Or why they could tweet news out instantly about Hurricane Sandy's effects on New York City but not find any Made-in-America electrical generators to supply power to people who desperately needed it.

Unfortunately, too many U.S. policymakers, right and left, bought into these arguments as they filled the Washington echo chamber, which then became the accepted truth.

The result was a trade policy that guaranteed the safety of U.S. companies' overseas investments without effectively opening foreign markets to U.S.-made goods; a tax code that favors offshoring and short-term financial speculation; a calculated attack on unions as the chief culprit in manufacturing's decline despite the fact that labor makes up just a fraction of the overall cost of production and workers have made tremendous sacrifices to enhance their employers' competitiveness; and an educational system that steers students toward four-year college degrees — which, according to conventional wisdom, now provide the only path to prosperity — and away from vocational training.

And what choice do educators have? Shop classes in high school — once a laboratory for tinkering and vocation — have essentially disappeared. Community colleges and technical schools have turned their focus to occupations that are likely to experience growth — such as health care and services.

None of this, I know, comes as a shock to anyone who's been awake and aware. But far too few policymakers and thinkers have examined the consequences of the country's shedding one-third of its manufacturing jobs in a ten-year period.

That's changing, as the experts that Richard McCormack has assembled for this book thoughtfully demonstrate in discussing topics ranging from energy and innovation to workforce training and capital formation.

A MANUFACTURING RESURGENCE?

In sum, I believe the good news to be this: a new American manufacturing is rising from the ashes. Detroit has never made better cars. American steel mills have never been so efficient. No other nation is better at making complex systems like aircraft or heavy machinery. The manufacture of sophisticated computer equipment, offshored over the past decade to Taiwan, Malaysia and China, is returning, ever so slowly, to America: Google's glasses; one line of Apple's Mac computer; Lenovo's laptops. Companies that long ago abandoned American factory workers are, without much accompanying irony and with a bit too much bravado, now complaining they can't find enough of them: see General Electric, Whirlpool or Caterpillar.

Outsourcing is out; insourcing is in.

Even former President Bill Clinton thinks so. He had the good fortune to preside over nearly eight years of economic growth, and manufacturing jobs grew during his administration. But he was one of the first American leaders to say, "Those jobs aren't coming back." He spearheaded and signed NAFTA and permanently lowered tariffs for Chinese-made imports. He steered kids toward four-year college degrees instead of vocational training. Through the repeal of Glass-Steagall, he gave unprecedented power to Wall Street, which then strangled Main Street manufacturing.

He refused to provide relief to America's beleaguered steel industry, which was headed toward mass bankruptcy. But the U.S. economy as a whole was growing, driven by low interest rates and massive speculative investment in real estate and high technology.

Fast forward to 2013, and even Bill Clinton has seen the light. He's bullish on American manufacturing. But more importantly, so is the current president: Barack Obama.

One of President Barack Obama's principal promises for his second term? Create a million new manufacturing jobs. His administration's tax strategy? Cut taxes for businesses that manufacture in America. He's launched initiatives to encourage public-private partnerships on manufacturing innovation and a skilled workforce. He rescued the auto industry. His administration has quietly embraced "Buy America" requirements for more federal investment. He's enforced American trade laws like no other recent president. There's a lot more he could be doing — tackling currency manipulation, working to reduce the trade deficit, making sizable investments in training. But no one can dispute that the Obama White House has given enhanced attention to American manufacturing.

And then look at the Republican Party. Its 2008 nominee, Senator John McCain, was contemptuous of efforts to boost American manufacturing before, during and after the campaign. And it cost him. He lost the heartland of America, and he lost an effort to strip "Buy America" requirements from the 2009 Recovery Act. The leading Republican candidates in 2012 couldn't get enough of "Made in America." Mitt Romney took a stronger position on China's currency manipulation than Obama. Rick Santorum put "Made in America" on his podium signs. Most of the contenders scrambled to find American-made campaign t-shirts after ABC News revealed that many campaign t-shirts had been made overseas.

And they paid to get the word out.

All told, Obama, Romney and their supporters spent nearly $700 million during the 2012 general election on ads focused around jobs, outsourcing and trade. They spent $45 million on "get tough on China" ads. Not a dime was spent on the opposite message. One of the most popular physical images in campaign ads? The factory. And in 2012, we saw politicians strolling through modern industrial workplaces in addition to the usual assortment of abandoned factories, padlocks and pink slips.

These ads played everywhere: nine of the top 16 markets for "get tough on China" trade ads were outside traditional industrial states, though the hottest market was, of course, Cleveland, Ohio.

Look as well at President Obama's State of the Union addresses in 2013 and 2012. Insiders know that every word in these speeches counts. There are dozens of critical issues, hundreds of federal agencies and thousands of federal programs, and the President has a finite amount of time in which to address them. Supporters of any program are thrilled with even a sentence's worth of praise or promise in a State of the Union address. So when manufacturing plays a starring role in two consecutive speeches, the signal sent to Capitol Hill, the business community and the American people is unmistakable: Manufacturing matters.

But if political rhetoric is not enough to persuade you, then perhaps pop culture is. ABC News launched a "Made in America" series that has generated unprecedented viewer engagement while arguing that buying American is not only possible, but also creates a lot of jobs. Chrysler's popular ads in the past three Super Bowls have trumpeted the comeback of industry: "Imported from Detroit," "Halftime in America" and Jeep's ode to returning war heroes. Companies such as Maytag, Brooks Brothers and the Container Store proudly promote their Made in America lines. Even foreign investors such as Hyundai and Honda make it a point in their ads to explain that some of their vehicles are made in America.

And if pop culture is not enough to persuade you, perhaps academics and management consultants will. My desk is stacked with reports on the benefits of "reshoring" and "rethinking your manufacturing strategy" from Harvard Business School, MIT's Sloan School of Management, Accenture, Boston Consulting Group, Booz, the Brookings Institution, the New America Foundation, the Information Technology & Innovation Foundation and the Council on Competitiveness, just to name a few. What makes this remarkable is that just a few years ago, offshoring was the default option. The only real debate among some in this crowd was over where to send the jobs.

Now to the numbers.

The measurable gains for manufacturing, while modest, have been more than rhetorical or political. Between its January 2010 low and the end of 2012, manufacturing employment expanded by nearly 500,000 jobs. That's 4 percent growth, which, according to the Commerce Department, is the strongest cyclical rebound since the early 1980s. (Mind you, the United States had shed nearly 33 percent of its manufacturing jobs between 2000 and 2009.) From mid-2009 through the end of 2012, the number of job openings in manufacturing grew by more than 200 percent, to nearly 260,000 openings.

What has contributed to the job growth?

The primary reason for it is the upswing in the business cycle. When consumers buy more goods, producers need to make more goods, and that requires more workers. America's post-recession rebound hasn't been strong, but it has been strong enough to support some growth in manufacturing jobs.

The rebound in the automotive manufacturing sector has also played a key role. After shedding jobs and factories, the Detroit Three have, since 2010, hired back workers and invested in U.S. manufacturing facilities at a fairly strong clip. The long tail of the automotive value chain has spread these benefits around to other sectors of the industrial economy.

The decision of the Federal Reserve Bank to pursue three rounds of quantitative easing (QE), which led to an expanded money supply and cheaper borrowing, temporarily enhanced the competitiveness of U.S. exports. Treasury secretaries for most of the past two decades have followed a "strong dollar" policy, which improves the purchasing power of American consumers by cheapening imports but makes U.S. exports less competitive, usually producing large trade deficits. A more competitively valued dollar helped to boost exports in 2010 and 2011, but weakness in Europe and China and currency manipulation by Japan have limited the impact of this policy more recently.

Finally, lower U.S. energy costs through the dramatic expansion of natural-gas production have propelled energy-intensive industrial

sectors to new heights of competitiveness, and the expansion itself
has supported a domestic market for equipment and material utilized
in exploration, extraction and transmission.

This employment rebound has been called a "resurgence" by some U.S.
political leaders and headline writers. But the country could be doing a lot
better. America's trade deficit with China reached a record $315 billion in
2012 right on top of a record $295 billion in 2011. Capacity utilization
in manufacturing is still below the modern average. That's not progress.

What's standing in the way of a real rebound? I have already outlined
a few of the misguided rationales for letting manufacturing go; now
let's explore these obstacles a bit more in depth.

1. China and other less-developed countries have provided multi-
    national retailers like Wal-Mart and producers like Apple with a
    virtually endless supply of highly exploitable workers and plenty
    of subsidies, both direct (tax relief) and indirect (lax enforcement
    of labor or environmental laws). A 2012 study by researchers at
    Yale and the Federal Reserve Bank concluded that the "certainty"
    provided by the 2000 law granting China's goods permanent,
    low-tariff access to the American market accelerated manufacturing
    job loss in the United States by nearly 30 percent. ·

    While some trends are shifting in America's favor, including the
    rise of labor costs in China, that nation's willingness — and ability —
    to pay any price needed to secure employment for its hundreds
    of millions of workers must never be underestimated. It's clear
    what the "tipping point" for Beijing is: any threat to its stability. But
    what's the tipping point for the U.S. government in this relationship?
    China's pervasive cyber-hacking? Its practice of intellectual-property
    theft? Millions of lost U.S. manufacturing jobs? Unacceptable
    levels of pollution? Counterfeiting? Constant currency manipulation?
    The largest trade gap between two nations in recorded history?
    Dependence on China to supply many materials and products
    in our defense industrial supply chain? Apparently, it has not
    yet been reached.

2. Financial deregulation in the late 1990s has made Wall Street
    the master of manufacturing rather than a provider of its capital,

which was its more traditional role. Quarterly earnings pressures and long-term growth strategies are often mutually exclusive in the world of capital-intensive manufacturing. Leo Hindery's chapter provides an excellent analysis of this challenge and possible approaches for freeing manufacturing from this relentless stranglehold.

3. Americans need to come to terms with the fact that new investments in manufacturing will, at least for some time, provide weaker employment gains than they might have hoped. It is true that automation, robotics and productivity mean that it takes fewer workers to produce the same amount of output. That means the U.S. government will need to support policies that will increase demand, turn product innovations into American production, expand the U.S. share of global exports and increase the percentage of consumer and government spending on American-made products.

4. The strong-dollar policy embraced by the Clinton administration and carried forward by the Bush administration made American goods less globally competitive. Consumers received short-term benefits because prices of imported products fell, but, on the flipside, workers in industries facing global competition have seen downward pressure on wages and income. It's hard to argue that America underconsumes during the healthy part of the business cycle; no one would argue, on the other hand, that America underproduces. Quantitative easing by the Fed has relieved some of this pressure, but it is an extraordinary intervention, not typical policy. Even with QE, the dollar has never been considered to be "undervalued" or below an "equilibrium" rate. At the same time, such global economic competitors as China and Japan support their industry through direct monetary policies that artificially undervalue their currency in order to gain a trade advantage. Will the United States change its monetary policy, and will it insist that consistent manipulators such as China and Japan compete fairly?

5. Over the past several decades, virtually all of America's economic policies, including its tax policy and trade agreements, have encouraged offshoring. The shifting focus of educational policy in favor of a four-year college degree for nearly everyone has helped to create the paradox that the nation faces today. There weren't many job opportunities in manufacturing during the last decade, but, with

demographic changes, there will be over the coming decade. Yet the pipeline for new talent has been severely constricted. Will federal economic and educational policies shift swiftly enough to support these new opportunities, as well as provide support for private-sector "reshoring" efforts?

Some will examine these challenges and say, "Forget about it. It's not worth it. Let's focus on making the service sector create good jobs." I'd say that's shortsighted.

Make no mistake, this will not be an easy transition. But it is an essential one. Not for the politics. Not for a nostalgic "saving" of manufacturing. At stake is nothing less than America's economic and national security.

Without more manufacturing, it will be virtually impossible to rebuild the middle class, reduce the trade deficit or innovate the next amazing generation of products. And smart observers have noted that the "race to the bottom" isn't the only way to compete in manufacturing. We know America will never win such a race, nor should it want to. America is very good at winning races to the top. Yet in manufacturing, it's not even in the race yet. Countries like Germany and Switzerland are characterized by stringent regulation, universal health care, high wages ($48 per hour compared to $32 per hour in the U.S. for manufacturing workers) and relatively strong industrial unions, but they still have more than 20 percent of their economies in manufacturing and a balanced trade account with China. While manufacturing employment and output have declined as a percentage of the overall economy in Germany, few in Germany see a future without manufacturing — nor without the public policies that support manufacturing.

Perhaps that's why, despite the odds, a manufacturing-policy debate has reignited in the United States. The result: Manufacturing's prospects look better than ever.

One reason is that recent periods of U.S. job and economic growth did not last: They were predicated on bubbles. The high-tech-sector bubble of the late 1990s, followed by the housing bubble of the 2000s, created temporary prosperity that was quickly dashed. What's the sustainable alternative? Manufacturing. It's been one of America's core competencies for more than two centuries, and the country led the world in manufacturing output for 110 straight years.

Another reason is that there is a plausible prospect for success. Loan guarantees and other assistance provided by the federal government to General Motors and Chrysler actually worked. Consumers have better choices. Employment in the auto sector is growing, with 160,000 more jobs expected to be added through the end of 2015. Industry, after years of opposition, agreed to a 54.5-mpg fuel-economy standard and embraced hybrid and electric vehicle technology.

The auto rescue was what I call "Emergency Room" industrial policy. President Obama and his team didn't do a perfect job, but the alternatives were far grimmer.

THE PUSHBACK

Still, there are some who say that manufacturing does not deserve a strategy. They've managed to get a lot of ink. Christina Romer, the former chairwoman of President Obama's Council of Economic Advisers, took U.S. manufacturing to task in a 2012 *New York Times* op-ed head-lined "Do Manufacturers Need Special Treatment?" Romer suggests that reasons to support manufacturing need to "go beyond the feeling that it's better to produce 'real things' than services."

She's asking the wrong question. Manufacturers don't need special treatment. Just a level playing field.

Romer takes an academic view of manufacturing, and that creates a problem. In the comfortable confines of a dusty textbook, her views may be fine. But in a cutthroat real world filled with competition, cheating and harsh mercantilism, this point of view is very limiting. It's a safe, mathematical view, which means Romer added her name to the long list of economists who have detached policy from reality.

Case in point: Romer uses arcane jargon like "efficiency grounds," "positive externalities" and "market failures" to justify her view that the manufacturing sector can be dismissed. In her op-ed she argues that service work is just as important as manufacturing: "American consumers value health care and haircuts as much as washing machines and hair dryers. And America's earnings from exporting architectural plans for a building in Shanghai are as real as those from exporting cars to Canada."

But extolling the virtues of a hair salon misses a fundamental point. Ultimately, the bottom line is jobs, and manufacturing supports more jobs, and pays better, than does the service industry. Those architectural plans being "exported" — how many jobs do *they* support? And what's to prevent that architectural work from being outsourced as well?

Romer continues on to argue against manufacturing. She says that "government intervention can be justified on efficiency grounds if the free market won't work well." But U.S. manufacturing advocates aren't asking for a handout. Instead, we're saying there isn't a free market at work, because the market in which American companies and workers compete is not "free."

I admire Romer's intellect, but I am shocked that she doesn't see the evidence of a market failure. The U.S. trade deficit in manufactured goods, which has nearly *tripled* since 1998, isn't a market failure? The fact that U.S. steel and semiconductor production is far more efficient than Chinese production on paper but America's market share is declining isn't a market failure? The fact that productivity of U.S. manufacturing workers has gone up while wages have not isn't a market failure? And, the fact that dollars invested in the American economy by venture capital are producing diminishing employment returns, as former Intel CEO Andy Grove has noted, isn't a market failure?

Let's consider why we need government policy in manufacturing in the first place. I borrow this from the Center for Budget and Policy Priorities' Jared Bernstein, formerly Vice President Joe Biden's economic adviser, who says that manufacturers face barriers to entry, expansion and innovation that no single, private firm can solve. Among the challenges businesses face are:

1. **Research barriers.** Basic R&D can be prohibitively expensive, and resulting profits hard to capture;

2. **Coordination barriers.** No single firm could coordinate national projects like infrastructure, the Internet or a smart electrical grid;

3. **Innovation barriers.** Firms need help getting academic innovations into production;

4. **Credit barriers.** Markets will underinvest when returns are particularly uncertain or occur over a long time horizon;

5. **Punitive measures against exports.** Firms need the federal government to push back against unfair trade practices and to reduce trade barriers overseas; and

6. **Workforce deficiencies.** While I view training as an ongoing obligation of employers, I also believe that employers should be able to access a talent pool of prospective workers who are proficient in basic math, reading and problem-solving skills upon graduation from high school.

I also point to the Brookings Institution's Howard Wial and Jonathan Rothwell, who did an outstanding job of emphasizing the importance of a strong manufacturing base to America's national ecology of innovation, research and development; and to the award-winning work of Willy Shih and Gary Pisano, who made this same connection in a 2009 *Harvard Business Review* piece. If the nation values expertise in engineering, science and technology, the pair argues, it must value manufacturing.

But, most egregiously, critics like Romer ignore perhaps the most important attribute of manufacturing: its job-multiplier effect. To paraphrase Gene Sperling, Director of President Obama's National Economic Council, a community that attracts an auto-assembly facility will also attract a Wal-Mart, while the opposite is not necessarily true. A typical manufacturing job supports four or five other jobs in the economy, directly or indirectly. Manufacturing plays an outsized role in our exports, and factories are often the largest local source of revenue for the public sector.

This leaves us with the argument that manufacturing policy prescriptions are not effective. Much of what President Obama is proposing would actually undo current disincentives such as the higher taxes that manufacturers face in the United States (which can drive them abroad), the lack of skilled workers to fill jobs, insufficient public investment in infrastructure and lax overall enforcement of trade laws. The President is proposing some smart policies — but they hardly rise to the level of industrial policy.

I would be interested in seeing Romer explain the phenomenon of Germany's thriving industrial sector. How does Germany accomplish this? It shapes its economic policies around supporting manufacturing. The United States, with better access to natural resources, immense human capital and breathtaking entrepreneurship, should be outperforming Germany on a per capita basis — but, without a focused manufacturing strategy, it is not.

Fortunately, President Obama appears to have rejected the advice of manufacturing's critics, if not for any of the above reasons then for this one: From a strategic (though perhaps not an economic) point of view, the United States does not want to depend on China to supply its military with vital parts, computer chips, rocket propellant and surveillance equipment. But if America loses the capacity to manufacture any of its key national security components, it won't have a choice. And China — which has ignored Romer's advice — will have won this argument, which is far from academic.

THE BLUEPRINT

There are concrete steps that Congress, the administration, governors, mayors and citizens can do to shape the future of manufacturing in America. Ultimately, success is built upon the imagination and ingenuity of the nation's businesses and workers. But their efforts can be turbo-charged by good public policies and thwarted by bad ones.

This section highlights some of the best ideas I've come across, many of which have been articulated in depth by the authors of the preceding chapters. You'll note detailed attention to many domestic economic issues. On trade, I just hit the highlights, as a more balanced approached to trade has been a longstanding priority of the Alliance for American Manufacturing and is covered in depth in many of its publications.

ACCESS TO CAPITAL

In the aftermath of the Great Recession, small and mid-sized manufacturers in particular have faced serious challenges in obtaining financing and working capital. While some of the most acute problems have abated, the principal source of friction between the finance community and manufacturers is quarterly-earnings pressure. Investments in capital equipment generally offer a slower rate of return than many of the latest "innovations" in financial instruments. Put simply, Wall Street would rather make a quick buck (or take a chance on making one) than allow capital to work more patiently. There are several public-policy approaches worth considering as carrots, sticks or workarounds.

The most essential of these is the creation of a significant revolving-loan fund for worthwhile investments in physical and human capital by small and mid-sized manufacturers. Congress could opt to change the tax treatment of capital gains to advantage assets that are held for a longer period of time, say, five to ten years. Similarly, Congress could choose to put into place a fee on certain financial transactions that have little or no bearing on job creation or economic growth in the United States. Finally, the Securities and Exchange Commission could limit guidance provided by corporations to an annual assessment, which would replace the quarterly guidance that is now standard.

But it's worth repeating: Wall Street has been partly or wholly responsible for inflating and then bursting various "bubbles." Manufacturing in America has never bubbled. It fluctuates with the business cycle, but that's far healthier than the booms and busts that have typically affected housing, high tech, commercial real estate and finance.

ECONOMIC DEVELOPMENT

No less a capitalist than General Electric's CEO Jeff Immelt has suggested that manufacturing should account for at least 20 percent of U.S. gross domestic product. To me, that sounds like the basis for a "topline" national manufacturing strategy: Use that as a goal with which to align major policies, such as that of the Federal Reserve, whose dual mandate requires it to keep both unemployment and inflation at low rates. There is also overwhelming public support for adopting a national manufacturing strategy — support that has grown dramatically from 2010 to 2013.

The second key economic-development task is to support communities engaged in high-road strategies for attracting manufacturing employment. If "low wages" are the selling point, then the economy will never have the opportunity to fully recover. Fortunately, there is some movement afoot to aid communities that have had the foresight to attract jobs through investing in infrastructure, education, innovation and quality of life. The Obama administration's Make It in America Challenge is one such effort. This competitive-grant process should be dramatically expanded to enable communities to build on their strengths rather than being forced to engage in a race to the bottom to attract new jobs.

ENERGY

One of the most critical new advantages for American manufacturing, particularly in energy-intensive industries, is the development of domestic supplies of natural gas and other resources. It's important for several reasons.

First, accelerated production of these resources has flipped the cost of energy from being a decided disadvantage in taking on some global competitors to being a tremendous advantage. For companies considering where to expand existing operations or to locate new ones, this could be a tipping point. Makers of durable goods and other energy-intensive products are already locating some new production in the United States. Look for this trend to continue.

Second, exploration, transmission and storage of natural gas themselves create markets for manufactured goods: think pipe and tube. Provided there is a level playing field for American pipe and tube makers in the face of subsidized competition from China and other nations, look for this market to grow.

Third, the byproducts of natural-gas production will incentivize the makers of resins, plastics and certain chemicals to locate production close to areas where natural gas is produced. In fact, the Boston Consulting Group has already identified chemical manufacturing as an industry likely to experience reshoring and employment growth in the very near future.

What does this say about policy? Chiefly, it suggests it would be foolish not to allow production of more natural gas. Cleaner than other fossil fuels, it offers a reasonable alternative to oil — depending on price levels, of course. But it would also be foolish to allow the production of natural gas to occur in a manner inconsistent with conscientious stewardship. Policymakers are still working to achieve this balance; they must arrive at it soon. Lastly, the U.S. stock of oil and natural gas is exhaustible. The lifespan of some of these new "plays" is no more than 25 to 35 years. That means pursuing cleaner, renewable alternatives remains essential.

One way to promote clean-energy production in the United States is through the use of clean-energy manufacturing credits and production tax credits. These credits are essential for ensuring that markets for wind, solar and other types of renewable energy remain robust. And to ensure that we aren't simply replacing imported oil with Made in China wind turbines or Made in Germany solar panels, the incentives for domestic manufacturing must stay in place.

But an energy policy would not be complete without a call for investment in energy efficiency. Paving the way to a greener economy can be done by promoting energy conservation and security, by providing incentives to retrofit public buildings with American-made materials and by supporting private-sector efforts to increase industrial energy efficiency.

EXCHANGE RATES

President Obama should convene a multilateral meeting to address global trade imbalances and, in particular, China's mercantilism. He should ensure that the proposed Trans-Pacific Partnership includes measures to prohibit trade-distorting currency manipulation and the market-distorting impacts of state-owned enterprises. China ships more than a quarter of its exports to the United States and finances less than 10 percent of U.S. public debt, so America has more leverage than some might suggest. Congress should pass legislation to deter foreign currency manipulation.

Designating another government as being a deliberate trade cheat is a serious charge. But doing this would be a first step by Washington toward addressing the problem, as it would initiate formal negotiations on the issue of currency between the accused government and that of the United States. And if those talks broke down, it would allow the U.S. government to seek redress through direct sanctions.

Unfortunately, the Obama administration's Treasury Department has let the most egregious trade cheating — that of the Chinese government —

slide despite numerous opportunities to do something about it since the start of the president's first term.

Currency manipulation is pretty simple: A country keeps the value of its currency deliberately low versus the U.S. dollar. This makes the country's exports artificially cheap when entering the U.S. market while simultaneously imposing a tax on U.S. exports entering its own market.

China does this.

And who is China's biggest trading partner? The United States of America.

In 2012, trade in goods between China and the United States totaled more than $536 billion. But it was unequal trade: America bought $315 billion more than it sold to the Chinese, which makes for the largest trade imbalance between two nations in recorded history. The two countries are already on a pace to surpass that record in 2013.

That total is pushed along in part by China's standing policy of currency manipulation, which is directed — by default — at American businesses and the workers they employ. Beijing has kept the renminbi below market value by hoarding U.S. dollars (to the tune of $191 billion in 2012 alone). China in 2013 had foreign-exchange reserves valued at a staggering $3.26 trillion.

If Congress or the President were to act, you could expect real results, because there's clear evidence that China responds to political pressure. A Senate procedural vote in 2005 that marked the first step toward addressing Beijing's currency manipulation provoked an immediate rise in the renminbi. When then-Treasury Secretary Timothy Geithner threatened action on currency ahead of a G-20 meeting in 2010, the renminbi rose again. It rose following House and Senate votes on currency legislation in 2010 and 2011. And when President Obama and Mitt Romney promised to combat Chinese trade practices during the 2012 campaign, the renminbi budged another time.

The takeaway? Pressure on China's currency works.

Now, you would be pressed to find a member of Congress who doesn't believe America's businesses and workforce deserve a guarantee of fair play in the marketplace. You will, however, find a few on Capitol Hill who balk at the notion of prodding the Chinese on currency because they claim doing so would risk a trade war. That was House Speaker John Boehner's excuse when he shelved an overwhelmingly bipartisan currency bill in 2010.

But that trade war hasn't happened yet, despite the aforementioned attempts at congressional action.

And while Americans wait for their political leaders to stand up to a country that is clearly cheating at trade, U.S. producers suffer from the hidden tax of currency manipulation, while the nation's unemployment rate remains frustratingly high and its trade deficit with China grows wider each day.

INFRASTRUCTURE INVESTMENT

The administration should work with congressional leaders to identify financing for, and to adopt, a large-scale, long-term infrastructure program of at least $500 billion over six years to follow on the more modest surface transportation reauthorization law, the Moving Ahead for Progress in the 21st Century Act, enacted in 2012.

The government should also leverage capital from private investors for large-scale transportation and energy projects by using creative investment measures, such as the establishment of a national infrastructure bank that would deliver low-cost loans or loan guarantees and place an emphasis on using domestic content to the maximum extent possible.

Both of these proposals have broad, bipartisan support, and the need is clear: America has more than 70,000 bridges requiring serious repair. We know that rebuilding America would create jobs: at least 18,000 for every $1 billion of investment. And it would boost manufacturing by providing a market for materials, improving logistics and distribution networks and making the U.S. economy more efficient overall.

MANUFACTURING-SUPPORT PROGRAMS AT THE COMMERCE DEPARTMENT

The Administration deserves enormous credit for initiating and funding several programs to promote best practices, collaboration, "high road" economic development strategies and the diffusion of innovation through America's manufacturing community. Among the initiatives it has launched are the Advanced Manufacturing Partnership, the National Network for Manufacturing Innovation, the Access Costs Everywhere online tool to promote reshoring, Make It in America challenge grants and supplier-scouting programs within the Manufacturing Extension Partnership. Taken together, these tools can help the private sector thrive by connecting it with innovation, process-improvement techniques, a skilled workforce and possible federal procurement opportunities. Congress would be wise to fully fund and support all of these valuable initiatives.

GOVERNMENT PROCUREMENT

The market for public procurement is a large one. Since the 1930s, "Buy America" laws have ensured that American workers and businesses receive a preference in many types of federal spending, including but not limited to road building, defense acquisition and vehicle fleets. Over time, these laws have attracted waivers and loopholes as special interests that have invested in outsourcing have sought to claim a share of U.S. tax dollars. There are three things Congress and the Administration should do to ensure that these tax dollars stay in the United States, supporting economic development and investment in the American economy:

1. **Support Buy America.** "Buy America" provisions should be applied to all federal procurement and to federal-aid infrastructure projects that benefit from Americans' hard-earned tax dollars. Doing this will ensure that tax dollars are reinvested within the domestic economy and thus used to create jobs here at home.

2. **Defend America with American-Made Products.** The Department of Defense should give more preference to contractors that commit to increasing the domestic content of the equipment, technology and supplies they sell to the military. This should commence with

a top-to-bottom assessment of the U.S. defense industrial base to identify critical items and materials that are at risk of no longer being available through domestic sources. (AAM's *Remaking American Security,* released in May 2013, provides an excellent starting point.)

3.   **Prepare for the Next Super Storm.** America should reevaluate how it prepares for and responds to catastrophic events in order to ensure that its increasing reliance on the complex and vulnerable global supply chain does not put future recovery efforts at risk. The risk of shortages or unavailability of critical materials and goods such as portable generators during natural and other disasters should be mitigated by adopting more pro-manufacturing policies like Buy America preferences at the federal level.

TAX POLICY

The tax code has a significant impact on the operations of U.S. companies and their decisions as to where to invest, innovate, produce and create jobs. Tax reform is receiving increasing attention in Washington as an issue that needs to be acted upon. Tax reform must not be driven solely by the misguided and simplistic notion that the primary goal should be lowering tax rates and broadening the tax base. More important, tax reform should enhance economic growth, improve the climate for the nation's productive sector and create a long-term path to prosperity for the companies that operate in the United States and their American workers.

Manufacturers have a particular stake in the shape of the corporate tax code for several reasons.

First, manufacturers face competitive pressures from overseas, whereas most service providers do not. Most foreign nations provide incentives for their exporters through a tax system that provides them with up to a 19 percent value-added tax (VAT) rebate, while applying that VAT rate to U.S. exports entering their markets. Since low tariff rates and investment guarantees make the relocation of manufacturing activity increasingly attractive, the U.S. tax code should be structured in such a way that it incentivizes domestic manufacturing activity.

Second, because manufacturing is capital intensive, substantial borrowing and a longer time-horizon for a return on investment are often required of manufacturers. The existing tax code recognizes this through accelerated depreciation and other mechanisms.

Third, manufacturing activity ebbs and flows along with the business cycle, which means the tax code should include mechanisms for allocating losses in a reasonable manner.

There is also compelling evidence suggesting that manufacturing activity should in fact be favored by the corporate tax code over other types of economic activity. Manufacturing jobs offer more middle-income opportunities for American workers than do jobs in other sectors of the economy. The "multiplier" factor for manufacturing activity — the number of additional jobs created by each primary job in manufacturing — far exceeds that for most other types of business activity. Manufacturing is responsible for nearly all of America's private-sector innovation, accounting for 90 percent of patent filings and two-thirds of private-sector research and development expenditures. And it accounts for about 60 percent of American exports.

Manufacturing activity cannot be replaced by any other type of economic activity, and that alone constitutes sufficient grounds for it to receive fair and reasonable treatment under the corporate tax code.

There are a number of misguided notions about today's corporate tax system, making it important to start any tax discussion with an understanding of the facts.

First, there is strong data suggesting that taxes on corporations in other developed countries are not dramatically lower than in the United States:

- U.S. corporate income and social insurance taxes are close to the OECD average.
- There is a big difference in consumption taxes between the U.S. and OECD counterparts. In the U.S., these taxes account for roughly 4.5 percent of GDP vs. an OECD average of 10.7 percent of GDP.

- As a percentage of GDP, U.S. tax revenues are lower than those of virtually every other OECD country — only Turkey's and South Korea's total burdens expressed as a share of GDP are less than that of the U.S.

- A comparison of effective tax rates on corporations provided in a 2012 Congressional Research Service study indicated that the U.S. effective rate was 27.1 percent while the weighted OECD average was 27.7 percent.

Second, broadening the tax base and lowering rates would primarily benefit less-productive and lower-hourly-wage industries.

A study published in *Tax Notes* presented the impact that a simplistic, base-broadening rate reduction might have on the tax burden for the following representative industries:

- Securities — 12.3 percent tax cut

- Insurance — 11.9 percent tax cut

- Retail — 10.1 percent tax cut

- Bank holding companies — 10.1 percent tax cut

- Construction — 0.9 percent tax increase

- Chemicals — 7.3 percent tax increase

- Metals, minerals and machinery manufacturing — 7.3 percent tax increase

- Transportation — 9.3 percent tax increase

- Agriculture — 16.8 percent tax increase

- Electrical products — 69.7 percent tax increase

Tax reform must support rather than undermine domestic production. As the facts above show, manufacturing, agriculture and other industries that produce things would see their tax burden increase significantly if tax reform simply eliminated deductions and credits, and used the resulting revenues to lower tax rates. America's long-term economic success and future opportunity for its workers depend on a tax code that supports and promotes investment in innovation, production and job creation in the United States. Tax reform must be focused on achieving those goals.

Any tax reform effort must preserve:

- A capital-cost-recovery system that promotes domestic investments in plant and equipment.

- The Section 199 manufacturing credit that stimulates domestic investments tied to domestic-job-creation criteria. Some proposals have suggested deepening this credit, which is an excellent idea.

- The research and development credit, while enhancing it to promote the deployment here in the United States of research funded through the credit.

- The ability of companies to utilize last-in/first-out inventory-accounting methodology so that they are best able to manage changes in input costs.

- The ability of companies to continue to deduct the interest they incur when borrowing to invest in their business. Just like homeowners who have to borrow to purchase the house in which they will raise a family, companies need to borrow to buy equipment. Robbing producers of the ability to deduct the interest they must pay on borrowed funds would decimate the economy.

- The ability of companies to utilize net operating losses against income in future years. The size of the investments that a company makes in plant and equipment, in addition to other factors, may subject it to a loss, thereby jeopardizing its ability to fully recoup the value of these investments. Such investments are critical to promoting innovation, production and job creation in the United States, and the full value should be eligible to offset income in future years.

- The ability of companies to plan for the future. Existing investments must not be penalized and uncertainty must be minimized. Large capital investments are made not to recoup in the next quarter, but over a multi-year period. Tax reform must promote long-term investment and success.

TRADE

American trade policy should be based on results, not philosophy. Textbook free trade is a good idea, but even Adam Smith acknowledged that there were limits to comparative advantage and that hitting back against market distortions is necessary. Unfortunately, his ideas have been distorted by history into something that he wouldn't recognize. I don't mind so much that Adam Smith's ideas have been warped, but I do mind the impact of these perversions: Massive trade deficits, a hollowed-out manufacturing base, rising inequality, wretched working conditions in many places overseas and dangerous global imbalances.

We need to revisit the way the our national leaders think about trade policy. A trade correction can be summarized in two points.

1.   **America Must Keep its Trade Laws Strong and Strictly Enforce Them.** We should refocus the trade agenda by giving American businesses new tools to counter currency manipulation, industrial subsidies, intellectual-property theft and barriers to market access by our trading partners.

2.   **America Must Reduce its Trade Deficit.** As the administration works toward President Obama's re-election campaign promise to double American exports, we should ensure that trade-deficit reduction receives a high priority. Lowering the trade deficit and creating manufacturing jobs will have a positive impact on federal revenues and will reduce the federal budget deficit.

WORKFORCE DEVELOPMENT

If you build it, they will come. A famous line from *Field of Dreams*, yes. But it's also the solution to the so-called workforce-skills gap. Like ballplayers emerging from the rows of corn, skilled workers will flock to manufacturing jobs if they are, in fact, available; if they pay well; and if the workers think those jobs will stay put.

There is no doubt that it will take some time to strip off the rust that the last few decades of neglect have left on vocational education for manufacturing careers. But too many just want to point fingers: at kids, for not being smart enough to realize the benefits of a manufacturing career; at schools, for not focusing enough on STEM education to prepare the workforce; at popular culture, for portraying factories as desolate and factory workers as desperate; or at the nation's leaders and counselors, for suggesting to students that a four-year college degree is the only path to success in America. Assigning blame may feel good, but it hasn't trained a single worker or filled a single position.

Here's what will:

- First, *a strong economy*. If consumers buy more goods, then factories must produce more goods. And that means, at some point, more workers to make those goods, even in this age of expanding automation. Manufacturing is recovering, but it is still below average capacity utilization.

- Second, *better wages*. Average starting wages in manufacturing have fallen since the start of the Great Recession. Given that most factory jobs take more than a couple of days, or perhaps hours, of training (unlike retail or food-preparation jobs), workers must invest time and money in their training, either on the job or at a community college.

  Imagine yourself as a 19-year-old, wondering whether you should take that wage-slave job at a fast-food joint, a job that will always be there for you if you work hard and demonstrate responsibility; or instead get a loan, train to be a machinist, face a daunting skills-certification exam and then hope to get placed in a job that can easily be outsourced. That machinist job used to be a factory job that came with paid health care, a retirement plan and a sizable wage premium, but perhaps no longer. That's one of the reasons that new entrants to the workforce prefer work in fast food over work in manufacturing.

  But if there were truly 600,000 unfilled positions in manufacturing — and believe me, there aren't — then wages would rise until supply and demand aligned. They haven't. As mentioned before, wages have headed in the opposite direction. Post jobs with better wages, and more qualified applicants will appear.

- Third, *continue working to expand the talent pipeline.* America's community colleges and vocational schools generally do a very good job of aligning their program offerings with employment offerings in the community. But when that spigot of job offerings has been more or less closed for more than a decade (like it has been in manufacturing), it takes a while to get back into alignment. Acquiring the latest training tools and well-qualified instructors and performing outreach to high schools demands time. The good news is that work is already well under way on this through programs like Skills for the Future, a public-private partnership created with the goal of training two million new workers in skilled professions like manufacturing, and through dozens of thoughtful, community-based efforts crafted by employers, foundations, civic leaders and others.

- Fourth, *provide more resources and innovation in matching small and mid-sized manufacturers with available talent.* Talk about a real issue: It's hard for the owner-operator of a small job shop to replace a skilled machinist who has been relied on for 30 years. That's where local Manufacturing Extension Partnership (MEP) centers and others can step in and provide "matching" services for qualified talent and openings at small manufacturers. MEPs do amazing work, but they are woefully underfunded when compared to similar institutions either abroad or in other sectors of America's economy, such as agriculture.

- Fifth, *America's leaders should use the bully pulpit to make clear that there is no shame in working with your hands as well as with your mind.* Workers in manufacturing report very high job-satisfaction levels compared to most of those in other careers. And Americans see the industry as the absolute most important in our economy: It's rated higher than high technology, banking and the service sector and, yes, seen as far more valuable than the media. It's time that manufacturing workers felt so valued around the clock, not just at election time.

- Finally, *enact economic policies that will form the foundation of a national manufacturing strategy.* For too long, America has willingly shed manufacturing jobs, even as Japan, Germany, China and other global competitors placed value on them. It's not the nature of the work or of the workplace that concerns Americans.

Aside from the desire to achieve a four-year college degree, not seeing a future in manufacturing because the jobs may not be there is the biggest sticking point for those considering a manufacturing career. The good news is that, by installing manufacturing-friendly policies, the country can do something about that.

There may be many obstacles that stand in the way of reshoring existing manufacturing jobs and creating new ones, but the oft-cited skills gap is not principal among them.

OTHER ISSUES

There are obviously many other policy matters that impact manufacturing. I'll touch on a few here.

Regulations can certainly be burdensome and lead to reduced competitiveness. And I know few business owners who think they are under-regulated. Some of them have legitimate complaints. But there will never be broad public support for deregulating in a way that exposes workers to more risk or the public to more air or water pollution.

Want to find a "paradise" of lax regulation? Go to China, where the air often isn't safe to breathe, the rivers run green and red, and millions of people die prematurely as a result of this pollution.

Such an environment isn't consistent with American ideals. The public acknowledges that smart regulation, such as the new fuel-economy standards for automobiles, can spur innovation, competition and domestic production, as well as amazing advances in the production of materials such as steel.

Innovation is the oxygen that feeds American manufacturing. Public policy must provide strong support for federally sponsored basic research, as well as mechanisms to commercialize the fruits of this research and to apply them in the private sector, as described previously in sections treating tax policy and efforts by the Commerce Department to boost manufacturing. Sridhar Kota in his chapter offers a fantastic idea, one that he perfected based on a suggestion by Robert Atkinson: Create a National Innovation Foundation.

IN THE STATES

Recommendations for public policy would not be complete without offering steps that states and localities can take to boost manufacturing. The good news is that a lot of work is already under way in this sphere. For instance, in May 2013 Maryland Gov. Martin O'Malley signed into law a bill overwhelmingly approved by the legislature in Annapolis that will expand the state's "Buy America" law to cover more types of manufactured goods. That will mean more jobs in Maryland and across the United States.

Here are ten policies that states and localities can pursue to boost manufacturing:

1. Link a state's incentives for research and development to domestic commercialization and production.

2. Establish a state-backed lending facility to provide access to capital for small and mid-sized manufacturers.

3. Expand a state's commitment to supporting trade beyond export promotion, so that it also includes ensuring a level playing field for manufacturers. For instance, former Pennsylvania Gov. Ed Rendell created a trade-enforcement office to provide assistance to man-ufacturers facing unfair subsidies, dumping and market-access or intellectual-property-theft challenges abroad. The State of Maine created a Citizens Advisory Council to inform the state government on international trade priorities. States should also seek standing in certain trade cases important to their economies.

4. More states should consider embarking on a "workshare" program that helps subsidize wages to replace unemployment insurance payments to workers idled by layoffs. This ultimately would boost the state's economy by preserving know-how and reducing other social insurance payments.

5. States that have established renewable-energy standards for power generation should also establish aggressive energy-manufacturing incentives for wind, solar and other renewables.

6. State governments often provide financing or permits for energy,

sports or development projects. To the maximum extent possible, states should establish standards to promote domestic sourcing of the materials used in the construction of such projects. The State of Minnesota did exactly this for the iron and steel used in a new stadium for the Minnesota Vikings.

7. States should refocus economic-development competition away from other states and toward reshoring manufacturing and service jobs. Employers are often willing to shift production stateside if they can pull costs to within 10 to 20 percent over what it would cost to produce overseas. There's a far larger potential market in reshoring than there is in seeking to attract business from another state.

8. Invest in infrastructure improvements through bonds, a state's capital budget or increased user fees such as fuel taxes. The cost of borrowing is low (in 2013), and the need is quite high. There may never be a better time to make such investments, and putting them off will only result in higher costs.

9. Revitalize vocational-education efforts by supporting manufacturing academies, secondary-level shop classes, community college industrial arts programs and skills certifications.

10. Enact state-level "Buy America" policies to ensure that state procurement budgets support domestic economic activity.

THE NEXT FIVE YEARS

Richard McCormack rightly points out that a considerable amount of policy work is now focused on manufacturing. I've mentioned how politics and pop culture have evolved to refocus on "Made in America." And we've touched on the academic and management-consultancy treatments of reshoring and manufacturing. The various authors of these chapters have offered ideas, as have I, for providing the right kind of public-policy support for American manufacturing. All of this is reason for optimism.

But there are also reasons to be pessimistic. The government of China will stop at nothing to employ the hundreds of millions of its citizens who need jobs. Wall Street and outsourcers profit from status quo trade and tax policies, and they will continue to stand in the way of progress. U.S. political leaders will pay lip service to "Made in America" during election time, but it remains an open question as to whether or not they really mean it.

So I offer a few suggestions for what you, as an individual, can do to make a difference. I think we've already made a pretty good case as to why it is important to support U.S. manufacturing: America's national security, its middle class, its innovation and its fiscal position for starters. But here's some food for thought:

1.   Next time you shop, make a point to purchase an item that is Made in America. You'll be frustrated if you try to find clothes in Wal-Mart or tools at Home Depot, but there are other choices, so select your stores wisely. It would be difficult to make all of your purchases American made, but once you start buying American, you won't want to stop.

2.   If you are ever in a position to provide advice on constructing a home, an office, a school or any structure at all, urge the contractor to purchase American-made materials.

3.   Participate in an action every few months on www.americanmanufacturing.org. We work to keep Congress honest on all these important issues.

4.   If you are buying a gift for someone, make it an American-made gift. You'll find lots of choices and a gift that is made in America is likely to bring a smile of surprise or delight to the recipient's face.

5.   Ask your friends and neighbors to read this book. It will arm them with (nearly) everything they need to know about the steps that must be taken to boost American manufacturing.

I'm confident that, together, we can keep it made in America.